Ballots for Freedom

Ballots for Freedom:

*Antislavery Politics
in the United States
1837-1860*

Richard H. Sewell

New York

OXFORD UNIVERSITY PRESS

1976

For Natalie

Preface

Better than any politician, perhaps, the scholarly Unitarian Theodore Parker stated the case for a politics of abolition. "Slavery is a moral wrong and an economic blunder; but it is also a great political institution," he wrote in 1858. "It cannot be put down by political economy, nor by ethical preaching; men have not only pecuniary interests and moral feelings but also political passions. Slavery must be put down politically, or else militarily. If not peacefully ended soon, it must be ended wrathfully by the sword. The negro won't bear Slavery forever; if he would, the white man won't."[1]

Long before Parker, in fact, American abolitionists had recognized the need to bring political as well as moral weapons to bear on the South's "peculiar institution." The American Anti-Slavery Society's original "Declaration of Sentiments," drafted by William Lloyd Garrison, conceded that Congress had no right to tamper with slavery in states where it was already established. At the same time, however, it called on all Northerners to topple slavery through "moral and political action" and outlined constitutional steps by which the job might be done. Although at first absorbed in tasks of organization and moral suasion, abolitionists at no time totally abandoned political tactics. And when earlier methods failed to produce the desired effect upon either of the major parties, a growing number concluded that the time had come to establish an independent antislavery party. In 1840, over the

[1] *The Present Aspect of Slavery in America and the Immediate Duty of the North* (Boston, 1858), 41-42.

violent objections of the Garrisonians (most of whom now espoused "nonresistance" beliefs that renounced allegiance to any human government) and to the dismay of Whiggish abolitionists who held high hopes for William Henry Harrison, such a party—the Liberty party—was born. Thereafter the antislavery impulse flowed increasingly within political channels.

As the political assault on slavery expanded, as Liberty men merged with Free Soilers and Free Soilers merged with Republicans, the tenets of political abolitionism inevitably lost some of their radical edge. Open declarations of abolitionist intent soon disappeared in favor of milder appeals for slavery *restriction* and an end to federal favors for slavery. Appeals to the self-interest of Northern white workingmen grew while protests against racial discrimination faded. Attacks on the "Slave Power" became as common as those on slavery itself. Yet, as I hope the following pages demonstrate, historians have often exaggerated the debasement of moral principle by Free Soilers and Republicans, and have overlooked striking continuities in the means and ends of antislavery politics. For not only did Liberty party abolitionists themselves concede constitutional barriers to immediate emancipation and develop a free labor ideology that underscored slavery's threat to whites, but Free Soilers and even Republicans held fast to the central idea of political abolitionism—that by preventing its spread and by breaking the Slave Power's hegemony over the national government, slavery might be driven down the road to extinction.

Racist notions unquestionably loomed larger among Free Soilers and Republicans than among Liberty party pioneers. Gone by 1848 was any official commitment to Negro rights. Free Soilers and Republicans often displayed a repugnance for blacks and a powerful attachment to white supremacy. Yet to a surprising extent, given the racism of the age and the demands of majoritarian politics, antislavery politicians continued throughout the 1850s to defend the basic civil rights of black Americans. Northern Negroes might complain of the bigotry of Democrats and Republicans alike, but they had no difficulty in deciding which party deserved their support.

With good reason, then, Southerners interpreted Lincoln's victory as a serious threat to slavery and hence to their region's social stability, economic prosperity, and political power. Despairing of fair treatment within the Union, the Confederate states broke loose, hoping through

independence to find security for their beleaguered way of life. The
Civil War which followed rendered purely political abolitionism ob-
solete. Peaceful solutions having failed, slavery was destroyed much as
Parkeɪ ɪ̣ad predicted: "wrathfully by the sword."

For all their attention to its moral aspects, historians have sorely
neglected the political side of the antislavery movement in the United
States. Only very recently have studies of the Free Soil party, the election of 1848, and the ideology of the Republican party—together with a
spate of instructive biographies—begun to correct this imbalance. In this
book I have taken a somewhat longer look at the politics of abolition.
By concentrating on the interplay between tactics, ideas, and the rush
of events, I hope to illuminate the process by which an avowedly antislavery party won control of the national government, making all but
inevitable a once unthinkable war.

A word about definitions. Like other students of the struggle against
slavery, I have tried to distinguish between those who stressed the institution's moral deformities, and pressed for its early demise throughout the land and those whose basic concern was merely to prevent its
extension into new pastures. For the most part I have followed convention in labeling the former type "abolitionists" and the latter "antislavery" advocates. Yet because attitudes toward slavery were susceptible
of nearly infinite variations and permutations, too rigid a dichot-
omy between "abolition" and "antislavery" risks distorting reality. I
have, therefore, tried to heed David B. Davis's sensible plea for "a
greater flexibility of language, which would recognize that abolitionists
thought of themselves as 'antislavery people,' and which would draw
distinctions according to historical context, rather than relying on ab-
stract and changeless categories."[2] In particular I have at times seen fit
to describe as "political abolitionists" men who, though never attached
to an antislavery society or insistent on *immediate* emancipation, nonetheless embraced non-extension in part because they thought it a perfectly constitutional way to hasten slavery's downfall.

[2] "Antislavery or Abolition?" *Reviews in American History*, I, No. 1 (Mar. 1973),
98.

Madison, Wis.   R.H.S.
February 1976

Acknowledgments

For aid and encouragement in writing this book, I am beholden to many persons. Librarians too numerous to mention, from Maine to Illinois, responded to my incessant queries and requests with a cheerful efficiency that made research a joy. I am particularly grateful to Carolyn Jakeman of Harvard University's Houghton Library, John Janitz of the Syracuse University Manuscript Depository, and the ever-obliging staff of the State Historical Society of Wisconsin—especially Ellen Burke, Gerald Eggleston, F. Gerald Ham, Josephine Harper, and Charles Shetler. Generous grants from the American Philosophical Society and the University of Wisconsin Graduate School helped keep a long task from becoming even longer. My thanks go also to a battery of secretaries in the University of Wisconsin History Department who meticulously typed and retyped my manuscript.

At Oxford University Press, Sheldon Meyer proved an unfailing source of reassurance and good will; Susan Rabiner, a most talented editor, gave my prose its penultimate polishing; and Caroline Taylor oversaw final preparations for publication with aplomb, good-humor, and professional skill.

I owe a special debt to Merton L. Dillon, Tilden G. Edelstein, James B. Stewart, and Bertram Wyatt-Brown. Distinguished historians all, they painstakingly read my original draft and offered wise suggestions for its improvement. Judah Ginsberg shared with me his understanding of New York politics and helped to sharpen Chapter 6. For the most part I heeded the shrewd and sensible advice of these friends. At times, however, I stubbornly went my own way. For that reason, among others, I accept sole responsibility for whatever errors and shortcomings may remain.

Finally, Alan, Deborah, and Rebecca, who would have preferred a book with pictures in it, somehow sensed my enthusiasm for this project and, in quiet ways, encouraged me to see it through. To Natalie, my wife and best critic, I owe most of all. The dedication of this book stands merely as a recognition—in no way a repayment—of that debt.

Madison, Wis.   R.H.S.

February, 1976

Contents

Abbreviations Used in Citations

BLD	Baker Library, Dartmouth College
BPL	Boston Public Library
CHS	Connecticut Historical Society
CLM	Clements Library, University of Michigan
FHL	Friends Historical Library, Swarthmore College
HLH	Houghton Library, Harvard University
LC	Library of Congress
MHC	Michigan Historical Collections, Ann Arbor
MHS	Massachusetts Historical Society
NHHS	New Hampshire Historical Society
NYHA	New York State Historical Association, Cooperstown
NYHS	New-York Historical Society
NYPL	New York Public Library
PHS	Pennsylvania Historical Society

SHSW   State Historical Society of Wisconsin,
       Madison

WRHS   Western Reserve Historical Society,
       Cleveland, Ohio

Ballots for Freedom

I

Toward a Politics of Abolition

To THE AGED JOSHUA LEAVITT, a veteran of more than thirty years in the antislavery crusade, the long-awaited victory seemed blessedly sweet. "Thank God!" he cheered, once the 1860 returns were tallied. "Lincoln is chosen! What a growth since 1840. . . . It is a joy to have lived to this day." Now that the "friends of freedom" had at last gained control of the federal government, the death of slavery appeared to be close at hand. Only the absence of departed comrades—Alvan Stewart, Myron Holley, Samuel Lewis, Gamaliel Bailey, James G. Birney, and many more who had not been spared to taste the fruit of their labors—marred the glory of the moment.[1]

Leavitt was justified in concluding that Abraham Lincoln's election meant that slavery's days were numbered—although neither he nor anyone else could foresee how swift and violent the end would be. He was also substantially correct in viewing the Republican triumph of 1860 as the culmination of efforts begun twenty years earlier by a small but dedicated band of Liberty party pioneers. Yet the roots of political abolitionism reached still deeper into the American past.

From its somewhat murky beginnings in North America, slavery had rested upon political enactments. Well before the American Revolution, statutory codes sanctioning human bondage and regulating the conduct of slaves were to be found in every American colony. The spirit of the Revolution rapidly undermined slavery in the North, but

[1] Leavitt to Salmon P. Chase, Nov. 7, 1860, Salmon P. Chase Papers, LC.

3

(except for a short-lived Virginia law permitting private manumissions) left Southern slave codes very much intact. The federal Constitution of 1787, while it pointedly shunned the word "slave" and gave promise of an early end to the African slave trade, tacitly recognized the "peculiar institution" by counting freemen and "three fifths of all other Persons" in apportioning congressional representatives and by requiring the return of fugitives from "Service or Labour." Pursuant to this latter clause, Congress passed in 1793 a fugitive slave law which empowered masters to seize runaways anywhere in the Union and levied a fine of $500 on anyone who obstructed the process of recovery.[2]

Inevitably, then, when men awakened to the evil of slavery they sought political as well as moral ways to attack it. The rationalistic, gradualistic temper of eighteenth-century philanthropy found political solutions particularly congenial. Later the legislative successes of British abolitionists and American reformers in many fields—Anti-Masonry, temperance, prison and school reform, among others—combined with habit to keep at least some of the antislavery impulse within political channels. The post-Revolutionary movement which swept away slavery in Northern states, passed the Northwest Ordinance, and abolished the foreign slave trade demonstrated that, given the right circumstances, political action could be remarkably effective.

Thereafter, as the egalitarian flames of the Revolution waned and Whitney's cotton gin strengthened the South's already powerful attachment to slavery, Congress and the state legislatures repeatedly turned cold shoulders to abolitionist proposals. Yet a great variety of such appeals continued to be pressed upon politicians from many sources and in many ways. Petitions—often used in colonial days to protest the importation of slaves—continued during the early decades of the new nation to be a common, if ineffectual, form of political pressure. The first antislavery petitions to Congress came in 1790 from Pennsylvania Quakers seeking an end to the slave trade. Other groups, North and South, also memorialized state and national legislatures, asking for a ban on foreign and domestic traffic in slaves, abolition of slavery in the

---

[2] Winthrop D. Jordan, *White Over Black: American Attitudes Toward the Negro, 1550-1812* (Chapel Hill, 1968), 103-10; Donald L. Robinson, *Slavery in the Structure of American Politics, 1765-1820* (New York, 1971); David B. Davis, *The Problem of Slavery in the Age of Revolution, 1770-1823* (Ithaca, 1975), chaps. I-IV, VI-VII, X.

District of Columbia, gradual emancipation (often tied to colonization), or better treatment of bondsmen.

Most antislavery societies before 1828 limited their political activity
to such polite entreaties, even though, as John Greenleaf Whittier later
observed, "their voice was too faint to be heard amidst the din of party
warfare, and the petitions too few and feeble to command attention."
At least two groups pressed further, however. The Tennessee Society
for Promoting the Manumission of Slaves, founded in 1814 by Charles
Osborn, and Benjamin Lundy's Union Humane Society (1815) each
framed constitutions insisting that members vote only for known opponents of slavery. Already some men recognized that to support "proslavery" candidates was to share in their guilt and that to petition unregenerate legislators was an exercise in futility.[3]

For Lundy and many others, the crisis over the admission of Missouri as a slave state further illustrated the need for political action by
abolitionists. Lundy himself had left Ohio for Missouri in 1819 to work
for the election of antislavery delegates to the constitutional convention. Although soundly defeated in this attempt, he came away from
Missouri pleased with the educational effect of the campaign and more
convinced than ever before of the utility of political antislavery action.
By 1823 Lundy was explaining to readers of his *Genius of Universal
Emancipation:* "I do not expect to *'persuade' the advocates of slavery*
to do justice. Such persons cannot be honest; and I am not for making
a covenant with dishonesty. WE MUST VOTE THEM DOWN."[4]

Throughout the 1820s Lundy and other reformers continued to seek
political solutions to the problem of slavery. In Maryland, where in
1825 Lundy and a group of associates organized a state antislavery society, this approach dominated all others. The new society's primary
purpose, Lundy explained, was to press the legislature "to alter and
amend the laws, and make them more favorable to manumission, colonization, and emigration." Such pressure would be most effective, he
believed, if brought directly to bear on the electoral process. The in-
transigence of slaveholders, when left to themselves, meant that the
ballot box remained "the ONLY means . . . by which slavery can be

[3] Gilbert H. Barnes, *The Anti-Slavery Impulse, 1830-1844,* Harbinger Books ed.
(New York, 1964), 109; Dwight L. Dumond, *Antislavery: The Crusade for Freedom
in America* (Ann Arbor, 1961), 136.
[4] Merton L. Dillon, *Benjamin Lundy and the Struggle for Negro Freedom* (Urbana,
1966), 58.

annihilated without commotion, rapine, and indescribable woe." Accordingly, the Maryland Anti-Slavery Society thrice nominated its president, Daniel Raymond, as a candidate for the general assembly. His platform of gradual emancipation stirred up much more hostility than support, and though his 1826 vote increased slightly over that of the year before, Raymond withdrew his candidacy in 1827. Swamped by the hoopla of Jacksonian politics, Maryland abolitionists never again made independent nominations.[5]

Elsewhere different tactics produced more tangible results. In 1824 Illinois antislavery forces succeeded, with the aid and encouragement of abolitionists everywhere, in voting down a proposed constitutional convention which they feared would seek to plant slavery in that hitherto free state. Once again, the utility of political action seemed demonstrable. That same year, the Ohio legislature responded to antislavery pressure by adopting resolutions—soon copied by several other Northern states—calling on Congress to recognize "that the evil of slavery is a national one" and to implement a scheme of gradual emancipation and colonization. Some abolitionists, perhaps partly out of fondness for John Quincy Adams, exhorted others to shun slaveholding candidates in the presidential election of 1824, and most (including young William Lloyd Garrison) opposed the election of Andrew Jackson in 1828.[6]

2

By the founding of the American Anti-Slavery Society in 1833, the nature of abolitionism had subtly though markedly changed. The incursion of romantic notions of the perfectibility of man and the absolute and uncompromisable distinction between good and evil, together with the failure of earlier, piecemeal attacks on slavery, produced a new emphasis upon the moral aspects of slavery and a demand for "immediate emancipation." At the same time, the tightening of the South's defense of its increasingly "peculiar" institution and the collapse of the always weak Southern antislavery societies gave a starkly sectional tone

[5] *Ibid.* 109-17. In 1825 Raymond received 624 of 10,711 votes cast. The following year he got 974 of 13,312.
[6] William H. Smith, *A Political History of Slavery* (New York, 1903), 23-24; Dillon, *Lundy*, 72-74.

to abolitionism and raised new obstacles in the way of political solutions to the slavery question.

No one, however, yet proposed the abandonment of political action. In its first annual report (January 1833) the New England Anti-Slavery Society forthrightly stated that "the people of New-England are . . . bound to use their moral and political power to overthrow slavery in the United States." And the American Anti-Slavery Society's Declaration of Sentiments, also drafted by William Lloyd Garrison, explicitly endorsed political campaigns against slavery. Congress, the Declaration conceded, possessed no constitutional right to tamper with slavery in states where it already existed. But, it went on, Congress had a right and a duty to suppress the domestic slave trade and to abolish slavery wherever the Constitution gave the federal government exclusive jurisdiction. And all good abolitionists recognized "the highest obligations . . . to remove slavery by moral and political action. . . ."[7]

Despite this official sanction of political activity, neither the American Anti-Slavery Society nor individual abolitionists directed much energy into political channels during the early 1830s. The formation of auxiliary antislavery societies, the training of agents and scheduling of lecturers, the circulation of tracts and periodicals, the conversion of press and pulpit, and boycotts of slave labor produce—all kept abolitionists too busy at first to allow much time for politics. Moreover, what limited political activity abolitionists did undertake during these years was intended to stimulate debate and to sway those already in positions of power more than to replace those in office with a better set of men.

Once again the petition became the favored instrument. The success of a widespread petition campaign in 1828-29 that forced Congress to debate and report on the question of abolishing slavery in the District of Columbia reawakened interest in such methods of political agitation, and by 1836 antislavery petitions had reached floodtide. Slave state representatives, aided by Northern Democrats who viewed the petition campaign as a Whig subterfuge designed to sabotage Democratic programs, responded by enacting a series of "gag rules" that effectively blocked Congress from receiving abolitionist memorials until 1844. But to antislavery forces the petition controversy, by advertising their

[7] *First Annual Report of the Board of Managers of the New-England Anti-Slavery Society, Presented Jan. 9, 1833* (Boston, 1833), 22; *Liberator*, Dec. 14, 1833.

cause on the floors of Congress and winning over many who saw the
issue as one of civil rights, proved a godsend. Fights over the gag rule
also helped to bind to the antislavery cause such powerful voices as
John Quincy Adams, Thomas Morris, and Joshua Giddings. It is hardly
surprising that for a time the petition campaign absorbed so much of
the abolitionists' attention.[8]

Not all petitions went to Congress. Throughout the North abolitionists also petitioned state legislatures, calling for the passage of personal
liberty laws, repeal of discriminatory Black Codes, opposition to the
annexation of Texas, abolition in the District of Columbia, constitutional amendments separating Northern citizens from all connection
with slavery, and other antislavery acts. Although no legislature ever
copied Congress' gag rule, such memorials usually got short shrift. But
once again petitions proved to be effective instruments of agitation,
and slavery's critics shipped them off to the statehouse at every opportunity.[9]

Before 1837 organized political action against slavery rarely went beyond such petition campaigns. Garrison lent some encouragement to a
proposal to amend the Constitution so as to excise the fugitive slave
clause, and in 1834 he spoke vaguely of establishing "a *Christian* party
in politics—not made up of this or that sect or denomination, but of all
who fear God and keep his commandments and who sincerely desire to
seek judgment and relieve the oppressed."[10] Most abolitionists continued to vote in public elections, supporting "honest and upright" candidates when they were to be found and occasionally scattering their
ballots or staying home when faced with a Hobson's choice. But seldom
was such activity concerted, even locally. Almost never had it any dis-
cernible effect.

The tentativeness and restraint with which abolitionists engaged in
political action during the early 1830s contrasted sharply with the boldness of their appeals to the nation's conscience. In part this disparity
stemmed from a conviction that a moral revolution—akin to Christian

[8] Barnes, *Anti-Slavery Impulse,* chaps. XI-XIII; Russel B. Nye, *Fettered Freedom:
Civil Liberties and the Slavery Controversy, 1830-1860* (East Lansing, 1949), 32-54.
In 1836 alone 100,000 petitions poured into Congress. Austin Willey, *The History
of the Anti-Slavery Cause in State and Nation* (Portland, Me., 1886), 62.
[9] Willey, *Anti-Slavery Cause in State and Nation,* 164, 207; Theodore C. Smith,
The Liberty and Free Soil Parties in the Northwest (New York, 1897), 20.
[10] Garrison to Thomas Shipley, Dec. 17, 1835 (copy), William Lloyd Garrison
Papers, BPL; *Liberator,* Dec. 20, 1834.

conversion—must come first if political assaults on slavery were to be effective. Indeed, some abolitionists assumed that right political action would so inevitably and automatically flow from universal awareness of the sin of slavery that debate over political tactics was pointless.

Even those who believed that moral witness and political action ought to move forward together, that parties and politicians might speed the work of moral regeneration, and that slavery might be forced to an early grave *before* a majority of Americans awoke to its sinfulness, at first endorsed only limited and indirect political involvement. For one thing, nearly all admitted that the Constitution safeguarded slavery from direct outside attack. As Whittier explained to one Virginia newspaper: "All the leading abolitionists of my acquaintance are . . . , without exception, opposed to any political *interposition* of the Government, in regard to slavery as it exists in the *States*. For although they feel and see that the canker of the moral disease is affecting all parts of the Confederacy, they believe that *the remedy* lies with yourselves alone."[11] Until the Southern blockade against antislavery literature tightened, many abolitionists devoted the bulk of their labors to arousing the North and propagandizing the South, restricting political action to modest forays against slavery's exposed outposts—particularly the District of Columbia, where Congress' powers were widely recognized.

Concern "to escape the polluting infection of party politics"[12] also curtailed antislavery political activity at the outset. Established parties, especially in the freewheeling age of Andrew Jackson, seemed to many abolitionists little better than engines for booty, and those who directed them practitioners in the arts of treachery and intrigue. "Your true party politician," contended one Ohio editor, "has never contemplated a moral end, never employed moral means—how then can he appreciate the meaning of the term *moral power?*" Thus the safest and wisest course for abolitionists to follow was to remain free of all partisan ties, making terms with no party, but letting "other Partisans and parties come to them." Garrison might advertise the virtues of Amasa Walker, a Democratic abolitionist, and recommend his election to Congress. But such endorsements were rare and no one yet advocated even occasional

---

[11] Quoted in the *Liberator*, Aug. 17, 1833. See also Utica *Friend of Man*, Dec. 29, 1836.
[12] *Friend of Man*, June 23, 1836.

independent nominations, much less the establishment of an antislavery party.[13]

3

By 1837, having planted antislavery societies throughout the North and launched an extensive campaign to proselytize the nation, abolitionists began to pay closer attention to politics. Creation of an antislavery third party was still far from men's minds. But during 1837 and 1838 disappointment with tried political methods together with a heightened awareness of the political dimension of slavery caused abolitionists to experiment with new ways of making their votes effective.

Although all deprecated "the political action of base and selfish men rising into power by the generalship of a party," antislavery reformers came increasingly to perceive a close and harmonious connection between political and moral action. "Politics, rightly considered, is a branch of morals, and cannot be deserted innocently," the Massachusetts Anti-Slavery Society's board of managers declared in 1838.[14] Moral pressure remained essential if Americans were to be aroused to the sinfulness of slavery. But, as Henry B. Stanton contended, "that does not abate the necessity of *political* action. It is but the cause of it. Moral feeling is but the *steam* by which we have been employed for 4 or 5 years in getting up; and political action is the *engine* to which it must be applied. For it is by legal means only, that slavery can ever be abolished."[15]

It was dissatisfaction with petition campaigns that first convinced many abolitionists of the need to develop a more efficient political engine. The parliamentary skills of flinty old John Quincy Adams, abetted by a handful of other antislavery representatives, meant that despite gag rules—or, rather, because of them—petitions to Congress remained for years useful means of agitation. And it was not long before antislavery memorials from ordinary citizens swelled the flood started by

13 Cincinnati *Philanthropist*, Nov. 11, 1836; Jabez D. Hammond to Gerrit Smith, Feb. 5, 1836, Gerrit Smith Papers, Syracuse University Library; *Liberator*, Nov. 8, 1834, Oct. 29, 1836.
14 *Fourth Annual Report of the American Anti-Slavery Society . . . 1837* (New York, 1837), 113-14; *Liberator*, Aug. 10, 1838.
15 *Friend of Man*, Aug. 15, 1838.

organized abolitionists. Yet many came bitterly to resent the insulting reception accorded antislavery petitions in Washington and concluded that to continue such appeals was both pointless and demeaning. This attitude was strongest in New York, where the volatile Alvan Stewart, president of that state's antislavery society, insisted: "We might as well send the lamb as an ambassador to a community of wolves. I would not lift my hand to sign a petition to Congress, to be insulted by that body."[16] Others, admitting that even rebuffed memorials might make good propaganda, lamented that the gag rule controversy had deflected the antislavery crusade from its central goal. "Instead of a struggle for the slave," complained the Cincinnati *Philanthropist*, "it has been a struggle for the right of petition."[17]

An even more fundamental objection to exclusive political reliance upon petitions was that to do so was "to throw away *power* and use *weakness*." The truth was, as more and more abolitionists admitted, that "all the strength our petitions ever had, they have derived from the *votes* to which they pointed, somewhere in the future."[18] Politicians might ignore moral arguments, but they could not help being impressed by numbers. Moreover, abolitionists soon discovered "the folly of petitioning our national and state legislatures, and at the same time sending men to represent us in these bodies who will treat our memorials with contempt, and turn a deaf ear to our petitions."[19] To make their weight felt, therefore, to force reluctant politicians to reopen channels of communication (by repealing gag rules and restrictions on the mailing of antislavery literature to the South), and to influence lawmakers on a wide range of slavery-related issues, abolitionists devised new ways of consolidating their suffrages.

By 1837 the usefulness of concerted action at the polling place seemed clear to most abolitionists. A few still held back, some insisting upon their independence to vote as they pleased, others warning of the danger of any efforts that resembled those of a political party.[20] But most willingly endorsed more aggressive steps. Although still few

[16] Barnes, *Anti-Slavery Impulse*, 149.
[17] Quoted, *ibid.* 148.
[18] Boston *Massachusetts Abolitionist*, July 4, 1839.
[19] Philadelphia *Pennsylvania Freeman*, June 28, 1838.
[20] See, e.g., the remarks of Leonard Gibbs and the Rev. Caleb Green at the 1837 convention of the New York State Anti-Slavery Society, reported in *Friend of Man*, Oct. 11, 1837.

in number (roughly one for every 250 Americans, according to one estimate), abolitionists boasted of appreciable strength in New England and parts of New York, Pennsylvania, and Ohio. Garrison expressed a common optimism when he noted late in 1836 that "Abolitionists are fast obtaining the balance of political power in every part of the free States."[21]

Since independent nominations—to say nothing of third *party* activity—still appeared dangerous and undesirable, effective voting meant concerted support for antislavery nominees in either party, Whig or Democratic. By voting as a bloc for "friends of the slave" wherever found, abolitionists could, without sacrificing their reputation for moral purity and disinterestedness, wield the balance of power and thus force existing parties to do their work for them. "A Whig abolitionist, or a democratic abolitionist," observed a prominent New York humanitarian, "will do the *party* work in congress as well as another and he will do *our work* besides." Once they understood that antislavery support meant the difference between victory or defeat, Whigs and Democrats, it was hoped, would go out of their way to respect abolitionists' opinions and to nominate candidates acceptable to them. In the process, sanguine Ohio abolitionists contended, "We shall, in some measure even reform corrupted politicians themselves, and thus do the country incalculable service."[22] So too, as Nathaniel P. Rogers took pains to point out, by withholding "votes from the enemies of our principles," abolitionists might "clear our own skirts from the guilt of their constituency."[23] Thus public welfare and personal morality might be served by a concerted policy of voting for none but proven friends of emancipation.

To determine accurately who those friends were among the Whig and Democratic candidates, abolitionists borrowed the system of interrogation earlier used with success by their British counterparts. Attempts "to call out" candidates' views on slavery and related issues received the endorsement of the American Anti-Slavery Society in 1837,

[21] Arthur H. Rice, "Henry B. Stanton as a Political Abolitionist," Ed.D. dissertation, Columbia University (1968), 115; *Liberator*, Oct. 29, 1836.
[22] E. C. Pritchett in *Friend of Man*, July 18, 1838; Report printed at the request of the Executive Committee of the Ohio Anti-Slavery Society, in *Philanthropist*, June 19, 1838. See also Seymour B. Treadwell to Gerrit Smith, Nov. 30, 1838, Smith Papers.
[23] *Emancipator*, Feb. 28, 1839. See also *Philanthropist*, Dec. 30, 1836.

and by 1838 these tactics were tried in most free states. To all nominees for important state and national offices, abolitionists sent questionnaires, asking that each declare his position on such key issues as the right of abolitionists to petition Congress, the desirability of annexing Texas, abolition in the District of Columbia, suppression of the domestic slave trade, recognition of Haiti, jury trial for alleged fugitives, and the repeal of laws discriminating against free Negroes. All responses were published in antislavery newspapers—with appropriate editorial comment. Abolitionists were then expected to back at the ballot box those who answered favorably and to deny their votes to all others. In the event that the nominee of neither party replied satisfactorily to their queries, abolitionists might either withhold their suffrages for that office altogether or "scatter" their votes by writing in at random the name of some known opponent of slavery. Thus abolitionists hoped to influence the outcome of elections—and, before long, the selection of candidates—without having to soil their own feet in the dirty waters of party politics.

At first the interrogation technique showed signs of promise. It worked best in New England, where antislavery strength was greatest and where, at least in Massachusetts, laws required that successful candidates receive a *majority* of all ballots, thus making it easier for reformers to hold the balance. Abolitionists in many states found encouraging the results of the interrogation of Rhode Island candidates in 1837, when, of six nominees queried only one failed to give satisfactory replies—and he lost the election.[24]

The next year Massachusetts humanitarians scored an even more impressive victory at the expense of Caleb Cushing, a Whig candidate for Congress. Although previously on good terms with Bay State abolitionists, Cushing answered their queries evasively in 1838. He affirmed "a devotion to liberty and equality, and an aversion to slavery in general," and to show that his deeds squared with his words he pointed to his votes against the admission of Arkansas as a slave state and against a resolution declaring that Congress ought not to abolish slavery in the District of Columbia. At the same time, however, he stressed constitutional restraints on political abolitionism and spoke of his "personal independence as the choicest of all possessions."

[24] *Friend of Man*, Sept. 27, 1837, July 4, Aug. 15, 1838.

At a meeting of the Essex County Anti-Slavery Society, Henry B. Stanton, roving representative of the national society, scornfully exposed the shortcomings of Cushing's reply, and at Stanton's urging the Society declared Cushing unworthy of its support. Unbeknownst to all, Cushing had himself witnessed these proceedings, sitting fretful but still in a shadowed corner of the gallery. Early the following morning when John G. Whittier went to call on the candidate to impress upon him the need for a stronger antislavery statement, Cushing was ready to comply. Still in his nightshirt, Cushing hastily drafted a letter affirming his support for the abolition of slavery and the slave trade in the District of Columbia "by the earliest practicable legislation of Congress." It was assurance enough for most abolitionists, and with their help Cushing returned to Washington.[25]

In Middlesex County, Massachusetts, concerted antislavery action produced a second heady triumph in 1838. Concluding that neither Democrat William Parmenter nor Whig Nathan Brooks deserved their support, abolitionists scattered their votes in the election for United States representative. As a result neither candidate received a majority, and Middlesex's seat in Congress went empty, to the great delight of antislavery men everywhere. Whittier, Gerrit Smith, and Nathaniel P. Rogers all sent their congratulations to the steadfast abolitionists who had fought and won the "Thermopylae of the cause."[26]

Hostile slave state reaction to growing antislavery political unity also helped to confirm some abolitionists in their faith in the interrogation system. In December 1838 the *Emancipator*, official voice of the American Anti-Slavery Society, pointed with satisfaction to an editorial in the *Richmond Enquirer* which complained that the pressure exerted on Northern candidates by the questioning tactic made abolitionism more dangerous than ever before.[27]

Yet the inherent flaws in the interrogation method were great and,

[25] Rice, "Stanton," 121-22; Henry B. Stanton, *Random Recollections*, 3rd ed. (New York, 1887), 57-58; Claude M. Fuess, *The Life of Caleb Cushing*, 2 vols. (New York, 1923), I, 251-54. Some abolitionists distrusted Cushing to the end and were angry at Whittier, without whose intercession "Cushing would have gone abegging for his election." See Charles T. Torrey to Amos A. Phelps, Nov. 16, 1838, Amos A. Phelps Papers, BPL.
[26] Rice, "Stanton," 123-25. Most Middlesex abolitionists preferred Brooks to Parmenter, and a few apparently voted for him. Phelps and Stanton to [antislavery voters of Middlesex County], Nov. 8, 1838 (copy), Phelps Papers; Phelps to Stanton, Nov. 8, 1838 (typed copy), Elizur Wright, Jr., Papers, LC.
[27] *Emancipator*, Dec. 6, 1838.

in the end, fatal. First of all, in relatively few districts did abolitionists in fact hold the balance of power. And even where they did, political candidates often refused to answer the questions put to them, or replied in vague platitudes. On one occasion a Whig county nominating convention in Michigan was delayed to within ten days of the annual election in order to spare candidates the embarrassment of antislavery interrogation.[28] When this sort of thing happened, abolitionists had no recourse but to scatter their votes or to boycott the polls—actions satisfying perhaps to one's conscience but painfully negative and in general politically ineffective. Second, the interrogation of candidates already in the field seemed to some abolitionists a tardy and left-handed manner of proceeding. Much better, as Leonard Gibbs advised the New York State Anti-Slavery Society, to get genuine abolitionists nominated in the first place—and then to elect them.[29] The problem here was that to secure the nomination of reliable antislavery candidates abolitionists would either have to act *within* existing political organizations or form a party and name candidates of their own.

Few were yet willing to risk the dangers of third party action, but some could justify working with, if not within, the major parties in order to obtain acceptable nominations. Alvan Stewart, long a leading spirit in New York antislavery circles, suggested in 1838 that abolitionists ought to concentrate on the nomination of fit men for Congress. Antislavery voters should first agree among themselves on some politician they would like to see in Congress. Having made their choice, Stewart argued to a Philadelphia friend, abolitionists ought then to go to the county and district caucuses of their man's party, and insist on his nomination. If the party bosses kicked, he advised, point out that "you must make a great sacrifice in voting for Assembly men, Senators, Gov. Lieut. Gov. and Presidential Electors who are not abolitionists." Then, by holding "in *Terrorem* over their heads" the danger of losing all contests without abolitionist support, the foes of slavery might get congressional candidates to their liking. "This will be a low motive," Stewart admitted, "but we must take the world as it is."[30]

Although most found such bargain-and-sale politicking repugnant

[28] Nathan M. Thomas, "Manuscript History of the Anti-Slavery Movement in Michigan," Nathan M. Thomas Papers, MHC, 25-26.
[29] *Friend of Man*, Sept. 27, 1837.
[30] Alvan Stewart to Samuel Webb, June 26, 1838, Alvan Stewart Papers, NYHS.

and continued to limit their political activity to sounding out those candidates already in nomination, a great many abolitionists undercut the
interrogation system by voting in the pinch as old party loyalties dictated. If the questioning of candidates was ever to be politically effective, slavery's opponents had to unite all their strength behind antislavery candidates of whatever party. Yet, as was repeatedly demonstrated,
many abolitionists found that on election day the influence of other issues and the strength of partisan ties were just too strong to be resisted. Antislavery conventions might resolve that an abolitionist who
voted for "proslavery" candidates risked bringing "suspicions on the
sincerity of his professions"; and staunch souls like Gerrit Smith might
deplore the "monstrous . . . inconsistency of talking and writing and
praying against slavery, at the same time, that we are voting *for* it!"
But old attachments died hard, and many were the lambs who strayed.[31]

To combat election day backsliding New York abolitionists experi-
mented with a pledge system, fashioned after the teetotal oath of temperance crusaders. Beginning in 1838, antislavery newspapers in New
York printed, along with the replies of candidates, lists of voters
pledged to support only those nominees who favored immediate emancipation.[32] The erratic but earnest Gerrit Smith, a wealthy reformer
committed equally to abstinence and abolition, went so far as to offer
$500 to promote the creation of new antislavery societies whose mem-
bers would be constitutionally forbidden to vote for proslavery candidates. In 1839 the New York State Anti-Slavery Society added such an
injunction to its charter, but few outside New York showed much interest and even some of Smith's closest associates were openly skeptical
of the value of pledges. Indeed, contended William Goodell, editor of
the Utica *Friend of Man*, "Some of our pledged abolitionists have given
us the greatest trouble."[33]

A final defect in the interrogation system, as abolitionists quickly
discovered, was that even when they succeeded in electing a candidate

[31] *Friend of Man*, Mar. 14, 1838; Gerrit Smith to Myron Holley, Jan. 17, 1839,
Miscellaneous Manuscripts, NYHS.
[32] *Friend of Man*, Oct. 31, 1838; *Liberator*, Nov. 23, 1838. For the importance attached to written pledges by temperance reformers, see Alice Felt Tyler, *Freedom's
Ferment: Phases of American Social History from the Colonial Period to the Out-
break of the Civil War*, Harper Torchbook ed. (New York, 1962), 325.
[33] Smith to Amos A. Phelps, Dec. 28, 1838, Letterbook, Smith Papers; Smith to
Elizur Wright, Jr., Dec. 13, 1838, Elizur Wright, Jr. Papers, LC; *Friend of Man*,
Nov. 29, 1838.

who had answered their questions satisfactorily, once in office he often betrayed them. Slavery's opponents soon learned to be leery of election-eve professions of good intent, "if made evidently for the mere purpose of obtaining our votes . . . ," and they cautioned one another to take special pains to investigate the past record of those who sought their suffrages.[34] But politicians, as ever, proved to be better at promises than performance, and abolitionists were often misled.

The experiences of New York and Ohio abolitionists most graphically revealed the pitfalls of interrogation and persuaded many of the need for more direct political involvement.

On October 1, 1838, Gerrit Smith and William Jay, acting for the New York State Anti-Slavery Society, put three test questions to the candidates for governor and lieutenant governor: (1) Do you favor a law granting a jury trial to persons in New York claimed as fugitive slaves? (2) Do you favor removal of all constitutional distinctions "founded solely on complexion"? (3) Do you favor repeal of the stat-ute which now permits persons to bring slaves to New York and hold them for as much as nine months? All nominees were advised that their replies would be published. The answers of Democratic incumbent Governor William L. Marcy and Lieutenant Governor John Tracy were almost insulting, and New York abolitionists (most already par-tial to Whiggery) at once wrote them off. William H. Seward, the Whig gubernatorial candidate, responded reluctantly and evasively. He declared his support for the principle of trial by jury, so long as no provision of the federal Constitution were violated, but upheld the nine months law on the ground that some time limit was better than none; and he approved, for the time being at least, restrictions on Ne-gro suffrage. Only Luther Bradish, Seward's running mate and, as it happened, a personal friend of Gerrit Smith, gave unqualifiedly affirm-ative answers to the abolitionist queries.[35]

Antislavery leaders moved quickly to reward Bradish for the "ele-vated and decided ground" he had taken and to punish the others. Smith damned Seward as "a pro-slavery man," no more deserving of support than the benighted Marcy. The executive committee of the

---

[34] *Friend of Man*, Sept. 26, 1838.
[35] Smith and Jay to Marcy, Tracy, Seward, and Bradish, Oct. 1, 1838 (copy), Smith Papers; *Emancipator*, Nov. 1, 1838; *Friend of Man*, Oct. 24, 31, Nov. 7, 29, Dec. 5, 1838; Ralph Volney Harlow, *Gerrit Smith: Philanthropist and Reformer* (New York, 1939), 138-40.

New York State Anti-Slavery Society publicly called upon abolitionist voters to stand behind their recent resolution to support only men fully committed to their cause. And the American Anti-Slavery Society's executive board pronounced Bradish the only candidate worthy of backing and suggested that ballots be prepared which omitted the other names.[36]

Gerrit Smith had hoped that his friend Bradish would poll 500 votes more than the recreant Seward. In this way abolitionists might rebuke the unfaithful and attest to their political strength. Yet on election day he and many other abolitionists were grievously disappointed. Seward bested Marcy by some 10,000 votes, and few bothered to scratch him from the Whig ballot. Smith himself glumly estimated that four out of five New York abolitionists had "shown their willingness to sacrifice the holy cause of crushed humanity on the polluted altar of party politics."[37] Not only had party ties and the argument that Seward represented a "lesser evil" than Marcy caused many abolitionists to overlook Seward's shillyshallying on slavery, but, apparently, a good many Whig *anti*-abolitionists deleted Bradish from their tickets. The real strength of the antislavery element was therefore still further masked. William Goodell tried hard to remain optimistic. "This is our first encounter," he observed. "And our forces were not prepared for it."[38] But the setback soured many on the workability of interrogation and inspired in some a search for alternatives that would soon result in truly independent political action.

Events in Ohio produced much the same effect. After both Whig and Democratic candidates for governor had declined to answer their queries, many abolitionists boycotted the 1838 election. Since antislavery voters usually supported the Whig ticket, such abstentions represented a windfall for the Democrats. Moreover, a fair number of those abolitionists who did vote crossed party lines and supported Democratic candidates in 1838. Some did so hoping thereby to ensure the reelection of Thomas Morris, a Democrat who had lately emerged as the lone, powerful antislavery spokesman in the United States Senate. Oth-

[36] *Ibid.* 140-41; *Friend of Man*, Nov. 7, 1838.
[37] *Ibid.;* Glyndon G. Van Deusen, *William Henry Seward* (New York, 1967), 51; Gerrit Smith to Editor of *Cazenovia Union Herald*, Nov. 23, 1838, quoted in *Liberator*, Dec. 21, 1838.
[38] *Sixth Annual Report of the Executive Committee of the American Anti-Slavery Society . . . 1839* (New York, 1839), 104; *Friend of Man*, Nov. 29, 1838.

ers were willing to reward Democrats who had indicated a willingness
to repeal the state's Black Laws. Still others came to the polls to protest Whig Governor Joseph Vance's election-eve arrest and extradition
of John B. Mahan, charged by Kentucky authorities with aiding a runaway slave. The result was a sweeping Democratic victory. Vance,
who the year before had coasted into office with a 6000 vote majority,
now found himself unseated by a full 5000; and Democrats gained several seats in Congress and the state legislature.[39]

Nearly all observers credited the outcome in Ohio to the abolitionists. Eastern antislavery presses extolled the principled independence of
their Western comrades, while at home chastened Whigs admitted the
power of antislavery voters and took steps to win them back. Abolitionists themselves seemed confirmed in their ability to shape the course
of politics without any compromise of principle. The future looked
bright.[40]

Within months, however, a profound disillusionment had set in. It
began in December 1838, when Democratic legislators, in a slap at abolitionists who had cast Democratic ballots to secure Senator Morris's
re-election, coolly passed Morris by and voted to replace him with
Benjamin Tappan, whose views on slavery were more orthodox.[41] A
second jolt came in January when the legislature, with the concurrence
of many lawmakers who before the fall election had professed antislavery sympathies, passed a series of resolutions that upheld the state's
Black Laws and denounced abolitionist schemes as "wild and delusive,"
incapable of producing good results, and tending "to disrupt the
Union." The following month, at the request of commissioners from
Kentucky, conservative legislators completed their work by enacting
a severe fugitive slave law: the "Bill of Abominations," outraged abolitionists dubbed it.[42]

The experiences of 1838-39 did not at once bring an end to the questioning of candidates. Even the badly burned Ohio reformers clung to

[39] Smith, *Liberty and Free Soil Parties*, 30-31; Smith, *A Political History of Slavery*,
44; *Philanthropist*, Nov. 6, 1838.
[40] Smith, *Liberty and Free Soil Parties*, 31; *Emancipator*, Nov. 15, 1838; Benjamin
F. Wade to Milton Sutliff, Dec. 8, 20, 1838, Milton Sutliff Papers, WRHS.
[41] *Philanthropist*, Jan. 1, 1839; B. F. Morris (ed.), *The Life of Thomas Morris*
(Cincinnati, 1856), 189-203; Bertram Wyatt-Brown, *Lewis Tappan and the Evangelical War Against Slavery* (Cleveland, 1969), 277.
[42] *Philanthropist*, Jan. 22, Feb. 19, 26, 1839; Smith, *Liberty and Free Soil Parties*, 22-
23, 31.

this system a while longer, seeing at first "no other course for abolitionists to pursue." And long after the formation of the Liberty and Free
Soil parties, antislavery voters occasionally resorted to interrogation
when for some reason they had neglected to make nominations of their
own. Yet increasingly after 1838 abolitionists soured on such methods
and, when they used them at all, did so only as a last resort.[43]

4

But disenchantment with the tactic of interrogation by no means meant
disillusionment with antislavery politics. Indeed, 1838 and 1839 witnessed a rising, clamorous debate over the proper political course for
abolitionists to follow. A majority felt a growing conviction that political action (preferably by *all* abolitionists) was necessary, and this majority wanted more direct, independent—even partisan—involvement.
Simultaneously, an influential minority, anchored by the fiery Garrison, began to espouse "nonresistance" notions that repudiated "all human politics" and labeled even voting a sin. Christian doctrine, such
men contended, demanded renunciation of all institutions based on
force—human government no less than slavery itself. This collision over
political means contributed to the schism which in 1840 left American
abolitionists openly and bitterly at war among themselves. It also hardened and intensified political attitudes on both hands and led inexorably
to the formation of the Liberty party.

   In its tangible results the election of 1838 proved to be dishearten-
ingly barren for most abolitionists. Yet its educational effect was immense. As never before—in antislavery conventions, newspapers, and
pamphlets—men urged upon one another the pressing need for "a
righteous and renovating *political action.*" William Goodell's temperate and well-reasoned articles entitled "POLITICAL ACTION AGAINST
SLAVERY," published in the Utica *Friend of Man* during August and
September 1838 and widely reprinted by other antislavery editors,
were especially influential. A kindly, peace-loving man with wide experience in reform journalism, Goodell enjoyed the respect of all abolitionists. Arguing now that politics need not be corrupt to be effective,

[43] *Ibid.* 31, 42, 189; Centreville (Ind.) *Free Territory Sentinel,* June 13, 1849; *Philanthropist,* July 23, 1839.

if abolitionists would only make known early their determination to vote for no lawmaker opposed to immediate emancipation, his essays set men to thinking. By denying the need for a third party or independent nominations, and by making no demands on those whom conscience kept from voting, he won endorsement even from Garrison, who found Goodell's arguments "not only conclusive, but irresistible."[44]

A few abolitionists, however, had already advocated more radical political steps. And before long Goodell and most others joined them in their independent course, while Garrison—blown by the winds of nonresistance—drifted rapidly in the opposite direction.

Slavery's foes prior to 1838 had invariably denied any intention of creating a political party of their own. Indeed, the matter was raised at all only because jittery Southerners sometimes accused them of such designs or because rigorous denials of partisanship were deemed helpful in burnishing the abolitionists' reputation for unselfishness. But in March and April 1838 little-known abolitionists in Ohio and New Hampshire came out foursquare for "a distinct and separate political party." Such proposals apparently envisioned no more than statewide organizations designed to make suitable nominations when left in the lurch by Whigs and Democrats; yet the outcry against them was instantaneous and deafening. "All that can safely be done in a political way, is to be done by questioning candidates," insisted the Cincinnati *Philanthropist;* and John G. Whittier, then editing the *Pennsylvania Freeman,* cautioned his readers against turning the antislavery crusade into "a mere scramble for office . . . a struggle for men rather than for principle."[45]

Yet the idea of an independent party, once advanced by abolitionists themselves, continued to germinate. Moreover, the arguments against third party activity came increasingly to rest not on principle but on expediency. Many, to be sure, shared Whittier's early concern that direct political involvement risked corrupting the moral purity of their undertaking. Many others, however, chose to warn against the abandonment of "safe and efficacious" measures for "an experiment which has never been tried and is therefore uncertain." Persuading major par-

[44] *Pennsylvania Freeman,* Apr. 5, 1838; *Friend of Man,* Aug.-Sept. 1838; *Liberator,* Aug. 31, 1838.
[45] *Philanthropist,* Sept. 8, 1837, Mar. 27, May 22, 1838; *Pennsylvania Freeman,* Apr. 26, 1838.

ties to put up candidates opposed to slavery, argued Goodell, would save abolitionists "the labour . . . of organizing any party of our own, which we know it is our best policy to avoid doing, though we have never relinquished the *right* of doing it; and think it might be done without 'dabbling in dirty waters.' " To say that political action was, of necessity, corrupt was, he added, to say "that civil government is a device of the devil, and not an ordinance of God. To such a doctrine we are not prepared to give our assent."[46]

Once the lessons of 1838-39 laid bare the shortcomings of earlier forms of political abolitionism, it was inevitable that many more would grow increasingly receptive to the creation of a distinct antislavery party. Even before the results of the fall election were known, New York's Oswego County abolitionists invited all who believed in immediate emancipation to meet in New Haven, New York, in February 1839 "to form an anti Slavery political association, the object of which shall be to secure the Election of men to office who are abolitionists and members of antislavery societies." In December 1838 Amos A. Phelps, who had just resigned his agency for the Massachusetts Anti-Slavery Society in protest against Garrison's perfectionist "peculiarities," broached to Gerrit Smith a plan to establish a new antislavery organization, "comprising voters only," which to some at least meant "a new political party." And although Smith discouraged the proposal— he still preferred to incorporate in the articles of existing societies a formal pledge against "proslavery" voting—his close associate Alvan Stewart worked hard to keep it alive.[47]

Before the movement to establish an independent party could get well under way, abolitionists clashed angrily over the more basic question of voting. Most heated in Massachusetts and other corners of New England where Garrison's influence was strongest, this conflict soon helped to divide Massachusetts abolitionists—and by 1840 all others— into two warring camps. Although other issues (women's rights, anticlericalism, the relation of state organizations to the parent society)

[46] *Philanthropist*, Mar. 27, 1838; *Friend of Man*, Aug. 1, 1838.
[47] Copy of a Call to the Abolitionists of Oswego Co., N.Y., Nov. 2, 1838, Slavery Manuscripts, Box I, NYHS; Smith to Phelps, Dec. 28, 1838, Letterbook, Smith Papers; Anne Weston to Deborah Weston, Jan. 31, 1839, Weston Family Papers, BPL; William Goodell, *Slavery and Anti-Slavery; A History of the Great Struggle in Both Hemispheres; with a View of the Slavery Question in the United States* (New York, 1852), 469; Harlow, *Smith*, 145; William Goodell to H. B. Stanton, Feb. 23, 1839, Phelps Papers.

also contributed to the schisms of 1839 and 1840, differences over political action were clearly the fundamental ones. And while men for and against party involvement could afterward be found in either camp, realignment greatly facilitated the development of a politics of abolition.

2

Garrison and His Critics

THE CRUX OF THE POLITICAL DISAGREEMENT between the Garrisonians and their abolitionist critics was not the wisdom or morality of antislavery politics—nor, except tangentially, whether nonresistance and abolition were compatible. Rather, the disagreement centered on two conflicting political strategies. By the late 1830s a majority of abolitionists were convinced that only the *collective* influence of antislavery votes could force cautious politicians into an awareness of the evil of slavery and the need to act against it. Whether or not an independent party was deemed necessary, most agreed that effective action on behalf of the slave required concerted pressure *within* the political system—even if that meant no more than rewarding friends and punishing enemies.

Garrisonians, on the other hand, persuaded that regeneration of the electorate must precede any lasting reform and that partisan involvement compromised moral influence, preferred to "work *through* both parties, but not *with* them."[1] Even the nonresistants in Garrison's following, although they spurned voting as a sin, refused to turn their backs on the corrupt and coercive governments from which they vowed to exclude themselves. Indeed, for many, and surely for Garrison himself, nonresistance and the slogans that followed in its train—

---

[1] Lydia Maria Child, quoted in Aileen S. Kraditor, *Means and Ends in American Abolitionism: Garrison and His Critics on Strategy and Tactics, 1834-1850* (New York, 1967, 1969), 162. See *ibid.* chaps. V-VII for a highly appreciative analysis of Garrisonian political views.

"no human government," "no union with slaveholders"—were not some utopian dogma, some doctrinaire perfectionist creed, but stood as symbols of the enormity of the sin America confronted. As such, they could serve as agitational devices to reform human government as well as to justify a saintly exodus from it.

William Lloyd Garrison's own fascination with politics began early. As a young New England editor he proclaimed the crusty Federalism he had acquired in his native Newburyport, demanding that Massachusetts be reimbursed for militia expenses incurred in the War of 1812 and attacking Jefferson's "notorious" and "unsound" religious beliefs. He delivered his first speech in support of Harrison Gray Otis's nomination for Congress. Even while editing the *National Philanthropist*, a reformist sheet ostensibly concerned with morality, not politics, Garrison lectured his readers on such matters as the wonders of Henry Clay's national economic system and the diabolism of Andrew Jackson. In 1828 his Bennington, Vermont, *Journal of the Times* beat the drums for John Quincy Adams. These early political ventures were more notable for their enthusiasm than for their astuteness, more backward-tending than forward-looking. But they revealed an interest in (and at times a suspicion of) politics which Garrison never really lost.[2]

Once Garrison became engaged in the antislavery movement, he quickly showed himself as willing as anyone to exploit political tactics. He in fact thought seriously at first of establishing the *Liberator* in Washington rather than Boston, because Washington was "the head of the body politic, and the soul of the national system" and because the District of Columbia was "the first citadel to be carried."[3] It was Garrison who drafted the first statements formally committing abolitionists to take political as well as moral action against slavery. It was he who called for "a Christian party in politics." "I know it is the belief of many professedly good men, that they ought not to meddle in poli-

[2] Walter M. Merrill, *Against Wind and Tide: A Biography of William Lloyd Garrison* (Cambridge, Mass., 1963), 20-21; John L. Thomas, *The Liberator: William Lloyd Garrison, A Biography* (Boston, 1963), 43-46; Wendell P. and Francis J. Garrison, *William Lloyd Garrison, 1805-1879*, 4 vols. (New York, 1885), I, 73-77.
[3] *Proposals for Publishing a Weekly Periodical in Washington City, to be entitled the Public Liberator, and Journal of the Times* [Aug. 1830], Garrison Papers. Garrison at first perceived no incompatability between attacking slavery and championing worldly schemes of political economy—not even when advanced by slaveholders. In this prospectus for the abortive Washington venture he announced that, besides plugging for abolition and other social reforms, "I shall give a dignified support to Henry Clay and the American system."

tics," he remarked in 1834, "but they are cherishing a delusion which, if it does not prove fatal to their own souls, may prove the destruction of their country." And when "A Friend" expressed his hope that, since antislavery was a moral undertaking, the *Liberator* would shun political advice, Garrison bristled. As he had penned the Declaration of Sentiments, he might be expected to know what it called for. Garrison endorsed the antislavery petition campaign and the questioning of candidates, and he urged the importance of scrutinizing the conduct of public officeholders. "Although we may not, in the technical sense of the term, become politicians ourselves," he counseled David Lee Child in 1836, "yet it is vastly important that we should watch and expose mere politicians." Garrison practiced what he preached. He not only watched and exposed with a vengeance, but instructed others how to vote and, on occasion, did so himself.[4]

Garrison voted for Amasa Walker in the 1834 congressional election, and perhaps again in 1836. But the presidential contest in New England between Martin Van Buren and Daniel Webster, both critics of abolition, seems to have soured him on participation within the existing system. To those who urged votes for one or another presidential candidate as a lesser evil, Garrison remonstrated: "No—no—vote for an honest and upright man, even if you vote alone, or do not vote at all. 'Let the dead bury their dead.' "[5]

Disenchantment with the presidential campaign of 1836 may well have helped to precipitate his decision to "come out" from a corrupt society. Perhaps it was then that Garrison vowed never to vote again so long as governments held men in chains. But not for many months— not until after the perfectionist teachings of John Humphrey Noyes provided him with an ideological base for his assault on human government, and not until the formation of the New England Non-Resistance Society in September 1838—would he seek to bind his followers to a boycott of elections. And at no time did he renounce democratic politics.[6] It was just that by 1838 Garrison had formulated a theory of es-

[4] *Liberator*, Dec. 20, 27, 1834, Oct. 29, 1836; Garrison to Child, Aug. 6, 1836, Garrison Papers. The phrase "a Christian party in politics" was coined by the Reverend Ezra Stiles Ely in 1827. Garrison was the first to give it an antislavery turn. See Bertram Wyatt-Brown, "Prelude to Abolitionism: Sabbatarian Politics and the Rise of the Second Party System," *Journal of American History*, LVIII, No. 2 (Sept. 1971), 316-41.
[5] *Liberator*, Dec. 20, 1834, Oct. 29, Nov. 6, 1836.
[6] Thomas, *The Liberator*, 220-21.

sentially agitational politics which sacrificed piecemeal and temporary success to the work of moral purification and broad-gauge, root-and-branch reform. All abolitionists, the Garrisonians expected, would by example and argument continue to prod errant politicos along righteous paths and to purify the springs of public opinion. Those whom conscience permitted to vote would do so, taking care to support only friends of abolition and to avoid the snares of third party action—or anything that smacked of it. "I have always expected, I still expect," Garrison insisted in June 1839, "to see abolition at the ballot-box, renovating the political action of the country. . . . But this political reformation is to be effected solely by a change in the moral vision of the people;—not by attempting to prove that it is the duty of every voter to be an abolitionist."[7]

Yet for all its outward tolerance, the new Garrisonian position on politics raised serious problems. It was all very well, as Wendell Phillips said, "to stand on the old broad anti-slavery program, and offer the right hand of brotherhood to everyone who gives the slave all the moral, political and religious action, which he can conscientiously exert, be it much or little, in one form or another." Garrison sounded wonderfully liberal when he insisted that he objected not to political action but merely to attempts to *prescribe* political conduct for all abolitionists.[8] But, as many reformers soon discovered, without *unity* of action many forms of political activity became difficult if not impossible. Interrogation, for instance, was a weak reed at best; yet without the *concerted* strength of abolitionism it had no chance at all. So too the effectiveness of any independent or third party action would be gravely weakened unless it could count upon the support of *all* abolitionists.

Many found Garrisonian nonresistance dangerous not only because it hobbled organized antislavery politics but also because it tended to tar all of abolition with its radicalism and thus frightened off many potential recruits. ". . . Garrison is doing us more mischief than his neck is worth," lamented Elizur Wright, Jr., in October 1837. "The wind of perfectionism has blown off the roof of his judgment, which was already somewhat started by indiscreet praise. . . . I have no more hope

[7] *Liberator*, June 28, 1839.
[8] *Ibid.* Mar. 8, 1839. See also Samuel J. May to Garrison, July 25, 1839, Garrison Papers.

from him in the future, than I have from the inmates of Bedlam in general." Garrison often strenuously denied that nonresistance and antislavery were in any way identical. Yet so symbolic was he of modern abolition that, say what he might, the notoriety of his new views inevitably attached itself to the cause of the slave. To the acute distress of many, Garrison not only introduced nonresistance and other "extraneous" topics in the *Liberator*, but sometimes seemed to be trading on a false union of antislavery and nonresistance. His boast that all good nonresistants were also true-blue abolitionists struck reformers like Orange Scott as a calculated attempt to aggrandize nonresistance by making it appear that all abolitionists endorsed such doctrines.[9]

Throughout 1838 and early 1839 many attempts were made to stimulate effective political action on behalf of the slave. At first most such proposals asked merely that abolitionists remain faithful to the cause and cast ballots for none but proven "friends of liberty." So long as the test of right political behavior remained couched in negative terms—no votes for proslavery candidates, no abandonment of political efforts, no distinct antislavery party—nonresistants had little cause to complain.[10] Gradually, however, as the 1838 election campaign gained momentum, those who perceived the need for unity at the polls and found Garrison's recent radicalism risky if not downright seditious brought forward stronger resolves, pointing to "the duty of abolitionists to vote at the polls. . . ." Although this harder line clearly impugned the integrity of nonvoting abolitionists, Garrisonians at first raised no objections. Indeed, the New England Anti-Slavery Convention approved "with great unanimity" a pair of resolutions offered by Alvan Stewart: one proclaimed it "the solemn and imperative duty of every abolitionist" to use his political influence to secure the nomination of antislavery candidates for Congress; the other demanded that all humanitarians "go to the polls in all cases and vote, irrespective of party, for such persons, and *such only*, as will promote the great cause of emancipation and human liberty. . . ." According to John Greenleaf Whittier, who played a prominent part in the convention, "These resolutions were advocated by Garrison himself, and the whole body of non-resistants

[9] Wright to Beriah Green, Oct. 17, 1837, Wright to Amos A. Phelps, Sept. 5, 1837, Wright to Garrison, Oct. 10, Nov. 6, 1837, Wright to his parents, Aug. 9, 1837 (all typed copies), Elizur Wright, Jr., Papers, BPL; Thomas, *The Liberator*, 261–62.
[10] *Pennsylvania Freeman*, Apr. 5, 26, 1838; *Philanthropist*, June 19, 1838.

voted for them, with the exception of C. C. Burleigh and two or three others—one a Van Buren man, who could not give up his party." And in early December, at a meeting in Concord of abolitionists from Massachusetts' Fourth Congressional District, Wendell Phillips eloquently endorsed, and Garrison declined to oppose, a resolve "that it is quite as important, and as such our duty, to . . . vote *for* a good and true man, as it is to *decline* voting for one who is not. . . ."[11]

Between December and mid-January 1839, however, the Massachusetts abolitionists split into two embittered camps. Anticipating a showdown on the question of political action at the upcoming yearly meeting of the Massachusetts Anti-Slavery Society, Garrison's critics—many of them clerical abolitionists distrustful of his perfectionism, angered by his vituperative assaults on churches for their alleged complicity with sin, and intolerant of his pleas for women's rights—set out to discredit nonresistance once and for all. If they could not rescue the Massachusetts Society from the "vortex of spiritual Quixotism," they stood pledged to set up a rival organization.[12]

In the weeks immediately preceding the state anniversary, the conservatives pressed their political program at local meetings throughout the state. At Fitchburg and Fall River, abolitionists embraced resolutions which strongly affirmed the duty to vote. Simultaneously pressure mounted for the establishment by the Massachusetts Society of a cheap official weekly newspaper devoted exclusively to the discussion of slavery. Garrison had tried to head off any weekly rival to his *Liberator* by prevailing on the board of managers to publish a *monthly* newspaper, the *Abolitionist*, to be edited jointly by Wendell Phillips, Edmund Quincy, and himself. But this proposition had understandably left Garrison's critics cold. What was needed, argued the Reverend Charles T. Torrey, long a thorn in Garrison's side, was a paper which would reach out to the estimated 20,000 antislavery voters in Massachusetts (fewer than 1500 subscribed to the *Liberator*, he contended)—especially one which would "take strong ground in regard to the *duty* in

---

[11] *Liberator*, June 8, 1838; Whittier to Elizur Wright, Jr., Mar. 14, 1840, in Samuel T. Pickard (ed.), *Whittier as a Politician* (Boston, 1900), 13; *The True History of the Late Division in the Anti-Slavery Societies, being part of the Second Annual Report of the Executive Committee of the Massachusetts Abolition Society* (Boston, 1841), 23-24.

[12] Elizur Wright, Jr., to William Lloyd Garrison, Nov. 6, 1837 (typed copy), Wright Papers, BPL.

carrying out our principles in our Ecclesiastical relations, and at the *polls.*"[13]

Led by Torrey and Phelps, and encouraged by members of the American Anti-Slavery Society's executive committee, the Massachusetts conservatives struggled to secure the election of delegates who were prepared to "urge political action as a *Christian duty*, in accordance with our original principles of association" and were favorably disposed toward their plan for a new antislavery paper. But Garrison soon smelled out the "deplorable and alarming" plot against him and quickly moved to baffle it. The threat to his leadership in Massachusetts and New England, to the well-being of the *Liberator*, and to the respectability of nonresistant abolitionists was clear and present. "Strong foes are without, insidious plotters are within the camp," Garrison proclaimed. "A conflict is at hand . . . which is to be more hotly contested, and which will require more firmness of nerve and singleness of purpose . . . than any through which we have passed to victory." Once again he called upon "our early, intrepid, storm-proof, scarred and veteran co-adjutors" to muster at the coming anniversary, "prepared to give battle to internal contrivers of mischief, as readily as to external and avowed enemies."[14]

The battle was joined on January 23, moments after Francis Jackson had called to order the immense throng which packed Boston's Marlboro Chapel to the rafters. In attendance were all the leading dissidents —Phelps, Stanton, Torrey, and Alanson St. Clair—as well as Garrison and his chief supporters—Jackson, Wendell Phillips, Samuel J. May, and Ellis Gray Loring. Deferring any vote on Garrison's annual report until the issues at hand could be disposed of, Garrison's lieutenants immediately moved for consideration of resolutions proposed by their rivals. The first of these called for the establishment of an official weekly paper, "to advocate political as well as moral action; to be ex-

[13] Thomas, *The Liberator*, 265-66; Garrisons, *Garrison*, II, 262-70; copy of circular letter from Charles T. Torrey to various persons in Norfolk Co., Mass., Jan. 4, 1839, Charles T. Torrey Papers, Congregational Christian Historical Society, Boston, Mass. Calls for a new, "truly A. S. paper" followed close in the wake of Garrison's perfectionist awakening. See, e.g., William Smyth to A. A. Phelps, Mar. 31, 1838, anon. to Phelps, Apr. 7, 1838, Charles T. Torrey to Phelps, Aug. 14, 1838, Phelps Papers.
[14] Copy of circular letter from Charles T. Torrey to some Massachusetts abolitionists, Jan. 7, 1839, Torrey Papers; A. A. Phelps to U. C. Burnap, Jan. 12, 1839, Phelps Papers; Garrisons, *Garrison*, II, 262; *Liberator*, Jan. 11, 1839.

clusively confined to the object of the Anti Slavery cause, and edited by a man or men, who can conscientiously, heartily and consistently advocate all the anti-slavery measures, political as well as moral action. . . ." Having set down requirements they knew Garrison could not abide, the anti-Garrisonians mockingly added that if the *Liberator* could be made to conform to these requirements there would be no need to look further.[15]

Inevitably, discussion of the need for a new journal soon slipped into a debate over the political principles it was designed to promote. Alanson St. Clair stressed chiefly the desirability of a cheap paper with broad circulation to publicize abolitionist activities. But Torrey and Stanton boldly contended that Garrison's nonresistance philosophy had atrophied political efforts against slavery, and that made a second weekly necessary. The resourceful Stanton freely admitted that political matter appeared regularly in the *Liberator*. But, he protested, the editor irresponsibly left it to others to gather all such commentary. Indeed, Stanton went on, Garrison undermined the political proposals in his own paper by accompanying them with no-government preachments calculated to nullify their effect. "It is not that other subjects are introduced into the *Liberator*," he explained, "—it is that *such* other subjects are introduced—subjects so injurious to the cause."[16] In sum, Stanton told the stunned assemblage, Garrison had "lowered the standard of abolition."

Garrison leapt to his own defense. "Am I recreant to the cause?" he asked. Shouts of "No! No!" cascaded from all corners of the chapel. The insurgents must have heard in these cheers their ultimate defeat, but Stanton pushed doggedly on.

"Let me ask him a question," Stanton requested the convention. "Mr. Garrison! Do you or do you not believe it a sin to go to the polls?"

"Sin for *me!*" came the reply.

---

[15] Except where otherwise noted, my account of the 1839 Massachusetts Anti-Slavery Society Convention rests on the following sources: *Seventh Annual Report of the Board of Managers of the Massachusetts Anti-Slavery Society. Presented Jan. 24, 1839* (Boston, 1839), i-viii; Maria Weston Chapman, *Right and Wrong in Massachusetts* (Boston, 1839), 93-113; Garrisons, *Garrison*, II, 271-76.

[16] Elizur Wright made the same point soon afterward. "With all due respect to G[arrison]," he wrote Maria W. Chapman (Feb. 18, 1839), "I consider his 'nonresistance' sheer lunacy—and sadly ill timed, as it cuts the hamstrings of abolitionism just at the crisis of battle—so far as it has any edge at all. But the worst of it is, *foenum habet in coma*—it scares needlessly." Wright Papers, BPL.

Garrison had wiggled too neatly off the hook, and Stanton pressed harder. "I ask you again, do you or do you not believe it a sin to go to the polls?"

"Sin for *me*," the editor answered once more.

There can be no doubt that Stanton's "treacherous interrogatory"— indeed, the basic strategy of the dissidents at the convention—was designed to force Garrison either to deny his own principles or to renounce as sinners the great majority of abolitionists who thought it proper to vote. Either course, as Garrison at once perceived, would grind him up and purge abolition of perfectionist heresies. In a sense, then, his cryptic rejoinder to Stanton was both a shrewd defense of his position and beliefs and a liberal refusal to make nonresistance the test of bona fide abolitionism. Yet it was more than that. It was also the boast of an unquestioned egotist and true believer, one who had discovered in nonresistance the purest and most effective way to demolish slavery in America. "Sin for so pure an abolitionist as me," he seemed to be saying. His opponents had long suffered his egotism (even friends sometimes called him "the Pope"),[17] and now they recoiled at the implied standard of *true* abolitionism his reply to Stanton maintained.

Garrison's friends, however, were both eloquent and numerous. By an overwhelming margin they set aside the proposition for a new paper, together with Stanton's resolution that every abolitionist who refused, "*under any pretext*," to vote for antislavery candidates was "guilty of gross inconsistency," and unfaithful to "the original and fundamental principles of the Anti-Slavery enterprise." So powerful were Garrison's legions that they easily defeated even Alanson St. Clair's mild resolution affirming it "the imperious duty of every abolitionist who could conscientiously do so, to go to the polls." The rub lay more in the resolve's source than in its language, though there were some who found sinister and potentially coercive such an affirmative substitute for earlier pledges against voting for proslavery candidates. In the end the delegates accepted with near unanimity Garrison's own "compromise" formula:

> Resolved, that those abolitionists who feel themselves called upon, by a sense of duty, to go the polls, and yet purposely absent themselves from the polls whenever an opportunity is presented

[17] Oscar Sherwin, *Prophet of Liberty: The Life and Times of Wendell Phillips* (New York, 1958), 73-74.

to vote for a friend of the slave—or who, when there, follow
their party predilections to the abandonment of their abolition
principles—are recreant to their high professions, and unworthy
of the name they assume.

By a vote of roughly 180 to 24 the convention then approved Garrison's annual report, and the rout was complete. " . . . The Society
hauled down its flag and run up the crazy banner of the non-govern-
ment heresy, and we had to rally around or be ostracised," lamented
Stanton. "The split is wide, and can never be closed up."[18]

2

Stanton's prophecy proved correct. While the Garrisonians celebrated
victory their critics moved to create a "new organization" to cleanse
abolition of all extraneous "isms." The first step was to establish a
weekly rival to the *Liberator*. Massachusetts insurgents must have made
preliminary plans in anticipation of defeat at the state antislavery convention, for arrangements for a new paper were complete within less
than a week of its close, and the *Massachusetts Abolitionist*, as it was
christened, first appeared in Boston on February 7, 1839. As its editor,
the weekly's backers chose Elizur Wright, Jr., who was at the time
corresponding secretary of the American Anti-Slavery Society, god-
father of the *Emancipator*, and, since 1837, an outspoken critic of
Garrison's "come-outer" notions. The Massachusetts dissidents were
particularly happy to land Wright because, in addition to his editorial
talents (even Garrison called him "an able, ready and caustic writer"),
he brought to the *Abolitionist* and the antislavery organization which
shortly formed around it a renown and reputation for integrity which
lent respectability to the new venture. The addition of Wright, Henry
Stanton assured A. A. Phelps, "inspires such men as Goodell, G. Smith,
Whittier, [Isaac] Knapp, [Gamaliel] Bailey, in truth everybody but
the Garrisonians, with the confidence that yours is *a real ultra abolition movement. This is worth its weight in gold.*"[19]

[18] Stanton to James G. Birney, Jan. 26, 1839, Dwight L. Dumond (ed.), *Letters of
James Gillespie Birney, 1831-1857*, 2 vols. (New York, 1938), I, 481-83.
[19] Garrisons, *Garrison*, II, 300; Stanton to Phelps, Sept. 2, [1839], Phelps Papers.
Wright did not undertake his editorial duties until May 23, 1839, after the annual
meeting of the American Anti-Slavery Society. Before then, however, he secretly

As its name suggested, the *Abolitionist* was devoted exclusively to the annihilation of slavery. The captive of no sect or party, its sponsors proclaimed in the first issue, it would shun "all irrelevant and extraneous questions." To Beriah Green, Wright explained: "My plan is not to enter the field to cut up the weeds—the *isms*—but to hoe the corn and till it well, and let the weeds look out for themselves."[20]

The "corn" which Wright and his associates proposed to cultivate was a hybrid of political and moral abolition. From the beginning, opposition to Garrison had come from those alarmed at the religious as well as the political implications of perfectionism, and ten of the *Abolitionist*'s twenty-seven-man publication committee were clergymen—including Phelps, St. Clair, and Orange Scott. Some, especially among clerical abolitionists, had rarely involved themselves in politics of any sort.[21] But most of those responsible for establishing the *Abolitionist* felt a strong need to carry antislavery convictions to the polling place.

The lead editorial in its first issue made clear the *Abolitionist*'s stand. Headlined "POLITICAL ACTION," it called for a return to the true principle of augmenting moral appeals with antislavery pressure at the polls. "The political action we ask of you," it said, "is to undo by your *votes*, the mischief that your votes have done, and those of your fathers. *Votes* make the men that make the laws that make the slaves. . . . *Votes* buy chains for slaves, and gags for freemen." More precisely, the keynote editorial proposed concerted political campaigns to destroy slavery in the territories and the District of Columbia and to ban the interstate slave trade. If, finally, such indirect measures did not force the slave states to uproot their peculiar institution, the federal Constitution would have to be amended.[22]

In subsequent weeks the *Abolitionist* refined and amplified its argument for antislavery politics. Far from detracting from moral suasion, political action actually heightened its effectiveness by securing a respectful hearing for abolitionists' appeals. So long as slavery's enemies had abstained from direct political involvement, Wright contended

---

wrote several editorials for the *Abolitionist*. See Stanton to Phelps, Jan. 29, 1839 (typed copy), Wright Papers, LC.

[20] *Massachusetts Abolitionist*, Feb. 7, 1839; Wright to Green, Feb. 9, 1839 (typed copy), Wright Papers, BPL. The *Abolitionist*'s mottos—"Supremacy of the Laws" and "Liberty, the right of all—law its defence"—bespoke its hostility to no-government heresies.

[21] *Liberator*, Mar. 22, 1839.

[22] *Massachusetts Abolitionist*, Feb. 7, 1839.

in his first pronouncement as editor, their proposals rarely received careful attention. But by rallying at the ballot box, abolitionists were beginning to be *"feared* as they never would have been had they remained in the quiescent land of abstractions. Their moral *power*," he claimed, "has been . . . multiplied tenfold by the political effort." Political action, moreover, was a remedy for moral callousness in the Massachusetts legislature (which had recently refused to consider revision in the state's miscegenation law or to protest the Atherton gag) as well as an instrument for change in Congress and the slave states.[23]

Capably edited, energetically promoted, and selling at less than half the *Liberator*'s price, the *Abolitionist* soon gained enough subscribers to frighten many Garrisonians.[24] To "hedge up the way of the *Abolitionist*," the Massachusetts Society began in March to publish the *Cradle of Liberty*, a cheap weekly made up of the best antislavery articles in the *Liberator*. Yet outside Boston and its coastal satellites the *Abolitionist* continued to make substantial inroads among pious reformers. "It must be put down or it will put down the Mass. Soc.," Maria W. Chapman, Garrison's most strident champion, warned in April. Putting the *Abolitionist* down, however, proved a difficult task. Not only did it receive moral support from antislavery leaders in other states, but Garrisonian attacks on it often backfired. "I am convinced that every move Garrison can make against the Abolitionist re-acts against the Liberator," observed the most shrewd and charming of all Garrisonians, Lydia Maria Child. "Friends at a distance *will* not believe that such men as Stanton and Phelps are plotters against the cause, and if you prove their narrow sectarianism, nothing is gained, at least for the present, for this seems a virtue in their eyes." From Northampton she wrote: "I think I may say I do not know *one* Garrison abolitionist here. . . . The abolitionists are honestly, sincerely frightened at the bearing of the Peace principles on governments; but more than that, I suspect they dimly perceive that these [perfectionist] ideas are shaking a belief in the literal sense of the Old Testament to its very foundations."[25]

23 *Ibid.* Mar. 14, May 23, 1839.
24 The *Abolitionist* numbered between 3000 and 3100 subscribers in 1839. Garrison (whose own circulation was perhaps 2300) credited his rival with only 1500 patrons and estimated that 5000 would be necessary to defray its expenses. See the report of George Russell to the Executive Committee of the *Massachusetts Abolitionist*, Aug. 12, 1839, Phelps Papers; Garrison to George W. Benson, Mar. 19, 1839, Garrison Papers; Garrisons, *Garrison*, I, 432.
25 Garrisons, *Garrison*, II, 284-85; *Friend of Man*, Feb. 20, 1839; Chapman to

The rift widened in March at the quarterly meeting of the Massachusetts Anti-Slavery Society. A long-smoldering quarrel between the state and national societies over the collection and control of finances produced most of the heat at this gathering, but sparks also flew over the political obligations of abolitionists. James G. Birney, who along with Lewis Tappan and Henry Stanton came to defend the interests of the parent society, provoked the Garrisonian majority by contending that it was the duty of all members of the American Anti-Slavery Society to take political as well as moral action against slavery and that anyone whose conscientious scruples barred him from voting ought voluntarily to withdraw from the Society. To repudiate the vote, Birney alleged in an amplifying letter, was as subversive as to reject moral suasion. "For if one of these modes may be rejected, so may the other," he argued, "and we might thus find ourselves an Association having a proposed end without any prescribed means for attaining it—which, in my view, would render the act of associating *useless*." He would forcibly exclude no one, but he thought it unworthy "in any *new* sect . . . to bend the constitution to suit their peculiar tenets." Stanton, who had earlier stressed the importance of making "a good defense, even tho' a packed jury condemn us," seconded Birney's remarks. Reading from back issues of the *Liberator*, he quoted Garrison himself on the duty of abolitionists to carry their principles to the ballot box.

Garrison disposed of these assaults easily and to the entire satisfaction of his followers. To Stanton's charge that he had strayed from the true path he had himself helped to blaze, Garrison merely replied that "whereas we were then blind, now we see; and greatly do we rejoice in the light." He parried Birney's plea for an association of abolitionists single-mindedly devoted to a political as well as moral crusade against slavery by resorting to what had already become a familiar tactic. Ignoring the implicit assumption of his critics that effective political action depended upon *united* pressure at the polls, Garrison defined the controversy as one over freedom of conscience. "The question is not what is or what has been our individual opinion respecting the use of the elective franchise," he maintained, "—but, whether those who de-

Deborah Weston, Apr. 4, 1839, Weston Family Papers; Child to Caroline Weston, Mar. 7, 1839, David and Lydia Child Papers, BPL. The *Abolitionist*'s subscription price was $1.00 per year, the *Liberator*'s $2.50. The *Cradle of Liberty* cost 75¢, or 50¢ in large quantities.

cline mingling in politics, for conscience sake, are henceforth to be regarded as disqualified from joining or remaining in the society."[26]

In May 1839 the warring factions carried their dispute to New York City and the sixth anniversary of the American Anti-Slavery Society. Expecting "a desperate struggle," the Garrisonians arrived in strength—nearly a hundred delegates, men and women, came from New England, and a good many more from eastern Pennsylvania and upstate New York. But those bent on "confining the Society to its *single* object—the *abolition of Slavery*" and on asserting the duty of right voting had also responded to pleas for full attendance; as a result control of the convention turned on whether Garrison's female supporters would be allowed to participate. The first day and a half of the convention was spent in a discussion of this question. When the yeas and nays were at last called for, 180 voted for the admission of women, 140 against. The Garrisonians had won an important victory; but since a fair number of political activists had also voted to seat the women the fate of other business to come was still hard to predict.[27]

The politically oriented executive committee set the terms of subsequent debate with an annual report (drafted by Lewis Tappan) which argued strongly that it was the duty of *all* abolitionists to use the ballot to provide "protection of law" to slaves as well as freemen. The anti-slavery movement now possessed the power to take effective political action, the report asserted, and to fail to use that power would be irresponsible and contrary to the Society's Declaration of Sentiments and constitution. To nonresistants, who countenanced certain indirect political tactics, notably petitions, the committee issued a direct challenge. The ballot, its report insisted, was an indispensable weapon; without it Congress could not be swayed. "The power of influencing Congress by mere petition has already failed. Four times have the ears of the popular branch been hermetically sealed. In both houses are the petitions regularly delivered over unopened to the dust and cobwebs of oblivion. . . . So far as practical means are concerned, if the ballot-box be given up, the cause is given up with it."[28]

[26] *Liberator*, Apr. 5, 1839; Stanton to Joshua Leavitt, Mar. 20, 1839, Weston Family Papers; Kraditor, *Means and Ends in American Abolitionism*, 124-27.
[27] Garrison to Mrs. Garrison, May 5, 1839, Garrison Papers; John G. Whittier to [?], Apr. 24, 1839, John G. Whittier Papers, FHL; Thomas, *The Liberator*, 272-73.
[28] *Sixth Annual Report of the Executive Committee of the American Anti-Slavery Society . . . 1839* (New York, 1839), 76-79.

Once again, Stanton and Birney (the latter already emerging as the most resourceful and effective spokesman for antislavery politics) took the lead in defending the committee's position against Garrisonian attacks. Stanton spent most of his energy in support of a resolution "that the power of the free States is sufficient, if properly exercised, to ultimately exterminate slavery in the nation." The power of which he spoke was political power, and the course he proposed—abolition of the slave trade and slavery in the District of Columbia, a ban on new slave states to make possible a constitutional amendment against human bondage, laws to protect runaways, and the like—implied concerted action at the polls. But because he stopped short of insisting that all abolitionists vote, and because Garrisonians had no objection to acts of political propaganda, Stanton's proposal passed without controversy.[29]

Birney, on the other hand, joined in a sustained and acrimonious battle against the Garrisonians on the most fundamental question raised by the executive committee's report: could one, out of conscience or otherwise, refuse to vote for the slave and still remain a faithful abolitionist? As a substitute for the committee's call for antislavery votes, Garrison had proposed a series of resolutions which endorsed petitioning, spoke loosely of the importance of electing to public office only proven friends of the slave, and put on record that it had never been the Society's intention "to exclude from its membership any persons, on account of their being prevented by conscientious scruples from participating in all the measures which the mass of the Society . . . may have contemplated as proper for the advancement of the antislavery cause."[30]

Unable to head off these resolves, Birney stubbornly brought forward one of his own. On the eve of the convention (Garrisonians thought it deliberately timed so as to avoid a rebuttal) he had published in the *Emancipator* a lengthy "View of the Constitution of the American A. S. Society as Connected with the 'No-Government' Question."[31] In it Birney made crystal clear his belief that nonresistance and the brand of abolition long practiced by the American Society were radically incompatible. It simply would not do, he argued, to contend that government and no-government men could act independently and

[29] *Ibid.* 12-19.
[30] *Liberator*, May 24, 1839.
[31] *Emancipator*, May 2, 1839; Garrisons, *Garrison*, II, 294-95.

harmoniously under a loose construction of the American Anti-Slavery Society's constitution. For the difference between no-government advocates "and those who prefer *any* government" to a state of virtual anarchy was vast. "When in obedience to the principles of the society, I go to the polls, and there call on my neighbors to unite with me in electing to Congress, men who are in favor of Human Rights, I am met by a No-Government abolitionist inculcating the doctrine, that Congress have *no rightful authority* to act at all in the premises," he complained. "How can we proceed together?"

To force the issue, therefore, Birney now asked the Society officially to proclaim "that to maintain that the elective franchise ought not to be used by abolitionists to advance the cause of emancipation, is inconsistent with the duty of abolitionists under the constitution."[32] Garrison's followers discerned a loophole in even this seemingly hostile resolution; they had never maintained that all abolitionists ought not to vote—only those whose consciences forbade it. Indeed, a common criticism leveled at the no-government men by Birney and others had been that "Proclaiming on one page that all human attempts to protect the innocent and punish the guilty by physical force are of the devil," they preached on the next "that those whose consciences approve of government are bound *to vote*." Conscience thus became "a chameleon-like thing," as Elizur Wright put it—an unstable guide which proclaimed to be right whatever men thought right.[33]

The Garrisonians correctly understood the intent of Birney's resolution, however, and were glad when parliamentary sleight-of-hand brushed it aside in favor of a more moderate declaration drafted by John G. Whittier and introduced by the business committee. This declaration simply reaffirmed the Society's position that voting "so as to promote the abolition of slavery, is of high obligation—a duty which, as abolitionists, we owe to our enslaved fellow countrymen, groaning under legal oppression." Garrisonians opposed even this compromise, preferring instead C. C. Burleigh's empty plea that all abolitionists do their duty as they saw it. But Burleigh's amendment was lost in the same procedural shuffle that buried Birney's. In the end Whittier's resolution carried, 84 to 77.

[32] *Sixth Annual Report of the Executive Committee of the American Anti-Slavery Society . . . 1839*, 42-44.
[33] *Emancipator*, May 2, 1839; Elizur Wright, Jr., to Beriah Green, Apr. 2, 1839 (typed copy), Wright Papers, BPL.

The vote on Whittier's resolution was by no means an accurate gauge of abolitionist opinion regarding political action. By the time the tally was taken on the fourth day of the meeting, many weary Garrisonians had already left for home. Moreover, as the *Liberator* later claimed, some who voted for Whittier's declaration might have supported Burleigh's watered-down substitute if given the chance.[34] And always, of course, there were many who believed strongly in the duty of anti-slavery voting but who objected to any attempt to force such action on their nonresistant colleagues. Still, the roll call[35] roughly indicated the regions of greatest interest in distinct antislavery politics and fore-shadowed the centers of Liberty party strength in the future.

VOTE ON WHITTIER RESOLUTION, MAY 10, 1839

	Yeas	Nays		Yeas	Nays
Maine	3	1	New Jersey	5	1
New Hampshire	2	—	Pennsylvania	6	9
Vermont	3	1	Delaware	1	—
Massachusetts	13	47	Ohio	2	—
Rhode Island	2	6	Illinois	1	—
Connecticut	4	2	Michigan	1	—
New York	41	10	TOTAL	84	77

The substantial "yea" vote from New York's delegation reflected a growing determination among abolitionists in New York City (where the executive committee's influence was strong) and in the "Burned-over District" to implement more effective political methods. So too the re-volt of Massachusetts conservatives against the anarchistic politics of the Garrisonians stood revealed in the roll call of that state. Phelps, Scott, and Torrey led the minority of thirteen whose support of Whit-tier's resolution hardened earlier divisions. Indeed, as the tally made clear, only in Massachusetts (where Wendell Phillips, Anne Weston, Henry C. Wright, Oliver Johnson, and others followed his lead) and in little Rhode Island could Garrison count upon truly solid support for his position on politics. In the West, where the duty of voting was nearly always taken for granted, Garrisonian strength was nil—as the unanimous vote for Whittier's resolve indicated.[36]

[34] *Liberator*, May 24, 1839.
[35] *Sixth Annual Report of the Executive Committee of the American Anti-Slavery Society . . . 1839*, 43-44.
[36] Smith, *Liberty and Free Soil Parties*, 33.

Yet the Garrisonians could look back on the 1839 convention as something of a victory. They had pulled off an immense tactical coup in the admission of women (over the strenuous objections of most though not all political activists),[37] they had extended a system of *voluntary* contributions calculated to strap the executive committee, and they had blocked Birney's attempt to make voting a test of membership. With good reason Garrison returned to Boston "with as light a heart as he brought."[38]

Garrison's critics certainly found little cheer in the convention results. Not only had they been repeatedly outflanked by their adversaries, but the decision to admit women as equals and the absence of any provision for proportional representation made likely continued Garrisonian domination of the American Anti-Slavery Society. Some were ready then and there to abandon the old ship to the Garrisonian pirates and to construct a new, more reliable vessel.[39]

Late in May, Bay State dissidents took the first step by seceding from the "old organization" and forming the Massachusetts Abolition Society. Dedicated to scraping away the perfectionist barnacles that retarded antislavery's advance, the splinter group received early assurances of support from the American Society's politically minded executive committee. "There is no doubt that our Comm. will recognize your Society as auxiliary in the fullest sense . . . ," Stanton advised Phelps four days after Garrison's rivals had hoisted their flag. "All our brethren here are specially anxious you should go ahead *abolitionally*, to make your movement felt on the State."[40]

In their own eyes, members of the Abolition Society were the true representatives of "Abolition-as-it-was in 1831-5"; and while a few new recruits signed up (among them Lewis Tappan's brother Charles), most "were the old *standbys*." Many, including Phelps and

[37] Most leading advocates of forceful political action had opposed "women's rights" as much because it seemed an extraneous and diverting issue—a "tin kettle" tied "to the tail of antislavery"—and because Garrison stood to benefit from their votes in convention as because of their distaste for "promiscuous assemblies." A good many anti-Garrisonians, moreover, among them Alvan Stewart, Joshua Leavitt, Gerrit Smith, William L. Chaplin, and Sherman Booth, all later active in the Liberty party, voted in favor of seating women delegates to the 1839 meeting. See Goodell, *Slavery and Anti-Slavery*, 463.
[38] Garrisons, *Garrison*, II, 299.
[39] Charles T. Torrey to Amos A. Phelps, Nov. 8, 1839; Phelps Papers.
[40] *Massachusetts Abolitionist*, June 6, 1839; H. B. Stanton to A. A. Phelps, June 1, 1839, Phelps Papers.

sixteen of the forty-one vice presidents, were clergymen. Yet all agreed on the need for thoroughgoing political war on slavery. Indeed, one of the new society's first acts was to send delegates to a convention at Albany in July 1839 to debate the merits of various plans of political action—among them one calling for the creation of an antislavery third party.[41]

[41] Charles T. Torrey to Ichabod Codding, June 3, 1839, Ichabod Codding Papers, FHL; *Massachusetts Abolitionist*, July 18, 1839; Goodell, *Slavery and Anti-Slavery*, 461-62.

3

Formation of the Liberty Party

IN RETROSPECT, the formation of an independent political party dedicated to the overthrow of slavery appears to have been almost inevitable. Once abolitionists acknowledged it a duty to carry their principles to the polls and to vote only for known foes of slavery, the creation of an organization to ensure acceptable candidates and to unify political action became a supremely logical and seemingly irresistible act. Certainly once the failure of interrogation became apparent—as it did to most abolitionists after 1838—the gate to independent nominations and separate political organization stood wide open.

Yet until the spring of 1840 the vast majority of American abolitionists saw third party politics as neither inevitable nor desirable. Garrisonians, of course, took a predictably jaundiced view of distinct party politics. But even among those who strenuously advocated political activity and who admitted the failure of previous attempts to influence existing parties, opposition to partisan action was at first powerful and widespread.

Garrisonians based their criticism of an antislavery political party chiefly on what they considered to be the inexpediency of such a venture. Both the instrumental nature of Garrison's own no-government beliefs and the fact that "the great majority" of his followers still believed in the duty of voting dictated their taking such a tack. Foremost among the arguments Garrisonians leveled against the establishment of a third party was that such a step would inevitably divide rather than unite abolitionists. At the same time, by advertising (indeed, exaggerat-

43

ing) their numerical weakness, the formation of an independent party would render contemptible the moral strength of abolitionists as well.[1] Moreover, despite the efforts of philanthropists, any such party would soon become a haven for spoilsmen and the political castoffs of other parties, "the floodgates of corruption would be opened," and the moral influence of abolition be all but destroyed. Clergymen, fearing that anti-slavery testimony would be mistaken for "electioneering harangues," would desert the cause; "and without the aid of the pulpit," Garrison somewhat surprisingly observed, "there is no hope of the peaceful or speedy abolition of slavery."[2]

All in all, Garrisonians repeatedly maintained, it would be the worst sort of folly to scrap the successful British model for "a hazardous experiment" in third party politics. Far better to limit antislavery political activity, as their English cousins had done, to interrogation and support at the polls for none but proven friends of the slave. In that way reformers might impress their views on the leading parties, both of which presently included antislavery members and were vying for abolitionist backing. "It is a fact, not less encouraging than undeniable," noted Garrison in 1839, "that both the Whig and Democratic parties have consulted the wishes of abolitionists even beyond the measure of their real political strength. More you cannot expect, under any circumstances." A third party, on the other hand, would only provoke the wrath of its powerful rivals. Finally, although never a conscious consideration, establishment of an antislavery political party would surely dilute Garrison's own influence. At every turn and in every way possible, therefore, Garrison and his disciples strove to head off "the party movement."[3]

From the time the issue first arose and for many months thereafter, most non-Garrisonian abolitionists also warned against the snares of distinct party involvement. Even in upstate New York, where the idea of independent political action first took root, support for so novel an

---

[1] David Lee Child, a Whiggish Garrisonian, opposed even antislavery bloc voting for major party candidates on this ground. "*We have got ourselves prematurely counted*," he complained in a letter to the American Society's 1839 anniversary. So long as the numbers of the abolitionists had been gauged by the goodness of their cause, "we have been thought stronger than we were; now, we are deemed weaker than we are." John Quincy Adams echoed this opinion. See Garrisons, *Garrison*, II, 312.
[2] Quoted in *Philanthropist*, Nov. 12, 1839.
[3] *Liberator*, Aug. 10, 1838; A. A. Phelps to H. B. Stanton, Nov. 26, 1839, Weston Family Papers; Charles C. Burleigh to James M. McKim, Dec. 27, 1839, Antislavery Collection, Cornell University.

undertaking was at the outset scant. At a meeting of the executive committee of the New York Anti-Slavery Society in January 1839, only Alvan Stewart came out "strong for a political party." Gerrit Smith, still hopeful that something might be salvaged from the interrogation system, vehemently countered Stewart's arguments. He warned of the corrupting effects of too deep an immersion in politics, "& spoke of *Caucus* & *party* management as necessarily at war with vital religion." Few were as emphatic as the excitable Smith, but most agreed with William Goodell that "some *grand reform* in the management of a political party" was essential before such a desperate step (which it was still hoped might be averted) could be taken. Accordingly, the executive committee recommended that *at present* no party be formed.[4] Goodell's *Friend of Man*, official voice of the state Society, aired arguments for as well as against an antislavery party, but the editor remained fixed in his misgivings throughout 1839 and early 1840.[5]

Another leading New York abolitionist who long held out against a third party was Lewis Tappan, like Goodell a founder of the American Anti-Slavery Society and, until he led the secession from it in 1840, the most influential member of its executive committee. Fully persuaded that abolition was an essentially religious enterprise whose ultimate success depended upon moral regeneration, Tappan strenuously opposed the creation of a separate party, which, he insisted, would compromise moral suasion by identifying idealists with spoilsmen. In November 1839 Tappan published in the *Emancipator* a detailed brief against the accelerating movement for a party which read as if written by Garrison himself. Indeed, although he voted for Liberty party candidates in 1840 and afterward, not until 1843 would he publicly espouse that new political organization.[6]

Hostility to third party action proved especially strong in the West, thanks partly to the solicitude of many antislavery Whigs for William Henry Harrison, but mainly owing to the outspoken opposition of Gamaliel Bailey and the Cincinnati *Philanthropist*. Cheerful, fair-minded,

[4] Goodell to H. B. Stanton, Feb. 23, 1839, Phelps Papers.
[5] *Friend of Man*, 1839–March 1840 *passim.*, but esp. Nov. 20, 1839, Feb. 12, 1840.
[6] *Emancipator*, Nov. 14, Dec. 12, 1839; Tappan to Gerrit Smith, Nov. 25, 1839, Mar. 24, 1840, Smith Papers; Tappan to John Scoble, Dec. 10, 1839, in Annie H. Abel and Frank J. Klingberg (eds.), *A Side-Light on Anglo-American Relations, 1839-1858* (Lancaster, Pa., 1927), 60-63; Tappan to William Goodell, Feb. 19, 1840, Letterbook, Lewis Tappan Papers, LC; Wyatt-Brown, *Tappan*, 193-94.

and staunchly independent, Bailey forsook a promising medical career in 1836 to help James G. Birney with the *Philanthropist*. Becoming sole editor the following year, Bailey fought "tooth and nail" against the independent party movement.[7] His opinions, imprinted on the Ohio Anti-Slavery Society and widely republished in abolitionist sheets throughout the North, presented yet another obstacle to advocates of a separate political organization.

To the already familiar allegations that party activity would invite corruption, undercut moral suasion, alienate the pulpit, and call down the fury of Whigs and Democrats, Bailey and his Ohio associates added persuasive arguments of their own. For one thing, Bailey concluded, an *abolitionist* party was an impossibility, since constitutional restraints limited national action to the *confinement* of slavery to states where it already existed. And, though he briefly advocated formation of a "Liberal" party whose "main object will be, to circumscribe the encroachments of the slaveholding power," Bailey soon decided that no party based purely on antislavery concerns could possibly survive.[8] Even if by some miracle such a party did endure, its capability to do mischief might well overwhelm its potential for good. For the "broken down, disappointed politicians, and cast-off demagogues" who flocked like buzzards around it would drive off pure and disinterested humanitarians, and "the reckless measures of mere partisans" might then seed a whirlwind. "Let the unprincipled demagogues of a political faction become the advocates of liberty in the face of slavery itself," Bailey warned, in words that distilled the slaveholders' own fears, "and where is the guarantee that the *slaves* might not be encouraged to take their emancipation into their own hands, and *thus* the bug-bear of insurrection becomes a terror of frightful reality."[9]

Most Westerners endorsed such views in 1839. At its annual convention in late May the Ohio Anti-Slavery Society voted to stick to present modes of political action "and to wear no party yoke, whether in church or state." Similarly, the executive committee of the Michigan Anti-Slavery Society pronounced it unwise, "at this crisis of our cause, to countenance a distinct Anti-Slavery political organization." So too

[7] Bailey to Birney, Nov. 28, 1839, Dumond (ed.), *Birney Letters*, I, 509-10.
[8] *Philanthropist*, Apr. 30, June 11, Nov. 19, Dec. 10, 1839.
[9] Report written at the request of the Executive Committee of the Ohio Anti-Slavery Society, printed in the *Philanthropist*, June 19, 1838.

in Indiana and Illinois, abolitionists uniformly stressed the duty of carrying abolition principles to the polls, but at the same time they chilled proposals for independent nominations. Indeed, at the end of 1839 the *Philanthropist* counted only three antislavery newspapers (all in the East) that freely endorsed a third party. As late as March 1840 Henry B. Stanton insisted to Birney that "19/20ths of abolitionists" opposed independent nominations.[10]

2

Against such opposition a small but growing band of determined abolitionists pressed forward their third party proposal. Rebuffed at first, they nonetheless persevered, slowly picking up adherents by the force of their arguments and the turn of events, by binding the meek with *faits accomplis*, and by brazenly ignoring the great odds against them until a Liberty party was born.

Faint rays of hope as well as disillusionment with previous courses of action contributed to the rise of interest in a distinct antislavery party. Political action by abolitionists seemed partially vindicated by the 1838 elections, which routed enemies like Ohio's Governor Vance and sent to Congress such staunch emancipationists as William Slade of Vermont, James C. Alvord of Massachusetts, Seth Gates of New York, and Joshua Giddings of Ohio. Antislavery men also credited political pressure with forestalling the annexation of Texas and making recognition of black Haiti's independence at least "an object worthy of national regard."[11] Political action, then, could be effective. But such effectiveness was still severely limited, as the defeat of Senator Morris, the 1838 failures of interrogation in New York and Massachusetts, and congressional gags on antislavery petitions made clear. The proper course seemed to be not to diminish political activity, but to devise better ways to implement it. An independent party was one way.

[10] *Ibid.* June 11, Dec. 10, 1839; Jackson *Michigan Freeman*, Oct. 23, 1839; Smith, *Liberty and Free Soil Parties*, 33-35; Stanton to Birney, Mar. 21, 1840, Dumond (ed.), *Birney Letters*, I, 542. The three unqualified champions of an antislavery party referred to by the *Philanthropist* were the *Emancipator*, *Massachusetts Abolitionist*, and *Rochester Freeman*.
[11] *Sixth Annual Report of the Executive Committee of the American Anti-Slavery Society . . . 1839*, 105-7.

In fact, the "treachery" practiced by both regular parties convinced some abolitionists that the creation of a separate antislavery organization was the *only* real option. Although many antislavery leaders—among them Thomas Morris, Amasa Walker, and Thomas Earle—came from Democratic backgrounds, most abolitionists had given up hope of that party's redemption even before the Atherton gag or the chastisement of Senator Morris. The great bulk of abolitionists, however, seem to have been Whigs, and on that party, it was expected, antislavery influence might leave its mark. Antislavery Whigs like Adams, Giddings, and Gates, after all, had led the fight against proslavery gags in the House of Representatives. Northern Whigs had always been more prone to protect Negro rights than had the Jacksonians. And even slaveholder Henry Clay, Whig presidential candidate in 1832, 1836, and, many expected, the choice for 1840, was as well known for his theoretical opposition to slavery as for his practical acceptance of it.[12]

Clay's violent attack on abolitionists and their principles, delivered in a speech to the United States Senate on February 7, 1839, therefore produced a sensation in antislavery circles. In what was correctly interpreted as a bid for Southern support, the Kentuckian condemned abolitionists for their reckless and misguided crusade against bondage. That crusade, he warned, "should no longer be regarded as an imaginary danger." Especially ominous was the movement toward antislavery politics. Indeed, Clay explained to the Senators, "It is because those ultra-Abolitionists have ceased to employ the instruments of reason and persuasion, have made their cause political, and have appealed to the ballot box, that I am induced, upon this occasion, to address you." He himself, Clay insisted, was "no friend of slavery." "But," he hastened to add, "I prefer the liberty of my own country to that of any other people, and the liberty of my own race to that of any other race. The liberty of the descendants of Africa in the United States is incompatible with the safety and liberty of the European descendants." Emancipation, he argued, could not succeed without trampling the rights of states, subverting the Union, and inviting amalgamation or a bloody war between the races. He beseeched the abolitionists "to pause in their mad and fatal course."[13]

---

[12] For Clay's views of slavery and emancipation, see Clement Eaton, *Henry Clay and the Art of American Politics* (Boston, 1957), 13, 118-36.
[13] *Congressional Globe*, 25th Cong., 3rd sess., Appendix, 354-59.

Clay's "infamous speech" jolted many abolitionists into a keener awareness that, in the Senator's own words, neither the Whig nor the Democratic party could be "justly accused of any Abolition tendency or purpose. . . ." The *Emancipator* reprinted Clay's address, together with Senator Morris's eloquent rebuttal and editorial remarks designed to make known the unreliability of the Whig party as a vehicle for anti-slavery. Other leading antislavery papers followed suit. William Goodell credited Clay with having singlehandedly brought to their senses nearly all the antislavery voters who had defected to Seward the previous fall. "There never was a more diabolical justification of a diabolical institution," Elizur Wright later recalled, and Lewis Tappan ascribed Clay's defeat for the Whig presidential nomination in December 1839 "chiefly to the increase of abolitionists . . . who would not vote for him."[14]

As important as the events of 1838 and 1839 in turning abolitionists toward an independent party was the tireless proselytizing by early converts—particularly Alvan Stewart. Born in upstate New York in 1790, Stewart attended Burlington College in Vermont, taught school for several years, and traveled briefly through the South before settling into the practice of law at Cherry Valley, New York. He dabbled in politics, winning election as mayor at the age of thirty-one. Sometime after 1829 he moved to Utica, where he soon distinguished himself as an able and resourceful lawyer. An imposing figure—tall, dark, and muscular—Stewart blended immense learning with mordant humor in ways which juries and, later, antislavery assemblies found marvelously effective. In 1834 he joined the antislavery movement and the following year took the lead in forming the New York State Anti-Slavery Society, serving during its early years as its president.[15]

Friends found Stewart a witty, companionable man, casual in manner and dress. But he had a violent, vindictive side as well, which made ridicule his stock-in-trade and laced his discussion of slavery with bloody

---

[14] *Massachusetts Abolitionist*, Oct. 31, 1839; *Emancipator*, Feb. 21, 28, Mar. 7, 21, 1839; *Friend of Man*, May 1, 1839; [Elizur Wright, Jr.], *Myron Holley; and What He Did for Liberty and True Religion* (Boston, 1882), 240; Tappan to Joseph Sturge, Dec. 14, 1839, Abel and Klingberg (eds.), *A Side-Light on Anglo-American Relations*, 66.

[15] Luther R. Marsh, "Sketch of Alvan Stewart," Alvan Stewart Papers, NYHA; Stanton, *Random Recollections*, 134-35; *Dictionary of American Biography*, XVIII, 5-6; Levi Beardsley, *Reminiscences . . . of Otsego County . . .* (New York, 1852), 67-70; Gerald Sorin, *The New York Abolitionists: A Case Study of Political Radicalism* (Westport, Conn., 1971), 47-57.

metaphor. As did few other abolitionists, he believed that murderous
slave insurrections were perfectly justifiable—indeed natural and inevitable unless human bondage was soon destroyed.[16] Perhaps Stewart's
violent attitude toward slaveholders had something to do with his advocacy of political action. He seems to have been readily convinced that
mere moral suasion was inadequate to the job at hand. "To hope to flatter, persuade, or convince a majority of slaveholders in this nation that
it is their duty to let their slaves go free," he concluded, "is a task beyond the highest conquest of moral suasion. We can never bring the
immorality and wickedness of Slavery as an argument for its abolition
with a people whose Priesthood hold Slavery a bible institution." Political pressure, therefore, marshaled by a separate antislavery party may
have seemed to Stewart the surest way of getting the "power" needed
to "behead the monster" slavery.[17]

It may also be that Stewart's radical antislavery interpretation of the
Constitution predisposed him toward the establishment of an independent political organization. As early as September 1837 Stewart had
broached before the New York Society the "new and startling" proposition that the Constitution, far from safeguarding the peculiar institution, was in letter and spirit an antislavery document which, together
with the Declaration of Independence, empowered Congress and the
federal courts to set all slaves free. At the 1838 annual convention of the
American Anti-Slavery Society, Stewart moved to amend the Society's
charter by striking from it a clause which admitted the constitutional
right of each slave state to exclusive control over slavery within its own
limits. For two days he argued the antislavery character of the federal
Constitution against William Jay, Birney, Leavitt, Wright, Wendell
Phillips, and others who, Stewart reported, "came down upon me like
thunder shower. . . ." The 47 to 37 vote in favor of his motion fell
short of the two-thirds required for amendment and appears to have
been more a tribute to Stewart's forensic skill than an accurate reflection of antislavery opinion. But Stewart understandably dubbed it an
"immense victory."[18] Buoyed by such tokens of acceptance of his un-

16 Stewart's sanguinary language is most pronounced in his private correspondence.
See, e.g., Stewart to Samuel Webb, May 20, 1838, June 25, Sept. 30, 1840, Dec.
1841, Alvan Stewart Papers, NYHS.
17 Stewart to Myron Holley, Dec. 16, 1839, Stewart to [Samuel Webb], Sept. 30
1840, Stewart Papers, NYHS.
18 *Friend of Man*, Oct. 18, 25, 1837, May 23, 1838; Stewart to Mrs. Stewart, May 2

orthodox constitutional views, Stewart may have turned his thoughts to the creation of a new party, one committed not only to antislavery action but to a radical view of the Constitution that immeasurably enlarged the scope of such action.

Whatever his reasons, by 1839 Alvan Stewart had emerged as the leading spokesman for an antislavery political party. He argued forcefully for such an organization at an executive committee meeting of the New York State Anti-Slavery Society in January, and although at first rebuffed he doggedly persevered. A new party was essential to the political war on slavery, he maintained. Present methods had proved to be woefully inadequate. Petitions, he became persuaded, were "a waste of labor." The whole campaign had boomeranged, resulting in the curtailment of abolitionists' liberties without in any way helping the slave. Interrogation of candidates had been no more successful. Stewart ridiculed the naïveté of those who still clung to the belief that Whigs and Democrats might be persuaded to nominate antislavery candidates in order to win abolitionist support. "That is to say these pro-Slavery parties who hate us more than they do each other, will come out & forsake their pro-Slavery candidates & nominate Abolitionists & elect them. Elect them for what?" he asked. "To do the very thing both of the great parties hate—to wit to abolish Slavery its roots and prongs. . . . Oh! infinite absurdity!" At best, Stewart insisted, the regular parties could be expected to nominate some "milk & water or a vainglorious nominal abolitionist" who would be next to worthless.[19]

During the late winter and early spring of 1839 most abolitionists fixed their attention on the duty of voting and prepared for battle at the national anniversary in May. That gathering, though it thwarted the plans of the most advanced political abolitionists, provided for a special national conference at Albany in July to discuss "the great principles" of the antislavery enterprise, especially those related to proper voting. To Stewart and other third party advocates the Albany conven-

---

1838, Stewart Papers, NYHA; Bayard Tuckerman, *William Jay and the Constitutional Movement for the Abolition of Slavery* (New York, 1893), 92-97; Jacobus tenBroek, *The Antislavery Origins of the Fourteenth Amendment* (Berkeley, 1951), 43-48. Luther R. Marsh, *Writings and Speeches of Alvan Stewart* (New York, 1860), includes most of Stewart's important public statements.

[19] Harlow, *Smith*, 145; Stewart to Myron Holley, Dec. 16, 1839, Stewart Papers, NYHS; Stewart to Edwin W. Clarke, Sept. 14, 1839, Box II, Slavery Manuscripts, NYHS.

tion offered the first opportunity to argue their case before an impor
tant antislavery assembly.[20]

Close to 500 abolitionists from twelve Northern states were presen
when the Albany convention met on July 31, 1839. Among them wer
William Lloyd Garrison and some four score of his disciples, but politi
cal activists dominated even the Massachusetts delegation (which in
cluded the Reverends Torrey, Scott, St. Clair, and Daniel Wise) an
tightly, at times highhandedly, controlled the meeting throughout. As i
to advertise their predominance they selected Alvan Stewart as presiden
of the convention.

Once Garrison's protest over the exclusion of women had bee
squelched, the delegates turned to a discussion of antislavery politics,
subject that engaged their attention for the better part of three swelter
ing days. Most of them enthusiastically affirmed the critical need fo
more effective political resistance to the Slave Power. "The politica
dominion which slavery has gained," the convention's Address declarec
"is not only a principal source of corruption and danger to the libertie
of the free; it is also a main pillar of support and tower of defence t
the system of slavery itself. Shorn of political power, slavery would fal
by its own weight, and die of its own imbecility." Slavery's politica
hegemony could only be met by political counterforce; only throug
the ballot could the slavocracy be destroyed. Without division, there
fore, the conference approved a resolution "intreating" every abolition
ist to carry his principles to the polls. (Birney's substitute, which de
clared it a *duty* to do so, ran into opposition—from Garrisonians an
from conservatives like E. D. Culver of New York, who demande
freedom to ignore the slavery question when more pressing issues aros
—and was set aside.) Likewise, the delegates approved by 238 to 1
(with many abstentions) a resolution declaring that they would vot
only for candidates who favored immediate abolition.

To men like Alvan Stewart, this commitment to support none bu
antislavery candidates made independent nominations for President an
Vice President imperative. Stewart himself contended as much, remind
ing the delegates of the utter prostitution of both existing parties to th
Slave Power and of the folly of "leaving every man to fish out his dut

[20] The following account of the Albany convention of July 31–Aug. 2, 1839 res
primarily on these sources: *Emancipator*, Aug. 8, 15, 1839; *Friend of Man*, Aug.
1839; *Liberator*, Aug. 9, 1839; Garrisons, *Garrison*, II, 307-9.

s best he might." But the objections to so radical a step were still mighty, and Stewart's argument was uncharacteristically tentative. Apparently it confused as many as it persuaded,[21] and in the end the convention worked out a compromise that left abolitionists in each section to settle this question for themselves. In this way, it was believed, political experiments could be tried without committing all abolitionists, and those that proved to be unsuccessful could easily be abandoned. It appeared to William Goodell, one of many still uncertain of the wisest course to follow, that a "considerable number of influential abolitionists seemed disposed, on the whole, to favor the *ultimate* organization of a third party."[22] And President Stewart quashed Garrison's resolution that any attempt to make independent nominations or to form a third party would imperil "the integrity and success of the anti-slavery enterprise." But many thought distinct party action premature, and many others continued to hope that abolitionists might somehow wield the balance of power without separate nominations.

The Albany convention proved something of a defeat for Garrison, who (together with 63 of his band) presented a formal "Protest" against its stress on political action, its exclusion of female abolitionists, and its implied rebuke of nonresistants. Yet many of Garrison's rivals were also dissatisfied. A large number complained that the pledge to vote only for candidates in favor of immediatism would straitjacket antislavery electors and rule out support for even a John Quincy Adams. One ought to be free to vote for any politician likely to advance the cause of freedom, they argued, whatever his views on immediatism. An Adams, as one Negro delegate observed, even if only five-sixths an abolitionist, was surely preferable to an Atherton.[23]

Those who went to the Albany convention hoping for a positive commitment to independent nominations also came away disappointed. Alvan Stewart, fully persuaded "that a third party or an abolition party is the only real available mode to prosecute our great undertaking politically," regretted the failure to establish a central committee for superintending political action. Goodell and Ellis Gray Loring, he grumbled, had sabotaged that measure. He lamented even more the delegates'

---

[1] Stewart to Edwin W. Clarke, Sept. 14, 1839, Box II, Slavery Manuscripts, NYHS.
[2] *Friend of Man*, Aug. 7, 1839. Italics added.
[3] Seth Gates to Gerrit Smith, Aug. 28, 1839, Smith Papers; *Liberator*, Aug. 30, 839; *Philanthropist*, Sept. 3, 1839.

unwillingness to make independent nominations for President and Vice President.[24] Still, those who agreed on the desirability of a new party could find satisfaction in the commitment to vote only for friends of immediate emancipation. For in the likely event that neither Whigs nor Democrats chose presidential candidates acceptable by this standard, abolitionists would have no choice but to select a ticket of their own or be disfranchised. The pressure for distinct nominations would thus become intense—perhaps irresistible. And with independent nominations would doubtless come an independent party. Although at the time none said so, it may well be that much of the opposition to the voting pledge came from men who saw it as a step which would lead inexorably toward creation of a third party.

Undaunted, the advocates of an antislavery party continued to press their views. Distressed at the heel-dragging of Goodell, Gerrit Smith, and other leading New York abolitionists, Stewart turned to his Quaker friend Samuel Webb, a prominent Philadelphia humanitarian. Pennsylvania, he reminded Webb, had once nominated Andrew Jackson before any other state lifted a hand. Now, he suggested, Pennsylvania abolitionists might improve upon that precedent by nominating a pair of good antislavery Whigs for President and Vice President and publicizing that ticket in the *Pennsylvania Freeman*. Other papers would soon "heartily respond" to this lead, Stewart cheerfully insisted, and "a stranger thing has happened, in this world, than to have these men elected, if the Whigs supposed they had no other hopes." At worst, he asserted, such a stratagem, if advertised before the Whigs' convention in December, might influence their selection of candidates.[25]

Nothing came of this proposal. But in the weeks and months following the Albany convention, support for a third party slowly but steadily grew. Among the new adherents to the idea of independent political organization, none was more influential than Myron Holley. Born and raised in New England, a graduate of Williams College, Holley had moved to Cooperstown, New York, in 1799 to study law with Judge James Kent. Soon thereafter he set up his own practice at Canandaigua. Once a Congregationalist, Holley gradually developed an eclectic, hu-

[24] Stewart to Samuel Webb, Aug. 5, 1839, Stewart Papers, NYHS; Stewart to Edwin W. Clarke, Sept. 14, 1839, Box II, Slavery Manuscripts, NYHS.
[25] Stewart to Webb, Aug. 5, 1839, Stewart Papers, NYHS.

manistic faith which rejected orthodox Calvinistic notions as "unscriptural, irrational and demoralizing" and postulated instead a benign and tolerant God who offered salvation to all men. "I never in all my life saw him in a church," his daughter Sallie later recalled. Instead he often held private services at home or in some civil building, preaching his hopeful creed to his family and "the poorer neighbors."

In 1816 Holley won election to the state assembly and, thanks to his early advocacy of the Erie Canal, appointment as treasurer of the canal commission. He held this latter post until 1824, when the discovery of a $30,000 shortage in his accounts, together with evidence of personal speculation with public funds, forced his resignation. Censured by both Clintonian and Bucktail factions for what he regarded as innocent and understandable slips, Holley may have taken a jaundiced view of established parties long before the question of slavery became prominent.

Like Alvan Stewart, Holley became embroiled in the Anti-Masonic movement, which burst into flame following the mysterious disappearance of William Morgan in 1826. He drafted Anti-Masonic addresses, served as a delegate to the new party's first national convention, and for four years edited Anti-Masonic newspapers. This experience seems not only to have reinforced his contempt for the major parties, but to have instilled in him a sense of the excitement and potential power of third party activity. Perhaps the conspiratorial outlook characteristic of Anti-Masonry also helped to heighten Holley's receptivity to abolitionist charges of a "Slave Power" conspiracy.[26]

Not until the winter of 1837 did Holley become seriously interested in the slavery question. And only after Henry Clay's anti-abolitionist blast in February 1839, which "struck at the foundation not only of his politics but his religion," did Holley throw himself wholeheartedly into antislavery politics. But once involved, he rapidly assumed a commanding position, and soon overshadowed even Alvan Stewart as a proponent of an independent abolition party. In June 1839 he began publishing the *Rochester Freeman*, which stressed the religious duty of political action on behalf of human rights. His profound disgust and alarm at what he called the toadying of both major parties to an increasingly

---

[6] For Holley's early life and career, see Wright, *Holley*, 29-225, 310-18; *Dictionary of American Biography*, IX, 150-51; Ronald E. Shaw, *Erie Water West: A History of the Erie Canal, 1792-1854* (Lexington, Ky., 1966), 59, 63, 169-72.

aggressive Slave Power lent urgency to Holley's editorials and speeches and brought him quickly to the side of Stewart, William L. Chaplin, and other pioneer advocates of a third party.[27]

Disappointed at the failure of the Albany convention to make an independent presidential nomination, Holley decided to take matters into his own hands. At a sparsely attended convention held at Rochester on September 28 to nominate antislavery candidates for the state assembly, Holley presented resolutions upholding voting as "the most effective, and in the last resort, the only conservative power of the republic . . . ," and calling for the establishment of a new political party devoted to "*equal rights.*" By a vote of 13 to 1 the group approved Holley's resolves and called upon the forthcoming national antislavery convention at Cleveland to nominate candidates for President and Vice President.

In support of its third party proposal, the Rochester meeting issued a lengthy Address, drafted by Holley. Only a new political organization, it insisted, composed of "disinterested, intelligent and virtuous men," could effectively stand up to the Slave Power. Both existing parties had shown themselves unwilling to oppose the encroachments of slavery, and all attempts to purify them had failed. Interrogation had been proved ineffective: where abolitionists were few, they were ignored; where many, they were consulted "in the spirit of that corrupt expediency, which surrenders principle for success." And invariably Whigs and Democrats selected candidates "as little fit for us to support as they think we can be induced to vote for." There could be no doubt of the propriety of collective action. "If political action be a duty in individuals," as most abolitionists would admit, that duty could hardly be lessened by association. Indeed, as the successes of Anti-Masonry had shown, a third party, so long as it remained open and independent, could work miracles beyond the power of individual men acting within the established system.[28]

Holley himself journeyed to Cleveland in late October hoping to impress these views on the special convention called by the American Anti-Slavery Society to pursue further the question of political action.

[27] Wright, *Holley,* 236-51 (quote on 243); *Rochester Freeman,* June 12, Sept. 25 1839; Holley to James G. Birney, Nov. 16, 1839, Miscellaneous Manuscripts NYHS; Goodell, *Slavery and Anti-Slavery,* 470.
[28] *Rochester Freeman,* Oct. 9, 23, 1839; *Friend of Man,* Dec. 18, 25, 1839.

He nearly succeeded. Most of the 400 delegates came from Ohio, where opposition to a separate party was especially strong, and most leading third party advocates, including Alvan Stewart, were unable to attend. Even so, those present chose Holley to preside, and his resolution in favor of independent nominations for President and Vice President touched off the longest and liveliest debate.

Delegates overwhelmingly rejected the proposition of one Whiggish abolitionist that moral suasion was "*all* that is necessary to blot the enactments of slavery from our statute book." Instead, they stressed the need for political action to rescind the laws by which slavery was artificially sustained and called on all abolitionists to march to the polls and vote only for candidates willing to "go to the utmost verge of their constitutional power for . . . [slavery's] immediate abolition." But Holley's resolution, after many hours of heated discussion, was narrowly tabled. Elizur Wright, Sr., father of the *Massachusetts Abolitionist* editor, who led a group of sixteen Oberlin College students to the convention, thought the resolution would have passed, except that "a few aspiring ones who are seeking promotion" feared to press so controversial an issue. Henry Stanton held a different—and probably more accurate—opinion. "The sentiment was quite general against making a nomination under present circumstances," he believed, because the great mass of abolitionists had been given no prior notice that the convention contemplated any such step. At the same time, he was convinced, most delegates admitted the necessity of an antislavery presidential ticket should Whigs and Democrats make unsuitable nominations. Stanton himself shared this cautious outlook. The wisest course was to wait and see. If Clay and Van Buren should be the only candidates, then it would be time for some group "to raise a standard worthy of being rallied around by a free and Christian people."[29]

Holley also believed that his proposal to select antislavery candidates "was manifestly regarded with favor by a majority of the convention," and that only the fact that there had been insufficient notice had prevented its implementation. Unlike Stanton, however, he was unwilling to await the outcome of the existing parties' conventions before moving

[29] *Emancipator*, Nov. 14, 1839; *Philanthropist*, Nov. 5, 19, 1839; Elizur Wright, Sr., to Elizur Wright, Jr., Nov. 6, 1839, Elizur Wright Papers, Case-Western Reserve University; Stanton to John G. Whittier, Oct. 26, 1839, quoted in *Philanthropist*, Nov. 19, 1839; Stanton to Elizur Wright, Jr., Oct. 28, 1839, Wright Papers, LC.

further.[30] Perhaps (though it seems improbable) he shared Stewart's hope that prior nominations by abolitionists would forestall the Whigs from making a slaveholder their candidate. More likely, he despaired of acceptable action from either Whigs or Democrats and saw nothing to be gained by delay.

3

By now, although the great bulk of abolitionists continued to be skittish about third party politics, the ideas of Holley and Stewart had won a respectable degree of acceptance. Support for independent action was strongest in the "Burned-over District" of upstate New York, where both men resided. Gerrit Smith, William Goodell, and others still hung back, but in Monroe, Ontario, and Oswego counties antislavery voters nominated independent tickets for state and local offices. Oswego abolitionists formally organized themselves as a party—complete with a central committee and town committees—and published an Address which justified separate organization as the most appropriate and effective way to show their commitment to liberty. In Dutchess County too, antislavery men had abandoned the interrogation tactic for independent nominations, as they did in New York City.[31]

Here and there in other states—New Hampshire, Pennsylvania, New Jersey, Ohio, and Michigan—abolitionists also organized in support of distinct antislavery tickets. Such nominations were often hastily made and frequently won only the most meager support. But in New Hampshire an "Independent Ticket" for governor and members of Congress, proposed by the *Herald of Freedom* and endorsed by the New Hampshire Anti-Slavery Society, tallied a highly respectable 1800 votes.[32] Although some viewed these local experiments in independent action

[30] *Friend of Man*, Nov. 13, 1839.
[31] *Emancipator*, Oct. 10, 31, Nov. 14, 1839; *Friend of Man*, Dec. 4, 1839; Myron Adams to Gerrit Smith, Nov. 20, 1839, Samuel Thompson to Smith, Dec. 9 [4?], Smith Papers; Edwin W. Clarke to A. Butterfield, Oct. 20, 1839, Clarke to William Goodell, Dec. 27, 1839, Box I, Slavery Manuscripts, NYHS. As late as mid-October 1839 Alvan Stewart described Gerrit Smith as "bitterly opposed to a 3*d* party." See Stewart to Edwin W. Clarke, Oct. 21, 1839, Box II, Slavery Manuscripts, NYHS.
[32] *Emancipator*, Oct. 10, 17, 31, 1839; Smith, *Liberty and Free Soil Parties*, 32; *True History of the Late Division in the Anti-Slavery Societies*, 43-44.

as merely temporary expedients, others found them promising beginnings and looked forward to the formation of a national antislavery
party.

Early support for such a party also came from "new organization"
leaders in Massachusetts—Charles Torrey, Orange Scott, and especially
Elizur Wright, Jr.[33] Before 1839, as he freely admitted to his Garrisonian critics, Wright had staunchly opposed the creation of a distinct
antislavery party. But soon after becoming editor of the *Massachusetts
Abolitionist* in May 1839 he had listened to arguments, "particularly by
Alvan Stewart," which convinced him that he had been wrong. When
Myron Holley's Rochester Address proclaimed the need for a new
party and called on the Cleveland convention to make independent
nominations, Wright confided to his friend Beriah Green that he found
this tack "above half right." He too, he confessed, "would like to see an
antislavery candidate for the Presidency—if we can find a 'proper man.'
We want a nucleus for pol. action—something for a practical man to
look at." Wright feared to commit the new organizationists to Holley's
scheme before the American Anti-Slavery Society had done so. His
newspaper did, however, defend local antislavery tickets when they appeared. "To undertake this work is very far from letting down the religious character of our enterprise," Wright assured his readers in October 1839. "Both politics and religion will gain by it. Politics will be
ennobled, and religion will be *humanized*."[34]

On the eve of the Cleveland convention, Wright wrote to Henry B.
Stanton, his former colleague on the American Anti-Slavery Society's
executive committee, and urged him to impress upon the other delegates
the importance of taking "a decided step toward Presidential candidates." Abolitionists, he maintained, had always realized that events
might some day force them to such a measure. Now the time had come.
The Slave Power's mastery over existing parties was painfully apparent,
and the sole alternative to an abolition ticket was "to back out" altogether. Confidently Wright outlined the benefits of an antislavery
nomination:

[33] Smith, *Liberty and Free Soil Parties*, 33; Orange Scott to Elizur Wright, Jr.,
Nov. 28, 1839, Wright Papers, LC.
[34] Garrisons, *Garrison*, II, 310-11; Wright to Green, Oct. 10, 1839, Wright Papers,
LC; *Massachusetts Abolitionist*, Oct. 17, 1839.

1. Something practical for every man to *do*.
2. Terror struck to the hearts of the South, from Clay downwards.
3. Concert of action—iron sharpening iron.
4. Leaving non-resistance abolitionism *hors du combat*. . . .
5. Politics ennobled—glorious object—clean skirts.
6. Interest, discussion and liberality increased a hundred fold—the matter being carried *home* to everybody.
7. Consistency—the jewel—the everything of such a cause as ours.

But more parochial, more selfish considerations also underlay Wright's third party enthusiasm. For, he confided to Stanton, "One thing I *know*. Unless you do take such a step, our New Organization here is a gone case. It has been *inter nos*, shockingly mismanaged." Everything had been made to turn on the woman's rights question, and political abolition had "been left to fall out of sight." It would be unwise for the Massachusetts Abolition Society to launch the new scheme, but if the parent society did so (preferably at its impending conference in Cleveland), new organization men would rally round, and by preempting so lively an issue drive off the irresponsible Garrisonians. "Take my solemn assurance," Wright concluded, "that it is life and death with us."[35]

If Wright was chagrined at the refusal of Stanton and the Cleveland convention to act upon his plea for independent nominations, it was as nothing when compared with the embarrassment he and his associates felt when his letter to Stanton somehow leaked to Garrison. Garrison gleefully pounced upon this evidence of frailty in the house of his defamers and, after forcing Wright to divulge the letter's full contents, ran it week after week in the *Liberator*. What better evidence, he asked, of the venality of the Massachusetts schismatics? Wright, driven now into the open, sought to regain the initiative with fighting editorials on behalf of third party politics. But his dream of rejuvenating the Massachusetts Abolition Society by means of a third party crusade against slavery was not to be. For by the time a new party did take the field, the new organizationists, their shortcomings advertised by the "pilfered" letter, had all but disbanded.[36]

In the rising debate over the wisdom of creating an antislavery political party, the executive committee of the American Anti-Slavery So-

[35] Wright to Stanton, Oct. 12, 1839, Wright Papers, LC.
[36] Thomas, *The Liberator*, 279-80; *Massachusetts Abolitionist*, Oct. 31, Nov. 28 Dec. 19, 1839.

ciety spoke in many voices. Some, notably the starchy, intensely pious
Lewis Tappan and Samuel E. Cornish, a distinguished Negro minister,
stood foursquare against the idea—Tappan even arguing that establishment of a new party would violate the Society's constitution. Others,
Stanton among them, blew hot and cold, wavering between the hope
that a strong abolition party might enlist the support of disgruntled
Whigs and the belief that the Whig party might yet assume a sufficiently antislavery position to justify abolitionist support. James G.
Birney, by now the most prominent advocate of political action in *some*
form, believed in the propriety of a separate organization but doubted
that the time for it was yet ripe.[37]

Of all the members of the executive committee, Joshua Leavitt was
the first and in many ways the most valuable convert to the idea of a
third party. Shrewd, dedicated, and pugnacious, Leavitt drifted steadily
away from an ill-fitting neutrality toward open support of independent
action. As early as September he had begun to challenge the efficacy of
existing tactics. By November he had lent such a pro-third party tone
to the *Emancipator* that Tappan felt obliged to print a lengthy critique
of the new movement and to explain that Leavitt's editorials did not
speak for all members of the executive committee.[38]

Apparently heartened by such signs of growing favor for antislavery
nominations, Myron Holley plunged boldly ahead. At Holley's bidding,
a convention of over 500 abolitionists meeting in Warsaw (Genesee
County), New York, on November 13-14 called for the formation of
an independent party and proceeded to nominate James G. Birney for
President and Francis J. LeMoyne of Pennsylvania for Vice President.[39]

To Holley, Stewart, Wright, Leavitt, and other early third party advocates the Warsaw nominations were profoundly encouraging. No
party had as yet been formed, but a declaration of political independence had been openly proclaimed. And some men, previously hostile or
aloof, now stepped forward to proclaim their approval of a distinct antislavery ticket and party organization, among them Gerrit Smith.[40] Most
abolitionists, however, remained opposed to such a course—at least for

[37] *Emancipator*, Nov. 14, Dec. 12, 1839; Betty Fladeland, *James Gillespie Birney:
Slaveholder to Abolitionist* (Ithaca, 1955), 182; Rice, "Stanton," 237, 239.
[38] *Emancipator*, Sept. 19, Oct. 10, 17, Nov. 14, Dec. 12, 26, 1839.
[39] *Ibid.* The resolutions passed by the Warsaw Convention may be found in Dumond (ed.), *Birney Letters*, I, 512n2.
[40] Harlow, *Smith*, 146.

the present—including, it soon turned out, the Warsaw nominees themselves. Both Birney and LeMoyne promptly declined their nominations. Although Birney agreed "that the great Anti-Slavery enterprise can never succeed without independent nominations," he asserted that the time had not yet arrived when that step could be harmoniously taken. At present, he believed, there was still "a large body—perhaps a majority —of abolitionists" who balked at third party action; and though most, given the opportunity for free discussion, would ultimately withdraw their opposition, to act now would "distract and divide" rather than unite the antislavery forces. To Holley, Birney confessed another, more personal, reason for his declination: the coolness with which his nomination had been received by Leavitt, Wright, Smith, and others who had preferred a more effective, better known candidate. "I saw in none of the Ab'n papers, the slightest commendation of the *particular person* nominated," he complained.[41]

LeMoyne, a distinguished physician and at the time president of the Pennsylvania Anti-Slavery Society, was much less optimistic than Birney about the chances for abolitionist victory. To him the third party movement seemed both inexpedient and premature. He was particularly afraid that so startling a departure as independent nominations might obscure the "emphatically religious" character of the antislavery enterprise and imply a lack "of confidence in the efficiency, and somewhat in the *propriety* of our past efforts in the use of moral means. . . ." Besides, he argued, abolitionists lacked the numbers to play politics successfully and a separate party would only expose them "to the ridicule and taunts of our opponents. . . ."[42] Birney had privately agreed to withdraw his declination if Holley and his associates insisted, but LeMoyne remained adamantly opposed to any use of his name in so doomed and misguided a venture, and he repeated in March his objections of December.[43]

The strongest protest against independent nominations, however, came not from such nonpartisan spirits as Birney and LeMoyne, but from antislavery Whigs. Starved for a presidential victory over the hated Jacksonians, caught up in the tumult of hard cider and log cab-

---

[41] Birney to Myron Holley, Joshua H. Darling, and Josiah Andrews, Dec. 17, 1839, Birney to Holley, Dec. 26, 1839, Dumond (ed.), *Birney Letters*, I, 514-16.
[42] LeMoyne to Holley *et al.*, Dec. 10, 1839, quoted in *Friend of Man*, Jan. 8, 1840; LeMoyne to Birney, Dec. 10, 1839, Dumond (ed.), *Birney Letters*, I, 511-14.
[43] LeMoyne to Birney, Mar. 24, 1840, *ibid.* I, 543-45.

ins, and prone to regard the nomination of Harrison over Clay as a concession to abolitionist feeling, they denounced third party action as *"unwise* and indiscreet." Since it was commonly agreed that most antislavery voters were Whigs ("49/50ths of our friends are in that party," claimed Henry Stanton), most of whom "would wade to their armpits in moulten lava to drive Van Buren from power," a separate abolition ticket could not help but fare miserably in 1840. Yet since most of what support it did receive would be subtracted from Harrison's total, a third party risked throwing a close election to the "proslavery" Democrats.[44]

Throughout the North, therefore, many leading abolitionists spurned independent nominations and professed confidence in Old Tippecanoe's antislavery instincts while they paid no heed to his slaveholding running mate. Complaining of "the deadness of those who ought to have shown their hearts ready to boil over for an anti-slavery nomination," Elizur Wright noted that many seemingly staunch Massachusetts abolitionists were "ready to take *Harrison* for a Godsend, because he is not *Clay!* They are so *excellent good* that they don't want to 'dabble in the dirty waters of politics' at all . . . ," he fumed, "but only presumably to vote the whole Whig ticket!" So strong was pro-Harrison sentiment among political abolitionists in Massachusetts that Wright's advocacy of a third party in the *Massachusetts Abolitionist* lost him many subscribers. "The whig, new organization abolitionists plainly tell us," he informed Gerrit Smith in March, "if we don't go against the distinct nomination they will go back to Garrison!"[45]

Smith could readily sympathize with Wright's predicament, for in his own state many prominent abolitionists, assiduously wooed by William Seward and Thurlow Weed, were declaring their support for Harrison and Tyler. Among them was Spencer Kellogg, chairman of the New York Anti-Slavery Society's executive committee, who resigned his post rather than embarrass his former associates. Likewise Seth Gates, a nominal Whig and an avowed abolitionist, refused entreaties to join the new party movement.[46] Matters were much the

---

[44] Joshua Giddings to [Milton Sutliff], Dec. 19, 1839, Milton Sutliff Papers, WRHS; Gamaliel Bailey to James G. Birney, Feb. 21, 1840, Stanton to Birney, Mar. 21, 1839, Dumond (ed.), *Birney Letters*, I, 531-32, 541-43.

[45] Wright to Beriah Green, Jan. 1, 1840, Wright Papers, LC; Wright to Smith, Mar. 20, 1840, Smith Papers.

[46] *Friend of Man*, Feb. 12, 1840; Seth Gates to Amos A. Phelps, July 14, 1840, Phelps Papers.

same in other states. In Michigan, moaned one humanitarian, "Harrison-ism rages like a pestilence." And even with an independent party at last in the field, he predicted that "not more than one [abolitionist] in ten will go for it being nearly all Whigs. . . ." In Ohio, Joshua Giddings preached the virtues of Harrison to receptive abolitionists on the West-ern Reserve.[47]

Even among such non-Whigs as Gamaliel Bailey, editor of the Cin-cinnati *Philanthropist*, hopes for Harrison ran high. Within weeks of the Whig nominations Bailey had persuaded himself that a "tolerably fair case might be made out for the General." Soon he was selling that case to all who would listen. "I am more, far more of a *real* Democrat in my notion of public policy, than a Whig," he insisted. But who could deny that Harrison—"emphatically the candidate of the free states"—was preferable to Van Buren, "*par eminence* the slaveholders' candidate"? The best course for abolitionists, therefore, and the one pursued in his own influential paper, was that of friendly neutrality to-ward Harrison, bitter enmity for Van Buren, and unbending opposition to a separate antislavery party. Two flattering visits from "the old gentleman"—who doubtless appreciated the support the editor could throw his way—did nothing to lessen Bailey's regard for the Whig candidate. Bailey found him honest and open-minded. He gave Harrison a copy of William Jay's *View of the Action of the Federal Government in Behalf of Slavery* (1839) and frequently sent him copies of the *Phi-lanthropist*, which the candidate at least pretended to read. In return Harrison gave private assurances that if elected he would do nothing to block abolition in the District of Columbia, and he provided informa-tion designed to offset the effects of his earlier anti-abolitionist remarks. "You under-rate Gen'l Harrison, I think," Bailey remonstrated to Bir-ney in March. "He is by no means a great man, but, he will not be a *tool* in the hands of anybody."[48]

Since the Harrison craze had sent so many otherwise solid abolition-ists to cavorting in coonskin—even cheering for hard cider—and since a good many others questioned the propriety of an antislavery party,

---

[47] A. L. Porter to S. B. Treadwell, Apr. 23, 1840, Seymour B. Treadwell Papers, MHC; Giddings to Milton Sutliff, Dec. 19, 1839, Sutliff Papers; Giddings to [?], Dec. 10, 1839, Miscellaneous Manuscripts, NYHS; James B. Stewart, *Joshua R. Giddings and the Tactics of Radical Politics* (Cleveland, 1970), 54-56.
[48] Smith, *Liberty and Free Soil Parties*, 38; Bailey to Birney, Feb. 21, Mar. 3, Mar. 30, 1840, Dumond (ed.), *Birney Letters*, I, 531-32, 535-38, 545-48.

either because it appeared to threaten the moral and religious character of the cause or because it might corrupt the souls of those caught up in political machinations, many men who shared Birney's opinion that independent nominations were ultimately essential agreed also that they were untimely. To launch so precarious an undertaking as a third national party at a time when a decided majority of abolitionists opposed it seemed the worst sort of madness. Indeed, argued John G. Whittier, after Birney had declined the Warsaw nomination it seemed unlikely that he or any other prominent abolitionist would accept another such offer. Even if a candidate "willing to stand the abuse, misrepresentation, and Indian warfare" that would be waged against him could be found, antislavery disunity would produce so crushing a defeat as "to bring contempt upon the party—turn the wavering to the popular side, and prevent the timid who fear proscription, from acting in conformity with their principles."[49]

The time to float a new party, Whittier, Stanton, and others argued, was after the fall elections. By then antislavery Whigs would have learned "the folly of their course by experience; and *then* they will repent and turn." Either Harrison would triumph (in which case his disregard for human rights would soon become transparent), or he would lose and free those abolitionists who had agreed "to make one more effort" to unseat Van Buren. These prodigal sons would be most likely to return to the antislavery hearthside if no third party were formed to underscore their dereliction to duty. "Do you not believe," LeMoyne asked Birney, "that if our people perpetrate a *pro Slavery* vote, *over the head* of a worthy and consistent anti Slavery ticket, under the present temptations, that their backsliding will be so gross, that they may not be expected ever to return to the faith?" For some, an added reason for postponing establishment of a third party was that to do otherwise would strengthen the Garrisonians' influence by handing them an issue—opposition to independent nominations—popular with antislavery Whigs as well as nonresistants.[50]

Despite the rebuff (somewhat coy in Birney's case) from the Warsaw nominees and the arguments advanced on every hand that a third party

---

[49] Whittier to Elizur Wright, Jr., Mar. 25, 1840, in Samuel T. Pickard (ed.), *Whittier as a Politician* (Boston, 1900), 16-20; *Philanthropist*, Mar. 31, 1840.
[50] Stanton to Birney, Mar. 21, 1840, LeMoyne to Birney, Mar. 24, 1840, Dumond (ed.), *Birney Letters*, I, 541-43, 543-45.

was premature, inexpedient, or just plain wrong, advocates of separate antislavery nominations refused to say quits. Further evidence of the failure of the interrogation system converted some and riveted others more strongly to the need for a distinct political organization. The votes cast by allegedly pro-abolitionist legislators for a "proslavery" United States Senator from New York, Nathaniel P. Tallmadge, had recently underscored the weakness of this old tactic. Likewise, the "unfaithfulness" of such antislavery Whig Congressmen as Giddings, Caleb Cushing, William Slade, and Seth Gates, who in December supported Virginia slaveholder R. M. T. Hunter in the House speakership election, seemed to demonstrate the extent to which existing parties had sold themselves to Satan and the folly of relying upon the abolitionism of their candidates.[51]

At all events, no sooner had Birney and LeMoyne declined the Warsaw nominations than efforts were begun to convene another, more broadly based antislavery political convention. Charles T. Torrey set the ball rolling late in January with a call for a national convention to meet in New York City in May. Birney complained that Torrey was "hardly sufficiently known to take such a matter as the call of a Convention in hand," and others protested that he ought to have sounded out all leading abolitionists before plunging ahead. Myron Holley and his associates in the "Burned-over District" raised still another objection. Although "exceeding gratified" at Torrey's proposal, they decided that a meeting in May would be too late. Holley and Gerrit Smith therefore prepared a call for a meeting of political abolitionists in Albany on April 1 to consider anew the question of independent nominations.[52]

To give this call as broad a base as possible, Holley and Smith presented it for endorsement to a convention of abolitionists at Arcade, New York, on January 28-29, 1840. Most of the 600 to 700 delegates (including "a large proportion of Ministers of various denominations") came from Genesee and surrounding counties, though a few arrived from adjacent parts of Pennsylvania. Antislavery Whigs appeared in

[51] *Emancipator*, Dec. 26, 1839; Gerrit Smith to William Goodell, Feb. 8, 1840, quoted in *Friend of Man*, Feb. 19, 1840; Gerrit Smith to Lewis Tappan, Mar. 14, 1840, Letterbook, Smith Papers; Brunswick (Me.) *Advocate of Freedom*, quoted in *Massachusetts Abolitionist*, Mar. 19, 1840; Gerrit Smith to S. B. Treadwell, Mar. 23, 1840, Treadwell Papers.
[52] Birney to Amos A. Phelps, Feb. 4, 1840, Henry B. Stanton to Phelps, Feb. 4, 1840, Phelps Papers; Holley to Joshua Leavitt, Feb. 3, 1840, in *Emancipator*, Feb. 13, 1840.

force, hoping to head off any denunciation of Harrison and Tyler and to block the formation of a third party. But the leadership of Holley and the debating skill of Smith and William L. Chaplin proved too much for them. By a 3 to 1 margin the convention condemned both Van Buren and Harrison, supported creation of an abolition party with candidates of its own, and endorsed the call for the Albany convention.[53]

In preparation for that gathering, third party advocates set to work to refute the criticism of opponents and to advance telling counter-arguments. To the accusation of inconsistency, recent converts to independent nominations devised two standard responses. One, anticipating Emerson, declared a foolish consistency the hobgoblin of small minds, the enemy of progress. "What should I have been, at the present time, had I resolved unalterably, a dozen years ago, on maintaining a consistency between my past and future conduct?" asked Gerrit Smith. "I should have been a rum-drinking colonizationist—and I leave it to any sober man of color to say whether I could be a much worse thing." A second way of replying to this common charge was to establish consistency not between past and present conduct or belief, but between antislavery professions and actions. If, as abolitionists had everywhere proclaimed, slavery was a sin, was it not then a religious duty to use *all* means—moral and political—to overthrow it? And if experience had shown the necessity of association to nominate true candidates and unite political strength, was not an independent party perfectly consistent with the goals of abolitionism?[54]

It was harder to answer the imputation that parties were always corrupt and that by establishing one of their own the abolitionists risked sullying the "moral sublimity" of their cause. Some were content to point out the moral pitfalls of the existing system. "As for corruption," Amos Phelps sarcastically observed, "to hang on to t[he] nomination of t[he] old parties for t[he] sake of avoiding it is like hanging on to the plague to keep clear of t[he] itch. The latter to be sure is rather uncomfortable, but it admits of an easy cure. Pardon the sublimity of my

[53] *Ibid.;* Myron Holley to Charles T. Torrey, [Jan. or Feb. 1840], Torrey Papers (quote); Gerrit Smith to William Goodell, Feb. 8, 1840, in *Friend of Man*, Feb. 19, 1840.
[54] Smith to Joshua Leavitt, Dec. 24, 1839, in *Emancipator*, Jan. 9, 1840; *Massachusetts Abolitionist*, Mar. 19, 1840; Myron Holley to Henry C. Wright, Feb. 24, 1840, Miscellaneous Manuscripts, NYHS.

figures. . . ." Others argued that corruption stemmed "not so much from politics, as the low intellectual and moral state of the country. . . ." Partisan involvement thus offered opportunities for reform as well as risks of moral contamination. A party of exalted purpose, one composed of godly men, might well raise the tone of American politics.[55] Moreover, such a party, far from alienating the pulpit, ought to win its enthusiastic support. Churchmen presently shunned party politics only because the issues involved seemed mere matters of expediency, "not having any strong moral bearings." Ministers had spoken out freely and forcefully during the American Revolution, and a new party dedicated solely to the cause of human rights might expect to find them once again on the side of freedom. Yet even among advocates of independent nominations, apprehension over the supposedly endemic depravity of political parties was deep and pervasive and did much to shape their view of the Liberty party soon to be born.

Typical of the soul-searching such fears produced were William Goodell's ruminations in the Utica *Friend of Man*. By 1840 Goodell was utterly disillusioned with the results of interrogation and fully persuaded that for abolitionists to remain attendant upon the Whigs and Democrats was in no way to escape political corruption, but he nonetheless admitted that the depravity of parties, *as then constituted*, made independent action risky. To Goodell, the corruption inherent in existing parties derived equally from their "usages and modes of nomination" and the selfishness of their goals. Leader-dominated and tightly organized, both the Whig and Democratic parties had become soulless *machines*, exalting regularity above principle, serving private ends rather than the public good, seeking victory at any cost. For abolitionists to copy such organizations, Goodell confessed, could prove disastrous unless reforms were made. In March he proposed creation of a temporary abolition "union," or "organization"—"we do not like to call it a party"—which would advocate "no partial or partisan objects," but only the destruction of slavery. In place of caucus or convention tickets, he suggested open nominations by any man or group, as had been the practice in the United States before 1800.

Like many other spokesmen for independent political action, Goodell anticipated that an antislavery party would be purely temporary. By

[55] Phelps to Gerrit Smith, Mar. 9, 1840, Smith Papers; "X.X." in *Liberator*, Feb. 21, 1840; *Massachusetts Abolitionist*, Oct. 31, 1839.

wielding the balance of power more effectively than the interrogation system had allowed, a third party would soon transform one of the major parties into an abolition organization. The very impermanency of the new party would ward off demagogues and political opportunists and provide a shield against corruption.[56] And, of course, the argument that a separate antislavery party need not itself seize the reins of power to force "repeal of slavery-sustaining laws" helped to blunt the allegation that the paucity of abolitionist voters made a separate party impractical.[57]

That great numbers of political abolitionists still found such arguments unconvincing was apparent in the difficulty Holley and Smith had in securing additional endorsements of their scheme from antislavery meetings in New York. Garrisonian emissaries Henry C. Wright and James C. Jackson dogged the steps of the third party men and twice swayed large abolitionist conventions (at West Bloomfield and Farmington) from sanctioning their proposal. Elsewhere too, antislavery societies either criticized the establishment of a new party or admitted a division of opinion on the subject. The antislavery press still bristled with letters and editorials more often against than for independent nominations.[58] Inevitably the *Liberator* sounded the harshest, most personal note. "It is evident," observed Garrison, "that there is, in the western part of New York, a small but talented body of restless, ambitious men, who are determined to get up a third party, come what may— in the hope, doubtless, of being lifted by it into office." The call for the Albany convention was presumptuous and unauthorized, he complained. "Let the meeting be insignificant and local, and thus rendered harmless."

In any event, more than just snow-clogged roads and the scarcity of money (the official excuses) kept attendance at the Albany convention low. Only 121 delegates from six Eastern states—Maine, Vermont, Massachusetts, Connecticut, New York, and New Jersey—were on hand when deliberations began on April 1; of these 104 came from New York. Most of the leading third party advocates showed up, including Holley, Stewart, Leavitt, Torrey, and Elizur Wright. (The sole important exceptions were Gerrit Smith, bedridden in his Peterboro

---

[56] *Friend of Man,* Feb. 19, 26, Mar. 11, 18, 25, 1840.
[57] Gerrit Smith to Joshua Leavitt, Dec. 24, 1839, in *Emancipator,* Jan. 9, 1840.
[58] *Friend of Man,* Feb. 19, 1840; Holley to Smith, Mar. 20, 1840, Smith Papers; *Michigan Freeman,* Mar. 25, 1840; Smith, *Liberty and Free Soil Parties,* 38; *Liberator,* Mar. 27, 1840; Garrisons, *Garrison,* II, 341.

home, and Birney, a likely nominee, who tactfully chose to remain in New York City.) But their presence was in part offset by the appearance of several quasi-abolitionists who came merely to defeat the creation of an antislavery presidential ticket. Garrisonians, most of whom boycotted the meetings, soon dubbed it the "April Fools'" convention.[59]

With Alvan Stewart presiding, the meeting quickly came to grips with the main order of business: the expediency of making a distinct nomination. At first it appeared that the dreams of Holley, Stewart, and Co. would be shattered once again. Many of the letters addressed to the convention by prominent political abolitionists counseled against independent action, at least at that time. "Were I with you," wrote John G. Whittier, "*I should vote against a nomination*, on the grounds of expediency. It would only furnish occasion for increased bitterness, and evil speaking among us. It would probably widen a breach already too visible to the enemies of our cause. The bare proposition to *discuss* the matter has been made the occasion, by some in our ranks, for impeaching, in a cruel and uncharitable manner, the motives of those concerned in it. A nomination under these circumstances, would be the signal for open, undisguised WAR, by a part of our organization, upon the candidates and their friends." Such internecine feuds, Whittier argued, would make it easier for "party-bound abolitionists" to stick with Van Buren or Harrison.[60]

Third party critics at the convention pointedly echoed such demurs. The Reverend Nathan S. S. Beman of Troy so wittily ridiculed the whole proceeding in an early address that, as Elizur Wright later recalled, "if the question of nominating had been voted on immediately after he sat down, the Convention would have been a failure and a joke worthy of the date."[61]

But the tide soon turned. One after another, Holley, Leavitt, Stewart, Torrey, Beriah Green, and Vermont's Benjamin Shaw (who had hiked ninety miles through snow and mud to reach Albany) elaborated on the pressing need for independent action. Holley's address, which followed hard on the heels of Beman's attack, did much to bolster the fainthearted. Neither of the existing parties, he contended, would ever

[59] *Friend of Man*, Apr. 8, 1840; *Emancipator*, Apr. 9, 1840; Wright, *Holley*, 259-61.
[60] *Emancipator*, Apr. 9, 1840.
[61] Wright, *Holley*, 261. See also letters of J. P. Miller and Oliver Clark, *Emancipator*, Apr. 9, 1840.

choose presidential candidates acceptable to abolitionists. "They will never forego *present* power for future victory. But *we* can." By making their own nominations, he insisted, the enemies of bondage would enhance their moral influence (which "must act itself out in consistent voting or disappear") and demonstrate the integrity of their cause. Abolitionists really had no other choice, insisted Alvan Stewart: "We cannot vote for either of the parties without voting for a slave-holder," since the Slave Power held sway over each. And the "scattering system," as experience had shown, "was of as little avail as it would be for a man to stand on an iceberg and whistle to the northwest wind to warm the atmosphere."[62]

Whig candidate Harrison's recent truckling letter to a slaveholding Congressman from South Carolina, which was read to the convention, may also have helped to win support for antislavery nominations. Moreover, the *Liberator's* strenuous attempt to head off the Albany convention and to impugn the motives of its proponents apparently backfired and made some delegates particularly receptive to the pleas of Holley and his associates. For, as Gerrit Smith had asserted, if through the efforts of the Garrisonians the convention "should prove a failure, it will be a failure most disastrous to our dear antislavery cause. The dogmatism and arrogance of Mr. Garrison will then know no bounds, and a fresh reason will then have been given for the loudest exultation of the enemies of our cause." But if successful, if a vital party of human rights were born, it would "give an impulse to our cause over which good men and angels will rejoice—over which, I trust, W. L. Garrison will himself yet rejoice."[63]

On the second and final day of the convention, a tally was at last taken on Holley's motion to nominate independent candidates for President and Vice President. Forty-four voted "aye," thirty-three "nay." More than a third of the delegates, undecided to the end, abstained. With near unanimity, the assemblage then nominated James G. Birney and Thomas Earle as standard-bearers of the new—and as yet unnamed—party.

Earle, a Philadelphia Quaker chosen chiefly for his Democratic col-

[62] *Friend of Man,* Apr. 8, 1840; Willey, *Anti-Slavery Cause in State and Nation,* 132-34.
[63] *Emancipator,* Apr. 9, 1840; Smith to Elizur Wright, Jr., and A. A. Phelps, Mar. 5, 1840, Wright Papers, LC. See also *Michigan Freeman,* Mar. 25, 1840.

oration, found scant favor with many abolitionists and soon slipped into obscurity. But in Birney the new party had found a distinguished (if not exactly prominent) candidate who had ably served its interests for years. A Southerner by birth, once a slaveholder himself, Birney had traveled slowly but steadily along an antislavery track—from gradual emancipation and colonization to full-throated indictment of the sin of slavery and a demand for its immediate abolition. In 1836 he moved to Ohio, editing the Cincinnati *Philanthropist* until the fall of 1837 when he left for New York City to become executive secretary of the American Anti-Slavery Society. Courageous and firm in his abolitionism, deeply religious, and skilled in the arts of propaganda, Birney instilled in his followers feelings of trust if not excitement. Indeed, many seem to have found his very drabness reassuring. Here, praise God, was no mere politician.[64]

Although in February 1840 Gerrit Smith had referred to an antislavery party as "the great 'Liberty party,'" and although for years abolitionists had freely used that label to distinguish their political efforts from those of the "slave party," the Albany delegates were content to leave the new organization unchristened. Not until 1841 was it formally designated the Liberty party. Throughout the 1840 campaign it appeared under several names—occasionally the "Liberty ticket," but most often the Abolitionist, or Independent Abolitionist, party.[65] Nor, except for the creation of a national committee of correspondence (composed of Stewart, Goodell, and Smith) and a recommendation that abolitionists call local conventions to nominate candidates for congressional and state offices, did the Albany meeting provide for the organizational needs of a political party.

Much of this inattention to party forms was apparently deliberate. Recognizing that many abolitionists who strongly opposed a permanent political organization were willing to support occasional independent nominations, the Albany party-makers took pains to distinguish their creation from traditional political machines. Likewise the

[64] Fladeland, *Birney*, 1-175. Birney's drab, unemotional side is amusingly revealed in the following consecutive entries in his diary (Birney Papers, LC): "Dec. 17 [1840] Engaged to be married to Eliz^h P. Fitzhugh. March 25 [1841] Married accordingly."
[65] Smith to William Goodell, Feb. 8, 1840, in *Friend of Man*, Feb. 19, 1840; Theodore Foster, "History of the Liberty Party," 17-18, Theodore Foster Papers, MHC; James Birney to James G. Birney, Aug. 15, 1840, James G. Birney Papers, CLM.

widespread apprehension among reformers over the corrupting tendency of party management, together with the desirability of remaining sufficiently open and permissive to lure recruits from existing parties, resulted in a platform which at times seemed to deny that a *party* had been formed at all. "Although in making distinct nominations we may appear in the attitude of a distinct party," the Albany convention proclaimed (apparently at the urging of William Goodell), "we disclaim adopting what some think implied in party management, to wit, the monopoly of the right of nomination by the caucus, and the bringing [of] the weight of party proscription to bear upon all who decline voting for the party nominees from conscientious scruples. . . ." Similarly, the platform declared that abolitionists—indeed, all Americans—had a duty "instead of supporting a first, second, or third *party*—to rise above all party" and to implement the egalitarian principles of the Declaration of Independence. The delegates were also careful to explain that while it was essential to take political action to destroy slavery—the source of most of the nation's evils—other measures ought still to be pressed. "We would urge on abolitionists everywhere," the convention stated, "renewed efforts to diffuse that information and apply that moral suasion and religious influence upon which alone all consistent political action and righteous legislation are based."[66]

The immediate response to the actions of the Albany convention was chilly. Few minds appeared to have been changed by the nomination of Birney and Earle. Predictably, most Garrisonians dismissed the whole proceeding as a "ridiculous farce," the work of a handful of deluded reformers who were not to be taken seriously. Others pointed to the skimpy turnout and the narrow margin by which the nominations carried as proof that abolitionists were not yet ready for a third party. Not one voter in five hundred would support the Abolitionist ticket in Massachusetts, Whittier informed Birney soon after the convention. "I do not know *one* in Essex County. This is to be deplored, but it is now too late to prevent it." He urged Birney to decline.

Gamaliel Bailey, perhaps the most influential antislavery spokesman in the West, also remained critical of independent nominations. Unrepresentative and poorly attended, the Albany convention had disre-

---

[66] *Emancipator*, Apr. 9, 1840. On the anti-party attitudes of political abolitionists, see Ronald P. Formisano, *The Birth of Mass Political Parties: Michigan, 1827-1861* (Princeton, 1971), 74-76.

garded the opinion of the great majority of abolitionists, he declared, and "must be regarded as a *failure*." He counseled Western abolitionists to "take plenty of time to deliberate on the question of political action, without suffering themselves to be driven into any hasty measures by the premature action of a few persons at Albany." Bailey was even more frank in a private letter to his old friend Birney: "So they have done the deed?" he wrote. "I am sorry—deeply sorry. The nomination will not be sustained by abolitionists generally; and I shall be mortified that the world should see how divided we are." Despite the nomination of one from their own ranks, and Joshua Leavitt's zealous endorsement of the Albany proceedings, the American Anti-Slavery Society's executive committee also remained divided over the wisdom of an abolitionist party.[67]

Few Whigs or Democrats took any public note of the Abolition nominations. Even the Albany *Argus* and *Evening Journal* published only curt announcements that an antislavery ticket had been formed. The *National Intelligencer* labeled the third party a "device of Mr. Van Buren to regain New York, and to recover Massachusetts. . . ." Some Whigs sought to discredit Gerrit Smith (and, through him, the new party) by spreading rumors of a deal with Democrats by which he would be elected to the United States Senate. Here and there Democrats were said to be pleased with the idea of Birney's candidacy. But outside antislavery circles the Albany nominations generated mainly indifference.[68]

4

No one, of course, expected the new party to make a strong showing in 1840. Birney himself looked upon his nomination as part of a staying action designed to steady antislavery lines for future political wars. The third party movement, he wrote when urging Earle to accept the

[67] *Liberator,* Apr. 10, 1840; Whittier to Birney, Apr. 16, 1840, Bailey to Birney, Apr. 18, 1840, Dumond (ed.), *Birney Letters,* I, 555-58; *Philanthropist,* Apr. 20, 1840; Lewis Tappan to William Goodell, Apr. 21, 1840, Tappan to Joshua R. Giddings, Apr. 24, 1840, Letterbook, Tappan Papers, LC.
[68] *Albany Argus,* Apr. 4, 1840; *Albany Evening Journal,* Apr. 4, 1840; Wright, *Holley,* 270; Harlow, *Smith,* 149; *Philanthropist,* Sept. 29, 1840; Jonathan Thomas to Jesse Thomas, Apr. 20, 1840, Thomas Papers.

Albany nomination, "was the only one that can now save the Abolition party from dissolution and from being lost in the Whig & Van Buren parties."[69] Some viewed the antislavery ticket as merely a stopgap—a desperate means of showing displeasure with the "proslavery" nominations of the regular parties. Others understood that it would take years before any new party could hope to sway masses of voters. And so great were the seductions of the hard cider campaign that most realistic observers foresaw a widespread reluctance among abolitionists to "waste" their ballots on Birney and Earle.

It was well that hopes were kept within bounds, for the fledgling party labored under staggering handicaps during its first campaign. Hopelessly outmatched by Whigs and Democrats in organization, experience, financial resources, and political savvy—not to mention popularity of program—the Abolitionist ticket came under heavy assault from within the antislavery host itself.

The Garrisonians, always critical of the third party movement, stepped up their attacks after their conservative, evangelical rivals, routed at the annual meeting of the American Anti-Slavery Society in May, seceded to form the American & Foreign Anti-Slavery Society. Many members of the new association (including its guiding spirit, Lewis Tappan) sharply disapproved of the Abolition party, while a few Garrisonians (notably Samuel E. Sewall and Isaac Clark) endorsed it. Yet in Garrison's eyes the new party was the handiwork of the same false friends who had sought to stifle his influence within the American Anti-Slavery Society. "The third party is only another name for new organization," he assured one friend. "They [sic] twain are one."[70]

From the presses of the *Liberator* and the *National Anti-Slavery Standard* (Garrison's voice in New York City) came salvoes, often indiscriminate ones, against those who threatened the integrity of the abolitionist cause and who wasted energy in a misguided political experiment. Garrisonian agents missed no opportunity to snipe at the new party. It was natural, Gerrit Smith bitterly complained, "that they,

[69] Birney, Diary, Apr. 4, 1840, Birney Papers, LC. For Birney's letter accepting the Albany nomination, see Dumond (ed.), *Birney Letters*, I, 562-74.
[70] Tappan to William Goodell, Feb. 19, 1840, Tappan to Seth Gates, Apr. 2, 1840, Tappan to Giddings, Apr. 24, 1840, Letterbook, Tappan Papers; Tappan to Gerrit Smith, Mar. 24, 1840, Smith Papers; *Massachusetts Abolitionist*, May 21, 1840; Samuel E. Sewall to Elizur Wright, Jr., Sept. 9, 1840, Wright Papers, LC; Garrison to John A. Collins, Oct. 16, 1840, Garrison Papers.

who hate all voting under our Government, should most hate that which is the most and only effective form of voting." Garrisonians urged abolitionists to return to the interrogation system, partly, Smith insisted, "because they know it is a farce." Yet he was forced to admit that the arguments of such old organization emissaries as James C. Jackson and Luther Myrick had turned many in upstate New York against the abolitionist slate.[71]

Much more crippling to the Liberty party cause were the wholesale defections of antislavery Whigs and Democrats and those nonpartisan reformers who, though at odds with Garrison, expressed misgivings at "the political turn of things" and feared that support of a separate political organization would intensify "discordance and division" among abolitionists.[72] Particularly distressing to the Birney forces was the virtually unshakeable determination of Whig abolitionists to "go this once" for Harrison and Tyler. The opportunity to unhorse the hated Van Buren and his "proslavery" minions was a temptation few Whigs could resist. Even such tested friends of the slave as John Rankin and Jonathan Blanchard (both former agents of the American Anti-Slavery Society) succumbed to the argument that as the lesser of two evils Harrison deserved antislavery support.[73] Gamaliel Bailey's eleventh-hour endorsement of Birney and Earle helped to wrest a few Western votes from the Whig ticket, but such leading Ohio abolitionists as Joshua Giddings, Benjamin and Edward Wade, Leicester King, Samuel Lewis, and Salmon P. Chase all backed Old Tippecanoe, and they carried many others with them. "Log cabins hard cider koon skins and corn doger has cought all the antislavery men here," observed one Ohioan from a township which gave Birney not a single vote.[74]

Matters were much the same in the East. Even in Madison County,

[71] *Liberator*, June 26, Nov. 6, 1840; *National Anti-Slavery Standard*, Sept. 17, 1840; Smith to Alfred Wilkinson, Oct. 19, 1840, Letterbook, Smith Papers. See also *Seventh Annual Report of the Executive Committee of the American Anti-Slavery Society . . . 1840* (New York, 1840), 11-12, 14.
[72] Alanson St. Clair to Amos A. Phelps, Nov. 6, 1840, Lewis Tappan to Phelps, June 25, 1840, Phelps Papers; *Philanthropist*, May 5, 1840; *Pennsylvania Freeman*, Sept. 10, 1840; Tappan to Gerrit Smith, June 29, 1840, Smith Papers; William Jay to Lewis Tappan, Sept. 22, 1840, John Jay Collection, Columbia University; Jonathan Thomas to Nathan Thomas, Oct. 22, 1840, Thomas Papers.
[73] Blanchard to Gerrit Smith, Aug. 5, Sept. 14, 1840, Smith Papers; *Philanthropist*, June 16, Dec. 9, 1840.
[74] *Philanthropist*, June 23, 30, Sept. 8, 22, 1840; Smith, *Liberty and Free Soil Parties*, 40; David Thomas to Nathan Thomas, Dec. 2, 1840, Thomas Papers.

New York—Gerrit Smith's home seat and long a hotbed of political abolition—a "Whig whirlwind" carried off many who had supported the Abolitionist ticket in 1839. From Utica Alvan Stewart lamented: "The defection is truly amazing," adding bravely: "But after all we must thank Heaven, for what is left in our ranks." In Massachusetts William Jackson turned down the Liberty nomination for governor, declaring that an independent party was premature and that the first task was to overthrow that lackey of the Slave Power, Martin Van Buren. Like many other antislavery Whigs, Jackson sought changes in economic policy—particularly important in a depression year—and shied away from a party which utterly ignored such mundane questions as banks and tariffs.[75]

Everywhere shrewd Whig politicos drove home their advantage. In some places well-known abolitionists were made presidents of Tippecanoe clubs. Prominent antislavery politicians like Giddings and Seth Gates portrayed Harrison as a man open to antislavery influences and the Whig party as the best hope for eventual emancipation. Whig newspapers, when they bothered to notice the new party at all, dismissed it as a locofoco tool designed merely to draw votes away from Harrison.[76] Shortly before the election in Ohio, Whig prints published reports that Democrats were distributing Birney tickets throughout the state. "The effect was what might have been anticipated," Gamaliel Bailey noted. "Abolitionists who had been hesitating between their politics and their abolition principles, without proof believed the report, and received it as conclusive evidence that after all, independent abolition 'was but a Van Buren trick.' " Most then presumably voted Whig in protest.[77] Indeed so solidly did Whig abolitionists stick by their party that in the West, at least, more former Democrats than Whigs seem to have cast ballots for Birney.[78]

[75] *Friend of Man*, Nov. 18, 1840; Stewart to Edwin W. Clarke, Oct. 17, 1840, Slavery Manuscripts, Box II, NYHS; William Jackson to Charles T. Torrey *et al.*, May 29, 1840, Phelps Papers.
[76] *Friend of Man*, June 24, Nov. 18, 1840; Stewart, *Giddings*, 52-56; *Philanthropist*, Sept. 29, 1840 (quotes *Cincinnati Gazette, Conneaut Gazette, Marietta Intelligencer*, and *National Anti-Slavery Standard*). Alvan Stewart later claimed that New York Whigs had spread false rumors that he and Gerrit Smith planned to vote for Clay so as to create "all possible distrust between abolitionists." Stewart to Lewis Tappan, Dec. 10, 1844, Stewart Papers, NYHS.
[77] *Philanthropist*, Nov. 11, 1840.
[78] *Ibid.* Nov. 25, 1840; Nathan Thomas to Joseph S. Thomas, Dec. 8, 1840 (copy), Thomas Papers.

Compounding all these problems was a shortage of funds, weak organization, and, more serious, a widespread reluctance to wage any campaign at all. Birney himself skipped off to England in May for the World Anti-Slavery Convention and did not return home until late November. His running mate, Earle, whose abolitionism some found lukewarm and whose locofocoism offended many, seemed more embarrassed by than proud of his nomination and bestirred himself no more than Birney did.[79] So it was with most of the rank and file. Some, apparently reacting against the demagoguery of hard cider politicking —viewing such campaigns, like caucuses, as manifestations of the corrupting side of party management, as violations of "the government of God"—refrained from making any attempt to sway the voters. Others saw no point in struggling against the Whig hurricane. "So strong has been the political excitement," observed one Ohio Birney man, "that for all the good to be accomplished it seemed like sailing against the wind." Even such basic tasks as the printing of Abolition tickets were often botched or ignored. Students and faculty members at Illinois College discovered on election day that, there being "no poll open for Birney" in Jacksonville, those who wished to support him would have to go elsewhere. And soon after the election William Birney advised his father: "Your third party politicians are better men than they are tacticians. The state [Ohio] was poorly supplied with tickets and half the people supposed that you had withdrawn from the canvass."[80]

Election returns reflected such handicaps. Of the nearly two and a half million votes cast, Birney and Earle received barely seven thousand. In no state did the new party tip the balance between the old; only in Massachusetts had it polled as much as 1 per cent of the total. Organizational deficiencies showed in the total absence of Abolitionist returns from many counties known to be friendly to the antislavery cause. (Indeed, not a single Liberty ticket turned up in all of Indiana.) Even where third party men had been active, most voting abolitionists —probably nine out of ten—resisted their appeals and voted for Tip or

[79] Fladeland, *Birney*, 188; Jonathan Blanchard to Gerrit Smith, Sept. 14, 1840, Smith Papers.
[80] Smith, *Liberty and Free Soil Parties*, 45-46; Lewis Perry, *Radical Abolitionism: Anarchy and the Government of God in Antislavery Thought* (Ithaca, 1973), 173-74; Samuel Willard to Julius Willard, Oct. 31, 1840, Samuel Willard Papers, Illinois State Historical Library; William Birney to James G. Birney, Nov. 15, 1840, Birney Papers, CLM. For the new party's financial problems, see Amos A. Phelps to Gerrit Smith, June 27, 1840, Smith Papers.

Van.[81] "The farce is equally ludicrous and melancholy," snorted Garrison, obviously gratified at Birney's crushing defeat. And yet, he added incredulously, the new party's spokesmen seemed bent on pressing ahead! Joshua Leavitt certainly showed no sign of abandoning the enterprise. Pessimism among the "faithful few" was unwarranted and out of place despite the tiny Liberty vote, Leavitt announced in a post-election editorial. "The fewer we have now, the more we have to gain before we carry our point. 'That's all.' "[82]

[81] Elizur Wright conservatively estimated that in 1840 there were at least 70,000 voting members of antislavery societies. Wright, *Holley*, 235. See also Smith, *Liberty and Free Soil Parties*, 46-47. W. Dean Burnham, *Presidential Ballots, 1836-1892* (Baltimore, 1955), 246, 248, places Birney's total at just 6225, overlooking Liberty votes cast in New Hampshire, New Jersey, Pennsylvania, and Michigan.
[82] Garrison to John A. Collins, Dec. 1, 1840, Garrison Papers; *Emancipator*, Nov. 12, 1840.

4

"The Right Sort of Politics"

MOST LIBERTY MEN shared Leavitt's optimism. Previous experience had hammered home the conviction that independent party action was essential if slavery were ever to be overthrown, and post-election developments did nothing to weaken that belief. Hopes that Harrison's Administration might soften the "proslavery" positions of his predecessors gained some life with the announcement of his Cabinet, which included only one member from the Deep South. But even Harrison's defenders among antislavery men professed low expectations of the new President; and his inaugural, which condemned those whose acts were "harbingers of disunion, violence and civil war," did nothing to disarm his critics.[1] "What a wet lid affair is Gen. Harrison's Inaugural Address!" scoffed Gerrit Smith. "We have reason to believe—have long had it—that his administration will be more devotedly proslavery than any which has preceded it."[2] The accession of John Tyler—a slaveholder and, ugly rumor had it, a father of slaves—snuffed out the last flickering hopes for an antislavery influence in the White House.[3]

Few Liberty supporters found the pitifully small vote for Birney cause for alarm. Better preparation and more effective campaigning would surely bring more impressive returns in the future. More important, even if the Liberty vote never rose very high it might accomplish a world of good. "Our cause is a plain one," declared one Pennsylvania abolitionist, "perseverance in what we believe right, wholly ir-

[1] Seth Gates to Gerrit Smith, Feb. 25, 1841, Smith Papers; Stewart, *Giddings*, 66.
[2] Smith to Theodore Weld, Mar. 14, 1841, Barnes and Dumond (eds.), *Weld-Grimké Letters*, 863.
[3] Alvan Stewart to John Frey, Sept. 3, 1841, Frey Family Papers, NYHS.

respective of results. I have no doubt of ultimate success, but whether successful or not I shall continue to vote none but Liberty tickets."[4]

There were many reasons for this willingness, shared by the vast majority of Liberty party pioneers, to support so inauspicious an enterprise. Foremost among them was the conviction that third party action was necessary to give point and purity to moral suasion. Slavery, as a moral evil entrenched in a political system, had to be attacked simultaneously on two fronts. To shun political weapons was morally irresponsible; to work within the major parties was morally contaminating. Hence the best course seemed to be to combine moral appeals with an independent politics designed to seek legislative cures for legislated evils. For voting abolitionists to come out from established "proslavery" parties would exalt their moral influence and greatly enhance the power of political abolitionism. "Such a universal sacrifice of party preferences among anti-slavery men," urged Bailey's *Philanthropist* during the 1840 campaign, "would prove them possessed of the true martyr spirit. It would win for their cause a consideration that could be attained in no other way, and multiply adherents to it far more than a thousand lectures or high-sounding resolutions. . . . *To vote right will be to proselyte.*"[5]

Once the Liberty party entered the field, its backers increasingly stressed its role as purifier of the political process. Far from corrupting those who endorsed it, the new party, by its adherence to lofty principle and disregard for boodle and swag, brought probity back to politics. Indeed, many argued that support for the Liberty party might regenerate individuals as well as political groups. "He who votes the liberty ticket," insisted the *Signal of Liberty*, "and by the force of moral principle bids adieu to his old party influences, and in the face of opposition gives his suffrages for the cause of human rights, greatly benefits himself. He raises himself in the estimation of [his] community." The notion that abolitionists would themselves become corrupted and lose moral power by engaging in party politics was the specious invention of "cunning and profligate officeseekers," claimed the Boston *Free American*. It was designed "to keep honest men away from

---

[4] Joseph P. Gazzam to James G. Birney, Feb. 7, 1843, Dumond (ed.), *Birney Letters*, II, 712.
[5] *Philanthropist*, July 21, 1840. See also Philadelphia *Pennsylvania Freeman*, Feb. 1, 1844; Ann Arbor (Mich.) *Signal of Liberty*, Feb. 19, 1844; Edwin W. Clarke to *Oswego Union Herald*, Feb. 17, 1841, Slavery Manuscripts, Box I, NYHS.

the polls, and has been solemnly re-echoed, these fifty years, by a certain portion of the clergy, who unwisely took it as a high compliment to their religion—a religion too pure for any day but the Sabbath."[6] This theme of regeneration—regeneration of abolitionist souls and political standards as well as of collective morality on the slavery question—helped to bind many abolitionists to the Liberty party and to give it something of the flavor of a religious crusade.

Yet it is misleading to say that "the Liberty party had been created more as a religious crusade than as a political party," or that the Bible was its "political textbook."[7] For although religious conviction unquestionably underlay many men's attachment to the new party, and scriptural quotations studded Liberty pronouncements, by no means all of the Liberty men were impractical moralists or political babes in the woods. Most possessed some understanding of political realities, and the hopes they held for their party, while often extragavant, were those of intelligent reformer-politicians, not those of doctrinaire visionaries unfit for the cold world of politics.

Nowhere was this realism more clear than in Liberty men's conception of what their party ought to be. A few dreamed heady dreams of a party of freedom which in no time could elect up to a hundred antislavery Congressmen and intimidate the South into voluntary emancipation. "Every thing wears a new & glorious aspect," gushed Alvan Stewart in 1841. "The matter is absolutely settled that we must abolish slavery, & as sure as the sun rises we shall in 5 or 6 years run over Slavery at full gallop unless she pulls herself up & gets out of the way of Liberty's cavalry."[8] Most early Liberty supporters, however, took a more modest view of their party's potential.

[6] *Signal of Liberty*, Sept. 22, 1841; Boston *Free American*, July 1, 1841. See also *Philanthropist*, Jan. 6, 1841; *Signal of Liberty*, Sept. 29, 1841. For a view of the Liberty party as a manifestation of "political come-outerism" explicitly designed "to enable the virtuous to symbolize their allegiance to God," see Lewis Perry, "Versions of Anarchism in the Antislavery Movement," *American Quarterly*, XX, No. 4 (Winter 1968), 779-80.
[7] Eric Foner, *Free Soil, Free Labor, Free Men: The Ideology of the Republican Party Before the Civil War* (New York, 1970), 78. For similar views see Dumond, *Antislavery*, 301; Wyatt-Brown, *Tappan*, 282n2; Perry, *Radical Abolitionism*, 166-87.
[8] Stewart to Samuel Webb, Nov. 13, 1841, Stewart Papers, NYHS. A year later, after his strenuous labors had produced only meager gains for the Liberty party in New York, Stewart showed a gloomier side: "Slavery has undone us. She has crawled into the Constitution, has paralized [*sic*] the church, broken the compact, silenced petition, overthrown morality, blotted out humanity, really dissolved the confederacy & left the Nation undone." *Ibid.* Oct. 10, 1842.

To many, in fact, the Liberty party seemed merely a *temporary* instrument of public enlightenment and political pressure upon the dominant Whig and Democratic parties. Gamaliel Bailey, Thomas Earle, and Gerrit Smith, among others, at first "looked upon the Liberty party as a mere temporary expedient, to draw or drive the other parties to adopt our principles." Once that was done, the antislavery party could be dismantled and its members could honorably return to the now purified and perhaps realigned major parties.[9] It seemed to Smith that only by avowing its transient nature could the Liberty party escape the corruption of conventional politics. "I have always flattered myself," he contended as late as 1845, "that the Liberty Party would be incomparably purer than other political parties; and that it would be so, not mainly because of its humane and holy object; but, rather, because, from its necessarily brief endurance, it would hold out little or no inducement to the ambitious and selfish to join it."[10]

This anti-party feeling was one reason why so many pioneer Liberty men at first looked upon their organization as merely transitory. The same suspicion of all political parties which had impeded formation of an antislavery party now led many of its early supporters to insist that its aims and tenure be strictly limited. A party of principle might, paradoxically, help to exorcise "the baneful spirit of partyism" in America, but only if its very impermanence helped to keep it pure. Such feeling was, of course, especially strong among the clerical element within the Liberty party. But many others shared a concern lest there "be too much of the *mere party* about this 'Liberty' business," and they worked to restrict the party's scope.[11]

The experience of the Anti-Masonic party (to which a good many Liberty leaders, including Smith, Stewart, and Holley, had once belonged) also contributed to the notion that a temporary coalition could

[9] *Emancipator,* Mar. 15, 1848; Foster, "History of the Liberty Party," 68; Gerrit Smith to Abby Kelley, July 24, 1843, Stephen S. Foster Papers, American Antiquarian Society.
[10] Quoted in *Signal of Liberty,* May 12, 1845.
[11] Salmon P. Chase to Joshua R. Giddings, Jan. 21, 1842, Giddings-Julian Papers, LC; Moses A. Cartland to John G. Whittier, Aug. 23, 1841, Martha H. Shackford (ed.), *Whittier and the Cartlands: Letters and Comments* (Wakefield, Mass., 1950), 30. For analyses of anti-party attitudes in nineteenth-century America, see Richard Hofstadter, *The Idea of a Party System: The Rise of Legitimate Opposition in the United States, 1780-1840* (Berkeley and Los Angeles, 1969), and Ronald P. Formisano, "Political Character, Antipartyism and the Second Party System," *American Quarterly,* XXI, No. 4 (Winter 1969), 683-709.

do all that need be done. So long "as masonry [had] reared its crest," a third party to combat it had been necessary. But, quite properly, once its mission had been accomplished and freemasonry put to rout, the Anti-Masonic party had been disbanded, its adherents moving back into the major parties from which they had originally come. Most Liberty men saw no reason why they might not duplicate Anti-Masonry's triumphs, and in much the same way.[12]

Still another reason for the early view that the Liberty party need not—perhaps ought not—be permanent was the conviction that the old parties were ripe for realignment along proslavery and antislavery lines. Traditional issues were fast dropping by the wayside, and President Tyler's falling out with the dominant wing of his party promised to abet a recombination of parties on the slavery question by further "confounding and finally putting to rest" many sources of conflict "between the contending national parties."[13] Having no basis in *principle*, and being composed of the most disparate factions, the major parties were themselves exceedingly fragile. With old issues—banks, tariffs, internal improvements—out of the way and with the vitality of abolition clearly revealed in Liberty party progress, one or another of the dominant parties might be induced to embrace a genuine antislavery position. Or, as Gerrit Smith speculated, a sectional realignment might occur in which Northern Whigs and Democrats would break their Southern ties and "identify themselves with our great doctrine of impartial and universal liberty: and then the Liberty party will die, as a matter of course."[14]

To a certain extent such speculation was highly fanciful and betrayed an ignorance of political reality. Yet that is not entirely so. For the issues which had created and sustained the second American party system had lost their compelling force by the 1840s, and Whigs and Democrats were already casting about for new platforms on which to unite. Moreover, the steady intrusion of the slavery question into national politics did set in motion a sectionalization of parties which within another generation would become an awful reality.

Garrisonians had argued that moral regeneration must precede politi-

---

[12] See, e.g., "X.X." to the editor, *Liberator*, Feb. 21, 1840.
[13] *Signal of Liberty*, Aug. 22, 1842.
[14] Gerrit Smith to Abby Kelley, July 24, 1843, Stephen S. Foster Papers.

cal reform, that no major political party could be expected to adopt antislavery principles until a majority of citizens had become abolitionists. Liberty men disagreed. The work of moral suasion had already produced an antislavery host strong enough, if it were politically united, to force fundamental concessions from the established parties. Full justice to the black man—slave *and* free, South *and* North—might well depend upon a national revolution in morals. But the war against slavery and legal discrimination need not await universal conversion. What counted, as Gerrit Smith put it, was not the proportion of abolitionists to the whole population, but "the proportion that the number of right-voting abolitionists bears to the difference between the aggregates of the voters in the [major] political parties." A small but tightly knit band, by wielding the balance of power, could "extort concessions, in the shape of the repeal of slavery-sustaining laws, from the [established] political parties, even whilst they remain unsubdued by antislavery truth, and continue pro-slavery in spirit."[15] To be successful, of course, the balance-of-power tactic would require the party practicing it to be impermanent. For, as Liberty men and their critics perceived, a ballot cast for the third party was in most instances the equivalent of no vote at all, so far as putting in or turning out a major party was concerned. What a Liberty vote did do was advertise the strength and resolve of political abolitionists and offer a potential reward to the party which adopted a sound enough antislavery platform to win them over.

The parity between Democrats and Whigs in most states encouraged Liberty men to believe in the possibility of "checking the ruinous measures of one party and aiding & carrying the beneficial propositions of another" by securing the balance of power in the free states and Congress.[16] In New England the antislavery party had the added advantage of laws requiring successful candidates to get a majority of *all* votes cast. At times a relative handful of Liberty voters were able to block the election of Whig and Democratic nominees. In 1841, for example, although the Liberty vote in Massachusetts amounted to less than 4 per cent of the total, over eighty legislative seats went empty because neither major party candidate received the requisite majority. In the fol-

[15] Smith to Joshua Leavitt, Dec. 24, 1839, quoted in *Emancipator,* Jan. 9, 1840.
[16] Salmon P. Chase to Joshua R. Giddings, Jan. 21, 1842, Giddings-Julian Papers.

lowing year Massachusetts Liberty men defeated the election of seven out of ten representatives to Congress and threw the contest for governor into the state legislature.[17] Elsewhere, however, the balance-of-power principle worked much less well. What Liberty men at first overlooked was that no party would be likely to bid strongly for abolitionist support when to do so meant risking defections from its conservative wing. So long as Whig or Democratic mossbacks outnumbered political abolitionists, the balance-of-power tactic in most states had little chance of success.

Interestingly enough, the victories of the Liberty men's nemesis, the "Slave Power," encouraged them in their often exaggerated faith in the miracles a minority party might work. If dedication and singleness of purpose could enable a small group of slaveholders (roughly equal to the number of voters in Ohio) to control the national government and run roughshod over free labor interests in North and South, might not similar unity and firmness crown the forces of liberty with success? One answer, of course, was that laws and constitutions gave special favors to the slave interest. But Liberty men had no doubt that, given "a corresponding and united effort," they could break slavery's iron grip on national parties and programs and replace it with the power of freedom. The purity of their principles and the numerical dominance of non-slaveholding interests, they believed, more than offset the Slave Power's advantage. And once Whigs and Democrats had been redeemed from their corrupt alliance with slavery, the Liberty party could safely retire from the field.[18]

This view of the Liberty party as the counterweight to the "slave party" raised the question of its proper orientation. Should it be a purely Northern party or should it portray itself as a truly national coalition? By and large, Liberty men chose the latter alternative. A few, most notably Gerrit Smith, argued that trusting national parties—whether ecclesiastical or political—to attack slavery was sheer folly. "Much as a geographical party in our country is to be deprecated," Smith maintained, "none other will abolish slavery." In the beginning,

[17] Foster, "History of the Liberty Party," 20-22; Nina M. Tiffany, *Samuel E. Sewall: A Memoir* (Boston, 1898), 94-96; Merton L. Dillon, *The Abolitionists: The Growth of a Dissenting Minority* (DeKalb, Ill., 1974), 147.
[18] Hallowell (Me.) *Liberty Standard*, Aug. 10, 1842; *Liberty Tract No. 9. The Compact; Or, What Have Our State Politics to Do with Slavery?* (Boston, n.d.), 4; Thomas, "History of the Anti-Slavery Movement," 44, 57-58.

at least, any real Liberty party must be a Northern party.[19] Most, however, took special pains to deny such particularism. This concern to
emphasize the national character of the Liberty party derived in part
from an understanding that voters found overt sectionalism alarming,
especially when it was linked to the explosive issue of slavery. It also
stemmed from the conviction that just as the Slave Power had allies in
the North, so Freedom had friends in the South.

> Let it always be borne in mind, that the Liberty party is not
> *sectional* in character [the Cincinnati *Philanthropist* reminded its
> readers]. We do not go for a *Northern,* but an American party.
> We war not against the South, but the Slave-Power. This power
> does not occupy the whole South, nor is it confined by southern
> limits. A large portion of the people of Kentucky, Western Vir-
> ginia, Eastern Tennessee, Maryland, and Missouri, will deeply
> sympathize with the Liberty party, whenever they can under-
> stand its principles and objects. Their interests are really op-
> pressed by the Slave-Power. . . . On the other hand, capitalists
> at the North, who own slave-property at the South, and others
> who from business, social connections or otherwise, are inter-
> ested in perpetuating the supremacy of the slave-interest, are
> constituent elements of the Slave-Power.[20]

In fact, some argued, the Liberty was the *only* truly national party—
both Whigs and Democrats being subservient to the sectional interests
of the South.[21] In any event, by 1843 the notion that "the Liberty party
is not a Sectional Party, but a National Party" was officially inscribed
in the party platform. Concerned as much with preaching an antislavery message as with rounding up votes, and as eager to describe future
tendencies as to analyze present prospects, few Liberty partisans were
much troubled at the nearly total lack of support from non-slaveholders in the South. Poor whites were bound in time to awaken to
their real interests, and when that happened they would inevitably
throw their strength behind a national antislavery party.[22]

Much of the Liberty party's effort went into the task of proksely-
tizing, of educating North and South alike to the evil of slavery, with-

---

[19] Smith to Alfred Wilkinson, Oct. 19, 1840, Letterbook, Smith Papers; Smith to
William H. Seward, Feb. 19, 1842, William H. Seward Papers, University of
Rochester.
[20] *Philanthropist,* Feb. 16, 1842.
[21] *Liberty Standard,* quoted in *Emancipator and Free American,* June 1, 1843.
[22] *Philanthropist,* Sept. 23, 1843; *Signal of Liberty,* Mar. 27, 1843.

out much regard for immediate political rewards. Liberty men looked upon their party as much as a vehicle of abolitionist propaganda as an instrument of political power. Joining appeals to conscience and self-interest, they strove as hard to persuade as to coerce.

2

In support of these twin aims, Liberty men developed a program which they confined in the beginning to the "one idea" of unremitting hostility to slavery and the Slave Power. Despite the objections of Thomas Earle, C. T. Torrey, and a few others who warned that a party so narrowly based could never succeed, and despite the ridicule of opponents who likened the Liberty platform to the Chinese map on which China nearly filled the whole, "but in a little corner stood the rest of the world," Liberty backers at first sternly resisted the temptation to add "extraneous" planks.[23] "Our enterprise embraces the preservation of the liberties of the free States, the interests of the free colored population, of two and a half million slaves, and of the non-slaveholders of the slave States," explained the *Signal of Liberty*, "all [of] whom are oppressed and harrassed [sic] by the Slave Power which we oppose." On all issues not directly related to slavery—trade, banking, land policy, internal improvements, and the like—the Liberty party would preserve a perfect neutrality.[24]

Liberty advocates justified this narrow base in many ways. Most commonly they contended that slavery exerted so corrupting an influence in national life that until it was destroyed other reforms were impossible or not worth undertaking. For not only did bondage rob millions of black Americans of their freedom, but it subverted the rights of most whites as well. As Birney noted in accepting his nomination in 1840:

> . . . For the last six years, we have seen [our civil liberties] invaded one after another—the administration aiding in the onset—

[23] Foster, "History of the Liberty Party," 12-13; Boston *Free American*, Sept. 30, Oct. 7, Nov. 11, 1841; *Signal of Liberty*, Feb. 19, 1844, quoting Mr. Millard, a Democrat of Adrian, Michigan.
[24] *Signal of Liberty*, Aug. 22, 1842. See also the Liberty platform adopted at the party's national convention in New York City, May 12-13, 1841, reported in *Emancipator*, May 27, 1841; Goodell, *Slavery and Anti-Slavery*, 473.

till the *feeling of security* for any of them has well nigh expired. A censorship of the mail is usurped by the deputy postmasters throughout more than half the country, and approved of by the administration under which it takes place. The pillage of the Post Office is perpetrated in one of our principal cities, and its contents made a bonfire of in the public square; no one is brought in question for the outrage. Free speech and debate on the most important subject that now agitates the country, is rendered impossible in our national legislature; the *right* of the people to petition Congress for a redress of grievances is formally abolished by their own servants! And shall we sit down and dispute about the currency, about a sub treasury or no-sub-treasury, a bank or no-bank, while such outrages on constitutional and essential *rights* are enacting before our eyes?[25]

Slavery, moreover, was seen not as passive and contained, but propulsive and unsettling. The other great questions could "never be equitably and permanently adjusted," until the "disturbing power of slavery" was crushed. "Change," insisted the *Granite Freeman*, "change is the law which the tyrant paupers of the south have written upon our national policy," and free labor could "never go to work confidently and safely in any branch of industry" while the Slave Power continued to manipulate government solely in its own interest.[26]

Practical political considerations seemed at first also to dictate adherence to an exclusively antislavery platform. For one thing, the introduction of other test questions might well drive off or shut out men who were sound on slavery. Equally dangerous, it might attract persons whose chief interest was not slavery, men with a nose for boodle who would compromise the party's reputation for high-minded benevolence. In either event, the Liberty party would quickly become a party of "antislavery and something else"—barely distinguishable from Whigs and Democrats—and, as had been true with those parties, antislavery would soon be swallowed up in the "something else." "Let us be content with the Liberty party as it is," Gerrit Smith urged his fellows in 1843. "Let us believe, that a party which is true to the essen-

[25] Birney to Myron Holley, Joshua Leavitt, and Elizur Wright, Jr., May 11, 1840, Dumond (ed.), *Birney Letters*, I, 566-67.
[26] Concord (N.H.) *Granite Freeman*, Oct. 31, 1844. See also Address of the National Liberty Convention, 1841, in *Emancipator*, May 27, 1841; James G. Birney to Russell Errett, Aug. 5, 1844, Dumond (ed.), *Birney Letters*, II, 831.

tial interests of man, may safely be trusted with his minor interests also. . . ."[27]

But even among those committed to a "one idea" program (and pressure for a broader platform quickly intensified), sharp divisions developed from the outset over the proper course for political abolitionists to steer. One basic disagreement involved the correct limits of the Liberty party's antislavery program. Should the party, as some suggested, restrict itself to "the deliverance of the government from the control of the slave power,"[28] or might it, in its capacity as a political force, justifiably press for emancipation in states where slavery already existed? The dispute was one among friends, since both sides equally desired the overthrow of slavery everywhere, but it nonetheless did much to sharpen men's perceptions of the legitimate function of an antislavery party and to define the party's relationship to the broader abolitionist crusade.

Westerners—particularly the Ohio group headed by Gamaliel Bailey, Thomas Morris, and, after 1841, Salmon P. Chase—insisted on the distinction between moral and political action, and maintained that the object of the Liberty party was not abolition in the South but merely the divorce of the federal government and the free states from the slave system. Such men were fearful lest, by advocating seemingly unconstitutional acts, the Liberty party appear more radical than it was and thereby frighten off potential supporters. Chase complained that matters had gotten altogether out of hand in New York, where in 1842 a state Liberty convention had officially endorsed Gerrit Smith's "Address to the Slaves," which justified illegal (if peaceful) acts by slaves in seizing their freedom.[29] Such a step was perfectly proper for an antislavery *society*, whose means were strictly moral and whose goal was universal emancipation. But "to avoid the appearance of evil," it was essential that an antislavery *party* confine itself to strictly constitutional proposals: it should not urge abolition in the South, for, as most

[27] *Signal of Liberty*, Nov. 13, 20, 1843; Smith to President, National Liberty Convention, Aug. 10, 1843, quoted in *Albany Weekly Patriot*, Sept. 12, 1843.
[28] Thomas Morris *et al.* to Joshua Leavitt, quoted in *Emancipator and Free American*, June 16, 1842.
[29] Chase to Thaddeus Stevens, Apr. 8, 1842, Thaddeus Stevens Papers, LC. Smith's "Address to the Slaves" advised chattels to flee from their oppressors and encouraged them to "use" such boats, skiffs, and horses as were necessary to make their escape, whether in slave or free states. See *Emancipator and Free American*, Feb. 4, 1842.

agreed, "we have no political power by the constitution which can reach that evil." Rather, as editor Bailey put it, the Liberty party should aim "to disenthral the laws, institutions and politics of the free states, from subjection to slavery influence; to rid these states of all responsibility in upholding the system of slavery; to give such power to the anti-slavery element in the General Government as shall be sufficient to free the domestic and foreign policy of the United States from slaveholding control, and withdraw all federal support, not absolutely demanded by the constitution, from the system of slavery."[30] As good abolitionists, Liberty men should, in their capacity as citizens, do all in their power to uproot human bondage everywhere. And if, after taking all steps constitutionally open to a political party, slavery continued "to disturb the business, corrupt the morals, and endanger the safety of the whole country," then Liberty men might legitimately press for constitutional amendments abolishing slavery throughout the land. For the moment, commonsense and constitutional constraints dictated that as a political instrument the Liberty party must stop short of a demand for universal abolition.[31]

Many others, especially in the East, thought this approach needlessly timid. Salmon Chase had suggested that the name "Abolitionist," often used in early years to describe the new party, was provocative and inappropriate and that it ought to be dropped. But Joshua Leavitt at once repudiated this cautious proposal. ". . . I *am* an abolitionist," he protested, "& expect to be one . . . until slavery is actually abolished. . . ." Discarding the designation "Abolitionist" after it had received popular currency would make people suspect that the third party men were "inclined to abandon the thing itself in our eagerness for political victory." Abolition was the ultimate goal of all Liberty men, whether or not political measures alone were adequate to the task. Why, then, not avow it and reap the rewards of boldness? Gerrit Smith, while admitting that the Westerners' narrow objective of hedging slavery within the slave states would probably lead quickly to general emancipation, also pressed for a broader appeal. Unless it invoked men's benevolence

---

[30] *Philanthropist,* Feb. 16, Apr. 13, 1842. See also *ibid.* Apr. 30, 1839, Jan. 6, 1841, Feb. 9, 1842; *Signal of Liberty,* Feb. 23, 1842.
[31] *Philanthropist,* Feb. 23, Mar. 16 (quote), Aug. 27, 1842. Chase also hinted that "in case of extreme necessity arising from war or insurr[ection]" the Liberty party might propose federal interference with slavery in the states. Chase to [John Quincy Adams], Sept. 24, 1842 (copy), Salmon P. Chase Papers, PHS.

as well as their self interest, he feared, the Liberty party would soon become a cold and stunted thing, no longer worthy of the trust of genuine abolitionists.[32]

This seemingly trivial dispute stemmed from fundamental disagreements over the purpose and direction of reform party politics. Men like Smith, Leavitt, and William Goodell stressed the propagandistic function of the Liberty party and strove for purity of program and membership so as to enhance the credibility of their arguments against slavery. The recruits they sought would come primarily from among already professing abolitionists. "We have seen enough to know that none but abolitionists should be trusted in the cause of impartial Liberty," said Smith.[33] That being so, it was axiomatic that the emancipation of all bondsmen, and not simply protection of the rights of free labor, should receive prime consideration. On the other hand, Westerners like Chase, Bailey, and Morris, more deeply schooled in conventional politics and representing a region notorious for its negrophobia, sought by more moderate appeals which emphasized the "Slave Power's" threat to free labor to draw enlightened Whigs and Democrats into the antislavery alliance. Barely visible in the party's early years, these divisions would grow during the mid-1840s until schism became inescapable: Chase and Bailey (joined now by Leavitt) engineering the Liberty party's fusion with free-soil Democrats and Whigs, Smith and Goodell forming a Liberty League to keep political *abolitionism* pure.

Whatever their differences over the proper extent of antislavery politics, however, nearly all Liberty men (and political abolitionists in the major parties) concurred in the constitutional steps by which slavery might be strangled. The first such step, most agreed, would be to deprive the peculiar institution of the aid and comfort it received from Northern states and the national government. Once deprived of such artificial support, once driven back within local bounds and revealed in all its "monstrous deformity," slavery would soon topple of its own weight.

The Liberty party spelled out in great detail its program for the "denationalization of slavery." First, of course, Congress should uproot

[32] Leavitt to Chase, Dec. 6, 1841 (quote), May 28, 1842, Chase Papers, PHS; Smith to Chase, May 31, 1842, Letterbook, Smith Papers; *Albany Weekly Patriot*, Sept. 12, 1843.
[33] Smith to Chase, May 31, 1842, Letterbook, Smith Papers.

slavery wherever its power constitutionally extended: in the District of Columbia; in the territory of Florida; in forts, arsenals, and navy yards; and on the high seas. The use of slave labor in public works projects ought to be discontinued at once. Measures ought also be taken to prevent slavery's spread into federal territories previously free of its blight. Creation of a *cordon sanitaire* against slavery expansion, in combination with repression of the interstate traffic in slaves, would soon force the upper South to free its bondsmen and make emancipation in other slave states merely a question of time. Indeed, some argued that even if only the *growth* of slavery were checked it would be cause for rejoicing. "It is a more important object to prevent a million of human beings from being made slaves," contended the *American Freeman*, "than it is to free an equal number who have already been half destroyed by being reared and long retained in the condition of slavery." Needless to say, Liberty men also strongly opposed the admission of any new slave states into the Union. "Every addition of a slave state," the Michigan *Signal of Liberty* warned, "increases the danger of foreign invasion, and domestic insurrection, and thereby weakens the nation."[34]

Other maneuvers by which slavery might constitutionally be outflanked included the election of "tried friends of Liberty" to key public offices. Thoroughgoing antislavery Congressmen, even if badly outnumbered, might turn the capitol into a forum on freedom and bondage. Adams, Giddings, and others had already demonstrated the possibilities for antislavery agitation in Congress; Liberty party representatives made of still sterner stuff might be able to carry the work of enlightenment even further. "A thorough discussion of this whole [slavery] question in the halls of our national Legislature," asserted the *Philanthropist*, "would be equal to its discussion in every slaveholding state in the Union." So too with appointive offices. Once in a position to exercise or influence such power, Liberty men should insist that federal and

[34] Salmon P. Chase to Charles D. Cleveland, Oct. 22, 1841, Chase Papers, LC; Milwaukee *American Freeman*, June 1, 1844; *Signal of Liberty*, Apr. 6, 1842. See also Thomas, "History of the Anti-Slavery Movement," 55; *Emancipator*, May 20, 27, 1841; *Liberty Standard*, July 12, Oct. 6, 1841, June 24, 1847; *Philanthropist*, Jan. 5, 1842; *Granite Freeman*, Oct. 31, 1844; *The Address of the Southern and Western Liberty Convention, Held at Cincinnati, June 11, 1845, to the People of the United States* (Cincinnati, 1845); *Proceedings of the Great Convention of the Friends of Freedom in the Eastern and Middle States, Held in Boston, October 1, 2, & 3, 1845* (Lowell, Mass., 1845); Thomas H. McKee, *The National Conventions and Platforms of all Parties, 1789-1904*, 5th ed. (Baltimore, 1904), 51-55.

free state appointments—especially to judicial posts—go only to opponents of slavery. "This principle," some held, "if practiced in earnest for a few years, would strike the death-blow to the accursed institution." Certainly, once the Liberty revolution had worked its way on the South, replacing slaveholding officers with philanthropists, slavery could not long endure. For, said Birney, "however slow a people may be, themselves, to put away wrong from among them, yet when once *justice* is boldly *done* upon it by their rulers, the act never fails to receive their heartiest approbation and sanction."[35]

Liberty men gave close attention to the party's position concerning fugitive slaves, without, however, reaching anything like full accord. The more conservative members (again centered chiefly in the West) stood ready to pledge noninterference with the return of runaways, apparently convinced that the Constitution spoke clearly of the slaveholder's right to pursue and reclaim footloose bondsmen. Others vehemently condemned the fugitive slave clause as "an offense against humanity, a sin against God," and called loudly for its nonobservance. "Few things have contributed more to keep alive the spirit of the abolitionists than the rescuing of slaves, and *interfering* with that infamous and bloody stipulation of the Constitution," Birney lectured Chase following an Ohio Liberty convention that took conservative ground on the question of runaways. "Whatever pledges of non interference may be given they will be disregarded—at least so long as our body has any life or humanity in it, or any greater fear of God than of man." At the party's national convention in 1843 the radicals triumphed. Despite resistance from the cautious business committee, the delegates adopted "by a rising vote, amid bursts of enthusiastic applause," a resolution declaring the fugitive slave clause contrary to the laws of God and the rights of man and hence "utterly null and void." At the time it stood as a highwater mark of Liberty party radicalism.[36]

From the first there had been a few political abolitionists willing to espouse even more radical doctrines. Most opponents of slavery (including, after a brief lapse, Garrison and his disciples) contended that the United States Constitution gave Congress no direct power over

[35] *Philanthropist*, Dec. 8, 1841; *Signal of Liberty*, Apr. 7, 1845; Birney to Russell Errett, Aug. 5, 1844, Dumond (ed.), *Birney Letters*, II, 831.
[36] Birney to Chase, Feb. 2, 1842, H. C. Taylor to Chase, Feb. 4, 1842, Chase Papers, LC; *Philanthropist*, Aug. 2, 1843; Foster, "History of the Liberty Party," 26; McKee, *National Conventions and Platforms*, 55.

slavery in the states. But some, especially in the East, followed the lead of Alvan Stewart and argued that the Constitution was in fact an anti-slavery document.[37] Constitutional guarantees of habeas corpus and republican government; the loose and libertarian Preamble; and above all the Fifth Amendment, with its insistence that no person "be deprived of life, liberty, or property, without due process of law," all convinced such men that Congress had a constitutional right—even a duty—to abolish slavery in the Southern states by direct legislation. Publication of William Goodell's *Views of American Constitutional Law, in its Bearing upon American Slavery* (1844) and Lysander Spooner's *The Unconstitutionality of Slavery* (1845), together with growing discouragement at the Liberty party's slow progress, won new converts to this dubious creed.[38] Yet before 1847 the vast majority of Liberty men, though they were personally certain that human bondage violated natural rights and were unwilling to admit that the Constitution *guaranteed* slavery, readily accepted constitutional limitation on outside interference with the institution where it was already established by local law. The Liberty party therefore directed its efforts toward hedging in slavery, depriving it of special favors, and stimulating emancipationist sentiment within the slave states.

3

The Liberty party formally pitted itself not only against slavery and the "slave oligarchy," but also against the oppression of blacks who were ostensibly free. Obliteration of racial discrimination seemed imperative to most Liberty men both because such discrimination con-

[37] For Stewart's pioneering arguments on the unconstitutionality of slavery, see Jacobus tenBroek, *The Antislavery Origins of the Fourteenth Amendment* (Berkeley and Los Angeles, 1951), 43-48; William M. Wiecek, *The Guarantee Clause of the U. S. Constitution* (Ithaca, 1972), 155-59; Luther R. Marsh (ed.), *Writings and Speeches of Alvan Stewart on Slavery* (New York, 1860); Dumond, *Antislavery*, 293-95; *supra*, p. 50. For other early acceptance of Stewart's doctrine, see James Appleton to J. C. Lovejoy *et al.*, Feb. 17, 1842, quoted in *Liberty Standard*, Feb. 23, 1842; *ibid.* Sept. 8, 1841, Dec. 21, 1842; Albany *Tocsin of Liberty*, Dec. 15, 1842; Harlow, *Smith*, 280-81.
[38] For analyses of Goodell, Spooner, and such like-minded pamphleteers as Gerrit Smith, Joel Tiffany, George Mellen, and James G. Birney, see tenBroek, *Antislavery Origins of the Fourteenth Amendment*, chap. III; Wiecek, *Guarantee Clause*, 159-65; Kraditor, *Means and Ends in American Abolitionism*, 186-95.

travened God's law and the American creed and because it stood in the way of abolition. For, as one Liberty convention declared, had Northern Negroes been "as honored and elevated as its white population—it would be found utterly impossible to reconcile the North to the enslavement of the colored man. . . . No proposition is more true, than that the wrongs which the North has done, and continues to do, to its colored people, enter most largely into the explanation of its proslavery spirit, and furnish the most influential argument in favor of Southern oppression."[39]

Since Northern discriminatory laws and habits, like Southern slavery, rested on a belief in the racial inferiority of blacks, Liberty spokesmen developed a two-pronged argument designed to lessen such prejudice. One line of attack—or counterattack—was to point to the accomplishments of distinguished Negroes like Frederick Douglass, Alexander Dumas, and Toussaint L'Ouverture as telling evidence of intellectual capacity. Similarly, some noted that no one race of men had at all times displayed a superiority over all others, suggesting that circumstance outweighed racial characteristics in determining relationships within the family of man. It had been the African, not the European, who in the days of Egypt's glory had held the upper hand.[40]

A second line of argument, often joined with the first, was that although Negroes were presently inferior to white Americans, they were by no means innately so. Again, condition, not color, had produced black backwardness. And once conditions changed—especially once the crushing effects of slavery were erased—Negroes might well rise to a station of equality. Or, if not equality, at least to respectability and a position warranting full rights of citizenship. In the meantime, any comparison between the white and black races was unfair. "So long as their minds are shrouded in superstition and ignorance," claimed Wis-

[39] *Proceedings of the Great Convention of the Friends of Freedom in the Eastern and Middle States . . . 1845,* 17-18. In its national platform (Aug. 1843) the Liberty party resolved "That this convention recommend to the friends of liberty in all those free states where any inequality of rights and privileges exists on account of color, to employ their utmost energies to remove all such remnants and effects of the slave system." McKee, *National Conventions and Platforms,* 54. See also *Signal of Liberty,* May 5, 1841; *Liberty Standard,* May 21, 1843.

[40] *American Freeman,* Aug. 25, Sept. 22, 1846; Elizur Wright, Jr., to Susan Wright, Mar. 31, 1840, Wright Papers, LC; John G. Whittier in *National Era,* June 3, 1847. Lydia Maria Child, a Garrisonian critic of the Liberty party, made much the same argument in *An Appeal in Favor of That Class of Americans Called Africans* (Boston, 1833).

consin's Liberty weekly, "—so long as the foot of the oppressor is planted firmly upon their necks, and so long as no efforts are made, either to leave them free to set about their own emancipation from the thraldom of ignorance, or to strike from them the galling chains of slavery,—we have nothing to guide us in our estimate of their capacity."[41]

Until such time as a Liberty party infiltrated the South, political abolitionists could do little for blacks in that region. But there were many avenues of uplift in the North, and there Liberty advocates, despite overwhelming opposition and a depressing lack of success, struggled hard against the causes and effects of racial discrimination. For the most part, their efforts (in keeping with the character of most antebellum reform) were designed merely to strike off the shackles which held Negroes back, not to provide special assistance. Discriminatory laws would be repealed, political rights extended, means of self-improvement—especially education—placed within the black man's reach. But thereafter self-help would be the chief reliance of upward-bound free Negroes. Paternalism, in short, had its limits, and once the blacks had been assured equal opportunity with whites they would be expected to stand or fall on their own merits. "The strong sympathy which the humane and benevolent naturally feel for the ill used has sometimes led them to caress and pet the Colored people," declared James G. Birney. This, he contended, was all wrong. "What the colored people really need and nearly *all* that they need to have done for them *separately*—is to be set up erect on their feet with full liberty to use their faculties of whatever kind, as others do, for their own improvement."[42]

Still, there was much that good-hearted whites might do. One needed reform was the extension of equal voting rights to blacks. Not only were discriminatory voting laws unjust in themselves—violating, for instance, the tenets of the Declaration of Independence and the basic American principle that taxation without representation was tyranny—but they paved the way for broader persecution. "This oppression by legislative authority in a political sphere," maintained the *American Freeman* during the contest over Negro suffrage in Wisconsin, "opens

[41] *American Freeman,* Sept. 22, 1846. See also *Philanthropist,* Apr. 28, 1841.
[42] Birney to William Wright, June 20, 1845, Dumond (ed.), *Birney Letters,* II, 945.

the way for injustice and insult in the market place, in the social circle, and in religious bodies. . . . It creates indeed a taint in the blood, that will descend from parent to child, to all future generations, while the Constitution endures."[43] Not only in Wisconsin, but also in Michigan, New York, Connecticut, and elsewhere, Liberty advocates took such arguments to heart and worked to open the polls equally to all men. They were uniformly unsuccessful, of course. But to those who waged it, the fight for black suffrage seemed both just in itself and useful as a way of showing that the grip of slavery reached even into the free states and tarnished Revolutionary ideals with an ugly and unnatural racism. Few, therefore, regretted their labors in a lost cause.[44]

Liberty men also decried, though they rarely organized to prevent, discrimination in economic and social affairs. For instance, they attacked barriers against the hiring of Negroes in federal projects. They also condemned Jim Crow schools. "Schools *exclusively* for . . . [blacks]," Birney proclaimed, "are useful to the prejudice and the pride of the whites, whilst they serve as symbols of the degredation [*sic*] of the class sought to be benefitted [*sic*]." Social mixing was a touchier matter. Liberty men were especially sensitive to the charge that their doctrines led inexorably to miscegenation—or, as it was then called, "amalgamation." Far from defending that prospect, they commonly spun the charge around and accused the slave system—one of "wholesale adultery"—with responsibility for most racial mixing. Even so, short of the bedroom door, at least, Liberty spokesmen took a decidedly tolerant stand. For, as Birney said, "if the professed friends of the colored people avoid social intercourse with them *only because they are colored* disregarding their individual intelligence and moral

[43] *American Freeman*, Jan. 5, 1847.
[44] Thomas, "History of the Anti-Slavery Movement," 55; Theodore Foster to James G. Birney, Dec. 14, 1841, Dumond (ed.), *Birney Letters*, II, 643; *Signal of Liberty*, Jan. 16, 1843; Alvan Stewart to Samuel Webb, Jan. 14, 1846, Webb to Stewart, Mar. 1, 1846, Stewart Papers, NYHS; *Granite Freeman*, Oct. 9, 1846; Foner, *Free Soil, Free Labor, Free Men*, 281. In New York attempts to include Negro suffrage in the revised 1846 constitution produced a collision among Liberty party supporters. Some, among them Gerrit Smith, Beriah Green, and William Goodell, insisted that political abolitionists vote a strict Liberty ticket whatever the view of other candidates on Negro voting. Others, like Alvan Stewart and Silas Hawley, argued in favor of backing Whigs and Democrats who would pledge to support equal suffrage at the constitutional convention. See Samuel J. May to Maria W. Chapman, Feb. 19, 1846, Weston Family Papers.

worth,—their professions will be suspected,—their sincerity will not be trusted in, and all hold on their confidence for good will be lost."[45]

As much as their Garrisonian cousins, Liberty partisans denounced the American Colonization Society's prescription for the nation's racial ills: deportation of Negroes to Liberia. Most had no objection to helping ex-slaves reach lands of their choice, whether in Liberia, Canada, or elsewhere. But for several reasons they damned colonization as a "hypocritical, slavery-begotten, pro-slavery scheme." For one thing, they objected to the unfair because unproven assumption "that the blacks can never be so elevated as to enjoy their rights in this country," a country for whose independence their fathers had fought. As citizens, Negroes deserved the same opportunities *at home* as white Americans enjoyed. Colonization, moreover, was in its very concept ludicrously inconsistent. "After slavery and prejudice and abuse have reduced the colored man to the lowest rank—not in society—but almost to a level with the brutes," the *American Freeman* sarcastically observed, "then he must be sent to Africa, to rise, and to convert the heathen." Finally, colonization would leave untouched the poisonous influence of slavery. It would "merely transport some of the victims of slavery to a land of exile, and leave the guilty oppressors steeped in their sins."[46] Among Liberty men only James G. Birney had a good word to say for colonization—and Birney's suggestions that exodus to Liberia might prove after all the wisest course for American Negroes came only in his embittered old age and derived solely from his despair over the depth and virulence of white prejudice, not from any sympathy with the racist principles of the Colonization Society.[47]

While Liberty party adherents were remarkably tolerant by the standards of the time, they were not all committed to racial equality. This was particularly true in the Old Northwest. In 1842 Birney com-

---

[45] *Liberty Standard,* Dec. 7, 1842; Birney to William Wright, June 20, 1845, Dumond (ed.), *Birney Letters,* II, 945-47. Lewis Tappan was an exception to the general skittishness of Liberty advocates on miscegenation. Wyatt-Brown, *Tappan,* 177.
[46] *Liberty Standard,* Oct. 5, 1842; *American Freeman,* Nov. 3, 1846.
[47] Birney's views are set forth in his pamphlet *Examination of the Decision of the Supreme Court of the United States, in the Case of Strader, Gorman and Armstrong vs. Christopher Graham, Delivered at Its December Term, 1850: Concluding with an Address to the Free Colored People, Advising Them to Remove to Liberia* (Cincinnati, 1852).

plained in his diary that the Liberty party of Ohio "professes no more sympathy with the free colored class than with any other class. . . ." Leicester King, the Liberty candidate for governor of Ohio in 1842, while admitting that blacks might not be excluded constitutionally, nonetheless publicly declared his preference for an exclusively white population in that state. No less a figure than Thomas Morris, Birney's running mate in 1844, had once opposed Negro suffrage, though by the time of his candidacy he had apparently undergone a change of heart. In Michigan, the Liberty party brought ridicule and charges of hypocrisy upon itself when at its 1843 state convention it denied two black delegates the right to participate in nominations because they were not legal voters. Such manifestations of race prejudice were exceptional and muted and might easily be used to demonstrate the remarkable toleration of Liberty men generally: King *did* defend the right of blacks to enjoy all the privileges of citizenship; Morris *did* soften his opposition to Negro suffrage in the face of great pressure from other party members; and Michigan's leading Liberty paper *did* feel "ill-concealed mortification" at the gagging of the black delegates. Still, these aberrations show clearly that not even abolitionists, whose party called officially for the legal equality of all men, could fully escape the racist temper of the age.[48]

More serious than occasional displays of prejudice or the patronizing tone antislavery politicians often used toward blacks was the fundamental inadequacy of the Liberty party's program for Negro advancement. Although aware of the stunting effects of slavery, Liberty men expected freedmen, once given equality before the law, to compete without favor with whites whose advantages of wealth, power, and education were staggering. After centuries of oppression, the black man needed more than a fair start. But political abolitionists proved unwilling or unable to move beyond the self-help verities of their antebellum world.

Whatever its shortcomings, the Liberty party appeared to most Northern Negroes distinctly superior to its rivals. Grateful alike for

[48] Birney, Diary, Apr. 19, 1842, Birney Papers, LC; King to J. W. Piatt, Aug. 22, 1842, Chase Papers, PHS; Gamaliel Bailey to Birney, Mar. 31, 1843, Birney to Bailey, Apr. 16, 1843, Dumond (ed.), *Birney Letters*, II, 726, 732; Lewis Tappan to Bailey, Mar. 20, 1843, Tappan Papers; Tappan to Gerrit Smith, Sept. 9, 1843, Smith Papers; Tappan to Salmon P. Chase, Sept. 20, 1843, Nov. 23, 1844, Chase Papers, PHS; Smith, *Liberty and Free Soil Parties*, 58.

the new party's goals and the cordial welcome it extended to their race, large numbers of blacks worked mightily to enlist support for Liberty candidates. *The Colored American* and such distinguished Negro leaders as Henry Bibb, Theodore S. Wright, Samuel Ringgold Ward, and Henry Highland Garnet all enthusiastically endorsed the Liberty party. Even Frederick Douglass, although still under Garrison's wing, defended the new party before antislavery audiences. The 1843 National Convention of Colored Men overwhelmingly acclaimed it. And at the national gathering of the Liberty party held at Buffalo soon afterward, Ward and Garnet both delivered formal addresses, and Charles B. Ray, a black New York minister, acted as one of the convention secretaries. Many black voters stuck to the old parties—especially the Whig—but few doubted the sincerity of the Liberty party's concern for Negro rights.[49]

4

In its desire to add as many recruits as possible, the Liberty party also made a special point of slavery's threat to the rights of *white* Americans. Indeed, to some it appeared that the party had scant interest in anything else.

> The basis of Abolition [wrote one Ohio abolitionist in 1842] is the wrongs of the negro through slavery. Abolition incidentally considered [*sic*] the encroachments of slavery on the rights of the white man, but his wrongs are not the real cause of action. Abolition is charitable—is philanthropic. . . . The Liberty Party proceeds on another, a more selfish principle. It views slavery chiefly as it affects the white man. The power which puts it in motion is self-interest. It may prefer that the condition of the slave should be bettered, but it stirs not for him. It seeks the welfare of the white race. . . . The abolitionist goes out to redeem the negro; the Liberty man stands up in self defence, and declares self-preservation to be the first law of nature.[50]

[49] Benjamin Quarles, *Black Abolitionists* (New York, 1969), 183-85; [Edmund Quincy] to [Caroline Weston], Mar. 9, 1844, Weston Family Papers; Foster, "History of the Liberty Party," 24ff; *Albany Weekly Patriot*, Sept. 5, 1843.
[50] Eli Nichols to Gamaliel Bailey, Apr. 3, 1842, quoted in *Philanthropist*, May 11, 1842.

Such a view grossly exaggerated the selfish motives of Liberty advocates. Even Westerners who were uncomfortable with antislavery radicalism evinced a concern for Negro rights which was both genuine and, by contemporary standards, exceptional. Yet self-interest undeniably animated many Liberty men and the party did take special pains to develop arguments showing the damaging effects of slavery on whites as well as blacks.[51]

The "overwhelming political ascendancy of the slave power" and "the consequent degradation and vassalage of the northern people" received particular attention from Liberty party opinion-makers. Slavery, complained Michigan Liberty men, in a typical mixture of materialism and idealism, was "not only a monstrous legalized system of wickedness of immense magnitude—but an overwhelming political monopoly, in the hands of an oligarchy of 250,000 slaveholders, which by holding the balance of political power in the nation, has long rigidly controlled its offices, its finance and all its great interests, and has thus tyrannically subverted the constitutional liberties of more than 12,000,000 of nominal American freemen."[52]

This oppressive political monopoly, Liberty propagandists maintained, derived from the absolute unity of slaveholders wherever their peculiar institution was concerned and from the "three-fifths clause" of the Constitution, which gave to the South an estimated twenty-five "extra" congressional seats based on its slave population. It also drew strength from the servility of free state politicians, who confused bluster for might and stumbled over one another in their haste to do slavery's bidding.[53] Nowhere was the Slave Power's political control more readily apparent than in its corner on key federal posts—from the presidency to the territorial governorships. Liberty newspapers time and again published elaborate tables to show that ever since the nation's birth many more Southerners than Northerners had fed at the public trough.[54]

---

[51] For a rigidly materialistic interpretation of the Liberty Party, see Julian P. Bretz, "The Economic Background of the Liberty Party," *American Historical Review,* XXXIV, No. 2 (Jan. 1929), 250-64.

[52] *Signal of Liberty,* Sept. 15, Oct. 13, 1841. See also "The Right Sort of Politics," *Emancipator Extra,* Sept. 14, 1843.

[53] *Tocsin of Liberty,* Oct. 5, 1842; *Liberty Standard,* Dec. 1, 1841.

[54] See, e.g., *ibid.* Apr. 13, May 25, 1842; *Liberty Tract No. 3. The Influence of the Slave Power* (Boston, n.d.). Revised and up-dated, such tables became a stock-in-trade of antislavery journalism until the Civil War.

The net effect of such political dominance was not merely to safe-guard slavery where it was already rooted and to thrust it into new territories from which additional slave states were formed, but also to limit the rights and heighten the burdens of all Northerners. An arrogant slavocracy, Ohio Liberty men remonstrated in 1841, had interfered in the domestic legislation of free states, "stifled the freedom of speech and of debate," promoted mob violence, and embroiled the nation in a war against the Seminole Indians for no larger purpose than to break up an asylum of fugitive slaves. Until the political hammerlock of the Slave Power was broken, true democracy—even among whites—was impossible.[55]

Liberty spokesmen also portrayed the social offshoots of slavery as pernicious and potentially dangerous to the moral health of the nation. The South, like any slave society, was sick: the bottom had been crushed out of shape, and the top was rotten to the core. Horse-racing, gambling, cockfighting, duelling, violence and murder, infidelity, self-indulgence—these were the malignant fruits of bondage. As slavery spread, its values would spread. For this reason if for no other, preached Liberty partisans, pious Northerners ought to cordon off and ultimately eradicate slavery.[56]

Since the birth of the Liberty party had coincided with the great depression of 1837-43, it was natural for its propagandists to give special emphasis to slavery's economic consequences. The Slave Power, charged the Address of the 1841 National Liberty Convention, "has manifestly sought to preserve the balance of power between the impoverished South, and the more prosperous and industrious North, by crippling the energies of the latter, and reducing them, as nearly as possible, to the level of the former. . . ."[57] Abolitionists had in fact put forth arguments concerning the peculiar institution's "ruinous" influence on the national economy even before the Panic of 1837.[58] But Liberty advo-

---

[55] Address of the Liberty Convention to the People of Ohio, Dec. 29-30, 1841, in *Philanthropist*, Jan. 5, 1842. See also *American Freeman*, Mar. 20, 1844; *Liberty Standard*, Aug. 3, 1842.
[56] See particularly the series of articles on "Manners of Slavocracy" in the *Signal of Liberty*, June-Sept. 1842. For an example of one Liberty leader's personal repugnance at the corruption of slave society, see Elizur Wright, Jr., to Beriah Green, Washington, D.C., July 8, 1842 (typed copy), Wright Papers, BPL.
[57] Quoted in *Emancipator*, May 27, 1841.
[58] See, e.g., John G. Whittier to Editors of the Richmond, Va., *Jeffersonian & Times*, quoted in *Liberator*, Aug. 17, 1833; *First Annual Report of the . . . New-*

cates, hoping to capitalize on the country's business slump, refined and elaborated such arguments to an unprecedented degree. In countless tracts, speeches, editorials, and platforms, they hammered home the Slave Power's responsibility for hard times.

The basic source of economic weakness, Liberty polemicists contended, lay in the inefficiency and prodigality of the slave labor system. "Slavery," claimed the *American Freeman*, "is, inherently, the parent of idleness and contempt for free labor, of luxury and lavish expenditure, of bad economy, both individual and social. . . ."[59] The wastefulness of slaves, who toiled solely out of fear of the overseer's lash, was matched only by the extravagance of their masters. Since, according to one estimate, slave labor provided no more than two-thirds of the South's sustenance, and since most Southern whites found work dishonorable because of its association with slavery, the South survived only by plundering the hard-earned wealth of Northern freemen. That is, Southern patriarchs, in order to make ends meet and still indulge their fondness for fine wines, imported silks, and fast horses, borrowed and bought on credit from Northern merchants. Such merchants were only too glad to extend credit, since planters, with their elegant manners, extensive plantations, and large gangs of slaves, gave the illusion of substance. In truth, however, they were *"sturdy paupers"* who often defaulted on their debts.[60]

> Go among the merchants or the manufacturers [wrote Joshua Leavitt in his influential pamphlet on the *Financial Power of Slavery*], and you will find one complaining of his ten thousand, and another of his hundred thousand, and another of his two or five hundred thousand dollars of southern debts. He would get along very well now, if it were not for that southern debt. And behind every one of these stands another class, who have sold goods, or lent money, or given their endorsement to others that have

England Anti-Slavery Society (1833), 19. Lewis Tappan dated his own conversion to abolitionism from a speech by Simeon S. Jocelyn in 1833 in which Jocelyn made much of slavery's sapping effect upon the national economy. Wyatt-Brown, *Tappan*, 102.
59 *American Freeman*, Nov. 20, 1844.
60 Alvan Stewart, [*Liberty*] *Tract No. 4. The Cause of the Hard Times* (Boston, [1843]); Stewart to Samuel Webb, Feb. 7, 1843, Stewart Papers, NYHS; *Liberty Tract No. 6. The Tyrant Paupers; Or, Where the Money Goes* (Boston, n.d.); Charles T. Torrey, *Liberty Tract No. 2. The War of Slavery on Northern Commerce and Agriculture* (Boston, [1843]); *Liberty Standard*, Oct. 20, 1841, Oct. 5, 1842, Oct. 26, 1843.

trusted their all to the South, and now cannot pay. And behind
these another class, and another, and another, until there is hardly
a remote hamlet in the free States that has not been directly or
indirectly drained of its available capital by the southern debt.[61]

The Slave Power sapped the prosperity of the North not only by
reneging on its debts, but also by using its enormous political influence
to retard Northern economic development. Tariffs, charged Liberty
pamphleteers, had invariably favored the South and injured the North
—by taxing the free laborer while exempting the planter, by protecting
cotton but not domestic industry, by closing off foreign markets for
Northern goods. Similarly, Liberty spokesmen blamed proslavery dip-
lomats for the loss of the rich West Indies trade and the failure to win
for free products the same access to overseas markets that Southern
cotton, tobacco, and rice enjoyed. The Deposit Act of 1836 and the
Distribution-Preemption Act of 1841 also benefited the South at the expense of the North by distributing the treasury surplus among the
states according to the "federal ratio" (which counted three-fifths of
slaves as well as all freemen) instead of dividing it simply on the basis
of free population.[62] By one means or another, Charles Torrey concluded, "The aggregate, in any ten years, thus plundered from the people of the *free labor* states is not less than $300,000,000, all of which
goes to make up for the pauperism of slave labor."[63]

The Liberty party's economic arguments were, of course, often
naïve, simplistic, or downright faulty. They grossly exaggerated the
extent and the impact of Southern indebtedness and belittled the importance of free white labor. (Alvan Stewart stretched credibility to
the breaking point when he coolly asserted that "Only one person out
of five labors in the Southern States, and that person *is a slave. . . .*"[64])
They seriously distorted the tariff history of the early republic, for example blaming proslavery interests for the Tariff of 1816 although in

---

[61] Quoted in Bretz, "Economic Background of the Liberty Party," 254.
[62] *Ibid.* 257-61; *Liberty Tract No. 3. The Influence of the Slave Power,* 3-4; *American Freeman,* Feb. 26, Mar. 5, 1845; *Signal of Liberty,* Sept. 2, 1842; *Address of the
Southern and Western Liberty Convention . . . 1845,* 10. The *Rochester Freeman*
(Aug. 14, 1839) pointed out that in 1836 distribution of the federal surplus according to the three-fifths formula had meant that South Carolina, Georgia, Alabama,
Mississippi, Louisiana, and Kentucky received $6,754,588, while Pennsylvania, with
a larger free population than these six states combined, got only $3,822,353.
[63] Quoted in *Albany Weekly Patriot,* Aug. 15, 1843.
[64] Stewart, *The Cause of the Hard Times,* 1.

fact Southern Congressmen had voted heavily against that measure. And they wholly ignored the repressive influence of the North on economic development in the South. Yet for all that—perhaps in part because of it—such arguments possessed substantial appeal, especially at a time of economic hardship. It is impossible to say how many voters were swayed by the Liberty party's economic analysis, but there can be no doubt that Liberty strategists found in appeals to the white man's pocketbook an effective weapon in the war against slavery.

Nonetheless, it would be wrong to let the presence of materialistic reasoning overshadow the real idealism of the early Liberty party. One must remember that political abolitionism long antedated the Panic of 1837 and that most Liberty recruits were men committed to emancipation before economic arguments gained much currency. Much of the Liberty party's attention to slavery's economic consequences was designed simply to fend off the charge that its platform was too narrow, that it ignored altogether the interests of white men. It is quite likely that its blasts against the economic aggressions of the Slave Power most influenced men who never came over to the Liberty party but remained moderately antislavery Whigs or Democrats. Almost never did Liberty advocates advance economic arguments against slavery at the expense of moral and civil ones. Alvan Stewart, in his tract on *The Cause of Hard Times*, used the fact of overwhelming Southern dependence on slave labor to ridicule the notion that, if freed, slaves could not fend for themselves. The Address of the 1841 National Liberty Convention, after listing the damaging economic effects of slavery on the North, pointedly denied that "mere *pecuniary* burdens, and embarrassments" were "the sole, or the most grievous items in our catalogue of complaints. . . . The same slave power that plunders our *purses*," it charged, "has declared open war upon our civil, political, and religious *freedoms*," not to mention those freedoms of the people it held in chains. And the voice of Maine Liberty men noted simply that "The Liberty party seeks the greatest good of the *whole* number, and of course includes the slaves, and gives the highest prominence to their claims because they are the greatest sufferers."[65]

[65] *Ibid.; Emancipator*, May 27, 1841; *Liberty Standard*, Apr. 5, 1843. See also *ibid.* Aug. 3, 1842; Liberty State Central Committee to the Freemen of Michigan, in *Signal of Liberty*, Sept. 15, 1841; *American Freeman*, Feb. 26, 1845; *Albany Patriot*, June 11, 1845; *Granite Freeman*, May 6, 1846; *Emancipator*, Feb. 24, 1847.

5

New Directions

ALTHOUGH THEY BEGAN THEIR ENTERPRISE bright with hope, Liberty men were soon forced to reckon with their party's sorry performance at the polls. While many doggedly resisted all attempts to abandon or modify the party's independent pursuit of the "one idea," arguing that so novel an experiment deserved an extended trial, a growing number of Liberty spokesmen called for new departures to make political abolitionism effective. One faction, headed by such religious-minded souls as Birney, Goodell, Gerrit Smith, and Beriah Green, sought to broaden the Liberty platform in the vain hope that "universal reform" might catch more voters than mere antislavery had. Even if it did not, such men reasoned, the party's dedication to human rights would be strengthened and its educative capacity enlarged. At the same time, political realists like Salmon P. Chase and Gamaliel Bailey pressed for a union of antislavery elements in all parties, even if it meant a partial lowering of the Liberty standard. By 1848 this latter group of coalitionists had carried the day, sweeping the bulk of Liberty men with them into the Free Soil party.

Liberty leaders did not perceive the limitations of their organization at once, however. At first all pitched enthusiastically into the work of building their party upon its original, solid but narrow, antislavery foundation. Six months after the Waterloo of 1840, delegates from all but two free states met in New York City to lay plans for the future.

Once again they nominated Birney for the presidency, but they dropped Earle as his running mate in favor of the more prominent and unequivocal Thomas Morris. A self-made Westerner, Morris was also expected to bring balance to the ticket. By way of justifying the new party's continued existence, the convention promulgated an *Address to the Citizens of the United States*. Drafted by Goodell, it indicted the Slave Power for every conceivable crime.

In addition, the delegates agreed to an elaborate plan of organization patterned after that of the Whigs and Democrats. Liberty committees were to blanket the land—a national committee which would watch over party affairs between elections, followed by a panoply of state, county, city, district, and finally township and ward committees. Each was to communicate with the next superior committee at least once a year. And town and ward groups were urged to canvass hard and to keep a Liberty Roll of voters pledged to support only abolitionist candidates. The idea, Alvan Stewart explained, was to make the Liberty organization "something like a self sharpening plough. We want something besides one of our orators addressing 50 or 60 already converted A.S. men, which has been the case except on great occasions for 2 years. A.S. men attend & hear an address, go home, do nothing, & call this carrying forward the cause. This must not be."[1] Clearly, some of the earlier antipathy to party machinery had by now evaporated.

As Stewart indicated, Liberty members strove after 1840 to reunite "the scattered parts of Abolition" and to enlist the services of large-hearted Democrats and Whigs. In 1841 and 1842 Liberty men initiated meetings between political and nonpolitical abolitionists in a move to restore harmony to antislavery ranks.[2] When it became apparent that old wounds made formal reunion impossible—that, indeed, shifting needs and the emergence of the Liberty party had robbed both the American Anti-Slavery Society and the American & Foreign Anti-Slavery Society of their vitality—Liberty leaders such as Lewis Tappan and Gerrit Smith proposed a scuttling of all antislavery organizations. They suggested that antislavery affairs be handled through "occasional

[1] *Emancipator*, May 20, 27, 1841; Fladeland, *Birney*, 211-12; Smith, *Liberty and Free Soil Parties*, 53; Stewart to Samuel Webb, Nov. 13, 1841, Stewart Papers, NYHS.
[2] Joshua Leavitt to Gerrit Smith, July 29, 1841, Smith Papers; L. P. Noble to Theodore Weld, Aug. 24, 1841, Barnes and Dumond (eds.), *Weld-Grimké Letters*, 877-78; Harlow, *Smith*, 164.

conventions," held as time and circumstance dictated, open to every "active, true hearted" abolitionist. On a personal level, too, third party advocates sought to persuade Garrisonian rivals of the rightness of their course.[3]

Liberty men worked even harder, since both the stakes and the chances of success were now greater, to wrest antislavery voters from the clutches of the major parties. The Whig and Democratic parties were equally corrupt, equally lackeys of the Slave Power, argued Liberty spokesmen. One might as well seek virtue in a whorehouse as look for genuine humanitarianism within either of the established political organizations. But since Northern Whigs made pretensions to antislavery principles which cut into the third party movement, Liberty propagandists trained their heaviest guns on Henry Clay and his followers. As the 1844 election approached, Liberty editors and orators portrayed Clay as, if anything, more dangerous than his Democratic opponent. Polk they insisted, was "too small a man, too openly committed, body and soul to the Slave-Interest, to seduce any anti-slavery voter into his support." Clay, on the other hand, was a man of talent and eloquence whose record Northern disciples had doctored so as to make him appear "anti-slavery in his feelings." So far, indeed, did Liberty men go in their unmasking of Whiggery that Henry B. Stanton warned: "We must be impartial, too, as between the parties. To the masses, our resolves and newspaper articles look rather Anti-Whiggish."[4]

In building their party, Liberty advocates had the advantage of an extensive and energetic newspaper network. All but three or four abolitionist papers endorsed the Liberty cause, and by 1844 the party boasted twenty-five regular news sheets: three dailies, twenty weeklies, and two semi-monthly publications. Financial distress plagued all of these journals. Some went under, many had trouble meeting payrolls, and all except Bailey's *Philanthropist* and Leavitt's *Emancipator* held editors and publishers close to poverty. Yet in 1844 some 35,000 Liberty copies appeared each week to bolster the faithful and enlighten the un-

[3] Lewis Tappan to Salmon P. Chase, Sept. 20, 1843, Chase Papers, PHS; Tappan to Gamaliel Bailey, Sept. 20, 1843, Letterbook, Tappan Papers; Tappan to David Lee Child, Sept. 21, 1843, Child Papers; Tappan to John Beaumont, Jan. 20, 1844, Abel and Klingberg (eds.), *A Side-Light on Anglo-American Relations*, 174.
[4] *Cincinnati Weekly Herald and Philanthropist*, Sept. 11, 1844; Stanton to John G. Whittier, Feb. 3, 1844, John Albree (ed.), *Whittier Correspondence from the Oak Knoll Collections, 1830-1892* (Salem, Mass., 1911), 86-87.

converted. After 1843 a series of short, pithy tracts broadcast the Liberty message more widely still.[5]

Yet for all their efforts at organization and propaganda, Liberty men found the harvests sparse. At first they took heart at evidence of progress, however slight. State returns in 1841 showed a threefold increase for the new party over the total Birney received the previous fall. By 1842 Liberty candidates had raised that count by another 50 per cent. If this rate of growth continued, political abolitionists told themselves, the Liberty ticket could expect 160,000 votes in 1844 and a vast majority in the free states by 1848.[6] The 1844 election brought Liberty prognosticators back to earth. Handicapped by the "Garland forgery" (a bogus letter which on election eve had made it seem as if Birney had been caught in bed with the Democrats) and by the allure which Clay's anti-Texas stand gave to Whiggery, the antislavery ticket polled only 65,608 votes—hardly more than Liberty candidates had received in the 1843 state contests.[7] (One Liberty stalwart, however, emerged from the 1844 campaign richer than he began: encountering Elizur Wright, Jr., on the train to Boston, Daniel Webster had bet $200 that the Garland letter attributed to Birney was genuine. Although then much in debt, Wright accepted the wager and won.[8])

Publicly, at least, Liberty men remained resolutely optimistic despite the disappointments of 1844. None proved more sanguine than Lewis Tappan, who, having finally endorsed the third party in 1843, now showed all the zeal of the convert. "The Anti-Slavery cause has had a wonderful impetus given to it during the Presidential Canvass," he informed an English friend. "The Whigs professed to be anti-slavery men, in order to gain abolitionists, & published Anti-Slavery matter far & wide. . . . We think that a slaveholder will never again be elected to the Chief Magistracy of this country."[9] Nor was Tappan the only

---

[5] Foster, "History of the Liberty Party," 18-19, 67; Joshua Leavitt to Salmon P. Chase, May 28, 1842, Chase Papers, PHS; E. Glover to Chase, July 29, 1842, Elizur Wright, Jr., to Chase, Feb. 3, 1844, H. B. Stanton to Chase, Feb. 6, 1844, Chase Papers, LC; Stanton to Amos A. Phelps, Sept. 23, 1843, Phelps Papers; Smith, *Liberty and Free Soil Parties*, 318-24.

[6] *Signal of Liberty*, Dec. 26, 1842; Foster, "History of the Liberty Party," 20-22.

[7] *Cincinnati Weekly Herald and Philanthropist*, Oct. 21, 1844; *Liberty Hall and Cincinnati Gazette*, Oct. 22, 1844; Lewis Tappan to Birney, Apr. 3, 1845, Letterbook, Tappan Papers; Fladeland, *Birney*, 227-51.

[8] Elizur Wright, Jr., to Mrs. Elizur Wright, Jr., Nov. 10, 1844 (typed copy), Wright Papers, BPL.

[9] Tappan to Joseph Sturge, Nov. 15, 1844, Letterbook, Tappan Papers.

skeptic who came around. William Jay, the learned New Yorker who complained in 1840 that "Birney's canvass will render abolitionists contemptible in the eyes of politicians, & perhaps in their own," admitted his error in 1843. "On all sides," he confessed to Salmon Chase, "I see indications of a change in public sentiment & I begin to think that the Liberty Party is effecting more than I formerly anticipated from its efforts. The politicians are certainly more cautious than formerly how they insult the abolitionists."[10] Others found it encouraging that of the 501 counties in free states in 1844, all but a hundred gave some ballots to Birney and Morris, "thus demonstrating that although the seed of political antislavery action might be but thinly scattered, yet it [was] generally and widely disseminated." And Gamaliel Bailey reassured his readers, saying that third parties should expect their biggest gains not in presidential elections, when stakes were large and partisan excitement high, but in off-years, "when the great parties are slumbering. While no party excitement disturbs the public reason, they must sow the seed, and at the local elections where no great interests are at stake, to arouse selfishness, prejudice or passion, reap the fruit."[11]

Yet although the Liberty total rose slightly in 1846, discouragement with the party's progress and with established modes of action steadily corroded such optimism and produced a search for new alternatives. Antislavery Whigs and Democrats had shown themselves stubbornly resistant to Liberty blandishments, reluctant to lose a voice on nonslavery issues and believing, in Joshua Giddings's words, "that it will be far easier to bring the present parties to support antislavery measures than it will be to form a new party on that ground."[12] Recruitment from among old organization abolitionists had proven equally unrewarding. If anything, Garrisonian hostility toward the Liberty party increased after 1840 as the nonresistant strain within the American Anti-Slavery Society became more pronounced. To be sure, some, like Ellis Gray Loring, kept an open mind and a very few braved Garrison's wrath to vote for Liberty candidates. But most Garrisonians condemned third

[10] Wyatt-Brown, *Tappan*, 273; Jay to Salmon P. Chase, June 5, 1843, Chase Papers, PHS.
[11] Foster, "History of the Liberty Party," 66; *Cincinnati Weekly Herald and Philanthropist*, Dec. 4, 1844.
[12] Giddings to Salmon P. Chase, Feb. 19, Oct. 12, 1843, Chase Papers, PHS. See also Seth M. Gates to James G. Birney, Dec. 11, 1841, Dumond (ed.), *Birney Letters*, II, 642-43; Gates to Gerrit Smith, Apr. 8, 1842, Smith Papers; *Cincinnati Weekly Herald and Philanthropist*, Feb. 21, 1844.

party followers as traitorous snakes who deserved more severe treatment than either Democrats or Whigs; for, as Maria Chapman explained, "they are one shade greener—one shade nearer the colour of the anti slavery grass."[13] Party building was proving harder and more frustrating than most political abolitionists had dreamed.

2

From the beginning, there had been some who insisted that to be effective the Liberty party had to go beyond balance-of-power politics. Its true mission, recalled Owen Lovejoy, brother of abolition's first martyr, had not been merely "to wring anti-slavery action from the other parties, but to obtain control of the government in order thereby to abolish slavery. . . ."[14] Pressure also developed early, particularly among those who looked upon the new party as more or less permanent, to expand the Liberty platform beyond the issue of slavery. The party's 1841 Address offered a precedent of sorts by tacking to its antislavery creed a demand for the popular election of the President and Vice President, and before the year was out there were proposals that Liberty men should take a common position on tariff reform, banking, and bankruptcy law.[15]

By 1842 several state gatherings had recommended a national conference at which Liberty advocates might consult on questions of national policy. Nothing came of such suggestions. Most still feared that a formal stand on other issues would belittle abolition and sow dissension in Liberty circles. But Ohio's Liberty convention that year independently promulgated a "statement of party principles" that outreached antislavery and called also for educational reform, adjustment of tariff policy, and federal help in securing markets for farm surpluses. This last proposition struck a responsive chord especially among hard-pressed Westerners, many of whom were captivated by Joshua Leavitt's

---

[13] Loring to Joshua Leavitt, Dec. 28, 1840, Letterbook, Ellis Gray Loring Papers, HLH; Loring to David Lee Child, Sept. 14, 1843, Maria W. Chapman to Child, Apr. 14, 1843, Child Papers; *Liberator*, Sept. 22, 1843; *Pennsylvania Freeman*, Sept. 26, 1844.
[14] Quoted in *American Freeman*, Nov. 3, 1847.
[15] *Free American*, Sept. 30, Oct. 7, Nov. 11, 1841.

pet program of free trade and repeal of the English Corn Laws.[16] At its national convention in 1843 the party took specific stands only on matters directly related to slavery, yet at the same time it announced a general concern for broader issues:

> Resolved, That the Liberty party has not been organized merely for the overthrow of slavery: its first decided effort must, indeed, be directed against slaveholding as the grossest and most revolting manifestation of despotism, but it will also carry out the principle of equal rights into all its practical consequences and applications, and support every just measure conducive to individual and social freedom.[17]

Such vacuous generalities left the party's one idea basically intact, but those who sought to make the Liberty platform more comprehensive found sanction and encouragement in this plank.

In the years after 1844 more and more Liberty men re-examined their original views and came to the conclusion that only as a permanent, broadly based party could they hope for success. There were several reasons for this reappraisal. Discouragement at the tapering off of Liberty votes inclined many to the belief that an exclusively antislavery party could not long survive. "Not to advance is to recede," Gamaliel Bailey had written; "no new and small party can live simply by holding its own."[18] By mid-decade it had become painfully clear that the Liberty party was doing little more than that. True, Birney's total had grown nine times between 1840 and 1844. Yet the Liberty count increased only slightly thereafter, actually declining in key states like New York, Pennsylvania, Massachusetts, and Michigan. Even in Ohio, which boasted four antislavery newspapers (including the influential *Philanthropist*), fewer than one voter in thirty had ever cast a Liberty ballot. In fact, after six years of trying, the antislavery party had carried not one of the five hundred counties in the North. The only remedy for such lassitude, a good many Liberty spokesmen came to believe, was to enlarge the party's creed. "Unless we join other interests

---

[16] *Signal of Liberty*, Jan. 26, May 9, 16, 1842; Foster, "History of the Liberty Party," 22-24; New Garden (Ind.) *Free Labor Advocate and Anti-Slavery Chronicle*, July 4, 1843.
[17] McKee, *National Conventions and Platforms*, 52. For a similar resolve of Maine Liberty men, see *Liberty Standard*, Jan. 25, 1843.
[18] Smith, *Liberty and Free Soil Parties*, 98.

to the cause of Anti-Slavery," Birney warned in April 1846, "it is in vain
for us to expect the progress that we *have* made. Indeed if we fail to
incorporate in to our party-creed, that which interests the majority, as
much as the sufferings of the slave interests the conscientious, we shall
only make such advances as will alarm the timid and discourage even
the boldest among us."[19]

Birney and others like him worried not only at the slow pace of Liberty progress, but also at the possibility of swift decline in the near future. This fear became especially acute in the months following the
election of 1844, when it appeared that the vanquished Whigs had
hatched a scheme to recoup their fortunes by persuading disgruntled
Democrats and frustrated Liberty men to join them. Signs of such an
attempt abounded. Soon after Polk's victory over Clay, leading Whig
sheets such as the *Albany Evening Journal* and the *Syracuse Journal*
urged the Whig party to "raise the Standard of Emancipation." This
phrase was apparently meant to apply solely to Texas (whose annexation most Whigs strongly opposed), and even so it received curt dis-
avowals from the bulk of the Whig press. Yet it was enough to keep
Liberty leaders on constant guard against defections from their ranks,
especially when, in the spring of 1845, the *Boston Courier*, the *Ann Arbor State Journal*, and other Whig prints loudly insisted that their
party was, or ought to become, a truly antislavery party. In June William H. Seward, one of Whiggery's most enlightened spokesmen, further aroused Liberty apprehensions by publicly endorsing Negro suffrage, abolition of the domestic slave trade and slavery in the District
of Columbia, and a ban on new slave states. By stealing *some* of the
Liberty party's thunder and offering at the same time an opportunity
to take a stand on other pressing issues, the Whigs might win over
enough abolitionists to defeat the Democrats and swallow up the Liberty party. Seward virtually admitted such designs in a letter to Salmon
Chase three weeks after the presidential election. The only defense,
some third party men concluded, lay in an enlargement of the Liberty
creed.[20]

---

[19] *Ibid.* 96-97; *Pennsylvania Freeman*, Jan. 29, 1846; *Signal of Liberty*, Feb. 16, 23,
Mar. 26, 1846; Birney to John V. Smith, Apr. 20, 1846, Dumond (ed.), *Birney
Letters*, II, 1011.
[20] *Signal of Liberty*, Mar. 13, Apr. 21, May 19, 26, July 7, 1845; Theodore Foster
to James G. Birney, Dec. 7, 1845, Dumond (ed.), *Birney Letters*, II, 982-84; Seward
to Chase, Nov. 27, 1844, Chase Papers, LC.

Pressure for a broader platform developed first and strongest in Michigan and New York. Theodore Foster, co-editor of the *Signal of Liberty*, started the kettle boiling in Michigan with a letter to Birney in July 1845. The time had come, he suggested, to permit—even to encourage—Liberty men to take public stands on *all* the pressing political questions of the day. Slavery ought to remain "the *paramount* question, and the *only test* of party membership." But unless Liberty voters were given a chance to express themselves collectively on all matters of public interest, atrophy was bound to set in. Birney responded enthusiastically to this proposal and soon joined Foster and his editorial partner Guy Beckley in convincing other political abolitionists of its merit. He wrote to Lewis Tappan in September 1845: "We must be prepared to apply the principles of the Liberty Party to every case as it may arise. Whilst the black man constitutes the first object of our consideration, the *white* must not be neglected. . . . We must be prepared to take on ourselves *all* the administration of the government or *none* of it. A party that does not take the *whole* of it—but seeks a particular object— will soon, in the strife of the other parties, become a lost party."[21]

Once again the salvation of the antislavery party was made to turn upon more forceful appeals to the rights and interests of whites. Hostility to slavery and legal equality for free blacks remained its prime concern, but well before the birth of the Free Soil or Republican parties, antislavery politicians, recognizing the racist nature of their society, conceded the need to float abolition in a larger vessel: the freedom of *all* men from monopoly and class legislation.

After successfully testing the new plan on a convention of Washtenaw County abolitionists, Birney and Foster carefully prepared an enlarged manifesto for the consideration of the Michigan Anti-Slavery Society at its anniversary meeting in February 1846. In addition to the abolition of slavery and the guarantee of equal rights for all citizens, Birney proposed a cut in the powers, patronage, and salary of the President; dismantling of the Army and Navy; eventual free trade; and economies in congressional allowances. To these proposals Foster added judicial reform, unlimited liability for corporate stockholders, and the single district system of electing legislators. Designed, in Birney's words, to make human government "concurrent with the divine gov-

[21] Foster to Birney, July 7, 1845, Birney to Tappan, Sept. 12, 1845, Dumond (ed.), *Birney Letters*, II, 950-53, 970-71.

ernment," this hodgepodge barely touched the bread-and-butter concerns of white Americans. Yet to Foster, who preferred that Liberty men also take stands on such basic matters as state taxes, railroad policy, and paper money, it seemed at least a step in the right direction. And to ideologues like Birney this broad creed served evangelical as well as purely political purposes, calling upon the righteous to battle injustice in all its forms.[22]

Despite Foster's prediction of easy adoption, the extended platform ran into heavy weather at the annual antislavery convention. Although it bore the endorsement of the Society's executive committee, only Foster and Beckley rose to defend it. On the other hand, those opposed to *any* dilution of the pure antislavery creed came forward in droves. Charles H. Stewart, state Liberty party chairman, argued that the "one idea" had not yet received a fair test and that the eradication of slavery would so alter the nation's political economy that reforms proposed now might well be inappropriate then. Seymour B. Treadwell, former editor of the *Michigan Freeman* and a pioneer Liberty advocate, angrily charged that the proposed new platform was the work of men of little faith who risked the party's ruin by burying its one big idea in an avalanche of small ones. The Liberty party, he insisted, had always been and ought to remain a temporary organization with a strictly limited, if transcendently important, purpose. Hard work and rigorous adherence to the great idea of abolition was the only medicine the party needed.[23]

In the end, such arguments carried the day. By an overwhelming margin, Michigan abolitionists (virtually all of whom, like their brethren in other Western states, belonged to the Liberty party) rejected the new propositions. Foster blamed their defeat on the influence of naïve and narrow-minded clergymen who bridled at the introduction of worldly concerns. Yet while antislavery ministers had undeniably been conspicuous opponents of an extended platform, there is no reason to believe that they controlled the 1846 convention. The most prominent critics had been laymen whose defense of the one idea

[22] Foster to Birney, Sept. 29, Oct. 16, Dec. 7, 1845, Birney to President of Michigan State Anti-Slavery Society, Jan. 1, 1846, Dumond (ed.), *Birney Letters*, II, 971-74, 978-81, 982-84, 990-96.
[23] *Signal of Liberty*, Feb. 16, 1846.

(while perhaps now as impractical as universal reform) rested more on political than on moral reasoning.[24]

Despite their setback at the state convention, proponents of diversification pressed ahead. With an eye to the Northwestern Liberty Convention, scheduled for Chicago in June 1846, Beckley and Foster sent to party leaders and all Liberty newspapers a circular advocating abandonment of the one idea, while keeping antislavery the "paramount object." The response was overwhelmingly negative. Only about half of the papers bothered to reprint the circular, and of those that did only the Pittsburgh *Spirit of Liberty* and one or two others seconded its views. The *Emancipator*, the Cincinnati *Herald and Philanthropist*, and other major Liberty journals roundly condemned the proposals, as did such influential spokesmen as Gerrit Smith, Lewis Tappan, and national Liberty chairman Alvan Stewart. Not surprisingly, the Chicago convention also repudiated the Michigan plan. Of all the Western states, only Wisconsin showed the slightest enthusiasm for the new doctrines. "The Liberty party," Foster glumly prophesied on his return from Chicago, ". . . are determined to be no party at all. They are intent on political suicide. . . ."[25]

Meanwhile, a somewhat more successful movement to elaborate the Liberty program had begun in New York. Led by William Goodell, W. L. Chaplin, and James C. Jackson (a recent third party recruit whose *Albany Patriot* gave them an effective voice), those dissatisfied with the one idea won a hearing for their views at a special state convention in Port Byron, New York, in June 1845. After much discussion, the delegates spurned the radical proposals, but not before the seed had been planted and allowed to take root. Before long the idea of platform extension had captivated a good many New York Liberty men, especially in the "Burned-over District." Among them, a tardy but wholehearted convert, stood the unpredictable Gerrit Smith.[26]

---

24 Foster, "History of the Liberty Party," 79-81, 83-84. Cf. Formisano, *Mass Political Parties*, 75-76.
25 *Signal of Liberty*, May 4, 23, June 6, 1846; Foster to Birney, Aug. 1, 1846, Dumond (ed.), *Birney Letters*, II, 1025; Fladeland, *Birney*, 258-60; Smith, *Liberty and Free Soil Parties*, 101.
26 Foster, "History of the Liberty Party," 79; *Albany Patriot*, June 11, 1845; Lewis Tappan to Gerrit Smith, July 29, 1845, Letterbook, Tappan Papers; Goodell, *Slavery and Anti-Slavery*, 475.

For years the Sage of Peterboro had fought against all attempts to enlarge the Liberty creed. "The party that is not willing to stake its all on the great question, whether a man shall be a freeman or a slave," he lectured his cohorts in 1843, "betrays, in that very unwillingness, a littleness of conception and an unsoundness of moral principle fatal to all its pretensions to the public confidence on any subject." As late as 1846 he circulated a leaflet which argued that Liberty men were still too negligent of their antislavery duties to warrant their taking stands on secondary issues. "What a farce," he scoffed, "and how fruitless of good, for several hundred Liberty men to come together at Port Byron, or elsewhere, with stolen clothes upon their backs and stolen food in their stomachs (for such are all slave-labor-products) and, to turn up the white of their eyes, and put on sanctimonious looks, and shudder and scowl at the violence done to sound morality by Banks and Tariffs and high salaries."[27]

Yet even as he wrote these words, Smith began to drift in the other direction, away from the one idea. To Birney he confided in April 1846: "I have for some months, been persuaded, that the time has come for the Liberty Party to discuss the application of its principle of human equality . . . in other directions—& especially in the direction of free trade." For a time he straddled the basic question, holding that the party might discuss but not act upon matters unrelated to abolition. But by 1847 he had taken the final step. To discuss public issues "under the foregone conclusion, that they shall not be acted upon," was, he decided, "the merest emptiness and hypocrisy." Just as important, the major parties had proved themselves "utterly incorrigible and hopeless," indicating that only a permanent, hence broadly based, party could effectively conduct political warfare against slavery.[28]

Buoyed by Smith's conversion, Goodell and his associates called for a national convention to be held at Macedon Lock, New York, in June 1847. Its purpose was to nominate a presidential ticket on a platform of "universal reform." Without a clear, consistent stand on *all* pressing national questions, Goodell's call maintained, the Liberty party could not

[27] Smith to Liberty National Convention, Aug. 1843, quoted in *Emancipator*, Aug. 18, 1847; Gerrit Smith, *To the Liberty Party* (Peterboro, N.Y., May 7, 1846), leaflet, Chase Papers, PHS.
[28] Smith to James G. Birney, Apr. 18, 1846, Birney Papers, CLM; Smith to Editors, *Emancipator*, Aug. 23, 1847.

"escape ultimate absorption in one of the other political parties, to the shipwreck of all the objects for which it was originally organized, including, signally, the defeat, for the present generation, of the anti Slavery enterprize [*sic*], so far as political action is concerned."

Accordingly, delegates to the splinter convention (which proceeded wholly without sanction from the regular Liberty organization) whooped their support for a platform which not only took a radical stand against slavery—an "illegal, unconstitutional, and anti republican" institution—but called as well for a rainbow of other reforms. Among them were the abolition of all legalized monopolies (including the postal service), dismantlement of the Army and Navy, retrenchment of government expenses, eradication of secret societies, the establishment of free trade, and distribution of the public lands "in small parcels, to landless men, for the mere cost of distributing." Reflecting both the Democratic predilections of many of the convention's organizers and a more general desire to curtail civil government so as to respect the government of God, the Macedon resolutions must have seemed a cold pudding to antislavery Whigs. This apparent disregard for the interests of the very group which had provided most of the early Liberty recruits was perhaps a hopeless blunder. Yet whatever its deficiencies, the platform did possess a certain political as well as religious logic. Certainly Democrats had of late shown themselves as receptive as Whigs to antislavery appeals, and the bitterness of Clay's abolitionist supporters at the third party's responsibility for his 1844 defeat made the prospect of future Whig crossovers dim.[29]

Not content merely to pass resolutions, the Macedon Lock delegates also nominated Gerrit Smith and Elihu Burritt ("the learned blacksmith") for the nation's highest offices. Burritt, already best known for his contributions to pacifism, was lecturing in England at the time of his nomination and hastily resigned from the ticket rather than jeopardize his effectiveness in the peace movement. Charles C. Foote, perhaps the most obscure of all vice presidential nominees, replaced him. Having formally seceded from the Liberty party, the Macedonians designated

---

[29] Call for a National Nominating Convention, quoted in Dumond (ed.), *Birney Letters*, II, 1047-57; *American Freeman*, July 14, 1847; Fladeland, *Birney*, 262-63; Kraditor, *Means and Ends in American Abolitionism*, 153-55; Perry, *Radical Abolitionism*, 171-72.

themselves the Liberty League and waited to see what others might do.[30]

Outside New York, the reaction of political abolitionists to the Macedon convention was decidedly hostile. Some objected to its frank assertion "that a party should be what the government should be"—enduring and comprehensive. "There ought to be no such permanent party," Austin Willey, editor of the Maine *Liberty Standard*, protested to Gerrit Smith, "but when an object is desired of sufficient importance, let the people unite to carry it through, then let the party die, and another object be undertaken in the same way. The people would then be free from partyism, demagogues be unhorsed, and slavery deprived of that very power—the power of party—by which it reigns."[31] Others protested what seemed to them an adulteration of moral principle in the new platform. "I dispise [*sic*] the craven spirit of that man who will not vote the fetters of the slave off unless he can at the same time 'vote himself a farm'!" fumed one Liberty editor.[32]

Many more complained that it was foolish and unnecessary to spell out all the implications of equal rights. Lewis Tappan cautioned against repeating the folly of the farmer who hitched his team to twenty stumps in an attempt to pull them all out at once, and Alvan Stewart warned that creed-making had undone many a good cause—including Protestantism. The time might come, predicted the *American Freeman*, when if Goodell insisted on making explicit all aspects of the doctrine of liberty as he saw it, he might find himself forming "a new party, consisting of Wm. Goodell, Esq."[33] Many thought it particularly galling that an unsanctioned minority—"a clique"—should attempt to impose candidates and new party tests upon the Liberty majority, especially so soon before a national convention. Even in Michigan support for the new Liberty League proved negligible.[34]

[30] Peter Tolis, *Elihu Burritt: Crusader for Brotherhood* (Hamden, Conn., 1968), 112-13.
[31] Willey to Smith, July 7, 1847, Smith Papers.
[32] Westley Bailey to Gerrit Smith, June 5, 1847, Smith Papers.
[33] Tappan to Smith, July 23, 1847, Smith Papers; Stewart to Samuel Webb, Nov. 6, 1847, Stewart Papers, NYHS; *American Freeman*, July 28, 1847.
[34] *Anti-Slavery Chronicle and Free Labor Advocate*, July 1, 1847; *American Freeman*, Aug. 10, Sept. 1, 1847; Tappan to Smith, July 23, 1847, Smith Papers; Smith, *Liberty and Free Soil Parties*, 101-2. James G. Birney endorsed the Macedon Lock convention, but did next to nothing to enlist support for the Liberty League or its candidates. See Fladeland, *Birney*, 262-63; Dumond (ed.), *Birney Letters, passim*.

3

At the same time that the "Macedon Lock-Smiths" sought to rescue the Liberty party by embracing "universal reform," another, more numerous, pragmatic, and farsighted group labored to heighten its effectiveness by forging alliances with antislavery men in other parties. Indeed, the work of alliance had proceeded so far by the spring of 1847 that Liberty Leaguers pointed to "unequivocal indications" of the rapid absorption of the Liberty party in some other, less principled organization as their excuse for independent action.[35]

An early move in this direction was the attempt of a group of Ohio Liberty men to replace James G. Birney with a more appealing candidate—even if it meant going outside the ranks of rock-ribbed abolitionists to find him. These dissidents, headed by Salmon P. Chase, Thomas Morris, Gamaliel Bailey, Samuel Lewis, Leicester King, and the Reverend Jonathan Blanchard, believed that someone better known and more politically seasoned than Birney, running on a moderate platform which emphasized the *quarantine* of slavery, might catalyze antislavery elements in all parties into a formidable new coalition. That coalition would, of course, continue to bear the Liberty name. And, they insisted, Liberty principles "would mould new adherents," not the other way around. Time, however, bore out the suspicions of the orthodox. By 1844 Chase had proposed changing the party's name to "True Democrat," and in the years that followed he and his Ohio associates took the lead in uniting Liberty men with antislavery Whigs and Democrats under the new banner: "Free Soil."[36]

The movement to replace the colorless, aristocratic Birney with a more "available" candidate began within a year of the Whig victory in 1840. Although renominated for the presidency by the party's national convention in May 1841, Birney dallied until the following January before giving the party his answer. The interlude allowed proponents of a more expedient choice (many of them, like Chase,

[35] Goodell, *Slavery and Anti-Slavery*, 475.
[36] Gamaliel Bailey to James G. Birney, Nov. 16, 1842, William Birney to Birney, Nov. 25, 1844, Dumond (ed.), *Birney Letters*, II, 711, 887; Joseph G. Rayback, "The Liberty Party Leaders of Ohio: Exponents of Antislavery Coalition," *Ohio Archaeological and Historical Quarterly*, LVII, No. 2 (Apr. 1948), 165-78.

Johnny-come-latelies to the Liberty cause) time to scout other possibilities. At the Ohio Anti-Slavery Society convention in December 1841, the names of Governor Seward and the venerable John
Quincy Adams surfaced as potential Liberty nominees, should Birney
decide to withdraw. Two weeks later Birney chilled such talk by at
last accepting his party's nomination, and to Chase he made clear his
own distrust of Adams and Seward. The thought "of going *out* of our
ranks for candidates for any office" he found repugnant. "Out of our
ranks," he argued, "all public men are of the Whig or Democratic party.
How can they be abolitionists? This was tried at the beginning of the
political movement of the abolitionists, and always failed, bringing
with it great injury."[37] Yet talk of recruiting a candidate from without
the party continued, and, as it happened, Birney's letter of acceptance
was partly to blame.

Always a complicated and reflective man, Birney had of late grown
increasingly pessimistic about the prospects not only of the Liberty
party but of democracy itself. And in his letter accepting the Liberty
nomination he made no attempt to conceal or minimize his doubts. The
domestic history of the last dozen years, he maintained—the gag rules
and lynch mobs, the persecution of Mormons and Cherokees, the craven
submission of Northern leaders to Southern "slaveholders and women-
whippers," the unpunished duels and assassinations—indicated a profound and spreading disrespect for the law. Indeed, he asserted, Americans had "so long practiced injustice, adding to it by hypocrisy, in the
treatment of the colored race, both negroes and Indians," that they had
begun "to regard injustice as . . . the chief element in our government." In place of law a new power, public opinion, had arisen, defy-
ing *"the solemn enactments of the people"* and subverting social order.
He had "but faint hope," Birney admitted, that the friends of liberty
would prevail against such degeneration.

To his confidants Birney spoke even more plainly. "What the end is
to be of our A.S. movement is hard to tell," he declared to Lewis Tappan. "There is no reason for believing that the virtue of our own people would ever throw off Slavery. Slavery has corrupted the whole
nation, so that it seems to me we are nearly at the point of dissolution.
I must say—and I am sorry to believe it true—that our form of govern-

[37] Chase to Birney, Jan. 21, 1842, Birney to Chase. Feb. 2, 1842, Dumond (ed.),
Birney Letters, II, 661-62, 670-72.

ment will not do. My confidence in it as a political structure is greatly impaired." By July Birney's hopes had hit rock bottom: churches corrupt, people corrupt, Judgment near.[38]

It took courage (as well as a peculiarly Southern sense of fatalism) for Birney to question the premises of democracy. But such statements understandably dismayed many Liberty men. "Some of our friends here," William Birney reported to his father from Cincinnati, "regret that you are so hopeless as to the success of the Liberty Party. If the trumpet of the leader give forth an uncertain sound, who shall arm himself for battle?" The leader's trumpet fluttered still more in 1843 as Birney made known his objections to manhood suffrage. The low state of political morality owed much to the ballots of the ignorant and the impure, he believed, and although it would be unwise now to withdraw rights already granted, it was regrettable that the Founding Fathers had not seen fit to restrict the franchise to those whom "the sober minded and law-abiding part of the community" pronounced worthy. The suffrage, Birney contended, should have been made "the birthright of none, but of easy attainment by all," a prod to good citizenship.[39]

To those Liberty leaders already inclined to seek someone with broader appeal to head their party's ticket, Birney's morose pronouncements on democracy seemed the last straw. While some secretly stepped up their search for a new face, Gamaliel Bailey openly and forthrightly urged Birney to step aside. "I have no doubt, as to your entire fitness for the presidential chair, so far as competency and perfect integrity are concerned," the editor insisted to his old friend. "But, I have had doubts, as to your being the most eligible candidate. You have always appeared in the character of a Moralist, a reformer, rather than a Politician or Statesman. Your letter of acceptance, I remember, so was written in the spirit of a prophet. You denounced the people—and, if I mistake not, gave them over to destruction; and you still, I believe, maintain the same views of their inability to govern themselves." These views, Bailey

[38] Birney to Joshua Leavitt et al., Jan. 10, 1842, Birney to Tappan, Jan. 14, July 8, 1842, ibid. II, 645-56, 656-59, 704. Birney's pessimism of 1842 contrasts strikingly with his optimism of a year earlier. In February 1841, after a swing through western New York, he had elatedly written Tappan: "I have, at no period of the Anti-slavery movement, felt such entire confidence in the speedy prevalence of our principles and the overthrow of slavery as I do now." Ibid. II, 623 (Feb. 5, 1841).
[39] William Birney to Birney, Mar. 1, 1842, Birney Papers, CLM; Birney to Gamaliel Bailey, Apr. 16, 1843, Birney to Samuel Lewis, July 13, 1843, Dumond (ed.), Birney Letters, II, 733-34, 744-45; Birney, Diary, Apr. 11, 1842, Birney Papers, LC.

argued, and the manner of their utterance, had made Birney "not the most eligible candidate that could be selected."[40]

By this time the man most favored by those of Bailey's persuasion was William Jay of New York, son of the first Chief Justice of the United States and a distinguished jurist in his own right. Seward and Adams had already been dropped from consideration, their own unwillingness to repudiate Whiggery reinforcing widespread doubts concerning their attachment to Liberty principles. In the months before the national Liberty convention in 1843, Chase, Bailey, Tappan, H. B. Stanton, Gerrit Smith, and other party leaders talked up Jay's candidacy. His ties to the Revolution, his long public career, his well-known political writings on slavery, all gave Jay greater eligibility than Birney. Moreover, some argued, the Judge's neutrality in the antislavery schism of 1839-40, together with his outspoken pacifism, made him the candidate most likely to make inroads among Garrisonian abolitionists.[4] Not all, however, welcomed the prospect of Jay's nomination. Elizur Wright disparagingly remarked that "I should eat & sleep only on a hatchet lest he should fall into a fit of prudence and *disclaim* us to death." Wright's misgivings were well founded. Despite the importunities of Tappan, Chase, and others, Jay (like Seward and Adams) clung to his conviction "that what little virtue there is in politicians is with the Whigs." No abolition candidate, he believed, could expect to win so much as a single electoral vote.[42] He was correct, but this was not at all what Liberty men wished to hear.

Rebuffed by their favorites and unable to sway the mass of Liberty men (including national party chairman Alvan Stewart and Joshua Leavitt, editor of the powerful *Emancipator*), Birney's detractors reluctantly acquiesced in his renomination and fatalistically stumped for him in 1844.[43] But the results of that election, together with Birney' alleged campaign blunders, convinced them as never before of the need

[40] Bailey to Birney, Mar. 31, 1843, Dumond (ed.), *Birney Letters*, II, 726-27.
[41] *Ibid.*; Salmon P. Chase to Lewis Tappan, Feb. 15, 1843, Chase Papers, LC; Henry B. Stanton to Gerrit Smith, Aug. 4, 1843, Smith to Stanton, Aug. 9, 1843 (Letter book), Smith Papers. Thaddeus Stevens tried unsuccessfully to sell Liberty leaders on Winfield Scott. See Stevens to John Blanchard, May 24, 1842, Stevens Papers.
[42] Wyatt-Brown, *Tappan*, 274-75; Tappan to Chase, Mar. 20, 1843, Chase Papers PHS.
[43] Wyatt-Brown, *Tappan*, 276; Harlow, *Smith*, 166-72; Leavitt to Chase, Dec. 31 1841, Jan. 29, 1842, Feb. 16, 1843, Chase Papers, PHS; Leavitt to Birney, Feb. 14, June 19, 1842, Feb. 28, 1843, Alvan Stewart to Birney, Apr. 14, 1842, Dumond (ed.), *Birney Letters*, II, 673, 699, 719, 689-90.

or a more magnetic candidate. When in the aftermath of Polk's victory
die-hard Birneyites once again promoted their hero's renomination and
sought to lure him out of self-imposed seclusion in Saginaw, Michigan,
and back to a command post in New York or New England, antislavery
coalitionists at once set up roadblocks. Gamaliel Bailey made plain the
opposition's position in an editorial he wrote at the end of 1844.
Birney, he admitted, had given faithful and honorable service to the
Liberty party. But, he went on, "he has no personal claim upon our
future support. . . ." Anyone who thought otherwise was doing a dis-
service to the antislavery enterprise. "We should feel ourselves just as
free now in regard to a choice of Presidential candidates, as if we had
never had one," Bailey insisted, "and the attempt to trammel this freedom we regard as unjust and impolitic." If an open and representative
national convention two or three years hence should decide to nominate Birney again, all well and good. "But . . . if by the action of certain cliques and influences, Mr. Birney be placed in such a relation to
our cause, that a National Convention should feel itself embarrassed,
and almost compelled to renominate him, we should feel ourselves entirely free from all obligation to the party."[44] Such warnings came
loudest and most often from Ohio, where, Leavitt reported, some Liberty advocates were "again getting bewitched after Seward." But they
came also from disenchanted Easterners, among them Henry B. Stanton
and William Jay.[45]

Birney himself, as it turned out, had concluded that the time had
come to step down. Late in January 1845 he announced his wish to be
considered henceforth as simply "one of the rank and file." He did not
bolt the door against a third nomination in 1848, but he asked Liberty
editors to refrain from espousing his name and privately suggested William Jay and Francis J. LeMoyne as the party's next standard-bearers.
A paralytic stroke following a fall from his horse in August 1845 permanently curtailed Birney's powers of speech, and although he recovered his strength of mind and body sufficiently to take a hand in party
affairs, never again was he to be a serious candidate for office.[46]

[44] *Cincinnati Weekly Herald*, Dec. 25, 1844, quoted in Rayback, "Liberty Party
Leaders of Ohio," 173.
[45] Dumond (ed.), *Birney Letters*, II, 922; William Jay to Salmon P. Chase, Mar. 24,
1845, Chase Papers, PHS; Harlow, *Smith*, 172.
[46] Birney to Leavitt, Jan. 25, 1845, Birney to Editor of *Albany Patriot*, Jan. 31,
1845, Dumond (ed.), *Birney Letters*, II, 922, 923; Fladeland, *Birney*, 253, 255-56.

Two months before his disabling stroke, in his final public appearance as Liberty chieftain, Birney had presided over the mighty Southern and Western Liberty Convention held at Cincinnati in June 1845. Attended by over 2000 delegates from Kentucky and western Virginia as well as the Old Northwest, this great assembly sought to attract not only the Liberty faithful, but "all who . . . are resolved to use all constitutional means to effect the extinction of slavery." In the event, antislavery Whigs and Democrats were conspicuously absent, though Cassius M. Clay, the maverick Kentuckian, Governor Seward, and a few others communicated with the gathering by letter. The convention's Address, penned chiefly by Salmon Chase, still insisted on the baseness of both traditional parties and advocated antislavery union solely on Liberty terms and under the Liberty banner. Even so, the Southern and Western Convention showed the growing strength of the coalitionists within the Liberty camp. Not just Chase, but also Bailey and Samuel Lewis had played prominent parts at Cincinnati. Only Birney's managerial skill kept out of the Address hints of a coalition with Democrats. And even in its purified form, Chase's report expressed a reverence for "the maxims of True Democracy" and intimated that purged of its present leadership and held to its professed principles the Democratic party might one day provide the rallying ground for all political abolitionists. In the years ahead, Chase's influence waxed while Birney's waned. Already, in fact, events were under way which would ensure that the new guard, with its moderate platform and coalitionist tactics, would prevail over the older advocates of strictly independent action.[47]

4

Ever since the Liberty party's inception there had been voices calling for a union of political abolitionists of every stripe. Kiah Bailey in Vermont, Elihu Burritt in Massachusetts, Jabez D. Hammond in New York —all had pleaded for an end to narrow-minded exclusiveness and the formation of a broadly based antislavery alliance.[48] The first actual concert of action, however, occurred in New Hampshire during 1845-46. There Liberty men joined hands with antislavery Whigs and Independ-

[47] *Ibid.* 253-55; Smith, *Liberty and Free Soil Parties,* 88-89; *Address of the Southern and Western Liberty Convention,* esp. 8-9.
[48] *Signal of Liberty,* Dec. 12, 1846; Jabez D. Hammond to Gerrit Smith, Dec. 7, 1844, Smith Papers.

ent Democrats to upend regular Democrats whose "sycophancy to the South" (as John Quincy Adams put it) was notorious. The success of that joint enterprise seemed to many Liberty advocates a model to be copied wherever circumstances allowed, in state and nation.[49]

Precipitating a union of antislavery forces in New Hampshire was the decision of John P. Hale, a rising young Democratic Congressman from Dover, to defy his party's commitment to the annexation of Texas. Believing, with good cause, that the admission of Texas would give new life to the peculiar institution (and not, as Granite State legislators had recently alleged, "add more free than slave States to the Union"), Hale boldly condemned annexation in an open letter to his constituents published early in January 1845. Before that time Hale had kicked over party traces to vote for repeal of Congress' gag on antislavery petitions. Now, confronted by yet another act of insubordination, Democratic leaders, headed by State Chairman Franklin Pierce, moved swiftly to ostracize Hale. At a special convention in Concord on February 12, Hale was formally censured for his "treachery" and read out of the Democratic party.

Having lost his place on the Democratic ticket, and with the congressional election but a month away, Hale threw over hope of a political future and made tentative plans to practice law in New York City. He reckoned, however, without the determination of many rank-and-file Democrats to avenge him. Ten days after the Concord meeting that "decapitated" Hale, a sizable group of Independent Democrats (as they now dubbed themselves) gathered at Exeter to denounce slavery and Texas and to launch a campaign for Hale's reelection to Congress.

Abolitionists everywhere watched these events with delight. Even Garrisonians applauded Hale's stand as "a miracle of political independence and uprightness." The *Liberator* printed his anti-annexation letter in full, and at a board meeting of the Massachusetts Anti-Slavery Society on January 25, Garrison disclosed that he "was *very* anxious to do something that should secure John P. Hale's election." Accordingly, notwithstanding its aversion to political involvement, the Society voted to send four agents into New Hampshire to plug for the Independent candidate.[50]

[49] Except where indicated otherwise, the following account of the New Hampshire Alliance derives from my *John P. Hale and the Politics of Abolition* (Cambridge, Mass., 1965), chaps. IV-V.
[50] Hale's votes against the gag rule had already disposed many abolitionists to look

Liberty men, who had lambasted "the iniquitous scheme of Texas annexation" for years, also rejoiced at Hale's defiant act. In New Hampshire, the Concord *Granite Freeman* cheered his "firm stand against the enlargement of the empire of oppression," and opened its columns to Independent Democrats who until May lacked a newspaper of their own. When Hale showed enough strength in March to block the election of his replacement on the Democratic ticket, New Hampshire Liberty men dropped their own congressional candidate and openly threw their backing to Hale. In this they had the blessing and encouragement of prominent Liberty advocates in all parts of the country. Antislavery poet laureate John Greenleaf Whittier, pleased with Hale's "burning and withering denunciations of slavery," worked tirelessly to drum up support for him among Liberty voters. So too did Henry Stanton, Lewis Tappan, S. E. Sewall, Elizur Wright, and others. Gamaliel Bailey urged New Hampshire Liberty men and Whigs to unite with anti-Texas Democrats to secure Hale's election. "If they do not do so," he preached, "they will prove themselves better partisans than patriots. *Party* is a thing of necessity, but when adherence to it would certainly defeat the very good it professes to labor for, we would put it under our feet."[51]

The union that Bailey called for emerged during the winter of 1845-46. It was agreed that Whig legislators would support Hale's election to the United States Senate in return for Independent Democratic and Liberty help in making Anthony Colby, an antislavery Whig, governor. At the annual canvass in March the New Hampshire Allies won a majority of seats in both houses, and when the legislature met in June they carried all before them. Not only were Colby and Hale elected as planned, but Whigs and Independents divided key state offices among themselves and sent Liberty man Joseph Cilley to Washington to serve out a short term in the Senate. Nor did the fruits of coalition end here. Sharing common views on slavery (if little else), the Allies exploited their dominance over state government to pass a resolution,

---

upon him with favor. See, e.g., Parker Pillsbury to Hale, Jan. 10, 1844, Hale Papers, BLD.
[51] James G. Birney to *Albany Evening Journal*, May 19, 1845, Dumond (ed.), *Birney Letters*, II, 939; *Granite Freeman*, Jan. 23, 1845; Whittier to Joshua Leavitt, Aug. 26, 1845, quoted in Boston *Emancipator and Weekly Chronicle*, Sept. 3, 1845; Elizur Wright, Jr., to Hale, Sept. 13, 1845, John P. Hale Papers, NHHS; Concord *Independent Democrat*, Mar. 26, 1846; Stanton, *Random Recollections*, 127; *Cincinnati Weekly Herald and Philanthropist*, Apr. 9, 1845.

drafted by Hale, which denounced the annexation of Texas and the Mexican War and pledged New Hampshire's "cordial sympathy" and active cooperation "in every just and well-directed effort for the suppression and extermination of that terrible scourge of our race, human slavery." In like spirit the coalitionists forced through the legislature a joint resolution calling on Granite State Congressmen to press for abolition in the District of Columbia, exclusion of slavery from federal territories, suppression of the domestic slave trade, and a ban on the admission of new slave states. To crown their labors, the Allies added to the statute book a personal liberty law which made more difficult the recapture and return of fugitive slaves.[52]

More than satisfied with such results and with the implacably antislavery tone of the Hale forces, New Hampshire Liberty men proceeded to enter into a formal union with Independent Democrats. At a joint convention held at New Market in September 1846 both groups agreed to a common commitment to the *extinction* of slavery, and made Hale their choice for President in 1848. The following spring they strengthened that union by merging the Liberty party's *Granite Freeman* with Hale's *Independent Democrat*.[53]

The success of the New Hampshire Alliance, exceeding the hopes of all but the most sanguine abolitionists, kindled great excitement within Liberty party ranks. "The Hale storm down east," Lewis Tappan and Whittier agreed, had "been felt far & wide." Many called for the "New Hampshireizing" of other states. In New York too, Liberty men struck bipartisan alliances, swapping votes for Whig candidates for pledges of assistance in lowering black suffrage requirements at the state constitutional convention of 1846. To be sure, some political abolitionists voiced misgivings at this trend, but even critics had to admit "that many, if not most of [our fellow-laborers] are looking for a kind of coalition similar to that in New Hampshire."[54] For the bulk of Liberty advocates

[52] This law, said one antislavery Whig, had been passed "rather to please the abolitionists than from any urgent need of it. We are so far north that few slaves reach this state. It was however proper in itself & goes to increase the growing mass of public opinion which is every day accumulating against slavery." William Plumer, Jr., Feb. 6, 1847, William Plumer Papers, New Hampshire State Library.
[53] *Independent Democrat*, Sept. 17, 1846; *Independent Democrat & Freeman*, May 6, 1847.
[54] Tappan to Whittier, Oct. 1, 1846, Tappan Papers; Simeon S. Jocelyn to John P. Hale, June 30, 1846, J. P. Land to Hale, Oct. 2, 1846, Hale Papers, NHHS; Joshua R. Giddings to Hale, July 25, 1846, Hale Papers, BLD; Harlow, *Smith*, 174-76; *Signal of Liberty*, July 18, 1846.

found in the New Hampshire Alliance a timely rejoinder to the Birney-Goodell group's recent queries of how, without enlarging the Liberty platform, abolitionists could ever gain sufficient strength even to influence—much less pass—needed legislation.

Already, in fact, some Liberty spokesmen were suggesting a *national* union of antislavery forces. While the New Hampshire Alliance was still in assemblage, Salmon P. Chase sounded out Hale on this notion. "I see that in New Hampshire the organization of the Independent Democracy assumes openly Liberty grounds," he wrote at the end of January 1846. "Now it seems to me quite useless to have two organizations contending for the same object. I am well persuaded moreover that the Liberty party can accomplish little as such, except indirectly. But by taking the name Democrats which justly belongs to us & uniting for Liberty for all as the consequence of Democratic principles, we can compel the whole body of the existing Democracy except such parts as are incurably servile to come upon our ground." The loss of proslavery "doughfaces" would be more than offset by the accession of antislavery Whigs, the Ohioan contended. "I desire to see the Liberty Party completely merged in a True Democratic Party," he remarked in closing, "organized not in one State only but in every State where there are freemen enough to organize it." Similar proposals, albeit minus Chase's pro-Democratic bias, soon appeared on many sides. From Massachusetts Whittier outlined a three-point program "on which all who love Liberty and abhor Slavery" might unite. And in Michigan the editors of the *Signal of Liberty*, having abandoned all hope of securing a broader Liberty platform, began early in 1847 to advocate cooperation with any man or party whose hostility to slavery was strong. Birney protested such wishywashiness, but without avail. Antislavery union now seemed too promising a stratagem to be easily tossed aside.[55]

[55] Chase to Hale, Jan. 30, 1846, Hale Papers, NHHS; Whittier to Hale, Sept. 16, 1846, Hale Papers, BLD; Whittier to John G. Palfrey, Sept. 21, 1846, John G. Palfrey Papers, HLH; *Signal of Liberty*, Jan. 9, 1847; Birney to Theodore Foster, Mar. 27, 1847, Birney to Guy Beckley, Apr. 6, 1847, Dumond (ed.), *Birney Letters*, II, 1041, 1057-61. Whittier proposed that the following propositions serve as the touchstones of "a great League of Freedom": (1) Abolition of slavery the leading & paramount political question. (2) No voting for slaveholders. (3) No voting for men who are in political fellowship with slaveholders.

6

The Revolution Moves On

THE EVENTS OF 1846-47 did much to brighten the hopes of Liberty party coalitionists. Annexation of Texas—itself a cause of lamentation and alarm among slavery's critics[1]—led directly and inevitably to war with Mexico. That conflict in turn raised the explosive question of the status of slavery in the vast territories American arms seemed likely to wrench from hapless Mexico. Congressman David Wilmot's proviso, which would have excluded slavery forever from all lands acquired by the war, provided a rallying point for antislavery men in all parties. It also touched off a bitter debate which both advertised the transcending importance of the slavery issue and jeopardized traditional political alliances.

"The Mexican War and slavery will derange all party calculations," prophesied Charles Sumner, a leading Massachusetts "Conscience" Whig. "The antislavery principle has acquired such force as to be felt by all politicians. In most of the free states it will hold the balance between the two [major] parties, so that neither can succeed without yielding to it in a greater or less degree. The Abolitionists have at last got their lever upon a *fulcrum* where it can operate. It will detach large

---

[1] In some political abolitionists annexation produced feelings of utter hopelessness. "But alas, my dear Sir, what are *now* the objects & expectations of the Liberty party?" William Jay asked Salmon Chase shortly after the American government approved the annexation of Texas. "Slavery has broken out of the enclosure within which we would *certainly* have hunted her to death, & she will now have the boundless regions of Texas, California &c in which to roam at large, & will there mock all our puny efforts to destroy her." Mar. 24, 1845, Chase Papers, PHS.

sections from each of the other parties. . . . The question of slavery advances upon the country with giant strides."[2] Together with a good many other free-soil Whigs and some Democrats, Sumner urged an end to antislavery factionalism and eagerly anticipated "a new crystalization of parties, in which there shall be one grand Northern party of Freedom."[3]

Leading Liberty coalitionists found such overtures profoundly exciting. During the summer of 1846 delegates to the Northwestern Anti-Slavery Convention in Cleveland, pursuing a suggestion made by Chase, approved the establishment of a committee of five (later changed to twenty) to prepare the ground for a convocation of antislavery men of all parties, with an eye to formal union.[4] No such gathering ever took place. A national fusion of antislavery elements still faced many obstacles, among them the reluctance of free-soil Whigs and Democrats to set aside pet economic concerns and the unwillingness of Liberty men to accept anything less than complete political union "based upon the substantial principles & measures" of the Liberty party.[5] By 1847, however, there were signs that at least in some states coalition sentiment was spreading. In Ohio Liberty advocates sometimes neglected to make their own nominations, supporting instead antislavery nominees from the old parties. In Indiana three Liberty congressional candidates withdrew in favor of their Whig opponents. And in New Hampshire the Allies of 1845-46 once again joined hands to send to Congress both Amos Tuck, Hale's lieutenant, and James Wilson, an antislavery Whig.[6]

By this time, moreover, Liberty party coalitionists could count upon the tactful support of abolition's newest and most widely read newspaper—the Washington *National Era*. Ably edited by Gamaliel Bailey, with assistance from John Greenleaf Whittier and Amos A. Phelps, the *Era* first made its appearance on January 7, 1847. Before the year was

[2] Sumner to George Sumner, Dec. 31, 1846, Edward L. Pierce (ed.), *Memoir and Letters of Charles Sumner*, 4 vols. (Boston, 1877, 1893), III, 138-39. See also Joshua Giddings to Sumner, Dec. 25, 1846, Charles Sumner Papers, HLH.
[3] Sumner to Salmon P. Chase, Dec. 12, 1846, Chase Papers, LC. See also Columbus Delano to Joshua Giddings, Aug. 25, 1846, Sumner to Giddings, Jan. 21, 22, 25, 1847, Henry Wilson to Giddings, Apr. 10, 1847, William Slade to Giddings, Dec. 15, 1847, Joshua R. Giddings Papers, Ohio Historical Society; Giddings to Sumner, Jan. 25, 1847, Sumner Papers.
[4] *Signal of Liberty*, Aug. 8, 1846; Chase to [?], Feb. 15, 1847, Chase Papers, LC.
[5] Salmon P. Chase to Joshua R. Giddings, Oct. 20, 1846, Chase Papers, LC.
[6] Smith, *Liberty and Free Soil Parties*, 115-16; Sewell, *Hale*, 87, 256.

out it boasted a weekly circulation of 11,000 copies and claimed a substantial readership in Border slave states as well as throughout the North. From the beginning, Bailey gave to his paper a moderate, hopeful tone which most, though by no means all, critics of slavery found appealing. And as part of his self-imposed task of reconciling differences among political abolitionists, he revealed from the outset a willingness—already familiar to readers of his earlier editorials in the Cincinnati *Herald and Philanthropist*—to scrap the Liberty organization in favor of a new, more broadly constituted, antislavery party.[7]

Yet despite Bailey's persuasiveness and the encouraging examples of interparty cooperation, most Liberty men remained, throughout 1847, wary of merging their party into any larger antislavery coalition. Joshua Leavitt's influential *Emancipator*, taking direct issue with the *National Era*, contended that only the Liberty party could be entrusted to carry out the *abolition* of slavery and argued that that organization was of itself worth preserving. "We are not now, as we were before we were organized," Leavitt lectured his readers. "The Liberty party becomes an object of strong attachment. . . . If a political organization is worth having, it is worth being supported, at any sacrifice, save that of a good conscience." Even Salmon Chase, the most eager and active of the coalitionists, insisted that while "willing to give up . . . names, separate organizations," he would never agree to a dilution of the Liberty party's stand on slavery. And in private correspondence he made clear his conviction that more than the Wilmot Proviso was called for. "What we want, in my judgment, is not resistance to encroachment, but direct aggression," he professed. "Abolish slavery in the District, on the seas, in all places of exclusive national jurisdiction—employ no slaves on public works—give a clear preference to antislavery men in public appointments . . . and all w[oul]d be well."[8]

Still, by 1847 a great many Liberty members were willing to con-

[7] Lewis Tappan to Salmon P. Chase, Mar. 9, 1846, Chase Papers, PHS; Tappan to George W. Alexander, Feb. 23, 1847, Tappan to John Scoble, Nov. 14, 1847, Abel and Klingberg (eds.), *Sidelight on Anglo-American Relations*, 218, 228; Joshua Giddings to Charles Sumner, Jan. 25, 1847, Sumner Papers; Horace Mann to Mrs. Mann, May 28, 1848, Horace Mann Papers, MHS; *National Era*, Jan. 7, Apr. 29, May 20, July 29, 1847. For comment critical of the *Era*'s moderate, coalitionist stance, see Beriah Green to James G. Birney, Aug. 2, 1847, Dumond (ed.), *Birney Letters*, II, 1078; *Liberty Standard*, May 13, 1847; *Emancipator*, Apr. 21, May 5, 12, 1847.

[8] *Emancipator*, Feb. 24, June 16, 1847; Chase to Joshua Giddings, Oct. 20, 1846, Chase to [?], Aug. 15, 1846, Chase Papers, LC.

template, if not the abandonment of their organization, at least the nomination of a presidential candidate from outside their original ranks. Not surprisingly, the man most often mentioned was John P. Hale. Convinced by his thunderous assaults on slavery that he shared the Liberty party's ideals, and hopeful that his newly won prominence and reputation for moderation would prove helpful in winning anti-slavery voters away from the major parties, Liberty men began to sound out Hale's availability as early as the fall of 1846. Hale responded coldly to all such overtures; he cherished no illusions of success in 1848 and preferred to enter the Senate an unfettered independent. But third party spokesmen continued to advertise his charms anyway.[9]

Conscious of the "very strong desire among a great many leading antislavery men" that Hale become their party's nominee, Henry B. Stanton, Joshua Leavitt, Lewis Tappan, John Greenleaf Whittier, and other prominent Eastern Liberty strategists arranged a meeting with the Senator-elect and his chief New Hampshire advisors at Boston in July 1847. Hale used the occasion to make plain his reluctance to become the Liberty candidate. At the same time, he convinced those present that he was "with the Liberty party in principles, measures & feeling," and hinted that he might accept a draft nomination. Support for Hale snowballed thereafter. "I think the nomination of Hale would combine all the scattered fragments of anti Slavery in the country," Whittier decided, and once again he put his pen to work on behalf of the recusant Democrat.[10] The *Emancipator*, now in Stanton's capable hands, quickly followed suit. It would be folly, Stanton editorialized in September, for the Liberty party, "which aims to govern the country," to select a standard-bearer offensive to antislavery men of other parties—especially when someone with Hale's credentials was available. "The aim of the Liberty party is not only to maintain a principle," he continued, "but to accomplish an object. It goes for SUCCESS, and if one candidate can carry us more rapidly, and as safely forward towards victory than another, is he not *the* man for our party and our cause?"[11]

[9] *Signal of Liberty*, July 11, 1846; *American Freeman*, Oct. 13, 1846; *Liberty Standard*, Jan. 14, 1847; Sewell, *Hale*, 88-89. Hale's popularity among Liberty men was enhanced by his congressional campaign to abolish flogging in the Navy. See, e.g., *Cincinnati Weekly Herald and Philanthropist*, Nov. 27, 1844.
[10] Stanton to Whittier, July 12, 1847, Whittier to Samuel Fessenden, July 26, 1847, Whittier Papers; Sewell, *Hale*, 89-90.
[11] *Emancipator*, Sept. 1, 15, 1847. See also Lewis Tappan to Salmon P. Chase, Oct. 6, 1847, Chase Papers, PHS.

More and more Hale seemed a kind of Moses who would lead the anti-slavery host out of the wilderness and, if not into the promised land, at least into a position of respectability.

To be sure, not all political abolitionists warmed to the prospect of an early Liberty nomination for Hale. A goodly number, including James G. Birney, protested that Hale's reluctance to affirm the constitutionality of both abolition in the District of Columbia and prohibition of the interstate slave trade unfit him for any place on a Liberty ticket.[12] Many more, while holding the New Hampshire maverick in high regard, sought first to stall off any Liberty choice until 1848 and, failing in that attempt, tried to dissuade Hale from accepting the nomination if it came his way. Now that the Mexican War and the Wilmot Proviso had set in motion antislavery men of all parties, it would be foolish, they contended, for Hale to shackle himself to a party which had all but outlived its usefulness.[13]

None felt this more strongly than did Salmon Chase. The Liberty party's chances of progress, he had concluded by 1847, were bleak indeed. "As fast as we can bring public sentiment right, the other parties will approach our ground, and keep sufficiently close to it to prevent any great accession to our numbers," he complained in a long letter to Hale in May.[14] This, in fact, had been the case in Hale's own backyard, where New Hampshire Democrats had recently endorsed the Wilmot Proviso. What course, then, ought Liberty men to pursue? For a time Chase toyed with the idea of scrapping antislavery action in favor of a national "anti-slavery league," with local affiliates, which would support anti-extension candidates in the traditional parties. He still had special hopes of regenerating the Democratic party, and briefly leaned toward Silas Wright of New York as one well qualified to "rally the anti-slavery sentiment" in all quarters.[15] Wright's death in August

---

[12] *Albany Patriot*, May 26, 1847; George Bradburn to Gerrit Smith, Oct. 23, Dec. 4, 1847, Smith Papers; Birney to Lewis Tappan, July 10, 1848, Dumond (ed.), *Birney Letters*, II, 1108-9.
[13] Joshua Giddings to Charles Sumner, Aug. 5, 1847, Sumner Papers; Henry I. Bowditch to Hale, Oct. 7, 1847, Hale Papers, BLD; Sewell, *Hale*, 90-91. The chief argument given in favor of postponing the Liberty party's convention till spring was to permit antislavery refugees from the other parties, as a matter of sound politics and justice, to have a voice in nominations.
[14] May 12, 1847, Hale Papers, NHHS.
[15] Chase to Preston King, July 15, [1847], Salmon P. Chase, *Diary and Correspondence*, published in the American Historical Association, *Annual Report for the Year 1902*, II (Washington, D.C., 1903), 120-22.

scuttled that scheme, however, and by September Chase was once again calling for an independent organization, "not of a Liberty Party, exactly, but of an Independent Party, occupying Liberty & Liberal ground, making Slavery or Freedom its paramount issue." He hoped to see Hale head such a party, "composed of ALL honest .opponents of slavery"—or so he told Hale. But he vigorously opposed any nomination before 1848, trusting that "the events of the winter" would expedite a more inclusive antislavery coalition.[16]

Despite the opposition of coalitionists like Chase and Bailey, the Liberty national committee, by a vote of 7 to 2, scheduled the party's convention for October 20-21 in Buffalo. It is questionable whether this vote reflected the actual extent of support for a fall convention among Liberty voters. In the West, at least, support for a spring convention was widespread. Yet once the decision was made, nearly all came around. On hand when the convention opened were 140 regular delegates from all Northern states, together with a good many voluntary delegates and Liberty Leaguers. Under a curious rule, all enjoyed equal rights and privileges.[17]

The first and sharpest fight came over the platform. Ably led by Gerrit Smith and William Goodell, the Liberty Leaguers sought to win recognition of the need to make abolition but the foremost of many reforms, and to commit the convention to their doctrine that slavery was everywhere unconstitutional—in states as well as in territories. In the end, after warm debate, the "expedient" faction beat down these proposals and passed instead more moderate resolutions which stuck closely to the "one idea." To the architects of coalition, it represented a critical victory. For, as one of Chase's friends put it, the incorporation of Smith's planks would have hindered antislavery union by making the Liberty party "like the man under the influence of mesmerism, and his bump of Benevolence excited. All heart and no head."[18]

On one point the Buffalo platform of 1847 was decidedly more con-

---

[16] Chase to Hale, Sept. 23, 1847, Chase Papers, NHHS.
[17] *National Era*, Apr. 22, May 20, July 22, 1847; *Liberty Standard*, May 6, 1847; *American Freeman*, June 2, 1847; Joshua Leavitt to Salmon P. Chase, Sept. 27, 1847, Chase Papers, PHS; Smith, *Liberty and Free Soil Parties*, 117-18. The national committeemen who voted against an early convention were Chase and Daniel Hoit of New Hampshire.
[18] *Ibid.* 118-19; *Emancipator*, Oct. 27, 1847; *American Freeman*, Nov. 3, 1847; D. H. Whitman to Chase, Nov. 2, 1847, Chase Papers, LC.

servative than that of 1843; although it called on antislavery Congressmen to work for repeal of the 1793 Fugitive Slave Act, the new creed no longer pronounced the fugitive slave clause of the Constitution "null and void." Otherwise, while more succinct and perhaps less radical in its rhetoric, the 1847 platform appeared much the same as the earlier model—hardly surprising, given Chase's key role in drafting both.[19] However much Liberty men may have coveted the disaffected votes of other parties, they as yet remained unwilling to buy ballots at the expense of their principles.

On the second day the Buffalo delegates turned to nominations. After once again beating back a motion by Chase that no choice be made until spring, Stanton, Leavitt, and Tappan formally placed before the convention the name of John P. Hale. Earlier there had seemed great hesitancy on the part of some delegates, particularly those from the East, to accept so tardy a convert to their cause. Hale's constitutional scruples about interfering with the domestic traffic in slaves raised doubts,[20] as did his obvious reluctance to become a candidate. ("I am anxiously & earnestly desirous of avoiding this nomination," he had apprised Whittier in August.) A few apparently protested Hale's lack of "evangelical sentiments on the subject of Christianity," and some feared that the Liberty nomination might complicate his activities in the Senate.[21] At the close of the first day, in fact, Leavitt reported that things had looked "somewhat dark & tangled." But the next day, after Tappan and others had sung Hale's praises, "the clouds all rolled off, everything looked bright & hopeful, & a most cordial unanimity of feeling pervaded the whole convention." By an overwhelming margin, the delegates picked Hale to head their ticket in 1848. After selecting Ohio's Leicester King as his running mate, and making provision for a subsequent meeting if necessary, the convention adjourned.[22]

Although some (mainly Liberty Leaguers) grumbled that the Buffalo conferees had dipped into "the class of slippery politicians" for their candidate, Hale's nomination sat well with most Liberty men. Their satisfaction grew once Hale entered the Senate (in December 1847)

[19] National Era, Nov. 4, 1847.
[20] William Day to Hale, Feb. 27, 1851, Hale Papers, NHHS; Goodell, Slavery and Anti-Slavery, 478.
[21] Hale to Whittier, Aug. 13, 1847, Lewis Tappan to Hale, Oct. 27, 1847, Hale Papers, BLD; Austin Willey to Hale, Nov. 5, 1847, Hale Papers, NHHS.
[22] Leavitt to Hale, Nov. 9, 1847, Hale Papers, NHHS.

and began a series of stinging attacks on slavery and the Mexican War. Even Garrison's *Liberator,* doubtless relishing the chance to make a distinction invidious to the old enemy, Birney, congratulated the Liberty party "on having got at last a reputable candidate."[23]

Although at the time few seem to have noticed, the candidate himself took a dim view of the Buffalo proceedings. Not until January 1, 1848, did he get around to accepting the Liberty offer, and even then his acceptance was grudging and provisional. Hale freely endorsed the Buffalo platform. But he emphatically denied that by accepting the Liberty nomination he in any way submitted his public conduct to party control. Moreover, Hale, mindful of the rising ferment over the Wilmot Proviso and the Mexican War, in his letter of acceptance declared that should a broader-based antislavery coalition form, "joining the good and true of every party," he would gladly step aside and march with the "humblest privates who will rally under such a banner." There is every reason to believe that Hale hoped that this would be the case —that he took the Liberty nomination purposely to avoid becoming the candidate of the free-soil alliance he expected soon to absorb the Liberty party.[24]

2

Certainly by New Year's Day 1848 there was ample cause to anticipate a political coming-together of antislavery forces. Raucous debate over slavery's status in territory conquered from Mexico had heated sectional antagonisms to the flash point, and in both major parties sizable free-soil factions stood ready to renounce old allegiances rather than acquiesce in the South's latest demands. Formerly, nearly all antislavery Whigs and Democrats would have agreed with Joshua Giddings that it was easier to convert the present parties to antislavery measures than to form a new antislavery party. Believing that by working within the traditional parties they could exert the greatest influence for human

[23] *Albany Patriot,* Nov. 10, 1847; *Liberator,* Dec. 17, 1847. For criticism of Hale's nomination, see also *American Freeman,* Nov. 10, 1847; William L. Chaplin to James G. Birney, Feb. 10, 1848, Birney to Lewis Tappan, July 10, 1848, Dumond (ed.), *Birney Letters,* II, 1091, 1108-9. For favorable reactions, see the sampler of Liberty press opinion in the *American Freeman,* Dec. 22, 1847.
[24] Sewell, *Hale,* 95-96.

rights, political abolitionists like Giddings and Gates, Bryant and King, had resisted appeals for an independent antislavery action.[25] The 1844 presidential contest between slaveholding candidates forced great numbers of abolitionists into the Liberty camp, but the election of Polk and the swift annexation of Texas merely confirmed to many antislavery Whigs the dangers of third party "meddling." Without Birney's candidacy, they were firmly convinced, Clay would have carried New York and with it the nation, thereby postponing indefinitely the incorporation of slavery-ridden Texas.[26]

Yet no sooner had war over Texas raised the question of slavery's extension into the vast provinces which Polk demanded as "indemnity," than free-soil Whigs and Democrats began to consider separation from their "proslavery" brethren. Among Whigs, this tendency was strongest in Massachusetts.

By 1846 a long-simmering dispute over the proper response to the Texas crisis had divided Bay State Whigs into two clearly defined and well-organized factions.[27] Conservative "Cotton Whigs," representing the new industrial order and conciliatory toward their economic and political partners in the South, cautioned tact and moderation in the fight against slavery and expansionism. Insurgent "Conscience Whigs," on the other hand, struck a belligerently antislavery stance. The peculiar institution, young dissidents like Charles Francis Adams, Charles Sumner, John Gorham Palfrey, Henry Wilson, Stephen C. Phillips, Charles Allen, and E. Rockwood Hoar strongly believed, was "a great moral, political, and social evil"—a cancer that threatened the health of all other institutions.[28] At the risk of antagonizing the South, therefore, they sought by word and deed to raise a moral and constitutional

[25] Giddings to Salmon P. Chase, Oct. 12, 1843, Chase Papers, PHS; Seth Gates to Amos A. Phelps, July 14, 1840, Phelps Papers; William H. Seward to Chase, Aug. 4, 1845, Washington Hunt to Chase, Mar. 18, 1846, Chase Papers, PHS.
[26] See, e.g., Giddings to Laura M. Giddings, Dec. 15, 1844, Giddings Papers.
[27] For detailed accounts of the Whig split in Massachusetts, see Martin B. Duberman, *Charles Francis Adams, 1807-1886* (Boston, 1960), chap. XII; Frank O. Gatell, *John Gorham Palfrey and the New England Conscience* (Cambridge, Mass., 1963), chap. IX; David Donald, *Charles Sumner and the Coming of the Civil War* (New York, 1960), chap. VI; Kinley J. Brauer, *Cotton versus Conscience: Massachusetts Whig Politics and Southwestern Expansion, 1843-1848* (Lexington, Ky., 1967).
[28] *Ibid.* 189. See also Henry Wilson to John P. Hale, June 27, 1846, Charles Sumner to Hale, Sept. 12, 1846, Hale Papers, BLD. Palfrey gave practical testimony to his hatred of slavery in 1845 by manumitting, at considerable effort and personal expense, twenty bondsmen he had inherited from his father, a substantial Louisiana planter. See Gatell, *Palfrey*, chap. VIII.

blockade which would isolate and ultimately destroy slavery. As Sumner put it in 1846:

> I think Slavery a sin, individual and national; and think it the duty of each individual to cease committing it, and, of course of each State, to do likewise. Massachusetts is a party to slave-holding, and is responsible for it, so long as it continues under the sanction of the Constitution of the United States. I would leave it to the *local* laws of each State. If the South persists in holding slaves let it not expect Massachusetts to aid or abet in the wrong.[29]

Such views squared so well with the Liberty party's position on slavery that Boston Liberty men offered Sumner their nomination for Congress. Sumner declined, but did so respectfully and without in any way impairing his good relations with third party leaders.[30]

In May 1846, the Conscience group acquired the struggling *Boston Whig* and thereafter the party's dirty linen hung in full public view. With Charles Francis Adams in the editorial chair, the new paper promptly set about to expose not only the machinations of the Slave Power (Palfrey provided a series of twenty-four articles on the subject), but also the failings—moral and political—of conventional Whiggery. Such party stalwarts as Abbott Lawrence and Nathan Appleton were roasted for "thinking more of sheep and cotton than of Man," for "truckling to expediency in every thing, for the sake of . . . slaveholding gold."[31] Congressman Robert C. Winthrop, who had reluctantly voted for a military supplies bill which blamed Mexico for the war just begun, received even rougher treatment. Hurt, angry, and surprised by the bitter attacks of the Conscience forces, the Cotton Whigs lashed back. Year's end found the regulars still in the saddle but the insurgents more than ever convinced that reform was imperative. "We do not mean to leave the Whig party . . . ," Adams editorialized at the end of November. "Still less do we propose to sanction the suicidal system of third parties. But no party ties shall bind us to sanction in Whig candidates for public office the desertion of Whig principles."[32]

[29] Quoted in Donald, *Sumner,* 134.
[30] *Ibid.* 148.
[31] *Ibid.* 142.
[32] Quoted in Brauer, *Cotton versus Conscience,* 204. On Adams's objection to third parties, see also *Boston Daily Whig,* July 9, 1846.

Events of the following year divided Whigs still further and caused even Adams to reconsider his aversion to third party politics. The principal irritant was the growing likelihood that Mexican War hero and Louisiana slaveholder Zachary Taylor would carry off the Whig presidential nomination in 1848. Convinced that "the people" were ready for "war upon the accursed system of human bondage," and scandalized at talk of Taylor's candidacy, the Conscience men tried to carry a resolution at the party's state convention at Springfield endorsing only candidates "known . . . to be opposed to the existence of Slavery." Defeated, they came away certain that the time had come for more radical action. "My own mind leans more and more to the conviction that little or nothing can be done with the old Whig party," Adams apprised Giddings soon after Springfield; ". . . something more decided must be resorted to than humoring their profligacy."[33]

Similar rumblings, though fainter, could be heard from Whigs in other quarters—especially in the Western Reserve. There Joshua Giddings, Columbus Delano, Daniel R. Tilden, and other free-soil Whigs worked to head off Taylor by promoting the candidacy of Senator Thomas Corwin.[34] In February 1847 this "Ohio ploughboy" had thrilled antislavery advocates across the North with a mighty, eloquent denunciation of the Mexican War. "If I were a Mexican," he had thundered, "I would tell you, 'Have you not room in your own country to bury your dead men? If you come into mine we will greet you with bloody hands, and welcome you to hospitable graves.' "[35] The speech was short on antislavery sentiment, but the fervor of his demand for peace clouded that fact and made Corwin for a time the darling of Wilmot Proviso Whiggery. "Tell him that there has not been in America since the revolution such a chance for a man to make an everlasting reputation as is now before him," Charles Francis Adams wrote Giddings. If Corwin embraced the Proviso, Henry Wilson asserted, he could carry every New England state in 1848.[36]

By autumn, however, the Corwin bubble had burst. Always more

[33] Samuel Gridley Howe to John G. Palfrey, Sept. 23, 1846, Palfrey Papers; Donald, *Sumner,* 158; Brauer, *Cotton versus Conscience,* 223.
[34] Giddings to Charles Sumner, Feb. 11, 21, 1847, Sumner Papers; Giddings to Horace Greeley, Apr. 16, 1847, Giddings-Julian Papers.
[35] Quoted in Louis Filler, *The Crusade Against Slavery* (New York, 1960), 186.
[36] Adams to Giddings, Feb. 22, 1847, Wilson to Giddings, Feb. 24, 1847, Giddings Papers.

concerned for the Whig party and the Union than for the reduction
of slavery, Corwin wrecked his credit among antislavery men with a
pussyfooting address at Carthage, Ohio, on September 18, 1847. De-
ploring abolitionist activity as a threat to national unity, and pronounc-
ing even the Wilmot Proviso "a dangerous question," Corwin joined
hands at Carthage with conservative Whigs who sought to dodge the
question of slavery expansion by opposing the acquisition of *any* new
territory—slave or free.[37] Giddings tried hard to convince himself and
others that the Senator might yet be brought right, and did elicit a letter
in which Corwin expressed a willingness to fall back upon the Proviso
should the non-annexation campaign fail.[38] But the damage was done.
"The No Territory movement, I fear, has played the mischief with
Corwin," observed a prominent Ohio Whig. "I . . . believe it has
killed him politically, so far as being a Candidate for President *at present* is concerned."[39] Increasingly, antislavery Whigs were being drawn
back to the harsh realization that they might have to turn outside their
organization for an acceptable nominee. Few showed much interest in
John P. Hale, now the official choice of the Liberty party. But already
an earthquake among New York Democrats had revealed astonishing
new prospects.

3

For years the political heirs of Andrew Jackson in New York and
other Northern states had been split—over canals, banks, and patronage
—into Conservative and Radical factions.[40] The intrusion of the slavery
question in the mid-1840s divided these groups still further and contributed to a growing antagonism among Radicals toward Southern
dictation of Democratic policy. Already bitter at the South's desertion
of Van Buren in 1844 and distressed at the political costs of sustaining
such "proslavery" measures as the gag rule, Radical Democrats seethed

[37] Corwin to Joshua Giddings, Aug. 18, 1847, Sumner to Giddings, Oct. 1, Nov. 1,
1847, Giddings Papers; Stewart, *Giddings*, 133-34.
[38] Giddings to Charles Sumner, Oct. 8, 18, 1847, Sumner Papers; Corwin to Giddings, Oct. 12, 1847, Giddings Papers.
[39] E. S. Hamlin to Charles Sumner, Oct. 26, 1847, Sumner Papers.
[40] William Trimble, "Diverging Tendencies in the New York Democracy in the
Period of the Locofocos," *American Historical Review*, XXIV, No. 3 (Apr. 1919),
396-421.

when, despite assurances to the contrary, President Polk acquiesced in John Tyler's decision to admit Texas as a single slave state. The feeling that legitimate Northern interests were being sacrificed to the corrupt claims of the Slave Power intensified in the months following the annexation of Texas. The Walker Tariff of 1846, with all its "free trade absurdities," struck a good many Northeastern Democrats as little better than "a bill of confiscation." John M. Niles, an old-school Jacksonian from Connecticut, bluntly called it "an act to bring down the free labor of the North, and to try to bring up the slave labor of the cotton planters & tobacco growers of the South." It particularly upset Gideon Welles that "arrogant" Southern Democrats had forced tariff reduction in the midst of war, leading to an enlarged national debt, unsound borrowing, and other evils. Northwesterners equally resented the Polk Administration's easy acceptance of the compromise with Great Britain that divided Oregon along the 49th parallel and the President's veto of a river and harbor bill beneficial to their section. "The time has come, I think, when the Northern democracy should make a stand," one of Martin Van Buren's confidants wrote in July 1846. "Every thing has taken a Southern shape and been controlled by Southern caprice for years. The Northern states are treated as provinces to the South. We have given in, too much, to their extreme [?] notions & abstractions. . . ."[41]

Therefore, when war with Mexico raised the question of slavery once more, Radical Democrats, especially in New York, were determined to resist the South's demands. In opposition to Southern insistence that planters be free to take their chattels into any new territory, Radicals pledged themselves to the principle of free soil, embodied in David Wilmot's Proviso of August 1846. They had no wish to make their antislavery creed a test of orthodoxy, but neither would they tolerate Southern attempts to make proslavery doctrines binding on all Democrats. Only by agreeing to disagree on slavery could the national party survive.[42]

[41] Gideon Welles to Martin Van Buren, July 28, 1846, June 30, 1848, Martin Van Buren Papers, LC. See also Joshua Giddings to [Oliver Johnson?], Dec. 15, 1843, Charles Francis Jenkins Collection, FHL; George D. Morgan to Welles, July 17, 1846, Gideon Welles Papers, NYPL; John G. Whittier to Elizur Wright, Jr., Dec. 15, 1845, Pickard, *Whittier as a Politician*, 40-42; Eric Foner, "The Wilmot Proviso Revisited," *Journal of American History*, LVI, No. 2 (Sept. 1969), 262-79.
[42] Martin Van Buren to Azariah C. Flagg, Oct. 12, 1847, John M. Niles to Van Buren, Dec. 16, 1847, Van Buren Papers; Niles to John Cochrane *et al.*, July 15,

Radical Democrats contended for "permanent perpetual barriers against the extension of Slavery" on grounds both of sound principle and political necessity. First, the Proviso merely restated, in essentially the same language, the principle Thomas Jefferson had originally laid down in the Northwest Ordinance of 1787. It sought merely to bar the *spread* of an institution that even Southerners had long considered a necessary evil; in no way did it threaten the right of slave *states* to regulate their domestic relations free from outside interference. But, as Silas Wright pointed out, "to contend that Congress should introduce, or engraft, slavery upon territory now free, is to ask the people of the Union to consider and treat slavery as a positive benefit and blessing to be diffused and extended by the action of Congress." This, he warned, the people of the free states would never do. Any politician, North or South, who thought or acted otherwise was gravely deluded and courted political disaster.[43] Congressman Jacob Brinkerhoff, a Van Burenite from Ohio, put the matter even more strongly:

> For years, [he told the House of Representatives in February 1847] Southern gentlemen have been permitted to shape our party issues for their own convenience, and have been floating upon the current of popular sentiment at home, and at our own expense. Are we required to father every wrong and outrage they may see proper to propose, and eternally to combat the inborn sentiments and native instincts of our people for their benefit? If we must descend to partisan considerations in connection with a question which ought to be and will prove to be *above* all party influences, I tell you, sir, the adoption of the principle of the "Wilmot proviso" is the only way to *save* the Democratic party of the free States.

If Northern Democrats surrendered the free-soil principle, he warned, "they are destined to defeat and doomed to a position in the minority,

1848, in *Albany Atlas*, July 21, 1848; William P. Pettit to Gideon Welles, June 30, 1848, Gideon Welles Papers, LC; Foner, *Free Soil, Free Labor, Free Men*, 152.
[43] Preston King to John A. Dix, Nov. 13, 1847, Silas Wright to Dix, Jan. 19, 1847, John A. Dix Papers, Columbia University. See also Wright to Dix, Mar. 22, 1847, Dix Papers; R. H. Gillet to A. C. Flagg, Jan. 18, 1847, Azariah C. Flagg Papers, NYPL; A. E. Burr to Gideon Welles, July 18, 1847, Welles Papers, NYPL; Welles to Burr, Mar. 24, 1849 (copy), Welles Papers, LC; Preston King to Welles, Sept. 11, 1847, Preston King Papers, St. Lawrence University; Hiram Ketchum to William P. Fessenden, Mar. 10, 1848, William Pitt Fessenden Papers, WRHS.

from . . . Iowa to . . . Maine. And this is not the worst of it, sir: they will deserve their fate."[44]

To this concern for voter attitudes at home was added mounting jealousy and apprehension over the extension of Southern power in national politics. It was high time, John Niles snapped, for the free states to regain "that influence, that equality, that control in the affairs of the Government, to which they are entitled."[45] Only by preventing the emergence of new slave states might the proper balance be struck.

So strong was such feeling in the North that even pro-Administration, or "Hunker," Democrats felt called upon to affirm a repugnance for slavery. "I respect with a feeling akin to reverence the sentiment entertained by the great masses of those I represent, upon the subject of slavery," insisted New York's leading Hunker, Senator Daniel Dickinson. "I know how deeply its existence is deplored by the true philanthropist."[46] Yet, solicitous of Southern opinion, anxious lest antislavery agitation abet the Whigs and jeopardize the Union, and more interested in Western expansion than in territorial government, most Hunkers reacted coolly to the Wilmot Proviso. When they supported it at all they did so tentatively, almost apologetically. Nearly all, moreover, quickly abandoned slavery restriction in favor of "popular sovereignty"—the notion, first broached by Vice President George M. Dallas in September 1847, that territorial settlers themselves ought properly "to determine their own institutions."[47]

In most states Democrats managed to hold their differences over slavery and other issues within bounds. In New York, however, a decade of intraparty acrimony had rubbed tempers raw, and disagreement on the Wilmot Proviso soon exploded into open warfare.[48] At the state

---

[44] *Cong. Globe*, 29th Cong., 2nd sess., 379.
[45] Quoted in Foner, *Free Soil, Free Labor, Free Men*, 153.
[46] *Cong. Globe*, 30th Cong., 1st sess., Appendix, 1202. I am indebted to Dr. Judah Ginsberg for directing my attention to this quotation.
[47] Chaplain W. Morrison, *Democratic Politics and Sectionalism: The Wilmot Proviso Controversy* (Chapel Hill, 1967), 87.
[48] The Hunker-Barnburner split in New York is chronicled in Herbert D. A. Donovan, *The Barnburners* (New York, 1925). See also Joseph G. Rayback, *Free Soil: The Election of 1848* (Lexington, Ky., 1970), 60-77; Arthur M. Schlesinger, Jr., *The Age of Jackson* (Boston, 1945), 454-64. Conflicting contemporary accounts are given in *New York Hards and Softs: Which is the True Democracy? A Brief Statement of Facts for the Consideration of the Democracy of the Union, Showing the Origin and Cause of the Continued "Division of the Party"* (New York, 1856) and *The Softs the True Democracy of the State of New York* (New York, 1856).

Democratic convention at Syracuse in September 1847, the Hunker faction wrested control of the party machinery from the Radicals—or, as they were popularly known in New York, the "Barnburners"—and, after a long and angry debate marked by shouts, "pugilistic feints, and pushing and crowding,"[49] beat down resolutions hostile to the extension of slavery. Furious, the Barnburners stormed out of the convention and arranged for a meeting of their own at the Herkimer railroad station in October. There, with the eyes of the North focused on their deliberations, they proclaimed their dedication to "Free Trade, Free Labor, Free Soil, Free Speech and Free Men."

The Barnburner revolt thrilled not only Proviso Democrats but Conscience Whigs and Liberty men, and inevitably heightened talk of coalition. None was more excited than Salmon P. Chase. "I know of no event in the History of Parties in this Country," he exulted to Charles Sumner, "at all approaching, in sublimity and moment, the Herkimer Convention, or rather the great movement of which the Convention was the most signal, visible expression." To be sure, many doubted the purity of the New Yorkers' motives, rightly recognizing that a desire to avenge the wrongs of Van Buren and Governor Silas Wright (whose 1846 defeat for reelection had been laid at the Hunkers' door) had prompted the Barnburners' bolt quite as much as principle had. But most advocates of free soil believed that, for whatever reason, the Herkimer schismatics had "passed the Rubicon" and would hold to the Wilmot Proviso at all costs. Quite likely their example would prove contagious. "The Revolution is moving on," sang one antislavery Whig to an immensely receptive Salmon Chase.[50]

In fact, applause for what John P. Hale called the Barnburners' "noble . . . demonstration . . . against the encroachments of slavery" was somewhat premature. For while young Radicals like Preston King, David Dudley Field, and William Cullen Bryant still insisted on free territory as the "cornerstone" of their party and confidentially sounded out Massachusetts Conscience Whigs about the feasibility of a national antislavery convention "to nominate a Northern candidate,'

49 *New York Herald*, Oct. 6, 1847, quoted in Morrison, *Democratic Politics and Sectionalism*, 81.
50 Chase to Sumner, Dec. 2, 1847, Chase, *Diary and Correspondence*, 125; Theodore Sedgwick, Jr., to Charles Sumner, [Nov. 1847?], E. S. Hamlin to Sumner, Oct. 26, 1847, Sumner Papers; Henry B. Stanton to John P. Hale, Oct. 30, 1847, Hale Papers BLD; Hamlin to Chase, Dec. 3, 1847, Chase Papers, PHS.

Barnburner greybeards hung back. Not only did the likes of John A. Dix, Benjamin F. Butler, Azariah Flagg, and Martin Van Buren discountenance all talk of an independent nomination for President, but they assumed an accommodating position on the Wilmot Proviso as well. Far from wishing to make support for the Proviso an article of party faith, old line Radicals were ready to tolerate differences on this and other aspects of the slavery question. Some, moreover, stood ready to support any presidential nominee who had not explicitly denied the constitutional power of Congress to prohibit slavery in the territories and who, if elected, would be willing to leave the whole issue to the legislative branch.[51]

So flexible were the Barnburners prepared to be, in fact, that many of them displayed a surprising fondness for the nomination of Zachary Taylor. The first choice of nearly all Barnburners had been Silas Wright, a plain-spoken man of the people, firm advocate of free soil, and, after Martin Van Buren, the most influential Democrat in New York. But Wright's death in August 1847 forced Radicals to seek another acceptable standard-bearer, and one of those most frequently mentioned was the slaveholding general from Louisiana. Although known to be a favorite of conservative Whigs and some proslavery Democrats, Taylor appealed to a good many Barnburners, young and old, for much the same reasons as had Andrew Jackson. A military hero whose political record was a *tabula rasa*, a man who reputedly "preferred honesty to intrigue, the true interests of the Country to the private interests of politicians, and a true and strict and faithful construction of the Constitution to pledges made to order," Taylor seemed a candidate ideally suited to the Barnburners' needs—provided, of course, he could be made to march to their drum. Only when it proved impossible to pin him down concerning slavery in the territories did the Barnburners drop Taylor from consideration. And even then there were many who insisted they preferred him to the Hunkers' favorite, Lewis Cass of Michigan.[52]

[51] Hale to Mrs. Hale, Dec. 5, 1847, Hale Papers, NHHS; Charles Sumner to Joshua R. Giddings, Nov. 1, 1847, Giddings Papers; Giddings to Sumner, Nov. 8, 1847, David D. Field to Sumner, May 31, 1848, Sumner Papers; Preston King to William P. Pettit, Mar. 16, 1848, John M. Niles Papers, CHS; Dix to Flagg, June 5, 1848, Flagg to Marcus Morton, June 19, 1848, Azariah C. Flagg Papers, Columbia University; Butler to Martin Van Buren, May 8, 1848, Flagg to Van Buren, June 19, 1848, Van Buren Papers; Dix to Thomas Hart Benton, Apr. 15, 1854, Dix Papers.
[52] James R. Doolittle to James W. Taylor, n.d. (photocopy), James R. Doolittle

Between the Herkimer meeting in October 1847 and the Democratic National Convention at Baltimore the following May, most Barnburners struck a basically moderate stance—emphasizing party regularity, endorsing Polk's war policy, calling for some territorial indemnity from Mexico, and agreeing to disagree on slavery expansion. In all of this they followed the advice of Martin Van Buren, who had moved to New York City early in 1848 to coordinate Barnburner strategy. Apparently the ex-President and his associates hoped by this strategy to strengthen their hand at the Baltimore convention—to win recognition of the Barnburner delegation at the expense of the rival Hunkers and thereby to influence the selection of a suitable ticket and sound platform.[53]

If so, they were sorely disappointed. After an extended squabble, the Democrats voted to recognize both New York delegations, splitting the state's vote between them. Angrily insisting on their exclusive right to representation as the regularly selected delegation, and charging discrimination on account of their free-soil views, the Van Burenites stalked out of the convention. Taking advantage of their absence, the remaining company then rubbed salt in the Barnburners' wounds by nominating Cass—the chief villain in Van Buren's downfall four years earlier—for President. The platform, which altogether ducked the question of slavery in the territories, still further alienated the New York dissidents.[54]

Suddenly gone was talk of conciliation and party regularity. Having resisted all attempts to pledge them in advance to support the national ticket, the Barnburners now rejected it as unfit for New York and issued a call for a state convention at Utica on June 22. There acceptable candidates might be chosen and future strategy plotted. A few old-time Radicals (notably Dix and Flagg) still counseled against an

---

Papers, SHSW; Theodore Sedgwick, Jr., to Charles Sumner, May 29, 1848, Sumner Papers; *National Era,* Feb. 24, 1848; Morrison, *Democratic Politics and Sectionalism,* 96-97.
[53] *Ibid.* 93-98. Not all Barnburners agreed with the moderate approach favored by Van Buren. Preston King, for one, spoiled for a showdown with administration Democrats and predicted "certain division" at Baltimore. King to William P. Pettit, Mar. 16, 1848, Niles Papers.
[54] Morrison, *Democratic Politics and Sectionalism,* chap. VII; O. C. Gardiner, *The Great Issue: or, the Three Presidential Candidates; Being a Brief Historical Sketch of the Free Soil Question in the United States, from the Congresses of 1774 and '87 to the Present Time* (New York, 1848), 96-101.

independent presidential nomination. Others agreed with Van Buren that New York had been "too grossly humiliated" by the Democracy of other states to turn back now, yet anticipated certain defeat for any third party in 1848. The great mass of Barnburners, however, moved equally by principle and revenge, were ready for war with the Slave Power and Northern "doughfaces" whatever the cost.[55]

By the time old Samuel Young gaveled the Utica gathering into session, it was a foregone conclusion that Martin Van Buren would be the Barnburners' choice for President. The only doubts of his suitability concerned his position on slavery, and these vanished with the reading to the convention of Van Buren's letter, which forcefully endorsed the Wilmot Proviso. Overriding, then, his avowed unwillingness to become a candidate, the Utica delegates noisily proclaimed Van Buren and Senator Henry Dodge of Wisconsin as their party's standard-bearers "in the momentous struggle" at hand. More stirring still to critics of slavery across the North, the Barnburners adopted by acclamation a platform that excoriated the peculiar institution "as a great moral, social and political evil—a relic of barbarism which must necessarily be swept away in the progress of Christian civilization . . ." and that ought therefore to be barred from territories now free.[56]

The Barnburner revolt was now complete and irreversible. The only question remaining was whether the New Yorkers would go it alone or join forces with antislavery factions in other states and other parties. Anticipating this latter possibility, the Utica platform urged Barnburner participation in any free state convention that might be called to unite all champions of free soil.[57]

A day or two earlier, in fact, a Free Territory Convention in Colum-

---

[55] John A. Dix to Azariah C. Flagg, June 5, 1848, Flagg to Marcus Morton, June 19, 1848, Flagg Papers, Columbia University; Martin Van Buren to Francis P. Blair, June 22, 1848, quoted in Rayback, *Free Soil*, 207; Benjamin F. Butler to Van Buren, May 29, 1848, Van Buren Papers.

[56] Gardiner, *The Great Issue*, 107-21. The Utica convention included a smattering of delegates and onlookers from five other free states and received telegrams and letters of good cheer from Mayor James H. Woodworth of Chicago and various free soil mass meetings. Several of these communications proposed a National Free Soil Convention to join Wilmot Proviso men of all parties. Dodge, a rugged frontiersman chosen to attract Westerners (and especially "the River & Harbor interest"), declined his vice presidential nomination as soon as he learned of it. See J. B. Elwood to Charles Sumner, June 24, 1848, Sumner Papers; Charles S. Benton to David Wilmot, July 10, 1848, Palfrey Papers; *New York Hards and Softs*, 12.

[57] Gardiner, *The Great Issue*, 120.

bus, Ohio, engineered primarily by Salmon P. Chase and composed of anti-extensionists from all parties, had issued just such a call—for a meeting of "all Friends of Freedom, Free Territory and Free Labor" at Buffalo on August 9 and 10.[58] Antislavery Whigs, moreover, whose enthusiasm for the Barnburner rebellion had previously been checked by lingering hopes that their party would see the light and select a sound free-soil presidential candidate (Supreme Court Justice John McLean was often mentioned), found those hopes shattered by Zachary Taylor's nomination at Philadelphia early in June, and they now eagerly sought some new alliance for freedom. "Stunned stupified outraged abased mortified and enraged to the last degree *beyond endurance* by the action of the Philadelphia convention," fumed an antislavery Whig on the Western Reserve, adding: "Can anything be done with the Barnburners? or Liberty party [?]"[59] In Massachusetts, Conscience Whigs cheered the defiance of Henry Wilson and Charles Allen, who had walked out of the Whig National Convention to protest its choice of candidates. At once they arranged for a meeting of their own at Worcester on June 28 to prepare the way for concerted action by antislavery men everywhere. There, meeting in the shade of the Worcester Lunatic Asylum (a fact Cotton editors never wearied of telling), some five thousand Conscience Whigs and sundry sympathizers from other states—including Joshua Giddings, Owen Lovejoy, and the New York City Barnburner John Bigelow—scored the conspiracy of lash and loom that had forced General Taylor "upon the late Whig party" and called on all "lovers of Freedom" to attend the impending convention at Buffalo.[60]

What had begun as a tentative, exploratory correspondence between

---

58 *Addresses and Proceedings of the State Independent Free Territory Convention of the People of Ohio, Held at Columbus, June 20 and 21, 1848* (Cincinnati, 1848). Chase had telegraphed Barnburners Preston King and John Van Buren on June 21 to inform them of the Ohio meeting's call. Whether this fact was generally known to Utica delegates is unclear. See Chase to John Van Buren, June 29[?], 1848, Samuel J. Tilden Papers, NYPL.

59 Albert G. Riddle to Joshua Giddings, June 12, 1848, Giddings Papers. See also Giddings to Salmon P. Chase, June 11, 1848, E. S. Hamlin to Chase, June 12, 1848, Chase Papers, LC; *Boston Daily Whig,* June 10, 1848. Some Northern Whigs apparently objected to Taylor as much for being an unreliable party man as for his suspected softness on slavery. See Myron Lawrence to Allen Bangs, Apr. 1, 1848 (copy), George Frisbie Hoar Papers, MHS; Richard Henry Dana, Jr., to Richard Henry Dana, July 11, 1848, Richard Henry Dana Papers, MHS.

60 Frank Otto Gatell, " 'Conscience and Judgment': The Bolt of the Massachusetts Conscience Whigs," *Historian,* XXI, No. 1 (Nov. 1958), 18-45.

men like Chase and Giddings, King and Field, Sumner and Adams was now a full-blown movement, strongest in Massachusetts, New York, and Ohio but reaching as well into every free state—a movement born of many complaints but united in opposition to the spread of slavery beyond its present bounds.

7

"Not Dead, but Translated"

To LIBERTY PARTY MEN, the Barnburner and Conscience Whig up-heavals seemed both promising and dangerous—promising because they appeared to place within reach a broader, more effective antislavery coalition, dangerous because they threatened to deflect attention and energy away from abolition and toward the lesser goal of slavery restriction. Therefore, while the more ardent fusionists (Chase, Bailey, and Stanton, among others) rejoiced at the recent turn of events, a great many third party regulars warned against involvement in any union not based squarely on Liberty principles. Free soil was fine so far as it went, they said, but it went not nearly far enough. "The *nonextension* of slavery where it is *not*, and the *maintenance* of slavery where it is!"—the real meaning of the Wilmot Proviso, insisted the *American Freeman*—fell far short of the true Liberty policy of using all constitutional means to restrict *and destroy* bondage in America. Unless Barnburner Democrats and antislavery Whigs were willing to go beyond the commitments of the Proviso and declare "eternal war to all government support of slavery," the Liberty party should resist coalition. To do otherwise would be to sacrifice principle, identity, and moral influence without materially advancing the cause of the slave. "Descend to the level of the Wilmot Proviso in 1848," warned the *Albany Patriot*, "and what will there be of you to rally in 1849?" Even Salmon Chase advised the Barnburners that "The Free Territory question, in discussion, must bring up the whole slavery question inevitably. Our contest is with the Slave Power, and it will break us down unless we break it down. The People will not stop with the exclusion of slavery from territories: they will demand its complete denationalization."[1]

The likelihood that the "Red Fox," Martin Van Buren, would become the Wilmot Proviso candidate of course did nothing to lessen Liberty mistrust of the free-soil enterprise. While third party men approved his anti-Texas stand in 1844 and his newly expressed hostility to slavery expansion, powerful objections remained. For too long Van Buren had been the doughface incarnate—the Northern man with Southern principles, or, in John Quincy Adams's words, "the catchpole of slaveholders." Liberty advocates bitterly recalled the ex-President's "proslavery" stand on the *Amistad* case (in which mutinous Africans, captured in American waters, sought freedom from Spanish slavetraders) and his support for a ban on the delivery of "incendiary" abolitionist mail in the South. In particular, they deplored his objections, reaffirmed in his recent letter to the Utica convention, to abolition in the District of Columbia. It seemed to Joshua Leavitt, for one, that "the Liberty party *cannot* support him, without deliberately giving the lie to all our own declarations for fifteen years past." "Van Buren is too old a sinner to hope for his conversion," thought Whittier. And even if the wily New Yorker did suddenly espouse more liberal principles, Amos Tuck maintained, "it will be difficult to *feel* that by-gones are by-gones."[2]

Yet as the Buffalo meeting approached, Liberty members warmed somewhat to the idea of a free-soil alliance—even to the prospect of Little Van's candidacy. Partly this softened stance reflected the persuasiveness of zealous coalitionists like Chase and Gamaliel Bailey, who made a strong case for meeting the Proviso men halfway. To those who warned against any lowering of the Liberty standard, Bailey replied with the familiar Western argument that, given constitutional restraints, "the real object of the Liberty Party" was not immediate abolition, but simply a divorce of government from slavery. It therefore made sense, he reasoned, for slavery's foes to concentrate "for a sea-

[1] *American Freeman*, June 14, 1848; Lewis Tappan to John P. Hale, June 20, 1848, Joshua Leavitt to Hale, July 3, 1848, Hale Papers, BLD; *Albany Patriot*, Apr. 26, 1848; Chase to John Van Buren, June [29], 1848, Tilden Papers.
[2] *Liberty Standard*, July 20, 1848; Leavitt to Joshua R. Giddings, July 6, 1848, Giddings Papers; Whittier to William F. Channing, July 1, 1848, quoted in Samuel T. Pickard, *Life and Letters of John Greenleaf Whittier*, 2 vols. (Boston, 1894), I, 333-34; Tuck to Gerrit Smith, Aug. 2, 1848, Smith Papers.

son" on the Wilmot Proviso. And while Liberty men should stick by
Hale as long as he remained in the field, Van Buren's "just, noble, and
patriotic" defense of free soil entitled him to serious consideration if
Hale stepped aside. Only the ex-President's reservations on abolition in
the nation's capital continued to give Bailey pause.[3]

The assurances of the Barnburners also won over a good many Liberty men. Ohio and Massachusetts free-soil men had for some months
approached the party's position that slavery be "denationalized," and
during July the Barnburners of New York showed signs of moving in
that direction. On the sticky point of abolition in the District, Van
Buren himself kept his peace. But his Radical associates insisted that all
was well. Indeed, David Dudley Field informed a Wisconsin correspondent: ". . . I *believe* he would assent not only to a repeal of the
Acts of Congress respecting slavery in the District, but to a removal of
the seat of government to a free soil." Typical was the growing respect
accorded the Proviso forces by the *American Freeman*. At first highly
critical of those whose antislavery principles asked no more than free
territory, by August the *Freeman* struck a decidedly more appreciative
tone. "The new movement is daily becoming more and more radical,"
concluded its editor, Sherman Booth. "The chief speakers at the various meetings begin to discuss the evils of slavery in all its phases, freely,
and to speak of it as a thing accursed and doomed to destruction—to
predict its entire overthrow as the result of the issue which the South
has forced upon the North." Moreover, he was convinced, "this movement is more radical at the bottom, than the outward manifestation of it
—than the leaders themselves dare avow."[4]

Caught in the middle of the Liberty debate over a free-soil alliance
was the party's reluctant nominee, John P. Hale. Still eager to escape
the burdens of candidacy if it could honorably be done, yet uncertain

[3] *National Era*, July 6, 13, 1848; Bailey to Van Buren, Aug. 2, 1848, Van Buren
Papers.
[4] Field to Charles S. Benton, July 25, 1848, Charles S. Benton Papers, SHSW;
American Freeman, June 28, Aug. 2, 1848. Charles Sumner had long predicted that
espousal of the Wilmot Proviso would inevitably lead to more radical goals. "They
have proclaimed Slavery to be *wrong*," he wrote of the Barnburners early in 1847,
"& have pledged themselves against its *extension*. It is difficult to see how they can
sustain themselves *merely* on that ground. The premise sustains a broader conclusion, that is, the duty of no longer allowing the *continuance* of the evil any where
within our constitutional action. They must become Abolitionists." Sumner to
Joshua R. Giddings, Jan. 21, 1847, Giddings Papers.

what duty and self-respect demanded, Hale was buffeted by advice from all sides. Some Liberty men, among them Bailey and Chase, pressed him to withdraw his candidacy so that his name might be placed before the Buffalo convention as one unaffiliated with any party. For as Charles Francis Adams had recently observed, Conscience Whigs and Barnburners would be more inclined "to create a candidate" than "to adopt one."[5] Others agreed with Lewis Tappan that Hale should stand firm. "Should you resign previous to the Convention," the New Yorker warned Hale, "it would look like conscious weakness on our part, & strengthen the feeling on the part of the Barnburners that Mr. Van Buren will be the nominee of the Buffalo convention."[6] Still others insisted that "the time has not yet come when we can coalesce with the Barnburners" without sacrificing "our moral position, in which our strength lies." They urged union with the antislavery Whigs of Massachusetts and Ohio, but without the New Yorkers, and they too entreated Hale to hold fast.[7]

By July Hale had plotted his course. Having carefully studied Northern opinion, he had realistically concluded that most antislavery advocates—Liberty men included—would unite at Buffalo, and that Martin Van Buren would probably be the convention's choice. He therefore proposed that Liberty representatives attend the Buffalo meeting so as to "exert as favorable an influence as possible." For his part, he would place in the hands of some reliable delegate "a letter declining to stand." If the convention adopted a platform satisfactory to Liberty men, the letter should be used. If not, it should be withheld and the Liberty party could proceed independently. Despite the objections of Lewis Tappan and others who mistrusted the Van Burenites and feared that a letter such as Hale suggested "might be used injudiciously—under excitement—even by your best friends," Hale stuck to his decision. So little encouragement did he give to those who sought his preferment that even Liberty stalwarts like Samuel Lewis of Ohio

[5] Hale to Chase, June 8, 14, 1848, Chase Papers, PHS; Bailey to Charles Sumner, May 31, 1848, Sumner Papers; Amos Tuck to George G. Fogg, June 1, 1848, Amos Tuck Papers, NHHS; Adams to John G. Palfrey, July 16, 1848, Letterbook, Charles Francis Adams Papers, MHS.
[6] Tappan to Hale, July 8, 1848, L. D. Catell to Hale, July 24, 1848, T. Gilbert to Hale, July 27, 1848, Hale Papers, NHHS.
[7] Amos Tuck to Hale, June 21, 1848, Rufus Elmer to Hale, July 7, 1848, Hale Papers, NHHS.

began to wonder whether Van Buren might not be, after all, the best man on whom "to unite all of antislavery influence."[8]

2

During the second week in August 1848 between ten and twenty thousand delegates and lookers-on poured into Buffalo to join in the creation of the Free Soil party. They came from every Northern state, three slave states (Delaware, Maryland, and Virginia), and the District of Columbia. Among those on hand when the convention opened were Barnburners Preston King, Benjamin F. Butler, David Dudley Field, and Samuel J. Tilden; antislavery Whigs Charles Francis Adams, Stephen C. Phillips, Richard Henry Dana, Jr., and Joshua Giddings; and Liberty men Chase, Leavitt, and Stanton. Also present were a motley assortment of disgruntled Clay Whigs, Liberty Leaguers, New York land reformers, workingmen, champions of cheap postage, and political freebooters seeking to repair broken fortunes. Because of the unwieldy number of spectators and delegates, the real work of the convention was left to a select "Committee of Conference" (composed equally of Whigs, Democrats, and Liberty men) which met in the Universalist church. Decisions made by these "conferees" were then referred to the mass convention, "consisting of all persons who had come up to Buffalo for Free Soil," which gathered under a huge tent in a nearby park.[9]

Speeches and formalities aside, the first major task of the convention was the framing of an acceptable platform. Much of this work fell to Salmon P. Chase, an old hand at such matters, although all factions had a voice in the preparation of resolutions. By the morning of the second day a draft platform had been hammered into shape. As was to be expected, it offered something for everyone. In addition to planks against slavery expansion and in favor of separating the national government from slavery, the new creed called for cheap postage and

[8] Hale to Lewis Tappan, July 6, 1848 (copy), Tappan to Hale, July 8, 14, 1848, Lewis to Hale, July 10, 29, 1848, Hale Papers, NHHS.
[9] The history of the Buffalo Free Soil convention is by now a well-told tale. See, e.g., Rayback, *Free Soil*, 223-30; Sewell, *Hale*, 99-104; Frederick J. Blue, *The Free Soilers: Third Party Politics, 1848-54* (Urbana, 1973), 70-80. Oliver Dyer's *Phonographic Report of the Proceedings of the National Free Soil Convention at Buffalo, N.Y., August 9th and 10th, 1848* (Buffalo, 1848) is full, fair, and surprisingly witty.

cheap government, river and harbor improvements, tariff reform, and free homesteads. As B. F. Butler read the proposed platform to the sweltering throng in the giant tent, "Every sentence, every paragraph was cheered into its legal existence." When the question was put on its adoption, the convention exploded in shouts, wild applause, a waving of hats and handkerchiefs. "In my whole life, I never witnessed such a scene," exulted the normally phlegmatic Adams.[10]

This done, the conferees repaired once more to the relative calm of the Universalist meetinghouse and undertook to nominate a candidate for President. Oliver Dyer, the convention's official reporter, contended that at the outset preference for John P. Hale "was strongly predominant and seemingly irresistible."[11] In fact, however, the Senator never had a chance. For not only had his own well-known reluctance to run dampened enthusiasm for his candidacy, but some of the most influential Liberty spokesmen came to Buffalo prepared to swap his claims for platform concessions. In exchange for Barnburner support of a "thorough Liberty platform," Chase, Leavitt, and Stanton privately agreed to back Van Buren's nomination and make it "harmonious & unanimous if possible."[12] Once it became known that Justice McLean, the first choice of most Conscience Whigs, had declined to stand, the New Yorker's selection was a foregone conclusion. Assurances that Van Buren had agreed to enter the convention on equal terms with all candidates and that the Barnburners would abide by whatever decisions were made placated many critics. So too did B. F. Butler's affirmation that if elected President, Van Buren would sign any bill outlawing slavery in the District of Columbia. After Stanton had reiterated Hale's willingness to forsake his Liberty nomination, a straw ballot was taken. It showed a clear preference for Van Buren: 244 votes to 183 for Hale, 23 for Giddings, 13 for Adams, and four votes scattered. Except for Stanton, Leavitt, and Chase, Liberty men stuck loyally by Hale. Whigs, who apparently concluded that the ex-President was "the best man to

---

[10] Richard Henry Dana, Jr., *Speeches in Stirring Times and Letters to a Son*, ed. by Richard H. Dana, III (Boston, 1910), 150-52; Adams, Diary, Aug. 10, 1848, Adams Papers.
[11] Oliver Dyer, *Great Senators of the United States Forty Years Ago (1848 and 1849), with Personal Recollections and Delineations of Calhoun, Benton, Clay, Webster, General Houston, Jefferson Davis, and other Distinguished Statesmen of that Period* (New York, 1889), 95.
[12] Stanton to Hale, Aug. 20, 1848, Hale Papers, NHHS.

knock in pieces the main prop of Slavery, the Northern Democratic party," gave Van Buren his edge.[13]

Mindful of their pledge to the Barnburners, Leavitt and Stanton now persuaded other Liberty leaders to make Van Buren's nomination unanimous. His brethren behind him, Leavitt then made his way to the platform. Amid great stillness, his voice taut with emotion, he pronounced the Liberty party "not dead, but TRANSLATED," and moved to make Van Buren's nomination unanimous. Another Liberty stalwart, Samuel Lewis, made a short seconding speech, and the conferees carried the motion by noisy acclamation. To balance the ticket, the Free Soilers selected rectitudinous Charles Francis Adams for Vice President. With "VAN BUREN AND FREE SOIL, ADAMS AND LIBERTY," they would carry their cause to the people.[14]

3

The Free Soil convention of 1848 has often been portrayed as a great turning point in the political war against slavery. Some say that by acquiescing in the nomination of rank outsiders, and by embracing a platform replacing direct abolition with mere non-extension "and a multitude of distracting demands that appealed only to the selfish interests of Northern whites," Liberty men destroyed political *abolitionism* forever. In their hunger for victory they had traded "moral purpose for votes." Thereafter, antislavery politicians directed their assaults more against the "Slave Power" than against slavery itself. What had begun as a crusade for black equality had become an opportunistic campaign for white Yankee supremacy.[15]

13 Sewell, *Hale*, 102-3. Theodore Foster claimed that "A large part of the Conferees would have preferred Chase as a candidate for Vice President," had his Democratic views not so closely resembled Van Buren's. Foster, "History of the Liberty Party," 114.
14 Leavitt to Hale, Aug. 22, 1848, Hale Papers, NHHS; Adams, Diary, Aug. 10, 1848, Adams Papers; George W. Julian, *Political Recollections, 1840-1872* (Chicago, 1883), 60-61; Dyer, *Phonographic Report*, 31.
15 Kraditor, *Means and Ends in American Abolitionism*, 182; Stewart, *Giddings*, 157. See also Wyatt-Brown, *Tappan*, 281; Goodell, *Slavery and Anti-Slavery*, 481-82; James A. Rawley, *Race & Politics: "Bleeding Kansas" and the Coming of the Civil War* (Philadelphia, 1969), 12; C. Duncan Rice, *The Rise and Fall of Black Slavery* (New York, 1975), 348-49. On the difference between slavery and the Slave Power, see Larry Gara, "Slavery and the Slave Power: A Crucial Distinction," *Civil War History*, XV, No. 1 (Mar. 1969), 5-18.

There is some truth in this view. Although Adams's record was better than Van Buren's, neither candidate, as William Goodell pointedly remarked, was famous for his abolitionism.[16] Horse traders as well as idealists (and at least one pickpocket) roamed the convention grounds: indeed, the striking harmony at Buffalo owed much to the backroom deal in which Chase, Leavitt, and Stanton threw their support to Van Buren in exchange for platform concessions. Despite such concessions, moreover, the Free Soil platform fell short of the official Liberty creed in several respects. Gone was any open declaration of abolition intent. Gone too were earlier denunciations of the Fugitive Slave Act, the three-fifths clause, and racial discrimination. And while Liberty men esteemed the planks that called upon the federal government to divorce itself from slavery and that forthrightly proclaimed "No more slave states and no more slave territory," they doubtless viewed as needlessly propitiatory a resolution that discountenanced congressional interference with slavery in states where it already existed.[17] Clearly, the Barnburners had not been the only ones to yield ground.

Yet what those who stress the "capitulation" of the abolitionist forces overlook is that the Liberty party—especially its Western wing—had been tending toward the Free Soil position for years, and that most of its adherents readily accepted the Buffalo platform as their own. A small group of Eastern radicals aside, the primary objective of most Liberty men had from the outset been not immediate abolition (which they maintained lay outside the constitutional powers of any party), but the absolute severance of government and slavery. And this cardinal doctrine—which went beyond mere free soil—was firmly embedded in the Buffalo platform. Even so radical an abolitionist as Sherman Booth, who on most issues sympathized with Gerrit Smith and the Macedonians, found the Free Soil creed more than acceptable. "It pledges the new party against the admission of any more Slave States, and to employ the Federal Government not only to limit, localize, and discourage, but to abolish slavery wherever it has Constitutional power to do so," he told readers of the *American Freeman*. "This is all the Liberty party, as such, ever demanded." So too Owen Lovejoy, brother of the martyred Elijah, assured readers of the *Western Citizen* that "the principles of Liberty are in this movement, undergird and surround it—

[16] Goodell, *Slavery and Anti-Slavery*, 478-79.
[17] McKee, *National Conventions and Platforms*, 66-69.

the immediate object aimed at is one which we cordially approve, and the ultimate object is identical—the extinction of slavery."[18]

As for the rights of black men, it is undeniable, as Eric Foner has pointed out, that "the Free Soilers were the first major anti-slavery group to avoid the question of Negro rights in their national platform." Yet even here less violence was done to Liberty principles than such a statement implies. For while many in the new party (particularly Barnburners) held openly racist views and looked upon free soil as a means of keeping *Negroes* out of Western territories, many others—including most Conscience Whigs and some ex-Democrats—found slavery a *moral* evil and shared Liberty notions on race. The omission of a platform statement in defense of equal rights indicated less an abandonment of principle than a tactical decision taking cognizance of Americans' nearly universal belief in white supremacy. At least that was the way most Liberty men looked at it. Despite the protests of some Barnburners, Liberty and Conscience Whig delegates saw to it that Negro leaders Frederick Douglass and Henry Bibb were allowed to address the convention, and although a few like Samuel R. Ward criticized the Free Soil party's shortcomings, most blacks gave it their support. Its greater likelihood of success apparently helped to offset misgivings about Van Buren and the platform's silence on Negro rights. "In this movement we see the beginning, the end of which will witness abolition of American Slavery," announced a group of Boston Negroes in founding a Free Soil club. "Even now it is causing slave holders at their homes to tremble, as the northern breezes bear to their ears the earliest sound of the buffalo's horn."[19]

In its attention to basic economic concerns—tariff reform, internal

18 *American Freeman*, Aug. 23, 1848; *Western Citizen*, Aug. 22, 1848, quoted in Edward Magdol, *Owen Lovejoy: Abolitionist in Congress* (New Brunswick, N.J., 1967), 89. See also *Liberty Standard*, Aug. 17, 24, 1848; *Anti-Slavery Chronicle and Free Labor Advocate*, Aug. 25, 1848. Although himself critical of the proceedings at Buffalo, Lewis Tappan explained to an English friend: "The natural desire of being in a large party, the hope that they should be able to guide the new party, & a belief that the Buffalo platform was substantially the Liberty platform, induced many, probably most, of the Liberty party" to acquiesce in the Free Soil merger. Tappan to Joseph Sturge, Nov. 8, 1848, Tappan Papers.
19 Eric Foner, "Politics and Prejudice: The Free Soil Party and the Negro, 1849-1852," *Journal of Negro History*, L, No. 4 (Oct. 1965), 239; Dyer, *Phonographic Report*, 21, 24; *Reunion of the Free-Soilers of 1848 at Downer Landing, Hingham, Mass., August 9, 1877* (Boston, 1877), 29; Philip S. Foner, *The Life and Writings of Frederick Douglass*, 4 vols. (New York, 1950), II, 71-72; Quarles, *Black Abolitionists*, 185-86; *Boston Daily Republican*, Sept. 16, 1848.

improvements, homesteads—the Buffalo platform also broke with Liberty practice. Yet once again, the change was less than radical and in no sense represented a caving in to Barnburner or Conscience Whig pressures. Support for a broader platform had been growing for years, and not only among Liberty Leaguers. By the end of 1847, for instance, the *American Freeman*, once swift to defend the "one idea," had come around to the position that the Liberty party had a responsibility for *all* men, white as well as black, and that that responsibility required opposition not only to slavery, but to "protection, tariffs, LAND MONOPOLIES, RUIN AND WAR." The Ohio Free Territory Convention in June had called for free farms as a corollary to free soil.[20] To many Liberty men, therefore, the extended Free Soil creed—particularly in its call for homesteads—represented a step forward, not backward.[21]

Martin Van Buren's candidacy was another, and to Liberty men less appealing, kettle of fish. Having so recently excoriated his softness on slavery, many now found it hard to sing his praises. Some turned their backs in disgust, nodding with approval when "Hosea Biglow" complained:

> I used to vote for Martin, but, I swan, I'm clean
>   disgusted,—
> He aint the man thet I can say is fittin' to
>   be trusted;
> He aint half antislav'ry 'nough,
>   nor I aint sure, ez some be,
> He'd go in fer abolishin' the Deestrict
>   o' Columby.

Others apologetically pointed to the "glorious" platform and the political advantages of union with the Barnburners as justification for support of the Little Magician.[22] A surprising number of Liberty men, however, ate crow as if it were quail and enthusiastically touted Van Buren's newly discovered virtues. "I am getting my steam up to the highest pitch (below the bursting point) in favor of *Van Buren & Adams*," Joshua Leavitt bubbled soon after returning from Buffalo. "I

---

[20] *American Freeman*, Dec. 22, 1847; *Addresses and Proceedings of the Free Territory Convention of Ohio*, 6.
[21] *American Freeman*, Aug. 2, 16, 23, 1848; *Liberty Standard*, Aug. 24, 1848.
[22] James Russell Lowell, *The Writings of James Russell Lowell*, Riverside ed., 10 vols. (Boston, 1890), VIII, 141; Sewell, *Hale*, 103.

visited our 'glorious old man,' on my way home, & have entire satisfaction that he is with us, heart & soul, & will be with us to the last battle against the Slave Power." Similarly, Austin Willey commended the former President as an "able statesman" of unimpeachable private character whose "antislavery objects are essentially those of the Liberty party." Sherman Booth, who had cast a straw ballot for Gerrit Smith at Buffalo, confessed to Wisconsin Liberty men that "had it been necessary to have secured his nomination, we should have changed our vote for Van Buren." For the New Yorker was not only the strongest available candidate, he insisted, but one whose principles were every bit as sound as John P. Hale's. Van Buren's letter of acceptance, although characteristically ambiguous, convinced many that Booth was correct—that even on the question of abolition in the District of Columbia, the Free Soil candidate's position differed little from that of the Liberty party.[23] In this they were doubtless deceived, by their own naïveté as well as by the Magician's congenital evasiveness. But most Liberty advocates supported Van Buren in good faith as the best man to rally the antislavery army, not as a calculated attempt to buy votes at the expense of principle.[24]

By no means did all political abolitionists agree, however, that the Free Soil party represented antislavery's best hope. Despite the arguments of Giddings, Sumner, and others, large numbers of Whigs continued to look to that party for effective assaults upon the Slave Power. The sole effect of the Free Soil alliance, warned Horace Greeley, would be to enhance the Democratic candidate Lewis Cass's prospects and, by undercutting antislavery representatives in Washington, to "enable the Extensionists to carry Slavery to the Pacific without a struggle in Congress." It was one thing "to be sacrificed for the sake of Principle," he wrote Giddings. But "to court ruin for the benefit of Cass I do not find so inviting." Many others found Van Buren's "new-

---

[23] Leavitt to Salmon P. Chase, Aug. 21, 1848, Chase Papers, PHS; *Liberty Standard*, Aug. 24, 1848; *American Freeman*, Aug. 23, 1848; Hallowell (Me.) *Free Soil Republican*, Aug. 31, 1848; *National Era*, Aug. 24, Sept. 7, 1848.
[24] As early as July 28, two weeks before the Free Soil convention, Henry Stanton had written to Salmon Chase: "I am satisfied that Mr. Van Buren must be the man for presidential candidate. There is no avoiding it. Nor am I satisfied that it would be well to do so if we could. He is strong in states & regions where the Antislavery aspects of the question have not taken very strong hold. Besides, the main prop of the slave power has been the northern democracy: & he is *the* man to shiver that in pieces & forever." John McLean Papers, LC.

born zeal for 'Free Soil' " unconvincing and bridled at the thought of union with the Barnburners. "Some of the scamps, I wish had stayed where they were," grumbled one antislavery Whig. "As prince [Achille] Murat said 'I have no prejudice—but I do *not* like Turkey Buzzard.' " Such men either boycotted the 1848 campaign or gave lukewarm support to the Whig ticket.[25]

Outside New York, Vermont, Wisconsin, and Illinois, few Wilmot Proviso Democrats endorsed the Free Soil enterprise. A good many like Gideon Welles, Thomas Hart Benton, and Francis P. Blair felt great affection for Van Buren and sympathy for the cause he now led. But, mistrustful of his new associates and reluctant to throw away their influence in a losing cause, they either sat out the election or cast a grudging vote for Cass. Notwithstanding his plentiful statements in support of popular sovereignty, Cass was at times sold to Northern Democrats as a Proviso man—a piece of political hocus-pocus that helped check defections to Van Buren.[26]

A small but notable group of Liberty men also rejected the Free Soil union. Of these the most important were Gerrit Smith and other Liberty Leaguers who protested that while the Free Soilers may have formed an antislavery party, "The Buffalo Convention was an anti-abolition Convention" because it failed to deny the right of property in man. Besides, as William Goodell later noted, such men had found it bad policy as well as poor principle "to set the claim of liberty on the lowest possible ground, that of the non-extension of slavery." To the Leaguers were added the likes of F. J. LeMoyne and Lewis Tappan,

[25] Greeley to Giddings, June 20, 1848, Miscellaneous Manuscripts, NYHS; Lewis D. Campbell speech to the United States House of Representatives, Feb. 19, 1850, *Cong. Globe*, 31st Cong., 1st sess., 177; Walter Mitchell to George F. Hoar, Sept. 25, 1848, Hoar Papers. See also Greeley to Schuyler Colfax, May 1, 1847, Sept. 15, 1848, Horace Greeley Papers, NYPL; William H. Seward to Salmon P. Chase, June 12, 1848, Chase Papers, LC; George N. Briggs to Charles Sumner, Sept. 1, 1848, L. D. Campbell to Sumner, Oct. 19, 1848, Sumner Papers; Benjamin F. Wade to Mrs. Wade, Oct. 27, 1848, Benjamin F. Wade Papers, LC.
[26] Welles to [A. E. Burr], Apr. 21, May 26, 1848, Welles to [Martin Van Buren], Sept. 30, 1848 (copy), Welles to Editor of [Hartford] *Times, c.* 1856, Welles Papers, CHS; Welles to [James T. Pratt], Mar. 1854 (copy), Welles Papers, LC; William P. Pettit to Welles, Oct. 28, 1848, Welles Papers, NYPL; Benton to Martin Van Buren, May 29, 1848, Van Buren Papers; Marcus Morton to Azariah C. Flagg, June 17, 1848, Flagg Papers, Columbia University; John A. Dix to Thomas H. Benton, Apr. 15, 1854 (copy), Dix Papers; Smith, *Liberty and Free Soil Parties*, 125-26. On the Vermont Barnburner movement, see David M. Ludlum, *Social Ferment in Vermont, 1791-1850* (Montpelier, 1948), 189-98; Montpelier *Green Mountain Freeman*, July 20, 1848.

pioneer abolitionists who found the Buffalo creed "not entirely satisfactory" and who shrewdly remarked Van Buren's very gingerly acceptance of its basic planks. Late in September 1848, at Canastota, New York, this "little remnant" adopted the League's broad platform and the Liberty party's name, preserving, so they thought, the true faith of political abolition.[27]

Yet although it lived on in name, the real Liberty party was now a thing of the past. Its accomplishments had hardly been such as to satisfy the hopes and expectations of its founders. ". . . It had a fair trial for eight years," Theodore Foster ultimately concluded, "and it accomplished nothing of any moment as a party until it had united with portions of other parties, and thereby ceased to maintain a separate existence."[28] Not once had a Liberty nominee gained office solely on the strength of Liberty votes. Only through bargains with other parties (as in New Hampshire) had abolition candidates won election, and even then victories were costly and exceedingly rare. Indeed, their inevitable price was loss of Liberty identity through absorption in some new coalition. Nor had the third party been very successful in imprinting antislavery principles upon the major parties by wielding the balance of power. Rarely had the Liberty vote influenced the outcome of an election, and when it had, as in the 1844 presidential contest, few could take satisfaction in the result. And while Northern Whigs and even Democrats grew increasingly receptive to antislavery (if not abolitionist) arguments, their change of heart owed more to internal pressures and the course of events—especially the gag rule, Texas, and the Mexican War—than to Liberty party leverage.

Even so, Liberty party pioneers could take pride in having prepared the way for mightier antislavery coalitions to come. Despite elaborate tables of organization, their party structures had been haphazard and incomplete. Only at election time were Liberty committees useful agencies of coordination. But the third party press, for all its troubles, proved remarkably effective in broadcasting antislavery doctrines throughout the free states. So too, Liberty party pamphleteers, lecturers, and well-advertised mass conventions, like the great Southern

[27] Smith to John W. North, Jan. 9, 1849, Letterbook, Tappan to Smith, Sept. 11, 1848, Smith Papers; Smith, *Letter to J. K. Ingalls, Editor of the* Landmark, *New-York* (Peterboro, N.Y., Aug. 15, 1848); Tappan to Joseph Sturge, Nov. 8, 1848, Tappan Papers.
[28] Foster, "History of the Liberty Party," 126.

and Western Liberty meeting of 1845, educated Northerners to the threat slavery posed to all Americans and developed a constitutional program for its destruction. In its essentials, moreover, that program outlived the Liberty party itself and became, with refinements and slight alteration, the keel on which the Free Soil, Free Democratic, and Republican parties, were laid. It was because they recognized this fact, this continuity of principle, that the vast majority of Liberty men continued in the years ahead to give such parties their undivided loyalty.

4

Intoxicated by the enthusiasm of the Buffalo proceedings, Free Soilers threw themselves into the 1848 campaign wholeheartedly and with high hopes. A swing through the Western Reserve on his way home from the convention convinced Salmon Chase that in that quarter, at least, Van Buren could count on the backing of antislavery men of all persuasions. Barring some unforeseen circumstance, he concluded, the Free Soil slate would sweep the Reserve by at least 13,000 votes. "This," he confidently assured Van Buren, "will ensure the vote of the state." George G. Fogg, editor of the Concord, New Hampshire, *Independent Democrat,* predicted that Van Buren would carry New York and enough small states to throw the election into the House of Representatives. Even John A. Dix, who harbored grave doubts about the independent movement, admitted that the free-soil impulse might well take the North by storm. To the very last, many Free Soilers held strong hopes of capturing New York, Massachusetts, Ohio, and Vermont.[29]

Such optimism, while extravagant beyond reason, was not wholly without basis. For one thing, as Dix and others observed, slavery restriction was an intensely popular issue throughout the free states. As the only party to endorse the Wilmot Proviso openly, the Free Soilers stood ready to reap rich harvests among Northern voters resentful

[29] Chase to Van Buren, Aug. 21, 1848, Dix to Van Buren, Oct. 7, 1848, Van Buren Papers; Fogg to John P. Hale, Aug. 21, 1848, Hale Papers, NHHS; Marshall M. Strong to H. A. Tenney, Sept. 11, 1848, Horace A. Tenney Papers, SHSW; Foster, "History of the Liberty Party," 118.

of "Slave Power" arrogance and determined to keep Western territories free from slavery's deadening grasp. Furthermore, the Free Soil
party could, as the Liberty party could not, count on the active support
of many prominent and seasoned politicians. Among those who
stumped energetically for Van Buren and Adams were Charles Sumner, Henry Wilson, Amasa Walker, and Anson Burlingame in Massachusetts; Senator Hale and Amos Tuck in New Hampshire; William
Slade and Edward A. Stansbury in Vermont; and John M. Niles in
Connecticut. David Wilmot, naturally enough, preached up Free Soil
in Pennsylvania, while in New York former Whig Congressman Seth
Gates and the young editor of the *Brooklyn Daily Eagle,* Walt Whitman, made common cause with Barnburner bigwigs. In the Old Northwest, one-time Democrats like Benjamin Tappan, Jacob Brinkerhoff,
and Flavius J. Littlejohn joined Joshua Giddings, Austin Blair, George
W. Julian, and other ex-Whigs to whip up enthusiasm for the new antislavery party. In Missouri, one of six slave states to field Free Soil
tickets, Frank Blair, Jr., beat the drums for Van Buren.[30]

Inevitably, a certain amount of friction developed within the Free
Soil camp, yet to a remarkable extent former Democrats, Whigs, and
Liberty men pulled amicably together—further heightening hopes for
the third party. The "Buffalo policy" of dividing nominations among
candidates from all factions was extended to the states as a spur to
harmony and cooperation. In Massachusetts, for example, Free Soilers
picked Stephen C. Phillips, a Conscience Whig, and John Mills, a Proviso Democrat, to head their slate. Likewise, New York Free Soilers
chose Barnburner John A. Dix for governor and Seth Gates, a Whig
turned Liberty man, for lieutenant governor. Nominations to lesser
offices were similarly spread around.[31]

Although handicapped by its late start and haphazard organization,
the new party waged an energetic campaign that skillfully averted internal differences by concentrating on a shared concern for slavery
restriction. Throughout the North, Free Soilers published documents
and addresses, circulated campaign newspapers, and held rallies to
pillory the "Slave Power," expose the weaknesses of Taylor and Cass,

[30] Smith, *Liberty and Free Soil Parties,* 142-45; Schlesinger, Jr., *Age of Jackson,*
466-67; Patrick W. Riddleberger, *George Washington Julian, Radical Republican:
A Study in Nineteenth-Century Politics and Reform* (Indianapolis, 1966), 37-40.
[31] Brauer, *Cotton versus Conscience,* 243-44; Henry S. Randall to Martin Van
Buren, Sept. 23, 1848, Van Buren Papers.

and tout the virtues of Van Buren and free soil. James Russell Lowell hurried to get his mordantly witty *Biglow Papers* in print in time to raise "the laugh at War & Slavery & Doughfaces to some purpose." And everywhere Free Soilers anticipated a strong enough showing on election day to strike terror in slaveholders' hearts.[32]

Despite such energy and gusto, the vote for Van Buren proved disappointingly small. On election day, Taylor won a narrow victory over Cass. Van Buren received barely 10 per cent of the popular vote, more than half of his total coming from Massachusetts and New York. In part, the Free Soilers' poor showing stemmed from organizational breakdowns and a shortage of funds.[33] But much more damaging, it seems, were the assiduous efforts of rival Northern politicos to preempt the Free Soilers' basic principle: resistance to slavery expansion. With Democrats playing up Cass's Northern background and insisting that popular sovereignty would keep the territories free, and Whigs like Tom Corwin telling the world "I *know* Gen. Taylor will not veto the Proviso," Free Soilers found it hard to break down old party loyalties. In the end, even the Sewards and Greeleys, Bentons and Blairs spurned the Free Soil alliance.[34]

In their post mortems on the election, most Free Soilers admitted disappointment at "the smallness of our vote," yet professed to see light on the horizon. To begin with, the 291,804 popular votes for Van Buren represented a nearly fivefold increase over Birney's 1844 total. Moreover, in two states Free Soil ballots had determined the outcome of the election, costing Cass New York and Taylor Ohio. Never before had the balance-of-power tactic looked so formidable. Here and there—in parts of Vermont, in Worcester County, Massachusetts, in the "Burned-over District" of upstate New York, in northeastern Illinois and southeastern Wisconsin, and on the Western Reserve—Van

[32] Smith, *Liberty and Free Soil Parties,* 143-45; James Russell Lowell to Mary Peabody Mann, Sept. 10, 1848, Mann Papers. So spirited was the Free Soil campaign that even some Garrisonian abolitionists seem to have been seduced. See Samuel J. May to Charles Sumner, July 12, 1848, Sumner Papers; May to [?], Aug. 2, 1848, Antislavery Collection, Cornell University; May to Sidney H. Gay, quoted in *National Anti-Slavery Standard,* Aug. 17, 1848; Garrison to Mrs. Garrison, July 18, 1848, Garrison Papers; *Liberator,* Aug. 25, 1848; Rayback, *Free Soil,* 250-51.
[33] See, e.g., B. F. Butler to Martin Van Buren, Oct. 3, 1848, Van Buren Papers; Adam Jewett to Chase, Oct. 24, 1848, Chase Papers, LC; Bradford R. Wood to Charles Sumner, Oct. 26, 1848, Sumner Papers.
[34] Salmon P. Chase to Charles Sumner, Nov. 27, 1848, Chase, *Diary and Correspondence,* 142-45; Rayback, *Free Soil,* 253-57, 294-97.

Buren won a plurality (occasionally even a majority) of the popular vote. Although he received not a single electoral vote, in Vermont, Massachusetts, and New York Van Buren finished second, ahead of Cass. Furthermore, Van Buren's count had come largely out of the hides of Democrats, and it seemed to many Free Soilers that his candidacy had, as hoped, rendered the Northern Democracy bankrupt— if not in numbers, then in doctrines on which to rally thereafter. Free state Democrats had no choice, Charles Sumner maintained, but to embrace the Buffalo creed. Simply by sticking to their principles, Free Soilers could insure an early triumph over the Slave Power.[35]

The Wilmot Proviso forces could also take pride and encouragement from the election of a dozen avowed Free Soilers to the Thirty-first Congress. A good many of these, lamented Ohio's abolitionist representative Joseph M. Root, seemed "more intent on imbuing their respective parties with the free soil spirit without disturbing their old organization than on building up a party devoted to the free soil principle." Yet with House Democrats and Whigs in near balance, the likelihood that Free Soilers might wield the balance of power seemed great. With luck they might even capture the speakership—a heady prospect, given the extensive powers of that office.[36] In February 1849 Salmon P. Chase was elected to the United States Senate, sending antislavery spirits soaring still higher. Together, the ponderous, learned, deadly serious Chase and the breezy, quick-witted Jack Hale would carry the Free Soil message into the heretofore unregenerate upper house.[37]

More important than immediate party gains, however, were the Free Soilers' impact on Democrats and Whigs and the lessons of the campaign for the future. By threatening to draw antislavery voters away from the traditional parties, the Free Soilers forced Northern Whigs and Democrats to proclaim their own dedication to non-exten-

[35] Salmon P. Chase to Mrs. Chase, Nov. 14, 1848, Sumner to Chase, Nov. 16, 1848, Chase Papers, LC; Rayback, *Free Soil*, 281-87.
[36] *Cong. Globe,* 31st Cong., 1st sess., 1; Root to Joshua R. Giddings, June 12, 1849, Giddings Papers. The Free Soil representatives were Amos Tuck (N.H.), Horace Mann and Charles Allen (Mass.), Walter Booth (Conn.), Preston King (N.Y.), John W. Howe and David Wilmot (Pa.), Joshua Giddings and Joseph M. Root (Ohio), George W. Julian (Ind.), Charles Durkee (Wis.), and William Sprague (Mich.).
[37] On Chase's election, see Frederick J. Blue, "The Ohio Free Soilers and the Problems of Factionalism," *Ohio History,* LXXVI, No. 1 (Winter 1967), 17-32; Smith, *Liberty and Free Soil Parties,* chap. XI; below, pp. 206-9.

sion more loudly. As a result, antislavery arguments acquired an un-precedented currency throughout the North. Many—including a goodly number of clergymen—who had formerly stood aside, now spoke out sharply on behalf of free soil, free labor, free men. Never again would they stand mute when presented with threats of slavery expansion. Moreover, the massive challenge Free Soilers laid down to the established parties helped to break "the thraldom of party" and to increase the likelihood of more successful challenges in the future. In more ways than one the Republican party would build upon the prece-dent of the Free Soil insurgency.

8

Free Soil

LIBERTY PARTY DIEHARDS and Garrisonian nonresistants had criticized the Free Soilers for limiting their concern to the *restriction* of slavery, for neglecting abolition and racial equality in their anxiety to protect free white labor against an aggressive slavocracy. Free soil, while not without its uses, was too narrow, too slow, too indirect, to serve as an effective antislavery instrument. At best, they alleged, it was "weaker than a spider's web," unable to survive "a single breath of the Slave Power."[1] At worst, it acted as a positive hindrance to genuine abolitionism. Non-extension sentiment, complained Wendell Phillips, had swept "over the land; 'like a mildewed ear blasting his wholesome brother'—I ought to say *mother*, for I mean the good old cause. It has sifted just enou[gh] of namby pamby Antislavery into the common papers to take off the edge of people's interest in ours."[2] Nor did the demand written into the Buffalo platform that the federal government divorce itself from slavery wherever constitutionally possible strike such men as a promising tactic, especially since many Free Soilers construed this plank so timidly as to rule out abolition even in the District of Columbia.[3]

[1] *Liberator*, May 26, 1848.
[2] Phillips to Samuel J. May, Apr. 20, 1848, Anti-Slavery Collection, Cornell University.
[3] Among those who harbored grave misgivings about abolition in the District was John A. Dix. See Dix to Thomas H. Benton, Sept. 9, 1848, Dix Papers, Columbia University. Martin Van Buren held to a position in favor of Congress' power to abolish slavery there, but "strongly against the expediency of exercising it." Still, he

Yet such criticism, while in some ways fair, was unduly harsh. Rightly or wrongly, nearly all contemporaries looked upon non-extension as a potentially deadly antislavery weapon, an "iron shroud" that would not only stifle slavery's growth, but place it on the way to ultimate extinction. In unguarded moments even Garrison spoke of the Wilmot Proviso as "a measure vital to . . . [the Slave Power's] existence."[4] Southerners clearly saw it that way.[5] And even the most racist Free Soilers, while stressing its advantages to whites, noted with satisfaction that the Proviso "would insure the redemption, at an early day, of the negro from his bondage and his chains."[6]

It has become fashionable in recent years to emphasize the racial bigotry of Free Soilers (and Republicans) and to insist that their chief concern was to rid the territories not of slavery as such, but of all *blacks*. Perfectly content to let the peculiar institution flourish forever where already rooted, Free Soilers, it is said, sought merely to quarantine a sickness arising as much from the presence of large numbers of depraved and backward Negroes as from the system of bondage itself. In short, racial prejudice, more than moral concern, underlay the Wilmot Proviso.[7]

---

noted in his letter accepting the Free Soil nomination, circumstances had changed in recent years and he would no longer find it his duty if President to veto a bill for the abolition of slavery in the District of Columbia. Van Buren to Benjamin F. Butler *et al.*, Aug. 22, 1848, quoted in Gardiner, *Great Issue*, 142-50, esp. 147-48.

[4] Garrison to Henry C. Wright, Mar. 1, 1847, Garrison to Richard D. Webb, Mar. 1, 1847, Garrison Papers. Most historians, from Ulrich B. Phillips to Eugene Genovese, Alfred H. Conrad and John R. Meyers, have concurred in contemporary arguments that slavery had to expand or die. For a recent contradictory view, see Robert W. Fogel and Stanley L. Engerman, *Time on the Cross: The Economics of American Negro Slavery* (Boston, 1974).

[5] See, e.g., Richard N. Current, *John C. Calhoun* (New York, 1963), 79-81; William L. Barney, *The Road to Secession: A New Perspective on the Old South* (New York, 1972), xiv-xv, 5, 71, 171.

[6] Speech of David Wilmot at Albany, N.Y., Oct. 29, 1847, quoted in *Albany Atlas*, Nov. 9, 1847.

[7] See, e.g., Rice, *Black Slavery*, 348-49; Blue, *Free Soilers*, 81, 87, 102, 290; Morrison, *Democratic Politics and Sectionalism*, chap. IV, esp. 70-73; Filler, *Crusade Against Slavery*, 187; Leon Litwack, *North of Slavery: The Negro in the Free States, 1790-1860* (Chicago, 1961), 47-48; Eugene H. Berwanger, *The Frontier Against Slavery: Western Anti-Negro Prejudice and the Slavery Extension Controversy* (Urbana, 1967); Rawley, *Race & Politics*; Leonard L. Richards, *"Gentlemen of Property and Standing": Anti-Abolition Mobs in Jacksonian America* (New York, 1970), 163; C. Vann Woodward, *American Counterpoint: Slavery and Racism in the North-South Dialogue* (Boston, 1971), 147-50. The best accounts of the racial element in free soil (though ones which to my mind still overstate the influence of negrophobia) are Eric Foner's "Racial Attitudes of the New York Free Soilers,"

Without question, some Free Soilers despised blacks and championed
the Proviso as a means of "keeping the territory clean of negroes."[8]
Such men, of course, merely reflected the dominant racism of the age.
As George W. Julian observed: "The American people are emphatically a *negro-hating* people. By their actions, politically, socially, and
ecclesiastically, they declare that 'the negro is not a man.' " Democrats,
especially, held blacks in contempt and had traditionally taken the lead
in curtailing their rights in the North and South. Thus, while less
prejudiced than their Hunker rivals, most Barnburners exhibited an
attachment to white supremacy far stronger than that held by other
Free Soilers.[9]

Repeatedly, Free Soil Democrats insisted that "The question is not,
whether black men are to be made free, but whether we white men are
to remain free."[10] In an editorial entitled "WHAT SHALL BE DONE FOR
THE WHITE MEN?" the *New York Post* asserted that free-soil advocates
"put aside the question how long the slave owner is to hold his negroes,
and how he is to get rid of them, if at all; and only demand that he shall
not take them into the territories to expel the free laborer by the repul-
sion of their presence."[11] Blacks, argued John A. Dix, in an oft-
reprinted speech, were an undesirable, innately inferior caste, beyond
hope of integration into the mainstream of American life. "Public
opinion at the north—call it prejudice, if you will—presents an insuper-
able barrier against its elevation in the social scale," he maintained. And
since "a class thus degraded will not multiply, . . . the slow but certain process of nature" would in a few generations humanely blot the
Negro race from American soil. That being so, said Dix, farsighted

---

New York History, XLVI, No. 4 (Oct. 1965), 311-29, and his "Politics and Prejudice: The Free Soil Party and the Negro, 1849-1852," *The Journal of Negro History*, L, No. 4 (Oct. 1965), 239-56.
[8] Thomas H. Benton, quoted in Morrison, *Democratic Politics and Sectionalism*, 70.
[9] George W. Julian to Colored Citizens of Illinois, Sept. 17, 1853, George W. Julian
Papers, Indiana State Library; Horace Greeley to Joshua R. Giddings, June 20,
1848, Miscellaneous Manuscripts, NYHS; Foner, "Racial Attitudes of the New York
Free Soilers," 312-13, 323-24; George M. Fredrickson, *The Black Image in the White
Mind: The Debate on Afro-American Character and Destiny, 1817-1914* (New
York, 1971), 26, 90-91.
[10] Speech of Martin Grover to the Utica convention, June 22, 1848, quoted in
Gardiner, *Great Issue*, 108.
[11] *New York Weekly Evening Post*, Apr. 27, 1848.

Americans had a "sacred duty to consecrate these [Western] spaces to the multiplication of the white race."[12]

Free Soil Democrats in other states also developed racist justifications for the Wilmot Proviso. Ohio's plain-spoken Congressman Jacob Brinkerhoff, for example, willingly confessed: "I have selfishness enough, greatly to prefer the welfare of my own race to that of any other, and vindictiveness enough to wish to leave and keep upon the shoulders of the South the burden of the curse which they have themselves created and courted." David Wilmot himself, a Democratic Free Soiler from western Pennsylvania, took great pains to deny that his Proviso had been framed especially for blacks.

> . . . The negro race already occupy enough of this fair conti-
> nent [he told a Barnburner rally at Albany]; let us keep what re-
> mains for ourselves, and our children—for the emigrant that seeks
> our shores—for the poor man, that wealth shall oppress—for the
> free white laborer, who shall desire to hew him out a home of
> happiness and peace, on the distant shores of the mighty Pacific.[13]

In the company of friends, Wilmot spoke more bluntly still: "By God, sir, men born and nursed of white women are not going to be ruled by men who were brought up on the milk of some damn Negro wench!" Small wonder that Barnburners often dubbed Wilmot's Proviso the "White Man's Resolution."[14]

On the home front, too, Barnburners joined Hunker Democrats in curtailing black freedoms. Most conspicuously, they fought success-fully against proposals to grant equal suffrage to New York Negroes, and raised cries of "Nigger Party," "Amalgamation," and "Fried Wool" against Whigs and Liberty men who espoused this reform. Of thirteen Free Soil leaders who had participated in the Constitutional Convention of 1846, which debated Negro rights, none endorsed the extension of black suffrage. Most, in fact, voted against a motion to reduce the property qualification for Negro voters from $250 to $100.

[12] Speech in the U.S. Senate on the Bill to Establish a Territorial Government in Oregon, quoted in Gardiner, *Great Issue*, 153-68, esp. 163.
[13] Brinkerhoff to Salmon P. Chase, Nov. 22, 1847, Chase Papers, PHS; *Albany Atlas*, Nov. 9, 1847.
[14] Charles B. Going, *David Wilmot, Free-Soiler: A Biography of the Great Advo-cate of the Wilmot Proviso* (New York, 1924), 174-75n.

"Prince John" Van Buren later explained: "I supposed the antipathy between the two races made that joint political action as impracticable and disagreeable as has always been a personal association between them."[15]

So far were they from extending to blacks full rights of citizenship that some Radical Democrats expressed a desire to be rid of Negroes altogether. Most subscribed to the notion that Northern states offered an "uncongenial clime" for blacks and did what they could to encourage the voluntary emigration of free Negroes to some tropical domain. The prospect of a reverse flow of freedmen into the North excited violent protest. When Governor William Smith of Virginia proposed shipping his state's freedmen northward, Barnburner George Rathbun coldly insisted: "there is no place for them. As far as New York is concerned, should the refuse part of the population of Virginia reach our territory, we will carry them back to Virginia." And Senator Dix, in the same speech in which he predicted the extinction of the black race in North America, denounced the influx of ex-slaves into the free states as "in the highest degree undesirable. They add nothing to our strength, moral or physical. . . . We desire and need independent, not dependent classes." The blacks' own best interest, such men alleged, dictated removal to some distant, tropical land where they might develop their (limited) potentialities unrestrained by discriminatory statutes and the competition of racially superior whites.[16]

Yet for all their racial prejudice, most Barnburners, like other Free Soilers, responded primarily to the menace of *slavery* and the "Slave Power," and only fitfully and secondarily to the "curse" of degraded blacks. Nearly all agreed that human bondage, if not a sin, was a "disgrace," "a great moral and political evil." "To buy and sell human beings," John Van Buren declared, "is revolting not only to a freeman and a democrat, but to a philanthropist and a christian."[17] Although there might be good reasons (besides constitutional constraints) for not interfering with slavery in Southern states, it was the *duty* of all decent

15 Foner, "Racial Attitudes of the New York Free Soilers," 313-14; *Albany Atlas*, Apr. 28, 1848.
16 Morrison, *Democratic Politics and Sectionalism*, 70; Gardiner, *Great Issue*, 164; Foner, "Racial Attitudes of the New York Free Soilers," 322-23.
17 *Albany Atlas*, Feb. 3, Apr. 28, 1848. See also *ibid*. Feb. 29, July 11, 21, 1848, Aug. 10, 1847; Foster, "History of the Liberty Party," 118; Address of the Herkimer Convention (Nov. 26, 1847), quoted in Gardiner, *Great Issue*, 49-55, esp. 52.

men to prevent this blight from spreading. "We may be wrong," professed the Van Burenite *Seneca Observer* in 1847, "but we could not regard with satisfaction the success of our arms [in Mexico], if the result of that success would be to deprive one human being of those rights which are his natural inheritance."[18]

Nearly always, moreover, Barnburners spoke of the need to protect white laborers against competition from "Negro *slaves*" or "black *chattels*."[19] This would seem to suggest that while the rights and privileges of white yeomen were uppermost in their minds, they found the slave *system*—which degraded free labor, fostered sloth and ignorance, and gave artificial preeminence to an elitist few—far more alarming than the mere presence of an "inferior race." Free Soil Democrats might be callous and indifferent in their attitude toward free Negroes, but they felt outraged and anything but indifferent when contemplating the corrupting "peculiar institution." And for some, including Wilmot, containment of slavery represented a first step toward universal emancipation, since without fresh lands to ravage, most believed, slavery could not long survive.[20]

2

Outside New York, the Free Soil party presented a markedly more liberal stance. The *Green Mountain Freeman*, for instance, exhorted Vermont Free Soilers to "Remember, as among the first articles of *our* creed and the CREED OF OUR POLITICAL FATHERS, THAT SLAVERY IS A SIN AGAINST GOD and a crime against man, which no human enactment can make right." Charles Durkee, spokesman for Wisconsin Free Soilers, passionately proclaimed in the House of Representatives: "Sir, you may take from . . . [a man] his wife, his children, and his friends,

[18] Quoted in *Albany Atlas*, Feb. 15, 1847. See also *Oswego Palladium*, quoted in *ibid.* Aug. 17, 1847; *Buffalo Republic*, quoted in Centreville (Ind.) *Free Territory Sentinel*, Feb. 21, 1849.

[19] See, e.g., *Albany Atlas*, Aug. 10, 1847; "Address of the Democratic Members of the Legislature of the State of New York," Apr. 12, 1848, Van Buren Papers. Eric Foner argues that "the seemingly unnecessary adjective 'black' before the word 'slave' testified to an aversion to the presence of any black men in the territories." Read in context, however, it would appear that "slave," not "black," was the operative word. "Racial Attitudes of the New York Free Soilers," 316.

[20] See Wilmot's speech to the Herkimer convention, Gardiner, *Great Issue*, 57-62, esp. 61; Seth H. Hunt to Martin Van Buren, July 13, 1848, Van Buren Papers.

and put handcuffs on his wrists and fetters on his feet, and brand him as your property . . . yet he is still a *man*—he is still our brother." And to E. S. Hamlin, a Whiggish convert to Free Soil, the antislavery struggle seemed a "far more glorious one than that of our Revolution." For, as he explained to Salmon Chase, "Our fathers' weapons were *carnal*, ours spiritual: they fought for *their own* liberty; we are fighting for that of *others*, a poor, despised, downtrodden race." Even skeptical Garrisonians noted that among Massachusetts Free Soilers "the prevailing spirit seemed to be one of opposition to slavery *per se*, and not merely on account of its interference with the rights and prosperity of white men."[21]

While willing for practical political reasons to leave the issue of Negro equality to voluntary local action, instead of including it in their party's national platform, Free Soilers managed to a remarkable extent to transcend the racism of the age. Far from seeking to strengthen or extend discrimination against blacks, many Free Soilers went out of their way to debunk conventional stereotypes of Negro inferiority and to preach the "equality of all men, of every climate, color, and race. . . ."[22] Free Soilers, editorialized Gamaliel Bailey, "are opposed to the spirit of caste, whether its elemental idea be a difference of color, birth, or condition—because, its inevitable tendency is to create or perpetuate inequality of natural rights."[23] Advanced sentiments such as these often provoked crude sneers from those who heard them. Even George W. Julian, a somewhat tardy convert to racial democracy, remembered years afterward the taunts of "amalgamationist" and "woolly-head" hurled at him during the 1848 campaign. "It was a standing charge of the Whigs," he recalled, "that I carried in my pocket a lock of the hair of Frederick Douglass, to regale my senses with its aroma when I grew faint."[24]

Notwithstanding such jeers, however, Free Soilers often took the lead in defending—and extending—the civil rights of black Americans. Although notably reticent on the question of social equality, and often

---

[21] *Green Mountain Freeman*, Aug. 25, 1853; *Cong. Globe*, 31st Cong., 1st sess., Appendix, 741 (June 7, 1850); Hamlin to Chase, Feb. 19, 1850, Chase Papers, PHS; *Liberator*, Sept. 15, 1848.
[22] Henry Wilson *et al.* to John P. Hale, Mar. 30, 1853, quoted in *Green Mountain Freeman*, Apr. 21, 1853.
[23] *National Era*, June 28, 1849.
[24] Julian, *Political Recollections*, 65.

patronizing in their relations with Negroes, many Free Soil advocates
perceived an embarrassing discrepancy between the Declaration of Independence and the Bill of Rights, which spoke of natural rights belonging to *all* men, and the web of legal and extralegal restraints that,
in every part of the land, consigned blacks to second-class citizenship.
As one Ohio Free Soiler remarked in denouncing his state's discriminatory suffrage law: " 'All men by nature are free and independent,' don't
look well by the side of 'every White male citizen.' "[25] Accordingly,
Free Soilers in many states and on many occasions damned political
costs and joined moral-suasion abolitionists in the battle against institu-
tionalized racism.

Most Americans would have agreed that the right to vote was the
most fundamental of all civil freedoms. Yet by the 1840s all but five
states—Maine, New Hampshire, Vermont, Massachusetts, and Rhode
Island—banned or severely restricted Negro suffrage.[26] Former Democrats aside, most Free Soilers, like Liberty men before them, deplored
such barriers to full citizenship and, upon occasion, worked to tear
them down.

The most nearly successful attempt came in Wisconsin. Although
few blacks were to be found so far north, the question of their political
rights inevitably surfaced during debates over the state's first constitution. Most Democrats followed the lead of Moses M. Strong, who
announced himself "teetotally opposed" to any form of Negro suffrage. A great many Whigs, however, as well as most Liberty men and
Free Soilers, pledged themselves to equal suffrage from the beginning.
At its annual meeting early in 1848 the Wisconsin Liberty Association
proclaimed that suffrage was an "inalienable right" belonging to all
men, that to deny this right to any would be to open the door to disfranchisement for all, and that the principle that robbed the Negro of
one right "only needs scope and opportunity to rob him of *all* rights."
Likewise, the next year Wisconsin Free Soilers forthrightly declared:
"We are in favor of equal and impartial suffrage, and are the friends of
man and the advocates of human rights the world over. . . ." The
principle, insisted the Milwaukee *Wisconsin Free Democrat*, was "one
of vital importance." For although exclusion of blacks from the polls

[25] Quoted in Berwanger, *Frontier Against Slavery*, 40. On Northern repression of
blacks, see Litwack, *North of Slavery*.
[26] *Ibid.* 91.

would have little practical effect, "it would sacrifice the vital principle of Democracy, by making *color*, and not *character*—factitious circumstances, and not manhood, the foundation of political rights." True democracy, it argued, implied equal rights, human brotherhood, and Christianity in government.[27]

That few Wisconsinites shared such liberal sentiments soon became clear. A special referendum on Negro suffrage and the right of blacks to hold public office, held in March 1847 showed 7664 for, 14,615 against. Defeat of the constitution to which this referendum was tied, however, presented advocates of equal suffrage with a fresh chance. A second state convention, meeting in 1848-49, drafted a constitution that limited suffrage to white males but authorized the legislature to "admit colored persons to the right of suffrage" after approval by a majority of voters at the next general election. Accordingly, Wisconsin's first legislature called for a plebiscite on black suffrage at the fall canvass of 1849.[28]

As the election approached, the Free Soil press urged "every true [Free] Democrat . . . to vote for this democratic principle of equal suffrage without distinction of color." The Free Soil gubernatorial candidate, Warren Chase, was touted as one who had in both constitutional conventions and in the legislature placed himself on record as a friend of equal political rights for all men. And many Whig newspapers, notably the *Milwaukee Sentinel and Gazette*, strongly endorsed free suffrage. Yet as the *Southport Telegraph* admitted afterward, "There seems to have been very little feeling among the people on this question." Even Free Soilers, embroiled in a quarrel with old line Democrats with whom they had hoped to coalesce, showed a good deal of apathy.[29]

Still, a clear majority of those who voted in the 1849 referendum backed Negro suffrage. When counted, the ballots showed 5265 in favor, 4075 opposed. However, since the language authorizing the referendum required approval by "a majority of all the votes cast at such election" before black men might receive the ballot, and since nearly

[27] Leslie H. Fishel, Jr., "Wisconsin and Negro Suffrage," *Wisconsin Magazine of History*, XLVI, No. 2 (Spring 1963), 180-82; *American Freeman*, Feb. 23, 1848; *Wisconsin Free Democrat*, Jan. 24, Apr. 11, 1849.
[28] Fishel, "Wisconsin and Negro Suffrage," 183-84.
[29] *Wisconsin Free Democrat*, Oct. 24, Nov. 7, 1849; *Southport Telegraph*, Oct. 19, Nov. 9, 1849.

32,000 had voted for governor, the State Board of Canvassers ruled that suffrage extension had failed for want of an *adequate* majority. Free Soilers protested this "back-handed blow" and argued for an interpretation that would give freedom the benefit of the doubt. With the clarity of hindsight they denounced the semantic trickery that had cheated blacks of the franchise, finding it rooted in "the indisposition of tyrants to concede the rights to the people which they have usurped and exercised. . . ." But their protests came to naught—at least until 1866, when in the case of Gillespie *v.* Palmer *et al.* the Supreme Court of Wisconsin belatedly overruled the Board of Canvassers and held that the simple majority in favor of black suffrage in 1849 had in fact been sufficient.[30] For Wisconsin Negroes, justice delayed had indeed been justice denied. But old Free Soilers and antislavery Whigs must have found special pleasure in this sudden flowering of their long-ago labors for equal rights.

Connecticut Free Soilers, led by William H. Burleigh, a long-time abolitionist and recently editor of the *Hartford Republican,* labored just as hard and with no greater success to restore voting rights withdrawn from Negroes in 1814. When Burleigh resigned his editorship in 1849, the Hartford Colored Washingtonian Temperance Society thanked him for his "arduous labors" on behalf of the slave and for advocating as well "the moral, social, and political right of the free colored man." Other Free Soil journalists kept up this fight. Burleigh's successor, John D. Baldwin, reported fully and favorably the proceedings of a convention of Colored Citizens of Connecticut at New Haven and took the occasion once again to urge votes for blacks. "The man who would deny the common rights of manhood to so much intelligence and moral worth as was represented in that Convention," he maintained, "deserves to be pitied for his subserviency to a blind prejudice." Prejudice, however, ran deep in the state that had earlier made a martyr of Prudence Crandall for daring to open a school for black girls, and despite the efforts of abolitionists and Free Soilers it took the Fifteenth Amendment to enfranchise Connecticut Negroes.[31]

---

[30] Fishel, "Wisconsin and Negro Suffrage," 184-96; *Wisconsin Free Democrat,* Nov. 21, Dec. 19, 1849; *Southport Telegraph,* Nov. 23, 1849; *Oshkosh True Democrat,* Dec. 28, 1849.
[31] *Hartford Republican,* Sept. 13, 27, 1849; James T. Adams, "Disfranchisement of Negroes in New England," *American Historical Review,* XXX, No. 3 (Apr. 1925), 545.

In Ohio and Indiana, Free Soilers battled not only against inequalities in the suffrage but against comprehensive Black Laws designed to ensure white supremacy. Few states north of Mason and Dixon's line oppressed blacks more systematically than did Ohio. In its earliest years of statehood (1804 and 1807) Ohio legislators had enacted laws deterring Negroes from entering the state, excluding them from militia service and jury duty, barring their testimony in cases involving whites, denying them poorhouse relief, and banishing them from public schools. Ohio's constitution deprived them of the right to vote. In 1839 the state assembly denied blacks even the right to petition the legislature "for any purpose whatsoever."[32]

For years Ohio's Negroes and white abolitionists, especially on the Western Reserve, had pressed for repeal of these repressive measures. Liberty men had made their revocation a party issue, and in the mid-1840s Governor Mordecai Bartley, a Whig, lent his name to the cause. In January 1845 a majority of the select committee appointed by the house to consider the question urged the annulment of the Black Laws as a matter of enlightened policy and simple justice. Pervasive racial prejudice, however, particularly among Democrats, together with the fear that if it offered equal citizenship Ohio would find itself swamped with free Negroes from other states, prevented the legislature from acting—at least for the time being.[33]

As it happened, Ohio's Free Soil party, which from its birth had denounced the Black Laws as "legalized injustice," became the instrument of repeal. Finding that Free Soilers held the balance of power in both houses of the state legislature in 1849, Salmon P. Chase contrived a deal whereby Democrats agreed to support his election to the United States Senate and revocation of the Black Laws in exchange for enough Free Soil votes to allow the Democrats to organize the house. Accordingly, most Democrats (acting grudgingly "under the most determined and rigid application of party discipline") as well as many Whigs and all Free Soilers, joined in rescinding the most flagrant laws of discrimi-

---

[32] Litwack, *North of Slavery*, 72-74, 93-94, 114; Foner, "Politics and Prejudice," 240; Blue, "Ohio Free Soilers," 23.

[33] "Report of a Majority of the Select Committee [of the Ohio House of Representatives], Proposing to Repeal All Laws Creating Distinctions on Account of Color, Commonly Called the Black Laws, January 18, 1845," Slavery Pamphlets, SHSW; *Documents, Including Messages and Other Communications Made to the Forty-Fourth General Assembly of the State of Ohio*, X, Pt. I (Columbus, 1931), 11; Frank U. Quillin, *The Color Line in Ohio* (Ann Arbor, 1913), 36.

nation. Henceforth, blacks might enter Ohio freely, testify in any legal proceeding, and attend common schools.[34]

Still, many restraints remained. The schools Negro children might now attend were, when feasible, to be strictly segregated. Senate amendments, moreover, had cut from the original reform bill (drafted by Chase and introduced in the house by John F. Morse, a Free Soiler from the Western Reserve) provisions granting blacks the right to serve on juries and to benefit from the poor laws. And the state's 1802 constitution still barred Negroes from holding office or casting ballots. Significantly, however, Ohio Free Soilers refused to settle for half a loaf where the rights of black citizens were concerned. All Free Soil delegates to the state constitutional convention of 1850-51 had campaigned on platforms urging equal political rights for Negroes, and when the question of black suffrage arose they backed it to a man. Well in advance of the racial temper of their time, Free Soilers saw this attempt fail resoundingly. Yet so long as their party remained alive, Ohio Free Soilers continued to press for the enfranchisement of *all* men.[35]

Even less successful, though scarcely less dedicated, were the attempts of Indiana's small band of Free Soilers to abolish that state's Black Laws. As in Ohio, Indiana Negroes faced a battery of discriminatory codes. The constitution of 1816 restricted the suffrage and militia duty to whites only. State statutes proscribed Negro testimony in cases involving whites and banned, under threat of severe penalty, interracial marriages. After 1831 blacks settling in the state were required to post bond "for their good behavior and self support." And public opinion effectively excluded Negro children from the common schools.[36]

---

[34] *National Era*, Feb. 8, 22, 1849; Blue, "Ohio Free Soilers," 20-23; Edgar A. Holt, *Party Politics in Ohio, 1840-1850* (Columbus, 1931), 400; E. S. Hamlin to Salmon P. Chase, Jan. 18, 19, 20, 30, 1849, Chase Papers, PHS. Repeal of the Black Laws, claimed Salmon Chase, "is an object dearer to me than any political elevation whatever; and is worth more to us as a Party than the election of any man to any office in the gift of the Legislature. It removes out of our path the greatest obstacle to our complete triumph, while it is in itself a great victory of humanity and justice." Chase to E. S. Hamlin, Jan. 20, 1849, Chase Papers, PHS. While Chase's senatorial hopes burned far brighter than he here admitted there seems no reason to question his idealism in pressing for repeal of Ohio's discriminatory code.

[35] Foner, "Politics and Prejudice," 241; Quillin, *Color Line in Ohio*, 39-40, 70.

[36] John W. Lyda, *The Negro in the History of Indiana* (Terre Haute, 1953), 15-17; Litwack, *North of Slavery*, 115; *Free Territory Sentinel*, Dec. 5, 1849, Jan. 30, 1850. Not until 1926 did Indiana drop its constitutional prohibition against blacks in the militia. Berwanger, *Frontier Against Slavery*, 122.

Condemnation of such statutes came primarily from antislavery Whigs like Schuyler Colfax, who favored African colonization and opposed equal suffrage but blamed the debasement of blacks on "the lust and avarice of the white race" and insisted that the Declaration of Independence guaranteed basic civil rights to all Americans.[37] But Hoosier Free Soilers, especially in the "Burnt District" of the upper Whitewater Valley—a region of strong Quaker influence—pushed hard for repeal of the "disgraceful" Black Laws. The Centreville *Free Territory Sentinel* (later the *Indiana True Democrat*) was especially active. Anticipating the constitutional convention of 1850, the *Sentinel*, in November 1849, began a petition campaign calling for annulment of the oppressive statutes. It kept up the pressure with a series of stinging editorials, and by the end of January some 3000 signatures had been affixed to memorials urging repeal of these statutes. Although admitting that "A considerable number of free-soil men are opposed to giving Negroes the right of suffrage," the paper's own editorials vigorously endorsed such a grant as a matter of "JUSTICE and RIGHT."[38]

Hopes for the liberalization of the Black Laws were soon shattered. With only one Free Soil representative present, the 1850 constitutional convention not only refused to modify discriminatory provisions already in effect (a motion to include in the constitution provision for Negro suffrage failed, 1 to 122), but added a new article 13 that henceforth prohibited all Negroes or mulattoes from entering the state and hinted at the removal of blacks already settled there. In a separate referendum in 1851, Indianans endorsed this article by more than five to one, in effect seconding the position of William C. Foster, a downstate Democrat, who had assured fellow delegates to the 1850 convention: "We cannot . . . be charged with inhumanity in preventing our State from being overrun with these vermin—for I say they are vermin, and I know it."[39]

Once again, however, Free Soilers conspicuously dissented from such

[37] *Report of the Debates and Proceedings of the Convention for the Revision of the Constitution of the State of Indiana*, 1850, 2 vols. (Indianapolis, 1850), I, 456-57.
[38] Riddleberger, *Julian*, 2-4; *Free Territory Sentinel*, Nov. 28, Dec. 5, 1849; Centreville *Indiana True Democrat*, Jan. 30, July 3, 1850.
[39] Smith, *Liberty and Free Soil Parties*, 193, 335-36; *Report of the Debates . . . of the Convention for the Revision of the Constitution of . . . Indiana, 1850*, I, 451. Only Randolph, after Wayne Free Soil's banner county, and La Grange (which also gave significant support to Van Buren in 1848) showed a majority against the exclusion clause.

blatant racism. The Free Soil *True Democrat* ruefully proclaimed: "The people of the State have thus voluntarily and *gratuitously* published to the world, that they are *barbarians*, by the adoption of this clause, which their own better reason will soon be ashamed of, and their own hearts would even now repudiate." The party's official platform denounced the "notorious 13th article" and bravely declared "That this is not less the *native land* of the negro than of the white man," and that it was "in every way as unjust and imprudent" to seek to expel the former as the latter. And when citizens of Cambridge, Indiana, attempted to drive all its Negroes out of town, ostensibly because many of them were suspected of thieving, Free Soilers caustically noted that there were lawful means of coping with theft, and urged the beleaguered blacks to stand fast.[40] Even in this most bigoted of free states, then, Free Soil advocates displayed an extraordinary willingness to admit—and to seek to protect—the Negro's rights and dignity.

Massachusetts offers still another example of Free Soil activity on behalf of racial equality. The Bay State had long since extended to blacks all basic civil rights, including the franchise. Yet even in this "cradle of liberty" prejudice against color worked its poison, sustaining a far-reaching system of social and economic segregation. Massachusetts abolitionists had warred against Jim Crow for years without appreciable success. In the 1840s, however, other antislavery groups—Liberty men, Free Soilers, and liberal Whigs—added their influence and energy to the efforts of the Garrisonians, winning at least token victories for racial democracy.

One such was the repeal, in 1843, of Massachusetts' statutory ban on interracial marriages. Prominent among those who effected this "staggering blow . . . to the monster prejudice," as Garrison termed it, were such proto-Free Soilers as Charles Francis Adams, John G. Palfrey, and Henry Wilson. Antislavery politicians, including Free Soilers, also joined indignant blacks and old organization abolitionists in a campaign against segregation in railroad cars. So successful were they that, though legislative remedies were thwarted, by 1849 Frederick Douglass could boast: "not a single railroad can be found in any part of Massachusetts, where a colored man is treated and esteemed in any other light than that of a man and a traveler." Less availing were attempts to open up the state's lily-white militia and to integrate its public schools.

40 *Indiana True Democrat*, Aug. 28, 1851, May 27, 1852, Oct. 4, 1850.

None labored harder for these reforms than did Charles Sumner. Together with Henry Wilson he pressed the matter of militia reform in
the constitutional convention of 1853, and in his argument in the celebrated Roberts Case of 1849 he attacked segregated schools as inherently unequal and damaging to all concerned. Conservatives tabled the
proposal for militia revision, and the Roberts decision upheld school
segregation in Boston. But Massachusetts Free Soilers continued to
press for the equal rights of all citizens, and in 1855 the state legislature at last outlawed racial or religious discrimination in the public
schools.[41]

Horace Mann, later Free Soil Congressman from John Quincy Adams's old district, took a great deal of abuse from abolitionists who protested his failure, as Secretary of the Massachusetts Board of Education,
to denounce segregated schooling. Yet in his private life Mann showed
himself anything but a friend of Jim Crow. When, for example, he discovered that the New Bedford Lyceum had refused to admit Negroes
to membership, he withdrew his previous agreement to lecture before
it. And when he learned of the predicament of Chloe Lee, a bright and
tough-minded Negro from Roxbury who won admission to the state
normal school at West Newton only to find that none in the village
would offer her shelter, Mann and his wife gave the girl their spare
room, making her "for all intents . . . a member of their family."[42]

At times the Free Soil concern for Negro rights cut across state lines.
When, for instance, in 1849 Secretary of State John M. Clayton denied
a passport to one Henry Hambleton solely on the basis of his color,
Free Soilers loosed a torrent of protest. Clayton's action they labeled
unprecedented, unauthorized, and unjust—an unforgivable infringe-
ment of Afro-Americans' inalienable rights of citizenship. The *Essex*
(Mass.) *County Freeman* went so far as to appeal openly for Negro
support on this issue. "Vote the free soil ticket," it urged, "in which
your INTERESTS are concerned."[43] Now and then Free Soil newspapers

---

[41] Litwack, *North of Slavery*, 104-10, 143-49; Foner, "Politics and Prejudice," 244-
46; Donald, *Sumner*, 180-81; Gatell, *Palfrey*, 95-96; Stanley K. Schultz, *The Culture
Factory: Boston Public Schools, 1789-1860* (New York, 1973), chap. VIII; *Boston
Weekly Commonwealth*, Mar. 19, July 2, Oct. 1, 1853.
[42] Jonathan Messerli, *Horace Mann, A Biography* (New York, 1972), 446-47.
[43] Salem *Essex County Freeman*, Aug. 8, 18, 22, 25, Sept. 1, Nov. 10, 1849; *Boston
Daily Republican*, Aug. 10, 21, 1849; *National Era*, Sept. 27, 1849; *Green Mountain
Freeman*, Oct. 25, 1849; John L. O'Sullivan to Martin Van Buren, July 25, 1849, Van
Buren Papers.

made it a special point to introduce evidence of Negro virtue and capacity for good citizenship. In Congress the more radical Free Soilers did what they could to block discriminatory legislation and to counter Southern charges of the innate depravity of blacks. Chase and Giddings strove throughout the 1850s to make blacks eligible for homestead grants, albeit without success. And John G. Palfrey, for one, pointed to the accomplishments of Hannibal, Dumas, and Douglass and cited statistics indicating rising sugar exports in the British West Indies since emancipation to demonstrate that Negro inferiority stemmed from "the depression and low culture of many generations," not "congenital incapacity."[44]

Attitudes toward colonization also provide an index to the racial views of Free Soilers. Like Liberty men earlier, most Free Soil spokesmen showed only animosity toward proposals to remove blacks from American soil. Most saw colonization as a "nefarious scheme" designed to tighten, not loosen, the chains of slavery. Its effect, they argued, was to intensify negrophobia and thus make emancipation more difficult. When Daniel Webster, in his famous speech on the Compromise of 1850, suggested that public land receipts might be used to transport the nation's free Negroes to Africa, Free Soil newspapers roundly condemned the idea. The *Independent Democrat* styled it the most inhuman and profligate proposition ever made in Congress and endorsed instead the *New York Evening Post*'s suggestion that it would be cheaper to transport the South's slaveholders instead.[45]

If colonization were a proslavery movement, some Free Soilers contended, then opposition to colonization might be made an antislavery measure. Indiana's George W. Julian advanced this notion most forcefully in a letter to Illinois Negroes in 1853. It was especially important, he argued, for the black man himself to resist colonization.

> He should resolutely demand his rights as a man and a citizen,
> and thus demonstrate that he *is* a man. . . . The degradation in
> this country of its free colored people, or their expatriation from
> it, is an essential part of the policy of the slave interest. The pres-

---

[44] *Independent Democrat*, Feb. 7, 1850; *National Era*, Mar. 16, 1854; Foner, "Politics and Prejudice," 242n.; *Cong. Globe*, 30th Cong., 1st sess., Appendix, 134-35, 33rd Cong., 1st sess., 504, 549.
[45] *Essex County Freeman*, Jan. 21, 1852; *National Era*, Jan. 23, 30, 1851; *Free Territory Sentinel*, July 25, 1849; *Indiana True Democrat*, May 22, June 5, 1851; *Portland Inquirer*, Apr. 24, 1851; *Independent Democrat*, Apr. 4, 1850.

ence of such a people is a perpetual danger to that interest, as well as a reproach to the slave holder; and therefore, by firmly and unitedly resolving to remain among us, they can perform an important work in the deliverance of their brother in chains.[46]

Blacks, of course, did just that, though it is doubtful that the resolution of *Northern* free Negroes caused slaveholders great alarm.

Not all Free Soilers, to be sure, viewed with such favor the eternal presence of the Negro race in America. Many who opposed compulsory colonization and objected to the statutory oppression of blacks nonetheless believed that God had intended a separation of the races. Salmon P. Chase candidly informed Frederick Douglass that in his opinion blacks and whites were adapted to different latitudes. Only the coercion of slavery had brought the two races together in the United States, and with emancipation one might anticipate a natural drifting apart. "I have thought it not unlikely," he asserted, "that the Islands of the West Indies & portions of South America would be peopled from the United States by the Black Race—that, by them, civilization would be carried back into Africa, not under the constraints of any colonization scheme, but of choice & free will." Chase thought the island of Jamaica would make "a most inviting field for colored enterprise." To an Ohio friend he wrote: "If I were a colored man I would go to Jamaica—buy one of those deserted plantations—sugar mill and all—divide the land away to colonists in fee—and have the mill for all to resort to just like one of our first mills, or old cotton spinning mills or wool carding mills. That's my notion."[47]

Julian to Colored Citizens of Illinois, Sept. 17, 1853, Julian Papers.
[47] Chase to Douglass, May 4, 1850 (copy), Chase to [N. S. Townshend?], Dec. 13, 1850, Chase Papers, PHS. Douglass would have none of Chase's advice. "It is my humble opinion that this is a question with which climate and geography have but little to do," he replied on May 30. "Experience, I think, has demonstrated beyond all reasonable doubt, that the black man's constitution as readily adapts itself to one climate as another. I think that the causes likely to influence or affect our destiny, are wholly moral and political, and although these do not appear very favorable to our remaining here viewed unconnected with the past, yet I think there has been no time in the history of our country when there were more favorable indications than are to be seen at this day." Chase Papers, LC. Chase clung to his climatic theory of race for years. During the Civil War he advocated federal use of Negro troops on the ground that they would make good soldiers "where Northern men could not serve without decimation by disease." William F. Messner, "The Federal Army and Blacks in the Gulf Department, 1862-1865," Ph.D. dissertation, University of Wisconsin, 1972, p. 304.

Gamaliel Bailey sounded the same note in the *National Era*. "While the white population of Europe is colonizing the United States and Canada," he suggested, "why should not the colored population of the United States colonize Mexico and the West Indies?" Full citizenship was open to blacks in both places and by importing democratic ideas they might enlarge the sphere of freedom.[48] Horace Mann was yet another prominent Free Soiler who advocated such notions of "white nationalism." Twice he shocked conventions of Northern Negroes by announcing his belief that although superior to whites in sentiment and affection ("the upper end of man's nature," Mann thought), blacks were intellectually inferior and best suited to more tropical climes. Similarly, Ohio Free Soilers prefaced their demand for repeal of the Black Laws by saying: "we desire a homogeneous population for our State, and believe that we shall have it whenever slavery shall cease to force the victims of its tyranny into the uncongenial North. . . ."[49]

While most Free Soil separatists were content to let time, emancipation, and Providence "whiten" the Northern landscape, a few, mainly in Ohio, sought to speed the process through "internal colonization." In 1851 a majority of Free Soilers in the Ohio senate backed a resolution calling for a federal law to reserve a portion of the public lands exclusively for Negroes. The *Cleveland True Democrat*, much under Salmon Chase's influence, also endorsed the establishment of a separate preserve for American blacks, somewhere "in the southern climate."[50]

To a good many Free Soilers, then, the Negro appeared an undesirable and quite likely inferior element in American society. Although a few like Connecticut's John M. Niles aroused spiteful talk by engaging in "cheek by jowl intercourse" with blacks, most antislavery men showed no interest in encouraging social mixing between the races.[51] Even one so radical as Charles Sumner, Frederick Douglass later complained, failed to recognize "the entire manhood and social equality of the colored people." And when in congressional debate Palfrey

[48] *National Era*, Mar. 13, 1851.
[49] Foner, "Politics and Prejudice," 247-48; *National Era*, Feb. 8, 1849. For an admirable account of white separatist attitudes, see Fredrickson, *Black Image   the White Mind*, chap. V, "White Nationalism: 'Free Soil' and the Ideal of Racial Homogeneity."
[50] Foner, "Politics and Prejudice," 243.
[51] A. E. Burr to Gideon Welles, Apr. 16, 1849, Welles Papers, CHS.

encountered the racists' chestnut—how would he like his daughter to marry a Negro?—he dodged the question and sought to have the exchange suppressed in Massachusetts—"for my poor daughter's sake," he lamely explained. To the influential *National Era*, blacks, as the descendants of "uncivilized Pagans, of brutish ignorance and loathsome practices," still lacked the intelligence, refinement, probity, and enterprise marking the Anglo-Saxon race.[52]

Once again, moreover, as was the case with Liberty men, Free Soilers offered no better prescription for Negro advancement than self-help. "Let them educate themselves—rely upon themselves—act for themselves—learn to move in concert," let them display old-fashioned American get-up-and-go, Gamaliel Bailey insisted, and all else would fall into place.

Yet the striking thing is not that Free Soilers betrayed signs of racial bias and shortsightedness. Not even moral suasion abolitionists escaped completely the racist currents of the day.[53] What is remarkable is that members of a political party needing majorities to put their program into effect braved prevailing opinion and insisted time and again that Negroes too were God's children, entitled to full rights of citizenship. Often, indeed, they went further, attacking the prejudice that sustained Jim Crow. The *National Era*, for instance, ridiculed the irrationality of negrophobia by likening it to discrimination practiced against the Cagots, a proscribed group of Spanish whites who differed from their neighbors, it was said, only by the absence of an ear lobe. Most often, while admitting the present inferiority of American Negroes, Free Soilers emphasized their capacity for improvement once the stones of oppression were rolled away. Isaac Kinley, sole Free Soil delegate to the Indiana constitutional convention of 1850, struck a common party note when he complained: "Instead of encouraging the [black] man to rise, you lay burdens upon him, and then insult him because he is degraded." Similarly, Gamaliel Bailey contended that a high rate of poverty and crime among free blacks "only proves that their release from slavery has been too recent and their disabilities are too heavy to allow

52 Douglass to Sumner, Apr. 24, 1855, Foner, *Writings of Douglass*, II, 362-63; Gatell, *Palfrey*, 155-56; *National Era*, Apr. 24, 1851.
53 William H. and Jane H. Pease, "Antislavery Ambivalence: Immediatism, Expediency, Race," *American Quarterly*, XVI, No. 4 (Winter 1965), 682-95; Wyatt-Brown, *Tappan*, 176-79.

their easy ascent to the elevation of a people whose fathers have never known the yoke of bondage, or the degradation of caste legislation."[54]

At least some of the apparent indifference of many Free Soil pronouncements to the plight of free blacks stemmed from an awareness that to link equal rights too closely to antislavery was to jeopardize both. As William Jackson, a pioneer Liberty man and Free Soiler, counseled Horace Mann, unless *white* interests received paramount attention, even the best antislavery speech would be hooted down as "a defence of the 'damned niger [*sic*] question.'" Once Northern whites came to understand free soil's benefit to *themselves*, he wrote, "the miserable principle of selfishness may be trusted for the completion of the work; but so long as appeals are made only in the name of charity and humanity, relying upon our moral principles and sense of Justice, the slave holders will continue to ride over us roughshod."[55]

But again, what is surprising is the extent to which Free Soilers disregarded the whisperings of expediency and doggedly pushed for what they thought was right.

3

Just as many Free Soilers sought on principle to extend the rights of free blacks, so most espoused the Wilmot Proviso primarily because they saw in it a perfectly constitutional way not merely to restrain, but ultimately to abolish, slavery. Although acutely sensitive to the "danger of frightening many disposed to join the movement with the cry of Abolition,"[56] the great mass of Free Soilers were as much committed to uprooting slavery everywhere as were the most dedicated Garrisonians. Their sense of outrage was less, their patience in the face of evil vastly greater. But their goal was the same. "Our mission," in-

54 *National Era*, Nov. 9, 1848, Apr. 24, 1851; *Report of the Debates . . . of the Convention for the Revision of the Constitution of . . . Indiana, 1850*, I, 586.
55 Jackson to Mann, Mar. 22, 1850, Mann Papers.
56 Stanley Matthews to Salmon P. Chase, June 12, 1848, Chase Papers, LC. Joshua Giddings cautioned Salmon Chase to "say nothing about the *abolition* of slavery. This is misunderstood and frightens many. I would go for the *separation of the federal government from all interference with that institution*. This in its effect and consequences is *abolition*, but in a much more acceptable form than the other." June 17, 1848, Chase Papers, PHS.

sisted E. S. Hamlin, the Ohio Free Soil editor, "is to overthrow slavery *in the States*, as well as to keep it out of the territories. . . ."[57] Likewise, Congressman Erastus Culver of New York declared in a rousing address to the Buffalo Free Soil Convention of 1848: "Now gentlemen, I say check slavery where it is and then I will show you a man that will go still farther. We have never guarantied [*sic*] that slavery shall rest on that 50 square miles [the District of Columbia] yet.—[No, no, no.] When my constituents sent me to Congress, I told them plainly just what I meant to do. I said as long as there is a loophole through which I can fire on this abominable old institution, I shall fire away. [Good, good, give 'em hell.]"[58]

Almost to a man, Free Soilers conceded that the North had no right "to act politically, on the local institutions of the South." Slavery, they admitted, was a purely local institution, a creature of state law, and as such was protected by the Constitution against outside assaults. Congress had no more power to abolish slavery in South Carolina than to abolish free schools in Massachusetts. At the same time, most agreed, antislavery men had a right and a duty to point out the moral wrong of slavery and, by denying the Slave Power fresh lands and government favor, force the South "to adopt some plan of gradual emancipation."[59]

To some, the Wilmot Proviso was simply a way of quarantining a contagion, of leaving the South to its own vicious devices so long as it refrained from aggression on lands already free.[60] Most Free Soilers,

[57] Hamlin to Salmon P. Chase, Mar. 11, 1850, Chase Papers, PHS. Six weeks later, provoked by a speech of Chase's that he found unduly cautious, Hamlin exclaimed: "I think we should let slaveholders understand that we make war upon the institution of slavery itself wherever it exists; and, when we have strength to legislate for its overthrow in the States, I think we shall find Constitutional powers through which to exert that strength." *Ibid.* Apr. 25, 1850.

[58] Dyer, *Phonographic Report*, 12. See also *Independent Democrat*, Feb. 28, 1850; *Green Mountain Freeman*, Nov. 2, 1848; *Boston Daily Republican*, Aug. 9, Sept. 29, 1849; William Whiting, *An Appeal to the Citizens of the Free States, Upon the Aspects of the Slave Question, and the Claims of the Free-Soil Movement, to Their Support* (Boston, 1848), 10.

[59] See, e.g., George W. Julian's speech in Congress, May 14, 1859, *Cong. Globe*, 31st Cong., 1st sess., Appendix, 574; *National Era*, May 24, 1849; *Independent Democrat & Freeman*, Aug. 3, 1848; *Free Territory Sentinel*, Aug. 16, 1848.

[60] Once again, free soil Democrats most often held this negative view of the Proviso. See, e.g., Wilmot's speech at a Democratic convention in Tioga Co., Pa., quoted in *Independent Democrat & Freeman*, Oct. 21, 1847; Jacob Brinkerhoff's speech in U.S. House of Representatives, Feb. 10, 1847, *Cong. Globe*, 29th Cong., 2nd sess., 377.

however, accepted uncritically the view that slavery must spread or die, and that the Proviso was therefore a sure-fire, if gradual, means of abolition. As Wilmot himself put it, "Slavery has within itself the seeds of its own dissolution. Keep it within limits, let it remain where it now is, and in time it will wear itself out." The reason, the *National Era* explained, was that Southerners had found slavery suitable chiefly for agriculture—especially cotton cultivation. And staple crop production, although profitable given ideal conditions, was "an exhausting process," which quickly impoverished the soil. Meanwhile, the natural increase of the slave population created new burdens for hardpressed planters and heightened the danger of insurrection. Lacking the time to reinvigorate lands through scientific agriculture, and unwilling or unable to funnel slaves into industrial pursuits, planters in the settled parts of the South would soon face a choice of moving on or releasing their slaves. By shutting off westward migration, the Wilmot Proviso would leave slaveholders only one option—emancipation. At the same time, of course, fencing in slavery would curtail the South's political power and hence its ability to fend off flanking attacks in the future. "The Black Hole of Calcutta was not more fatal to its inmates," Gamaliel Bailey editorialized, "than would be a limited area to slavery."[61]

A great many Northerners who shared the Free Soilers' desire to keep slavery within present bounds nonetheless argued that the Wilmot Proviso was unnecessary and hence undesirable. God Himself, some maintained, had set natural limits beyond which slavery might not go. Climate and soil, said Daniel Webster in his celebrated speech on the Compromise of 1850, had made the question of slavery in the territories acquired from Mexico "a mere abstraction." "The whole controversy," another observer insisted, "related to an imaginary negro in an impossible place." It was a grave mistake, such men argued, to risk sectional discord merely "to reaffirm an ordinance of nature . . . , to reenact the will of God."[62]

For many reasons, Free Soilers thought otherwise. To begin with,

[61] Wilmot's speech at Albany, Oct. 29, 1847, quoted in *Albany Atlas*, Nov. 9, 1847; *National Era*, Feb. 4, 1847, Feb. 20, 1851. See also *Boston Daily Whig*, Aug. 21, 1847; *Independent Democrat & Freeman*, Oct. 21, 1847, Oct. 12, 1848; James Wilson to Moses A. Cartland, Dec. 11, 1848, Moses A. Cartland Papers, HLH.

[62] *Cong. Globe*, 31st Cong., 1st sess., Appendix, 269-76; Arthur Bestor, "Patent Office Models of the Good Society: Some Relationships Between Social Reform and Westward Expansion," *American Historical Review*, LVIII, No. 3 (Apr. 1953), 505-26.

they contended, the Proviso gave men a chance to pass moral censure on a barbaric institution. To permit its spread to any other quarter (as an extension of the Missouri compromise line would have done), or to allow mere numerical majorities to determine its future (the essence of popular sovereignty), or even to duck the issue by opposing any new territorial acquisitions would be to compromise with evil, to overlook the question of right and wrong. The Wilmot Proviso, Charles Francis Adams admitted, was "an abstraction to be sure." But, he went on, "so was Magna Charta an abstraction. So is the idea of right and justice and the truth of God an abstraction. And it is these abstractions that raise mankind above the brutes that perish."[63]

More, too, than Northern consciences and souls were involved, for slavery's reputation bore a direct relation to its vitality. As the Barnburner *Oswego Palladium* observed, the failure to place a ban on slavery expansion was causing "slavery itself . . . to lose its abhorrent features in the eyes of many, and its advocates, emboldened by the timidity of those who entertain different views, claim for it unlimited extension and perpetuity of duration."[64] To Free Soilers the Wilmot Proviso represented an effective antidote to the poisonous notion that slavery was a positive good, a blessing to be spread far and wide.[65]

Not only was the Proviso desirable, Free Soilers alleged, but it was absolutely essential if the territories were to be preserved for freedom. Webster's thesis that "Slavery, like the cotton-plant, is confined by natural laws to certain parallels of latitude," struck Free Soil spokesmen as dangerous nonsense, and they went to great lengths to refute it. "Slavery," said Whittier, sounding a common note, "is singularly cosmopolitan in its habits. The offspring of pride and lust and avarice, it is indigenous to the world. . . . It has the universal acclimation of sin."[66] Taking a less metaphysical tack, David Wilmot warned Congress that ". . . wherever labor is in demand—wherever there is work to do, there the slave is valuable, and there he will be taken, unless legal barriers are interposed to prevent it." Only strong and farsighted action by the Founding Fathers had purged slavery from Northeastern states and barred its encroachment into the Old Northwest; only the Mis-

[63] Dyer, *Phonographic Report*, 7.
[64] Quoted in *Albany Atlas*, Aug. 17, 1847.
[65] See, e.g., Jacob Brinkerhoff's defense of the Proviso, Feb. 10, 1847, *Cong. Globe*, 29th Cong., 2nd sess., 378-79.
[66] *National Era*, May 2, 1850.

souri Compromise had kept slavery from overspreading the whole of the Louisiana Purchase.[67]

As for California and New Mexico, even if one conceded that soil and climate ruled out staple crop production (a point not all Free Soilers were willing to grant), the threat of slavery remained great. For, it was argued, history proved bondage to be admirably suited to mining operations. Southern newspapers openly admitted as much. Why, then, not anticipate the migration of slaveholders with their chattels into the gold fields of California and the mineral-rich regions of New Mexico?[68] Slaves might also be brought to the Southwest as domestic servants. And, as Horace Mann noted: "If individuals do not desire to carry slavery into New Mexico, for *personal* profit, may not communities & states desire it for political aggrandizement?"[69] Surely there was nothing to suggest that Southerners recognized natural barriers to the establishment of slavery in the newly acquired territories. Indeed, Senator James M. Mason of Virginia was quoted as saying in 1850 that had California been organized first as a *territory* "the people of the Southern States would have gone there freely, and have taken their slaves there in great numbers."[70]

To many Free Soilers, the peril of slavery in the West seemed not only conceivable, but actual and immediate. Pondering the "momentous crisis" of the times, John P. Hale perceived in the summer of 1849 a "great and imminent danger" that slavery would overrun all the newly won territories, including California. The threat, he warned,

> is even now upon us and while the interested & venal are lulling us with the syren song that there is "no danger" slaves are being carried into those territories, the clanking of whose chains, and the cries of whose agony shall fill the ear of the Most High, call-

[67] *Cong. Globe*, 31st Cong., 1st sess., Appendix, 515 (May 3, 1850); *Albany Atlas*, Nov. 9, 1847; *Independent Democrat*, May 2, 1850; *National Era*, Feb. 27, 1851; Charles Sumner to Lord Morpeth, May 21, 1850, Pierce (ed.), *Letters of Sumner*, III, 214-15. Free Soilers were not, of course, the only antislavery group to take issue with the natural limits argument. See, e.g., William H. Seward's Senate speech of March 11, 1850, *Cong. Globe*, 31st Cong., 1st sess., Appendix, 266; *Liberator*, Mar. 22, 1850; Wendell Phillips, *Review of Webster's Speech on Slavery* (Boston, 1850), 19ff.
[68] *National Era*, Mar. 14, 1850, Feb. 27, July 24, 1851; Horace Mann to Mrs. Mann, Mar. 10, 1850, Mann Papers.
[69] Mann to S. Downer, Jr., Mar. 21, 1850, Mann Papers.
[70] Quoted in Horace Mann, *New Dangers to Freedom, and New Duties For Its Defenders: A Letter by the Hon. Horace Mann to his Constituents, May 3, 1850* (Boston, 1850), 18.

ing for vengeance upon us, if through timidity, party spirit or
any other cause, we hold our peace, and do not do what we may
to prevent so great a wrong.

At the same time, the *Essex County Freeman*, under the headline
"THERE IS DANGER," cautioned that Southerners were "adopting every
device to insinuate slavery into the territories recently acquired. . . .
They have actually sold slaves there."[71]

Such accounts may have exaggerated the threat of slavery's encroachment on the Southwest, but they by no means invented it.
Throughout 1849, as gold-mad prospectors stormed westward, reports
circulated in the Northern press that companies of Southerners, "armed
to the teeth," were being formed "for the express purpose of carrying
slaves into California."[72] Quotations from Southern papers like the
Kosciusko (Miss.) *Jeffersonian* to the effect that "The idea that slave
property cannot be sufficiently profitable to permit negroes to be taken
to California, is turning out to be untrue," fueled antislavery apprehensions. So too did reports that a Negro woman and her child had recently been sold for $1000 in San Francisco, and that a widely reprinted
article from the *Natchez Free Trader* had revealed that General Bris-
coe, one of the biggest planters in Mississippi, had lately set out with
his slaves for California to test the theory that bondsmen might profitably be used "on the placers, where nothing but physical labor is required."[73] Not unreasonably, Free Soilers and other critics of slavery
insisted that eternal vigilance and congressional action remained the
price of liberty—even in California.

Indeed, not even California's admission as a free state in 1850 wholly
stilled such fears. What more than anything kept them alive were reports (emanating particularly from the *San Francisco Evening Picayune*) of a scheme to split California into two states, making one free,
one slave. At first, claimed the *Picayune* (whose editors opposed "fa-
natical abolitionism" and showed scant concern over slavery elsewhere), this plan was dismissed as the "offspring of diseased imagina-

---

[71] Hale to Moses M. Davis, Aug. 25, 1849, Moses M. Davis Papers, SHSW; *Essex
County Freeman*, Aug. 11, 1849. See also *National Era*, July 5, 1849; *Green Mountain Freeman*, Nov. 8, 1849.
[72] *Independent Democrat*, May 3, 31, 1849; Lynn (Mass.) *Bay State*, quoted in *National Era*, Nov. 22, 1849; J. H. Allen to Theodore Parker, Mar. 14, 1850, Letterbook, Theodore Parker Papers, MHS.
[73] *Kosciusko Jeffersonian*, *Natchez Free Trader*, quoted in *Green Mountain Freeman*, Sept. 6, 1849, May 23, 1850.

tion on the part of a few restless, ambitious, ultra southern disunionists."
By the middle of 1851, however, it had behind it "many of the most
enlightened and responsible men in the Democratic party." The danger
was clear and present. Unless Californians rallied to the side of freedom, warned the *Picayune*, "the day will not be far distant, when free
white men will be forced to stand aside, and yield the mines to southern slaves, while their wealthy owners will quietly sip their wine
beneath the magnolia and palmetto trees of Louisiana and South
Carolina."[74]

In point of fact, the movement to divide California antedated the
American presence there and apparently owed more to longstanding
regional enmity than to conflict over slavery. As the French vice-
consul observed in 1851, southern California differed from the rest of
the state not only in its greater receptivity to slavery, but in its overwhelmingly agricultural economy and in the strongly Mexican flavor
of its religion, customs, and people. The few great landholders who
dominated the southern counties complained that the more populous,
commercially-oriented north taxed them unfairly yet disregarded their
needs in such matters as crime control.[75]

Yet whatever the motives of those who pressed for division, those
who opposed the creation of a second California did so chiefly out of
fear of slavery expansion. And throughout the 1850s recurrent proposals of division, together with continued reports that Southern slaveholders still hoped for a slave state on the Pacific, kept Free Soilers and
Republicans on guard.[76] In April 1859 their worst fears seemed con-

[74] *San Francisco Evening Picayune*, June 10, 1851, quoted in *ibid.* July 31, 1851.
About the same time, Francis P. Blair, Sr., took note of Pennsylvania Free Soilers'
abhorrence of James Buchanan "on account of his design (not yet relinquished) of
dividing California by the line of 36°30′ giving one half of this free state to slavery.
There is now an active movement going on in California to effect the division."
Blair to Gideon Welles, Oct. 5, 1851, Welles Papers, CHS.
[75] J. Lombard to Monsieur le Ministre, Secrétaire d'État en Département des Af-
faires Étrangères de France à Paris, Aug. 30, 1851, in A. P. Nasatir (trans.), "A
French Pessimist in California: The Correspondence of J. Lombard, Vice-Consul
of France, 1850-1852," *California Historical Society Quarterly*, XXXI, No. 4 (Dec.
1952), 319-20; Rockwell D. Hunt, "History of the California State Division Controversy," *Annual Publications*, Historical Society of Southern California, XIII
(1924), 37-53; J. Gregg Layne, "Annals of Los Angeles," *California Historical Society Quarterly*, XIII, No. 4 (Dec. 1934), 346.
[76] *Green Mountain Freeman*, Apr. 22, Aug. 12, 1852, Jan. 20, 1853; *National Era*,
Feb. 19, Mar. 11, Apr. 29, May 20, 1852; *Essex County Freeman*, Mar. 27, 1852;
New-York Daily Tribune, May 11, 1859.

firmed when the California legislature voted to allow five southern counties and part of a sixth to form a separate government to be known as the Territory of Colorado. Californians approved this measure by the required two-thirds and sent it along to Congress for final endorsement. Before any action could be taken, however, the Civil War intervened, and when in later years proposals to divide the state surfaced again the question of slavery was but a memory.[77]

Free Soilers were even more convinced that, if given the chance, slavery would fix its blight upon Utah and New Mexico. "Unless a sprout of opposition is set," Horace Mann confided to a friend early in 1851, "slavery is as certain to invade New Mexico & Utah, as the sun is to rise."[78] Left free by the congressional acts of 1850 to legislate on slavery as well as other "rightful" subjects, the Southwestern territories struck antislavery men as being especially vulnerable to proslavery influences. For if, as the *National Era* remarked, slavery threatened California, a state "composed generally of enterprising, intelligent citizens," what might be expected in New Mexico and Utah, where "the populations are much lower in the scale of civilization, and which no constitutional provision shields against aggression?"[79] By 1851 the peculiar institution had gained a toehold in the Southwest, and the appointment of slaveholders to key territorial offices heightened fears that its influence would steadily rise. Henry Clay's proposal that Congress refrain from interfering with the interstate slave trade was interpreted by some Free Soilers as a determination "to facilitate the passage" of slaves into New Mexico. And when Governor William Carr Lane himself purchased two black slaves at Santa Fe in 1852, Free Soilers felt even more sure that nothing short of positive congressional barriers could keep slavery out of the Southwest.[80]

That there were never more than a handful of Negro slaves in New Mexico and Utah and fewer still in California in no way eased Free Soil anxiety. For, the Proviso's champions believed, if slavery were accorded equal rights with freedom even a relatively small band of slaveholders could overwhelm vastly larger numbers of nonslaveholders and

[77] Layne, "Annals of Los Angeles," 346.
[78] Mann to Samuel Gridley Howe, Jan. 28, 1851, Mann Papers.
[79] *National Era*, Feb. 20, 1851.
[80] *Ibid.* June 19, 1851; *Boston Weekly Commonwealth*, Aug. 16, 1851; Mann, *New Dangers to Freedom*, 11; Holman Hamilton, *Prologue to Conflict: The Crisis and Compromise of 1850* (Lexington, Ky., 1964), 175.

mould the institutions of the infant West to their own satisfaction. Since, it was argued, free and slave labor were fundamentally incompatible, once a few thousand slaves had been introduced to a territory the most enterprising free men would be driven off and the country surrendered to masters and slaves. "One slaveholder with his gang of negroes," maintained the *New York Post*, "elbows out thousands of free settlers who bring only the implements of their toil and their own hardy families."[81] Those poor, slaveless whites who remained would be no match for the powerful and imperious planters who, perhaps aided by fresh waves of slave immigration, would quickly gain political—as well as social and economic—dominance. Moreover, Free Soilers professed: "Just as the twig is bent so the tree's inclined."[82] Once slavery was rooted in the territorial stage, the question would no longer be should it exist, but should it be abolished? With slaveowners in the saddle, who could doubt the answer? To those who found this logic unconvincing, Free Soilers responded by pointing to Missouri, where "the bare permission" given planters to enter with their chattels "fixed its character as a slave state." Not even Oregon had been safe, antislavery men insisted, until Congress extended the Northwest Ordinance to it in 1848.[83]

Admittedly, some of this dismay may have been bogus, produced for effect. Free Soilers doubtless understood that to insist on the need for the Proviso *everywhere* was the best way to secure its application at least somewhere. Likewise, they probably discovered that warnings of slavery's danger to Oregon or California, if nothing else, effectively advertised the image of the "Slave Power's" insatiable greed and the magnitude of the threat slavery posed to all Northerners. Yet it also appears that the apprehensions voiced by most Free Soilers—that slavery might force itself upon any territory not protected by congressional ordinance—were genuine. Certainly they knew that Southern representatives fought against having their peculiar institution banned in any ter-

---

[81] *Essex County Freeman*, Mar. 23, 1850; *New York Weekly Evening Post*, Mar. 23, 1848.
[82] Speech of Preston King at Canton, N.Y., July 4, 1848, quoted in *Albany Atlas*, Aug. 11, 1848.
[83] *Speech of Hon. W. Collins, of New York, on the Bill to Establish the Territorial Government of Oregon. Delivered in The House of Representatives, July 28, 1848* (Washington, D.C., 1848), 4, 8-9; Amos Tuck to John G. Palfrey, Apr. 13, 1850, Palfrey Papers; *New York Weekly Evening Post*, Feb. 17, Apr. 27, 1848; Sewell, *Hale*, 119-21.

ritory, however arid or mountainous, and they took such resistance, not illogically, as evidence of expansionist hopes if not designs. Lest one discount overmuch Free Soil fears of slavery in the Southwest, it is also well to remember that in 1859 New Mexico actually provided itself with a slave code.[84]

While non-extension was the Free Soilers' dominant concern, it was not by any means the whole of their antislavery program. Both the party platform of 1848 and that of 1852 demanded that the federal government "relieve itself from all responsibility for the existence or continuance of slavery" wherever it had the constitutional power to do so. What this might mean if practiced, Free Soilers spelled out on many occasions. Typical was the response of the *Boston Daily Republican* to challenges in 1849 from two neighboring newspapers, one accusing Free Soilers of ignoring the problem of slavery in the states, the other roasting the *Republican* for advocating assaults on slavery even where safeguarded by the Constitution. To the first complaint the *Republican* (then edited by Henry Wilson) replied by citing the goal of the 1848 Buffalo convention not merely to limit but to *discourage* slavery, and added: "There is a *power* in the INFLUENCE of the Federal Government which is now almost entirely exerted for slavery. We mean it shall be exerted for freedom." To the charge that it proposed outside intervention in the domestic institutions of Southern states, the *Republican* answered:

> We would have the National Government pass an organic law, that should *forever* preserve all the territories to freedom; we would have it abolish slavery and the slave trade in the District of Columbia—forbid the interstate slave trade—repeal the [fugitive slave] law of 1793 and all other acts that in any way make the people of the free States responsible for the existence of slavery—exercise all its constitutional power to discourage, localize, and destroy slavery—and use its patronage and influence to sustain the friends of emancipation in all lawful, constitutional, and just means, to free the slave States from the wrongs and evils of a system that blasts their prosperity, disgraces the country, and destroys the rights and happiness of three millions of our fellow men. If this is interference with slavery in the States, so be it.[85]

[84] Harry V. Jaffa, *Crisis of the House Divided: An Interpretation of the Issues in the Lincoln-Douglas Debates* (New York, 1959), 390-91.
[85] *Boston Daily Republican*, Aug. 9, Sept. 29, 1849.

Once slavery lost its special privileges, Free Soilers maintained, once the influence of government were brought to the side of freedom, the corrupt and corrupting peculiar institution would quickly fall. Naked to its enemies, it could withstand neither the currents of nineteenth-century humanitarianism and republicanism nor the competition of a free labor economy.

4

Aware of and to some extent affected by the racial biases of their day, Free Soilers, like Liberty men earlier, often couched their antislavery message in language that was directed strongly toward the self-interest of white Americans. Some took this tack because of their own negro-phobia; others did so because it seemed the likeliest way to win new recruits. For all, the concept of a conspiratorial Slave Power possessed a propagandistic value too great to pass up.

No one calculated the potential of this approach more clearly than did Joshua Leavitt. Impressed at the currency the term "Slave Power" had gained even among Whigs and Democrats, Leavitt concluded in 1848 that its "incessant use" would "do much to open the eyes & arouse the energies of the people." To Salmon Chase, whom he had once chided for camouflaging the Liberty party's abolitionist bent, Leavitt now advised:

> *The Slave Power! Delenda est,* is the response of every patri-
> otic bosom, the moment it is brought to comprehend the *reality*
> of the existence & extent of this Slave Power. We must keep our
> eyes upon this, & familiarize the people to the facts. . . . Let it
> appear that it is the *Slave Power* which we wish to restrict & to
> curtail; that it is the *Slave Power* whose demands we resist, whose
> growth we deprecate, whose usurpations we will put down.[86]

In exploiting the Slave Power concept, Free Soilers generally fol-lowed the lead of earlier Liberty party pamphleteers. Once again they published detailed accounts of the South's dominance of federal offices and policies. Once again they chronicled slavery's ruinous influence upon private morality and social order. But whereas Liberty men had

[86] Leavitt to Chase, July 7, 1848, Chase Papers, PHS.

concentrated on the Slave Power's responsibility for the depression of 1837-43, Free Soil propagandists, writing in flush times, warned chiefly of the South's conspiracy to force slavery into fresh pastures and of the irresistible conflict between slave labor and free labor.

Behind the plot to extend slavery's sway, Free Soilers believed, stood the Slave Power's inherent restlessness. "The word 'peace' is not in its vocabulary," argued the *Independent Democrat*. "Slavery being itself a system of war upon all the higher and holier rights of man, can have no peace with any who do not acknowledge its supremacy." So ceaselessly aggressive was the Slave Power in pursuit of its interests, Charles Sumner observed, that the cause of peace as well as of abolition depended upon its overthrow. "As soon as it is distinctly established that there shall be no more slave territory," he maintained, "there will be little danger of war."[87]

With so voracious a foe, Free Soil publicists cautioned, constant vigilance was imperative. Accordingly, the party's newspapers and pamphlets bristled with detailed exposés of "The Gigantic Plans of the Slave Power." Not only did planter oligarchs plot the conversion of New Mexico and Utah into slaveholding territories and the partition of California into slave and free halves, but, Free Soilers claimed, schemes were already afoot to counterbalance Northern influence through new conquests in Mexico and the Caribbean. By 1849 if not sooner, antislavery voices gave warning of behind-the-scenes attempts to bring Cuba (with its heavy slave population) into the American Union. Haiti and Santo Domingo were also said to figure in Southern dreams of empire. If not checked, the Slave Power might well commit the United States to ruinous and reactionary actions throughout Latin America.[88]

Such Free Soil apprehensions, while at times exaggerated, were by no means baseless. Both Presidents Polk and Taylor had lately sought acquisition of Cuba by purchase. The adventurer Narciso Lopez had risked (and lost) his life in the same cause. And although "The Pearl of the Antilles" offered strategic and economic resources appealing to men of all sections, there remained little doubt that the South would

[87] *Independent Democrat*, July 31, 1851; Sumner to Richard Cobden, July 9, 1850, Pierce (ed.), *Letters of Sumner*, III, 216-17.
[88] *Portland Inquirer*, June 19, 1849, June 26, 1851; *National Era*, June 19, 1851; *Green Mountain Freeman*, Sept. 8, Oct. 6, 1853.

benefit most from its annexation. Surely most slaveholders thought so, and Free Soilers slipped easily into the argument that what devils propose angels should oppose.[89]

It was essential to resist the aggressions of the Slave Power, third party men maintained, because the peculiar institution not only crushed blacks but degraded free labor as well. Indeed, as the Massachusetts party declared in 1849, wherever slavery took root the whole social fabric unraveled: "labor loses its dignity; industry sickens; education finds no schools; religion finds no churches, and the whole land of Slavery is impoverished." One had only to compare the "unexampled growth of population, wealth, intelligence, and power" in the Old Northwest (rescued from slavery's blight by Jefferson's farsighted ordinance) with the corruption and decay of its slave state neighbors to appreciate fully the blessings of freedom. Much of the Free Soil propaganda effort, therefore, went into explanations of slavery's depressing effect upon the dignity and profitability of free labor, of its burdensome influence on the march of civilization. Slavery *and* the Slave Power remained, as before, the twin enemies of political abolition.[90]

---

[89] For an excellent account of Southern plans for tropical expansion, see Robert E. May, *The Southern Dream of a Caribbean Empire, 1854-1861* (Baton Rouge, 1973). On Lopez, see *ibid.* 25-30; Robert G. Caldwell, *The Lopez Expedition to Cuba, 1848-1851* (Princeton, 1915).

[90] *Boston Daily Republican,* Sept. 14, 1849; *National Era,* Sept. 16, 1847, June 29, Nov. 2, 1848; *Independent Democrat & Freeman,* Oct. 12, 1848; Isaac N. Arnold *et al.* to Martin Van Buren, June 16, 1848, Van Buren Papers; speech of Lewis D. Campbell in U.S. House of Representatives, Feb. 19, 1850, *Cong. Globe,* 31st Cong., 1st sess., Appendix, 181.

9

Coalitions

DEFEAT IN 1848 RAISED HARD QUESTIONS for Free Soilers. Though the party improved significantly upon earlier Liberty votes for Birney and sent a dozen representatives to Congress, the tally for Van Buren and Adams revealed bluntly how slight was the Free Soil impact upon the North—to say nothing of the nation. While outwardly optimistic, a good many Free Soilers had begun to wonder privately whether an antislavery third party was still viable. Especially among the Barnburner faction there early emerged a predisposition to conclude that the defeat of Cass made a return to old party attachments the most natural and effective course. Even many who continued to advocate an independent antislavery organization now weighed the moral advantages of going-it-alone, of strict detachment from Whigs and Democrats, against the likelihood that through coalition with one or another of those parties reliable antislavery candidates might be elected to key public offices, and the work of political regeneration quickened.

Of those who continued to press for a truly autonomous Free Soil strategy, none was more articulate or influential than Joshua Giddings. Drawn into social reform by personal crisis and religious conviction, Giddings publicly dedicated himself to the antislavery cause in the summer of 1838. That fall, running as a Whig, the strapping, broad-shouldered young lawyer won election to Congress from Ohio's Western Reserve—already a hotbed of abolitionist activity. Though at first "determined to soothe and reconcile" conflicting opinion on slavery, in the naïve hope that reform might be effected "without contention

and noise," Giddings soon became outraged at gags on antislavery petitions from his constituents and the sight of coffles of bondsmen being
driven insolently past Capitol Hill.[1] Thereafter he grew increasingly
bold in his attacks on slavery and the "Slave Power." Fearless and resourceful, a rough-and-ready debater thoroughly versed in all aspects
of the slavery question, he quickly established himself as "Congress'
vocal catalyst," next to John Quincy Adams (with whom he formed a
warm friendship) the most respected antislavery voice in Washington.[2]

Giddings had been critical of the Liberty party since its beginnings,
believing it easier to convert existing parties to antislavery positions
than to build a new organization. As well, he was convinced that his
own influence was greatest as a Whig.[3] Taylor's nomination in 1848,
however, on a platform that dodged the slavery question, drove Giddings reluctantly into the Free Soil alliance. Once there, once having
choked down his long-standing dislike of Martin Van Buren, he refused
to turn back. Had Taylor been defeated and had the Whig party
sought new leaders and programs, Giddings's old loyalties might have
reasserted themselves; he might conceivably have returned, vindicated,
to help in the work of renovation. As it was, he found little incentive
to rejoin an unreconstructed party now headed by a slaveholder
President.[4]

Indeed, Giddings not only kept his identity as a Free Soiler but, in
the aftermath of Van Buren's drubbing, urged others of that party to
resist all proposals of amalgamation or coalition with Whigs or Democrats. "It strikes me that we should stand entirely independent of both
parties," he observed in the spring of 1849. "Any alliance with either
would at once disband us." At the very least, political deals with tainted
older parties would water down Free Soil principles. Besides, Giddings
insisted, "Our mission is to *correct public opinion,* not at present to
control political action." Once public sentiment had grown sufficiently
enlightened to sustain a thoroughgoing antislavery program, reformers

---

[1] Giddings to [Gamaliel Bailey?], Feb. 26, 1839, Miscellaneous Manuscripts, NYHS.
[2] Giddings's life is perceptively examined in James B. Stewart, *Joshua R. Giddings
and the Tactics of Radical Politics* (Cleveland, 1970).
[3] Giddings to Salmon P. Chase, Feb. 19, Oct. 12, 1843, Chase Papers, PHS.
[4] President Taylor's fight against Henry Clay's compromise plan of 1850 ultimately
won grudging praise from Giddings and other Free Soilers. "Old Tai's" sudden
death, however, followed by the accession of the acquiescent Fillmore and the
swift passage of the Compromise, left Giddings more alienated from his former
party than ever. Stewart, *Giddings,* 185-86.

might legitimately exalt partisan maneuver above moral instruction—
not before.[5]

Echoing as it did the methods and postulates of the early Liberty
party, Giddings's position found support among a number of pioneer
political abolitionists. The great mass of Free Soilers, however, at first
preferred the fusionist or coalitionist policy laid down most cogently
by Giddings's Ohio rival, Salmon P. Chase.

Chase's fascination with coalition politics was, of course, nothing
new. Almost from the moment he joined the Liberty party he had
worked to advance its (and his own) interests through alliance with
antislavery elements in other parties. His unsuccessful effort to find a
more "available" candidate than Birney in 1844, his sponsorship of the
Southern and Western Liberty Convention of 1845 (which sought the
support of all political abolitionists), his enthusiasm for the New Hampshire Alliance, his early and zealous labors in forging the Free Soil coalition of 1848—all displayed Chase's restless, pragmatic quest for the
strongest possible antislavery union.

Nearly as long-standing was Chase's conviction that the true maxims
of the Democratic party offered potentially the soundest basis for such
a union. As early as 1844 he had proposed changing the Liberty party's
name to "True Democrat," and by 1847 he was writing that whereas
"the Whig party will always look upon the overthrow of slavery as a
work to be taken up or laid aside . . . as expediency may suggest," the
Democrats, once awakened to the idea that slavery's destruction was "a
legitimate and necessary result" of their principles, could be counted
on to see the job through.[6]

As he surveyed the political landscape in the aftermath of the 1848
campaign, Chase found himself more than ever convinced that personal
interest and antislavery advancement would best be served by fasten-

[5] Giddings to Chase, May 6, 1849, Chase Papers, PHS.
[6] William Birney to James G. Birney, Nov. 25, 1844, Dumond (ed.), *Birney Letters*,
II, 887; Chase to John P. Hale, May 12, 1847, Hale Papers, NHHS. Chase had, in
fact, begun his political life as a Whig. In 1832 he served as a delegate to the National Republican convention which nominated Henry Clay and in 1836 and 1840
he threw his support to Harrison. But on many issues—the tariff, money, and banking—he stood shoulder-to-shoulder with the Jacksonians. Had it not been for
Democratic backwardness on the slavery question, he might well have switched to
that party instead of the Liberty party once his hopes of exerting an antislavery
influence over President Harrison died. See Chase to [?], July 10, 1853, Chase Papers, LC; Albert B. Hart, *Salmon Portland Chase* (Boston, 1899), 86-90.

ing the Free Soil party to the Northern Democracy. Early signs persuaded Chase that Hunker Democrats, having been defeated in the recent presidential election by Cass's popular sovereignty doctrine and
cut off now from the spoils that had formerly bound them to the
South, might begin to cast "a wistful eye toward the Buffalo platform."
To facilitate a merger of the regular Democracy and the Free Democracy (as he now dubbed the Free Soilers), Chase urged third party men
to adopt "a liberal and conciliatory" attitude toward old line Democrats. He also began to trumpet his own predilections and to describe
the Buffalo platform as merely traditional Democratic dogma cleansed
of its proslavery heresies. If Democrats made good their faith by ap-
plying the "great cardinal doctrine of equal rights" in all ways, he for
one would cast his lot with them.[7]

In theory the strategies of Chase and Giddings were not wholly contradictory. Although Chase was prepared to believe the best concerning Democratic intentions he, as much as Giddings, insisted on "the indispensable necessity of maintaining the antislavery character of our
Free Democracy." Any lowering of the Buffalo creed would be "a
deplorable mistake"—a forfeiture of political strength and moral
power.[8] Similarly, Giddings, while opposed to merger or coalition at
present, held no selfish hopes for the Free Soil party and foresaw some
sort of reconstitution of parties in the future. And after 1850, like
Chase, he viewed the Whig party as defunct, beyond hope of redemption.

In practice, however, the two men and their followers pursued
strikingly different courses. Whereas Giddings and a portion of the
old Liberty host pointedly held themselves aloof from political dealing
of any kind, Chase called for a more "realistic" approach. As he professed to Charles Sumner:

> I fear that this world is not to be redeemed from its ten thou-
> sand self inflicted curses so easily as we flatter ourselves at the
> outset of any reform enterprise, and, especially, before brought

[7] Chase to James H. Smith, May 8, 1849, Chase to Charles Sumner, Nov. 27, 1848,
Chase, *Diary and Correspondence*, 144, 171-72; Chase to Albert G. Riddle, Feb. 24,
1849, Albert G. Riddle Papers, WRHS; Chase to Thomas Bolton, Apr. 17, 1849,
Chase to George Reber, June 19, 1849, Letterbook, Chase Papers, LC.
[8] Chase to E. S. Hamlin, July 26, Dec. 15, 1849, May 27, 1850, Chase Papers, LC;
Chase to Benjamin F. Butler, July 26, 1849, Chase, *Diary and Correspondence*,
180-82.

much in contact with the machinery behind the scenes, by which
the movements in view are regulated.[9]

By the time that he penned these lines Chase had proved himself a master of backstairs diplomacy and through an arrangement with Ohio Democrats had won election as United States Senator. His victory represented a setback for Giddings's political strategy and personal ambition.

Chase found his opportunity in a stalemated state legislature and what the *Cleveland True Democrat* tagged "a little dirty squabble about an apportionment law."[10] The facts, briefly, were these. Early in 1848 Ohio Whigs, in an attempt to strengthen their hand in the legislature, forced through passage of a law dividing Hamilton County (which included Cincinnati) into two districts. Democrats refused to acquiesce in the flagrant gerrymander, with the result that in the fall election both new districts sent rival sets of representatives to Columbus, each claiming legitimacy. Since control of the legislature depended upon which set was seated, the stakes in the Hamilton contest were high. And since the Free Soilers held the balance between Whigs and Democrats in both houses, they found themselves in an enviable position. Among the prizes that might be claimed in return for their assistance in organizing the legislature was a place in the Senate of the United States.[11]

Both Giddings and Chase coveted that powerful and prestigious office. While admitting that he might be most effective in the House, where he had "established an influence," Giddings confessed to his journal that "the moral effect of my election would be great, and on that account I feel a desire to succeed to that office."[12] Chase was even more ambitious, and, though outwardly modest and discreet, much less willing than Giddings to leave his fate to chance. While the high-minded Giddings sat passively in Washington, discountenancing all deals on his behalf, Chase and his agents contrived an arrangement with Ohio Democrats designed to advance simultaneously his own fortunes

[9] *Ibid.* 183.
[10] Quoted in Smith, *Liberty and Free Soil Parties*, 180.
[11] *Ibid.* 162-63; Hart, *Chase*, 104-5; Blue, "Ohio Free Soilers," 20-21. The composition of the house was 32 Democrats, 30 Whigs, 8 Free Soilers, and 2 contested seats representing Hamilton County. Of the Free Soilers 5 had been elected with the aid of Whig votes, 1 with help from Democrats, and 2 as independent third party men. The senate included 17 Democrats, 14 Whigs, and 3 Free Soilers.
[12] Quoted in Smith, *Liberty and Free Soil Parties*, 170.

and those of free soil. "Reliable" Free Soilers would cooperate in seating the Democratic representatives from Hamilton County, thus giving to that party control of the state's house. In return, Democratic legislators would support repeal of the state's Black Laws and Chase's election to the Senate. To see that nothing went awry, Chase for a time joined his principal henchmen—Stanley Matthews, Eli Nichols, and E. S. Hamlin—in Columbus, buttonholing, cajoling, testing the political waters. As the senatorial decision approached he withdrew to his home in Cincinnati whence he pelted his backers with helpful arguments and advice. Giddings, meanwhile, continued to exalt party unity above self-interest so as to make it almost appear that he too endorsed Chase. And although friends kept up negotiations on his behalf, Ohio Whigs, fearful of offending the incoming Taylor Administration and angry at Giddings's defection in 1848, coolly put them off.[13]

Not surprisingly, all went as Chase had hoped. After Norton Townshend and John F. Morse, independent Free Soilers from the Western Reserve, had provided the votes necessary to elect a Democratic speaker and to seat that party's Hamilton County claimants, the Democrats made good their part of the informal bargain. First came revision of the Black Laws. Then, after a series of delays and four ballots, all fifty-three Democrats joined Townshend and Morse in selecting Chase as Senator from Ohio. (The rest of the Free Soilers voted down the line for Giddings, whose chances orthodox Whigs destroyed by backing the conservative Thomas Ewing.) In final payment for such favors Morse and Townshend cooperated in elevating two Democrats to state judgeships.[14]

Outside Ohio news of Chase's triumph caused widespread rejoicing among Free Soilers. To Charles Sumner it seemed to mark "the beginning of the end" of the war against slavery. John P. Hale, previously the lone Free Soil voice in the Senate, confessed "that I do not remember when I heard of an election which has afforded me more pleasure than that of Mr. Chase." And Bailey's *National Era*, which had touted Chase from the beginning, now commended him as a clearsighted, uncompromising champion of the antislavery cause.[15]

---

[13] Stanley Matthews to Chase, Jan. 11, 1849, Chase Papers, LC; Stewart, *Giddings*, 74-75; Blue, "Ohio Free Soilers," 21-22.
[14] Smith, *Liberty and Free Soil Parties*, 164-72; Hart, *Chase*, 106-11.
[15] Sumner to Chase, Feb. 7, 27, 1849, Chase Papers, LC; Hale to Mrs. Hale, Feb. 23, 1849, Hale Papers, NHHS; *National Era*, Mar. 1, 1849.

At home, however, opinions were sharply divided. Indeed, there can be little question that the manner, if not the result, of Chase's victory "nearly ruined the Ohio Free Soil Party."[16] Whiggish Free Soilers (to say nothing of free-soil Whigs) reacted furiously, though less to the fact of Chase's election than to the coalition with Democrats that had produced it. As one former Whig complained: "For myself when I mounted the 'Free Soil' platform I did not thereby intend to transfer myself to LocoFocoism *Boots* and all. . . ."[17] Townshend and Morse became targets of special abuse for their alleged sellout to the Democrats, particularly their role in the Hamilton County dispute and their abandonment of Edward Wade, a true-blue Free Soiler, in the selection of judges.

Chase himself received congratulations and grudging praise from many who had beforehand opposed his election. Among them was the selfless Giddings, who assured Charles Sumner: "I felt neither mortification nor disappointment at . . . [Chase's] success over me. On the contrary I regard his election as a great victory." Yet the recent events had awakened old antagonisms between Whig and Democratic Free Soilers and Chase, as much as the antislavery party, would become their victim. As Albert G. Riddle, a prominent Whig Free Soiler, later recalled: "Whatever may be said of the morality or the expediency of the course pursued . . . , no doubt can exist of its effect upon Mr. Chase and his career. It lost to him at once and forever the confidence of every Whig of middle age in Ohio. Its shadow never wholly dispelled, always fell upon him, and hovered near and darkened his pathway at the crucial places in his political after life."[18]

Bitterness and mistrust worked both ways. The Chase faction too found cause to complain: in the "unjust" attacks on Townshend and Morse who had sought merely to "save the Free Soil party from being dissolved in Whiggery," and in the refusal of Whig Free Soilers to honor an informal but binding agreement to line up behind Chase once Giddings's chances had proved hopeless. So deep was the resentment on both sides that some wondered whether the Free Soil union would survive. Samuel Lewis, for one, worried that the organization had been

[16] Smith, *Liberty and Free Soil Parties*, 173.
[17] John French to Albert G. Riddle, Mar. 6, 1849, Riddle Papers.
[18] Giddings to Sumner, Mar. 30, 1849, Sumner Papers; A. G. Riddle, "The Election of S. P. Chase to the Senate, February, 1849," *The Republic*, IV (1875), 183. See also Thomas Bolton to Chase, Apr. 17, 1849, Chase Papers, LC.

"thrown into such confusion" by the senatorial question "that free-soilers losing confidence in each other will incline to relaps [*sic*] into their old party associations. . . ."[19]

To guard against any such dissolution of the Free Soil alliance, whether through internal bickering or the sort of willful fusion Chase seemed bent upon, Joshua Giddings undertook a vigorous campaign of reconciliation. In his own correspondence and through the *Ashtabula Sentinel* he preached the need to "let bygones be bygones," to forget the Hamilton County quarrel, and to get on with the work of party building. In May he presided over an amity convention at Cleveland attended by Townshend, Morse, Riddle, Edward Wade, and other Western Reserve Free Soilers. At his prompting that gathering issued a call for a national Wilmot Proviso convention to meet at Cleveland in July. It was Giddings's fond hope that this assembly might restore unity and a sense of purpose to the entire Free Soil enterprise.[20]

Yet although many were on hand to hear speeches from the likes of Austin Willey, "Prince John" Van Buren, Henry Bibb, and Giddings himself, and to endorse resolutions forcefully reasserting the Buffalo platform, the July meeting fell far short of revivifying the Free Soil party. For not only were most prominent Free Soilers conspicuously absent (or, like Chase, present out of politeness only), but everywhere on the horizon there loomed signs that the Free Soil party was prepared to alter—even surrender—its identity in search of success. From without if not from within, the fruits of the Ohio coalition looked delicious beyond words, and in state after state Free Soilers sought out Whigs or (more often) Democrats in hopes of striking similar bargains for themselves. Indeed, within Ohio itself, fusion rather than righteous independence continued for several months to be the rule. To the unbounded delight of Salmon Chase, during the spring and summer of 1849 in nearly every county of the state Free Soilers (now calling themselves Free Democrats) made common cause with old line Democrats whose antislavery attitudes had of late grown increasingly radical.

The following year witnessed setbacks for Free Democratic coalitionists, however, and men like Chase discovered that fusion had its

[19] Smith, *Liberty and Free Soil Parties*, 166; Chase to Albert G. Riddle, Feb. 24, 1849, Riddle Papers; Lewis to Joshua Giddings, Mar. 20, 1849, Giddings-Julian Papers.
[20] Stewart, *Giddings*, 176-79; *National Era*, May 17, 1849.

perils as well as its rewards. Not only were Whiggish Free Soilers re-
pelled by talk of the third party's affinity for the Democracy, but former Democrats found in such arguments an excuse to flock again to
the original nest. Coalition took even harder knocks in 1851. Although
they once again held the balance in the state legislature, the Free Democrats of Ohio were unable to secure for their candidate, Giddings, the
United States Senate seat which became vacant that year. Instead they
joined with Ohio Whigs to elect Benjamin F. Wade, an outspoken
critic not only of slavery but of Giddings and the Free Soilers as well.
("I hate him and all his friends and despise them," Wade had confided
to his wife.)[21]

The other half of Ohio's senatorial contingent took cold comfort in
Wade's victory. Having built his hopes around union with the Democrats and used all his influence to defeat any Whig, Salmon Chase found
equally depressing the manner and the result of Wade's election. It did
not, however, modify in any way his opinion concerning the right road
to antislavery success. His reflexive reaction to the legislature's decision was to assert once again his conviction that "our Party must
be a democratic party in *name* and *fact:* that we should act with
the old line Democracy as far as practicable without a sacrifice of
principle. . . ."[22]

To Chase's chagrin, fewer and fewer Free Soilers seemed inclined to
share this view. The meager dividends of coalition and disillusionment
over the praise leaders of both national parties had heaped on the Compromise of 1850 sparked a renewed determination to preserve Free Soil
autonomy. When, therefore, a series of third party meetings on the
Western Reserve, followed by the state Free Soil convention at Columbus in August, all rejected cooperation with either of the "corrupt" old parties, Chase saw no recourse but to follow his conviction
and his personal ambition into the Democratic party. Early in September he published in the *National Era* a letter announcing his decision to
support Reuben Wood, the moderately antislavery Democratic candi-

---

[21] Smith, *Liberty and Free Soil Parties*, 235-37; Wade to Mrs. Wade, Mar. 14, 185c
Wade Papers. Once law partners and friends, Giddings and Wade had long since
fallen out. Of Wade's election Giddings observed: "In regard to Senator we hop
for the best but expect little good to our cause, at least such are our fears that M
Wade will be of little service to the cause of humanity." Giddings to Salmon F
Chase, Apr. 3, 1851, Chase Papers, PHS.
[22] Chase to Joshua Giddings, Mar. 24, 1851, Giddings Papers.

date, instead of Free Soiler Samuel Lewis for governor. Although Norton Townshend, Stanley Matthews, and a few other Chase loyalists
followed him into the Democratic camp, most Free Soilers did not. In
the fall election Wood carried Ohio with ease, but the Free Democrats
swept the Western Reserve and tallied three thousand more votes than
they had the previous year. Putting both coalition tactics and the "late
Mr. Chase, our lamented friend," behind them, Ohio Free Soilers
looked toward the next presidential canvass with renewed enthusiasm
and the sense that their enterprise was back on track.[23]

2

Even before the Ohio alliance paid off in Chase's election to the Senate,
Wisconsin Free Soilers embarked on an ill-starred fusion course of their
own.[24] Conscious of the difficulty of improving upon their performance in 1848, owing to the decidedly antislavery stance of both major
parties, Free Soil leaders moved quickly to form a partnership with one
or another of their rivals. At the Free Soil state convention at Madison
in January 1849 third party delegates passed resolves reaffirming the
Buffalo platform and calling for land reform, free trade, direct taxation,
economy in government, and the popular election of all federal officers.
They then announced themselves "ready to unite and co-operate with
any party or the members of any party that cordially approve the principles embodied in the foregoing Resolutions." When Moses M. Strong,
a "regular" Democrat given leave to address the convention, spoke out
for union, the path to a new antislavery partnership seemed open. Whig
Free Soilers displayed understandable misgivings about the new free
trade plank and talk of union with the Democrats. But their demurs
were quickly brushed aside as the Free Soil host glimpsed the possibility of success without sacrifice of principle.

On March 30 Free Soil and Democratic members of the Wisconsin

[23] Stewart, *Giddings*, 200-205; Smith, *Liberty and Free Soil Parties*, 238-43; Chase
to C R. Miller (Editor of *Toledo Commercial Republican*), Aug. 25, 1851, re-
rinted in *National Era*, Sept. 11, 1851.
[24] Except where otherwise noted, the following account of Free Soil maneuvers in
Wisconsin rests on Theodore C. Smith's *Liberty and Free Soil Parties*, 208-16, and
The Free Soil Party in Wisconsin," *Proceedings of the State Historical Society of
Wisconsin, 1894* (Madison, 1895), 97-162, esp. 119-38.

legislature met in the senate chamber in Madison and set in motion plans for the merger of their parties. After adopting a set of resolutions that added to the key articles of the Buffalo creed a demand for land reform, cheap postage, free trade, river and harbor improvement, and "equal and impartial suffrage," the legislators agreed to ask each state committee to call for a joint convention early in September to effect a Free Soil–Democratic alliance. Although some Free Soilers remained leery, suspecting Democrats of seeking merely to coopt them, most strongly endorsed this move. "For a union on the basis of these Resolutions," proclaimed the *Wisconsin Free Democrat*, "we have been prepared ever since the nomination at Buffalo."[25]

Late in June, however, the Democratic State Committee slammed the door on coalition with Free Soilers—except on terms many in the third party found degrading. Repudiating the March 30 agreement, the Democratic bosses invited Free Soilers to work individually with Wisconsin's Democracy, but refused to deal with them collectively or as partners. "We are coolly told that we went off without reason," protested the *Kenosha Telegraph*, "and the most we can ask is the privilege of coming back unquestioned." The only honorable course left, Free Soilers now concluded, was to "Hold their Convention, make their nominations and elect their ticket if they can." All Wisconsinites must now understand, the *Oshkosh True Democrat* angrily proclaimed, that the real fanatics were not political abolitionists like Sherman Booth who championed union, but Hunkers like George B. Smith, chairman of the Democratic State Committee, "who would rather rule in Hell than serve in Heaven."[26]

Accordingly, the Free Soilers invited "all the friends of Freedom and True Democracy" to gather at Madison on September 7, two days after the regular Democratic convention. By the time this "union" meeting convened, however, Wisconsin Democrats had deftly cut the ground from under the Free Soilers, leaving them divided, disorganized, and thoroughly on the defensive. In their convention on September 5, the Democracy, though it had nominated a full slate of Cass Democrats and had barely acknowledged the Free Soil party's existence, had brazenly adopted the Madison platform of March 30. Having

[25] *Wisconsin Free Democrat*, Apr. 11, May 2, 1849; *Southport Telegraph*, Apr. 13 July 20, 1849; *Oshkosh True Democrat*, Apr. 6, 13, 20, 1849.
[26] *Oshkosh True Democrat*, June 29, 1849.

already offered to merge with any party endorsing their principles, the Free Soilers now had no choice but to switch colors or, by standing aloof, invite charges of spoilsmanship.

At their sparsely attended convention on September 7, the third party risked the latter course. A good many delegates, led by A. W. Randall and A. E. Elmore, urged fusion with the Democrats, and when the gathering decided otherwise they walked out. The rump group remaining (fewer than thirty in all) then selected an independent ticket headed by Nelson Dewey (already the Democrat's choice for governor) but otherwise composed of new names, nearly all of them Barnburners. In justification of this action the Free Soilers blasted the Democrats' inconsistency in having nominated doughfaced Hunkers on an antislavery platform. Even this excuse for continued independence fell flat, however, after the Randall-Elmore faction elicited from all Democratic candidates public statements in favor of their party's strong antislavery platform. "In all the history of political maneuvering in the Northwest," writes Theodore C. Smith, "there is nothing to surpass the consummate ease and skill with which Wisconsin Democrats in this year took the Free Soilers at their word, deprived them of logical consistency, and put them in the wrong."[27]

Not surprisingly, the Free Soil vote fell sharply in the fall election. Warren Chase, the party's gubernatorial candidate once Dewey spurned the Free Soil nomination, polled merely 3761 votes, less than 12 per cent of the total and 64 per cent fewer than Van Buren received the previous year. Some four thousand Free Soilers apparently returned to the Democratic fold, a few rejoined the Whigs, and a couple of thousand sat the election out. Year's end found the Wisconsin Free Soil party in tatters. Nor did its fortunes improve substantially in 1850, although a temporary alliance, this time with Whigs, did produce Free Soiler Charles Durkee's reelection to Congress. From time to time the *Wisconsin Free Democrat* floated trial balloons to test chances of union with the Democrats. But by 1851 Badger State Democrats had repudiated their earlier radicalism and Free Soilers (now reduced to the old Liberty party remnant) concluded for the time being "to maintain an independent position, and not coalesce with either of the old political organizations." Whistling in the dark, Sherman Booth editorialized that another defeat in the 1852 presidential race might make Wisconsin

[27] Smith, *Liberty and Free Soil Parties*, 212.

Democrats once again receptive to the principles of freedom. Then, he implied, Free Soilers would gladly reconsider some form of union.[28] Any fair-minded Free Soiler would have had to admit, however, that in Wisconsin the coalition tactic, for all its early promise, had thus far been a cruel disappointment.

Things went little better in other Midwestern states. In Michigan, where Lewis Cass's powerful presence ruled out cooperation with the Democratic party, Free Soilers entered into an alliance with the Whigs. A good bit of ticket-mixing occurred in local elections in 1849 and, following the resignation of their first choice, the Whigs grudgingly agreed to support the Free Soil gubernatorial nominee, Barnburner Flavius J. Littlejohn. Littlejohn's defeat touched off a flurry of mutual recriminations, but in the 1850 congressional campaign Free Soilers decided against independent nominations and supported instead the three Whig candidates, all solid antislavery advocates. This time the informal union was touched with success. Two conservative Democrats (including Cass's henchman A. W. Buel) went down to defeat and the third narrowly squeaked by. Thereafter most Michigan Free Soilers submerged themselves in Whiggery, hoping for triumphs and recognition that, unfortunately, never came, while a corporal's guard of ex-Liberty men kept the faith against a better day to come.[29]

The Free Soil party of Indiana, after one strikingly successful venture in coalition politics, also quickly fell apart. In the immediate aftermath of the 1848 election, Hoosier Free Soilers pledged themselves to the perpetuation of an independent antislavery party. Yet as their own systematic questioning of political candidates soon made clear, most Indiana Democrats and Whigs were as firmly committed to non-extension and the divorce of slavery from government as any Free Soiler. Understandably, then, many third party men slipped quietly back into the traditional organizations. Other Free Soilers clung to their own identity, but, with the blessing of party leaders, refrained from making independent nominations in the congressional and local races of 1849.[30]

Only in the "Burnt District" of the upper Whitewater Valley did

[28] *Wisconsin Free Democrat*, July 9, 16, Sept. 10, 24, 1851.
[29] Smith, *Liberty and Free Soil Parties*, 198-208; *National Era*, Oct. 4, 11, Nov. 22, 1849.
[30] *Free Territory Sentinel*, June 13, 1849; *Indiana True Democrat*, Jan. 9, 1850; Smith, *Liberty and Free Soil Parties*, 187-90.

Indiana Free Soilers remain strong and active. There, with support from Democrats who saw no hope of carrying a candidate of their own, they succeeded in electing George W. Julian (a former Whig who had endorsed Van Buren in 1848) to Congress. It was a heady victory and one that apparently vindicated the policy of coalition. But the circumstances attending it were very nearly unique (only Ohio's Western Reserve presented similar political conditions), and the 1849 gubernatorial race canceled out much of the satisfaction Free Soilers derived from Julian's triumph. In a turnout of over 147,000, the Free Soil candidate, James H. Cravens, received barely 3000 votes—hardly more than a third of Van Buren's total the previous fall. Once having accepted the propriety of backing right-minded Whigs and Democrats in most congressional and many local contests, Free Soilers found it hard to invoke party loyalty even in support of regularly nominated candidates. By the close of 1849 Indiana's Free Soil party seemed well along the road to oblivion.[31]

In Illinois the third party faced a special problem. Feisty after a respectable first showing, Prairie State Free Soilers were left to spar with shadows for two years when the state's new constitution (adopted in the spring of 1848) scheduled the next elections of any consequence for 1850. By then, however, the backsliding of Free Soilers in other states and the tranquilizing influence of Henry Clay's compromise had worked a perverse magic. So that although here and there they made a stand, most Free Soilers simply gave up the ghost, working (if they worked at all) for antislavery goals within the established parties.[32]

Iowa's tiny band of Free Soilers found the going just as tough, but they responded with greater resilience than did their fellows in most other states. Disillusioned with coalitions after an unsuccessful sortie in that direction in 1849 and taken aback by their inability to poll so much as six hundred votes in the following year's gubernatorial race, Iowa third party men (most of them abolitionists) nonetheless refused to quit. In 1852 their persistence was rewarded to the extent at least that theirs was the only state in the Union to return more Free Soil votes than in 1848. It was a small distinction, but sufficient to keep Iowa's outnumbered abolitionists bravely plugging away.[33]

[31] *Ibid.* 190-93; Riddleberger, *Julian*, 45-50.
[32] Smith, *Liberty and Free Soil Parties*, 193-97.
[33] *Ibid.* 216-19, 266.

3

In no state, perhaps, did the antislavery impulse run so wide and deep as in Vermont. Governor Carlos Coolidge accurately described the temper of his fellow citizens when he observed early in 1849 that "hostility to slavery is, in them, an instinct."[34] One recent sign of that hostility was the state's substantial vote for Van Buren in 1848. Receiving nearly 30 per cent of the popular ballots, the Free Soil ticket finished second, ahead of Cass, in the presidential canvass. It was Free Soil's strongest showing anywhere. Although some Whig stalwarts like ex-Governor William Slade backed the Free Soil slate, Van Buren's candidacy cut most deeply into the ranks of Vermont Democrats.[35] By the spring of 1849 the mauled remnants of that party (even in the best of times outnumbered by Whigs) were also willing to make common cause with the Free Soilers, hoping in that way to rescue their blasted fortunes.

The Free Soilers, having before them the examples of their brethren in Ohio and Wisconsin (where hopes for fusion still burned bright), encouraged the Democrats' overtures, demanding only that any alliance rest on the bedrock of Free Soil principles. In May 1849, therefore, Vermont Democrats proposed, and Free Soilers gladly accepted, political union on the basis of a thoroughgoing antislavery platform. Declaring "that American Slavery is a great evil and wrong, which ought to be repented of and abandoned," the Free Democracy (as the consolidated party now styled itself) called for passage of the Wilmot Proviso, a ban against new slave states, and the abolition of slavery wherever Congress had constitutional power to act, including the District of Columbia. The new union also endorsed cheap homesteads for actual settlers, cheap postage, and free public education. At the same time, however, it stressed the paramountcy of the slavery question and pronounced "settled" such formerly divisive issues as the National Bank, an Independent Treasury, and the distribution of funds from public land sales. The Free Democrats also agreed on a common slate for state offices, headed by Horatio Needham.[36]

---

[34] Quoted in Walter H. Crockett, *Vermont: The Green Mountain State*, 4 vols. (New York, 1921), III, 372.
[35] Ludlum, *Social Ferment in Vermont*, 194–97; Rayback, *Free Soil*, 284.
[36] *Green Mountain Freeman*, June 21, 1849; *National Era*, June 7, 14, 1849.

The new alliance attracted much attention in state and out. "It is formidable and an extraordinary effort will be required to defeat it," cautioned the *New-York Tribune*. "Sweeping into the dragnet men of the most extreme contrariety of opinions—the ultra-Abolitionists—and the ultra-opponents of Abolition—the supporters of Birney and the zealous adherents of Polk—it is quite possible, should all the screws hold as calculated and stipulated that they may even carry Vermont away from herself."[37] Fearing the worst, Vermont Whigs drew on every means at their command (including a series of rallies featuring native son Horace Greeley) to head off their opponents. Not all Democrats were pleased with the Vermont merger either. Almost at once some Hunker Democrats, with strong encouragement from outside the state, set about to break up the newly forged coalition, complaining of the neglect of old Democratic issues and charging that the Free Soil element was riddled with Whigs. Enough Hunker die-hards eventually refused to go along with the Free Democratic nomination to throw the 1849 election to the Whigs. Yet the new party nearly doubled the Free Soil turnout of 1848 and forced the gubernatorial election into the legislature before bowing out. Although old line Democrats held their own convention soon after the campaign's close, the future looked bright for Vermont's Free Democracy.[38]

Yet although the Free Soil–Democratic union held firm, the experience of 1850 and 1851 somewhat deflated earlier hopes. In both years Free Democratic state candidates, while swamping their Hunker rivals, ran well behind the Whig nominees. More serious, support for the coalition slate showed signs of erosion, the party's vote for governor slipping from 23,250 in 1849 to 18,956 in 1850. Most of this loss went to the Democrats, for as one Free Soiler explained, "some of the Cass men who united with us on our glorious platform in 1849" had jumped back "upon the Hunker car, which they fancy is whirling on to certain victory in 1852."[39] In 1851, in an attempt to check these defections, the Free Democrats reversed themselves and added to their platform several planks which gave attention to such traditional Democratic

---

[37] Quoted in Crockett, *Vermont*, III, 378.
[38] *Ibid.* III, 379; *Green Mountain Freeman*, Aug. 9, Sept. 13, 20, Oct. 25, Nov. 1, 1849.
[39] E. A. Stansbury to George W. Julian, Oct. 30, 1850, Giddings-Julian Papers. See also Edward D. Barber to Salmon P. Chase, Feb. 24, 1851, Chase Papers, LC. Election returns are given in Crockett, *Vermont*, III, 379, 386, 397.

issues as the Bank, the tariff, economy in government, and internal improvements. This accommodation, however, failed to stem the party's slide. In the gubernatorial election that year the Free Democratic candidate won only 14,950 votes, a 21 per cent drop from the previous total. Vermont Free Democrats therefore approached the 1852 campaign somewhat apprehensively—their alliance was still intact but they were uncertain how well it would weather the storm of presidential politics. The boast that theirs was the nation's only "integral party on a free soil platform" still held true. Whether it could long retain both its unity and its principles was another question.[40]

4

Coalition continued also to yield rewards in New Hampshire, where Amos Tuck and a free-soil Whig were twice returned to Congress, and in Maine, where Free Soilers combined first with antislavery Democrats to keep Hannibal Hamlin in the United States Senate and then with Whigs to elect Isaac Reed, a powerful critic of slavery, to the United States House of Representatives.[41] In Connecticut, too, cooperation between Free Soilers and Democrats, though short-lived, sent three reliable antislavery representatives to Congress in 1849 and secured several victories in state contests as well.[42] It was in Massachusetts, however, that the policy of combining with other parties paid off most handsomely—though not without severe strain to the Free Soil party itself.

The results of the 1848 election in Massachusetts had been promising enough to persuade many Free Soil leaders that continued independ-

40 *Green Mountain Freeman*, May 29, Oct. 9, 23, 1851.
41 Sewell, *Hale*, 143; H. Draper Hunt, *Hannibal Hamlin of Maine: Lincoln's First Vice-President* (Syracuse, 1969), 72-74; Edward O. Schriver, *Go Free: The Anti-slavery Impulse in Maine, 1833-1855* (Orono, 1970), 68-69.
42 A. E. Burr to Gideon Welles, Mar. 19, May 14, 1849, John M. Niles to Welles, May 13, June 10, 1849, Loren P. Waldo to Welles, Feb. 24, 1850, J. D. Baldwin to J. M. Niles, Sept. 21, 1841, Welles Papers, LC; Gideon Welles to C. F. Cleveland, Mar. 9, 1849, Jan. 21, 1850 (copies), A. E. Burr to Welles, Apr. 16, 1849, Welles Papers, CHS; A. E. Burr to Welles, July 12, Aug. 9, 1849, Welles Papers, NYPL; Calvin W. Philleo *et al.* [Connecticut State Free Soil Committee] to [Free Soil state representatives], Apr. 10, 1849 (printed circular), Philleo to Edmond Perkins, Oct. 22, 1849, Calvin W. Philleo Papers, CHS; *National Era*, Apr. 5, 12, 1849. The successful coalition congressional candidates were Wilmot Proviso Democrats Loren P. Waldo and Chauncey F. Cleveland and Free Soiler Walter Booth.

ence was the proper course. Not only had the new party drawn over 38,000 votes, outpolling the Cass forces statewide, but its support had come more or less evenly from all classes and all sections. Just as basic to high-minded souls like Adams, Palfrey, and Dana was the fear that union with Whigs or, worse, Democrats would rob the Free Soil party of its moral character.[43]

Others drew a far different lesson from the first Free Soil campaign. To them the overwhelming vote for the slaveholder Taylor (more than half again Van Buren's total) plainly demonstrated that the only way for Free Soilers to become effective was to combine with one or another of the major parties. Some urged a marriage of Free Soil and Whiggery. The influence of voices like Sumner, Palfrey, and S. C. Phillips would be incomparably greater *within* their former party, argued Horace Mann, than hostilely arrayed against it. "For heaven's sake heal this breach, instead of widening it," he implored, "and bring the whole force of the north to bear upon the subject of freedom."[44]

Talk of reunion with Whigs, however, ignored both the proved dominance of Cotton over Conscience in Massachusetts and the fact that some 45 per cent of the state's Free Soilers were former Democrats. The most convincing advocates of coalition, therefore, were plain and practical Free Soilers like Amasa Walker, John B. Alley, Francis W. Bird, E. L. Keyes, and Henry Wilson, who preached the advantages of union with Bay State Democrats. What could make more sense, they asked, than for the state's two minority parties, each dedicated to equal rights for all, to wage a joint crusade against the Money Power of the North and the Slave Power of the South?[45]

One of the earliest, most influential, and in the end most self-interested converts to this point of view was the eloquent and egotistical Charles Sumner, chairman of the Free Soil state committee. Although he found the social and intellectual resources of Boston Whiggery more appealing than Democratic crudities, Sumner had long displayed a preference for Jacksonian economic policies. He stood on good terms with Democrats in Massachusetts and other Northern states, notably New York. And under the subtle tutelage of Salmon Chase he had come in recent

---

[43] Donald, *Sumner*, 177-78.
[44] Mann to Samuel Downer, Jr., Mar. 21, 1850, Amos Tuck to Mann, Apr. 30, 1850, Mann Papers.
[45] Donald, *Sumner*, 178-79; Duberman, *Adams*, 159; Richard H. Abbott, *Cobbler in Congress: The Life of Henry Wilson, 1812-1875* (Lexington, Ky., 1972), 35-37.

months to appreciate the antislavery potential of a purified Democracy. "We must have a *true* Democratic party—not a sham—which pledges itself to Humanity and to the Future," he parroted to Chase in May 1849.[46] Finally, Sumner's own political ambitions may unconsciously have inclined him toward union with the Democrats. Well aware of the bounty just such a coalition had conferred upon his friend Chase, he also knew that Massachusetts too would soon be choosing a United States Senator. Although he kept his own aspirations a secret—perhaps even from himself—Sumner began early in 1849 to mouth opinions which Whigs deemed "nothing more or less than old fashioned Jacobinism, or new-fashioned loco-focoism, dressed up in more gentlemanlike habiliments than they are wont to wear."[47]

At the Massachusetts Free Soil convention in September 1849, Sumner, as chairman of the resolutions committee, drafted a platform adding to antislavery a raft of Democratic planks—cheap postage, economy in government, and popular election of all civil officials—as well as river and harbor improvement and free homesteads. Under Henry Wilson's shepherding hand, the convention approved them all. About the same time Bay State Democrats, still smarting over Southern defections to which they attributed Cass's defeat in 1848, promulgated a strong set of antislavery resolves. One by one the barriers to coalition were coming down.[48]

For the time being, however, the Adams-Palfrey faction remained strong enough to forestall "amalgamation," and although joint Free Soil–Democratic tickets appeared in many counties, the Whigs carried the state easily and the Free Soil vote showed a slight decline from 1848. Local fusion broke down most conspicuously in Middlesex County, where despite Free Soil–Democratic cooperation in state races Democratic defections robbed Palfrey of his bid for reelection to Congress.[49]

Eighteen-fifty brought better things for Massachusetts coalitionists. In the first place, Daniel Webster's Seventh of March speech in defense of Clay's compromise proposals (including a more stringent fugitive slave bill), and his party's subsequent acceptance of those measures,

46 Sumner to Chase, May 9, 1849, Chase Papers, LC; Donald, *Sumner*, 179-81.
47 Quoted in *ibid*. 181.
48 *Ibid*. 182.
49 Duberman, *Adams*, 161-62; Gatell, *Palfrey*, 188-89.

eliminated any possibility of cooperation with Massachusetts Whigs. All summer, therefore, Wilson and others labored to secure an alliance with the Democrats. Once again Adams and his friends succeeded in preventing formal union. However, the Massachusetts Free Soil convention in October left individual party members free to make deals on their own, and in the November election, though the Whigs received a substantial plurality, Free Soilers and Democrats together won a majority of seats in the state legislature. And since no candidate for governor or lieutenant governor claimed a clear majority, the new legislature would have at its disposal both the highest state offices and a coveted place in the United States Senate. Even the moralistic Adams rejoiced that "the domination of Daniel Webster" had at last been broken.[50]

Soon after the 1850 election Henry Wilson, the Natick cobbler turned professional politician, opened negotiations with leading Democrats (notably George Boutwell and Nathaniel Banks) with an eye to a division of spoils. By the first week of the new legislature a formal understanding had been reached. The Free Soilers would back Boutwell for governor along with the Democratic candidates for lieutenant governor, clerk and speaker of the house, and a majority of the council seats. In return, the Democrats agreed to support Free Soilers for the United States senatorship, presidency of the state senate, and the remaining places on the governor's council.[51]

At first all went smoothly. Free Soil diehards protested the "unholy combination" to the end, Palfrey contributing a stinging open letter denouncing the proposed pact as an abandonment of principle and denying that it was in any way binding on individual representatives. But most third party men found the rewards of coalition irresistible, and, bucked up by their constituents, Free Soil legislators willingly made good their part of the bargain. By mid-January Boutwell had won with ease election to the governorship and all state offices had been parceled out according to plan. First indications also pointed to

---

[50] Duberman, *Adams*, 170-73; Ernest McKay, *Henry Wilson: Practical Radical, A Portrait of a Politician* (Port Washington, N.Y., 1971), 62-65.
[51] Donald, *Sumner*, 189; Abbott, *Wilson*, 38-39. The Free Soilers also agreed to elect a Democrat, Robert S. Rantoul, to serve out the few remaining weeks of Daniel Webster's term in the United States Senate. Webster's seat, left vacant by his resignation to become Millard Fillmore's Secretary of State, had been filled temporarily by Whig Robert C. Winthrop.

the quick election of a Free Soil Senator. At their caucus on January 7 Free Soil legislators overwhelmingly nominated Charles Sumner for the position and the next day all but six Democrats gave him their approval.[52]

No sooner had the Democrats received their share of the booty, however, than Sumner's fortunes were thrown very much in doubt. For although the coalition held firm in the state senate (where Sumner passed muster on January 22), in the house it became apparent that a group of some thirty "indomitable" Democrats, led by Caleb Cushing and buttressed from without by such Democratic Free Soilers as ex-Governor Marcus Morton, was bent on scuttling the Free Soil candidate. Cushing protested that Sumner was a "one-idead abolitionist agitator" whose election would be a "death-stab to the honor and welfare of the Commonwealth," and Morton complained of awarding the senatorship to any Whig Free Soiler, most of whom he found "ultra" and "impracticable" except on slavery.[53] Holding the balance in the house, the "irreconcilables" blocked any choice on ballot after ballot. As winter turned to spring and the deadlock persisted, Free Soilers grew alarmed that the legislature might adjourn without making a decision—leaving the state short a Senator and Sumner in limbo. Most Democrats also became concerned, less over the senatorship stalemate itself than over the way it obstructed pet legislative programs whose passage seemed essential to their future success at the polls. Concern bred pressure, and with Henry Wilson (now president of the state senate) buttonholing Free Soilers and Democrats alike, the needed votes were finally scraped together. On August 25, by the slenderest of majorities, Charles Sumner was elected United States Senator from Massachusetts.[54] "Laus Deo!" shouted Salmon Chase. "Now I feel as if I had a brother colleague—one with whom I shall sympathize and be able fully to act." And upon receipt of the good news in neighboring Vermont, Montpelier Free Soilers met at the courthouse "pursuant to the call of Town Criers, and the ringing of bells" to adopt measures suitable to honor the event. Even Charles Francis Adams expressed satisfaction at this conclusion to the deal he had taken such pains to oppose—reveal-

[52] Gatell, *Palfrey*, 194-95; Stephen C. Phillips to Sumner, Jan. 9, 1851, Sumner Papers; *Essex County Freeman*, Jan. 8, 1851.
[53] Donald, *Sumner*, 192-93; Morton to Frederick Robinson, Nov. 22, 1850, Morton to Caleb Cushing, Nov. 28, 1853, Letterbook, Marcus Morton Papers, MHS.
[54] McKay, *Wilson*, 68-73; Donald, *Sumner*, 195-202.

ing, in his son Henry's uncharitable words, a nature "too good to take part, but not too good to take profit."[55]

Yet despite its initial success, the Massachusetts coalition soon showed signs of stress. In the legislature Free Soilers joined Democrats in enacting a string of reform measures, among them laws providing for the secret ballot, regulation of banks and corporations, and state control over Harvard College. But when Free Soilers sought support for a stronger personal liberty law to protect runaway slaves and for resolutions condemning the new Fugitive Slave Act, only a minority of Democrats were willing to go along and both measures were lost. At the Democratic state convention in August Boutwell again won nomination for governor, but Hunkers like Cushing and Benjamin Hallett —"by tact, cunning, trickery and impudence," the *Essex County Freeman* alleged—secured a platform that fully endorsed the 1850 Compromise. In the fall election, running separate tickets, the coalitionists once again gained control of the state house and once again divvied up the treasure.[56]

For the time being, at least, most Massachusetts Free Soilers found the rewards of coalition sufficient to warrant their continued participation in it. Few, however, trusted the Democrats fully or were willing to move from coalition to a fusion of parties. It remained to be seen whether this common-law marriage could survive the strain of a presidential contest in 1852. All one could say with assurance as the election year began was that Free Soilers were "standing by . . . [their] guns in a state of 'masterly inactivity,' " determined to support no party or candidate not solidly committed to the containment of slavery.[57]

5

Nowhere was the policy of coalition carried so far and nowhere did it do such great harm to the Free Soil party as in New York state. The

[55] Chase to Sumner, Apr. 28, 1851, Sumner Papers; *Green Mountain Freeman,* May 1, 1851; Henry Adams, *The Education of Henry Adams,* James T. Adams (ed.), Modern Library edition (New York, 1931), 49.
[56] Blue, *Free Soilers,* 224-26; Donald, *Sumner,* 223; *Essex County Freeman,* Aug. 23, 1851.
[57] Anson Burlingame to Charles Sumner, Feb. 10, 1852 (quote), Henry Wilson to Sumner, Feb. 3, 1852, Sumner to F. W. Bird, Feb. 8, 1853, Sumner Papers.

Barnburners had contributed over a third of all the votes for Van Buren in 1848. Quite obviously the future of the Free Soil movement depended heavily on whether the New Yorkers would continue to stand firm or would slip back into Democratic traces.

Signs of Barnburner intent appeared early. Within weeks of the election Van Burenite spokesmen had made it clear that while they were not yet willing to dismantle their own organization or to abandon the Buffalo platform, they craved reconciliation with their Hunker rivals. One indication of this desire emerged from the post-election editorials of leading Barnburner newspapers. The *Albany Atlas*, for example, called for the perpetuation of the Free Soil organization so long as it was necessary to restore "the creed of a pure Democracy." And the *New York Evening Post* spoke of the recent canvass in such triumphant terms that Barnburners could only wonder what need remained for continued separation. The Free Soil campaign, claimed the *Post*, had determined the outcome of the presidential race, "emancipated the Democratic party from the control of the Slave Power," compelled Northern Democrats to recognize the validity of the free-soil principle, and "in all probability decided the question of Freedom or Slavery in the Territories" by debating it so widely. So successful a revolution, the *Post* seemed to imply, hardly needed to be pursued. A time for mending was at hand.[58]

A second hint that the New Yorkers sought reunion with their Democratic brethren lay in their resistance to suggestions that they forcefully reassert their commitment to the Free Soil organization. Preston King, Samuel J. Tilden, and David Dudley Field all replied to Charles Sumner's proposal for some such declaration by insisting that the wiser course was to sit tight and watch events. Hunker Democrats might be expected to take higher antislavery ground, King argued, especially now that a slaveholding Whig claimed the White House, and nothing should be done which might alienate potential allies.[59]

Not that the Barnburners threw themselves at once into the arms of Democratic conservatives. Especially among younger party men, Free Soil zeal continued to burn high. One such, Henry S. Randall of Cort-

[58] Quoted in *National Era*, Nov. 23, 1848.
[59] King to Sumner, Dec. 5, 1848, Field to Sumner, Dec. 6, 1848, Tilden to Sumner, Dec. 18, 1848, Sumner Papers.

land, told Van Buren at the end of 1848 that the "holy war" for slavery restriction would continue no matter what party sachems might decide. "When the buffalo herd rush across the prairie," he warned, "the leader who pauses is instantly trampled to death by the advancing masses behind." Yet even the most zealous Barnburners viewed the Free Soil party as a temporary expedient and looked forward to an early reunification of the state Democratic party on the principles of '48. Even Henry B. Stanton, who had recently moved from Boston to Seneca Falls, New York (leaving, critics sneered, his principles behind him), now counted on a united and purified Democracy to "read a lecture to the South compared with which the admonition of Cotton Whiggery will be but gentle cooings of a sucking dove."[60]

One obstacle only blocked reunion. "In all the great questions of state and national policy," Benjamin F. Butler observed in June 1849, "the two sections of the party will be able without difficulty to harmonize—save one": slavery. Even here there was enough common ground to give hope of some healing compromise. Hunkers insisted as they had before that they were as much opposed as the Barnburners to slavery or to its extension into territories now free, though many continued to regard the Wilmot Proviso as "a needless agitation of a dangerous and irritating sectional question."[61] For their part, most Barnburners continued through the spring and early summer to insist that there be no lowering of free-soil principles. At the same time, however, many (especially those who had always harbored misgivings about the third party adventure) betrayed such zeal for reunion that Free Soilers in other states grew apprehensive that the New York Radicals might "be drawn into some unworthy compromise."[62] Such fears grew stronger after a meeting of New York City Barnburners in June approved resolves that endorsed a ban on slavery in territories *then free* but that stopped short of the Buffalo ultimatum: "No more slave states and no more slave territory." By July the *National Era* nervously

[60] Randall to Van Buren, Dec. 18, 1848, Van Buren Papers; Stanton to *Boston Daily Republican,* July 31, 1849, quoted in Rice, "Stanton," 312. See also Stanton to Salmon P. Chase, Feb. 24, 1849, Chase Papers, LC.
[61] Butler to Charles S. Benton, June 2, 1849, John V. S. Pruyn to Benton, July 4, 1849, Benton Papers.
[62] John G. Whittier to Lewis Tappan, July 14, 1849, Tappan Papers. See also Salmon P. Chase to B. F. Butler, July 26, 1849, Chase, *Diary and Correspondence,* 180-82.

noted a disposition among Empire State Democrats "to blink the great question" of slavery and urged their strict adherence to the Free Soil creed.[63]

Most Hunkers were also eager to mend party differences. Seizing upon a proposal from the Free Soilers for peace talks, the Hunker Central Committee suggested that both factions meet separately but concurrently at Rome, New York, in August. There they might confer informally and, if all went well, join forces and select a common state ticket for the fall elections. The Barnburners accepted their rivals' invitation, but although joint talks were held as planned, the Rome convention failed to produce the hoped-for reconciliation. Both groups agreed that slavery was an evil, and the Hunkers openly declared their opposition to its extension into free territory. But the Barnburners insisted that the Wilmot Proviso be included in the party's state platform —a political test that Conservatives rejected as unnecessary and unwise —and on that rock the assemblage split.[64]

Pressure from rank-and-file Democrats for reunion remained strong, however, and in September the Hunker faction took a long step in that direction. At their convention at Syracuse on September 6, the Hunkers, despite bitter protest from the more conservative delegates, expressed a willingness to replace half of their nominees for state office with Barnburner nominees if the Barnburners would endorse the rest. To sweeten this proposition, the convention also resolved "that opinions upon slavery should not be made a test nor a persistence in antislavery agitation deemed a heresy." This time the Barnburners went along. Meeting at Utica on September 12 they reaffirmed their free-soil principles and agreed to cooperate with the Hunkers in the impending campaign. Two days later the two factions gathered at Syracuse and, after a hitch or two, settled on a joint ticket.[65] On the nagging slavery issue they agreed to a statement adroitly skirting the reefs and shoals on either shore:

> Resolved: That Congress has the constitutional power over
> Slavery in the District of Columbia, and has no power over the

[63] *National Era*, July 5, 12, 1849.
[64] Donovan, *Barnburners*, 113-14; Blue, *Free Soilers*, 157-58; Ernest P. Muller, "Preston King: A Political Biography," Ph.D. dissertation, Columbia University, 1957, pp. 490-91; *National Era*, Aug. 23, 1849.
[65] *Ibid.* Sept. 20, 27, 1849; Donovan, *Barnburners*, 114; Blue, *Free Soilers*, 159-60.

subject in the states. That it possesses, in the opinion of this Convention, full power over the subject in the Territories of the United States, and should exert that power on all occasions of attempts to introduce it there; but, as the constitutional power is questioned, we are willing to tolerate the free exercise of individual opinion upon that question among members of the Democratic family. . . .[66]

Why had the Barnburners agreed to rejoin their conservative rivals on such terms? Beyond doubt the hunger for spoils was basic. Practical politicians all, Radical leaders found intolerable the prospect of extended Whig domination made possible by the Democratic schism. As John Van Buren bluntly remarked: "We are asked to compromise our principles. The day for compromise is past; but, in regard to candidates for state offices, we are still a commercial people."[67] Yet as even this quotation makes clear, the Barnburners expected to rejoin their old party without doing violence to their antislavery principles. Indeed, it seemed to many the most effective way of extending and strengthening those principles. "Old friends" of the free-soil cause, reported the *National Era,* had been most prominent in the Syracuse union convention, and such men—Preston King and Henry B. Stanton among them—assented to its actions in "hope of seeing the important State of New York united and upon the right side in the great contest for human freedom."[68] Lest such pronouncements be written off as so much self-serving claptrap, it is worth bearing in mind that so independent a source as James Gordon Bennett's *New York Herald* saw the reunion as a victory for free soil, converting the Northern Democracy into an antislavery party "to a very remarkable and dangerous extent"—a view shared by several Southern journals. Similarly, Hunker mossbacks like Daniel S. Dickinson grumbled afterward: "We [Hunkers] are emphatically used up by this amalgamation."[69]

[66] *National Era,* Sept. 27, 1849.
[67] Stanton, *Random Recollections,* 165. In the event, Hunkers fared better than Barnburners in the 1849 election. Of the 4 Democratic candidates to win state office, 3 were Hunkers. Together, the factions gained control of the assembly by a majority of 2. And although the Whigs still controlled the state senate, among the Democratic minority in that body stood Henry B. Stanton. Muller, "Preston King," 494; Stanton to Charles Sumner, Nov. 8, 1849, Sumner Papers.
[68] *National Era,* Sept. 27, 1849; Muller, "Preston King," 492. See also Rice, "Stanton," 315; King to Joshua Giddings, Sept. 19, 1849, Giddings Papers.
[69] Muller, "Preston King," 493.

Still, as Azariah Flagg observed, "The failure to unite on *principles* at Rome, and the junction on men at Utica, has a bad aspect to the faithful in other states. . . ." In fact, although some Free Soil papers like the *Boston Republican* and the *Cleveland True Democrat* severely censured the Barnburners for selling out the antislavery cause, most Free Soilers took a more tolerant, wait-and-see attitude. Gamaliel Bailey, while denying the wisdom of the Radicals' actions, convinced himself of the purity of their motives and in his correspondence and in the columns of the *Era* preached the need for lenity and understanding. "They meant well, and their movement may turn out to be all they intend," he advised Joshua Giddings. "Why cast them off and denounce them? This certainly is not the way to influence them for good." Many Free Soil newspapers took heart from the role men like King and Stanton had played in the merger, felt sure that the union represented a triumph of young Hunkers over old, and predicted that the Barnburners would now sway the entire New York Democracy. "If they do succeed in laying Croswell and Co. on the shelf, and waking in the Democratic masses of New York an enthusiasm for a Democracy that *is* a Democracy," the *Hartford Republican* proclaimed, "they will deserve all praise."[70]

Eighteen-fifty, however, brought a closer and less principled fusion of New York Democrats, one which left Free Soilers in other states no choice but emulation or denunciation. By spring sentiment in favor of reunion was so strong that the more radical Barnburners, fearing still further dilution of the Buffalo platform, declared themselves "disheartened and depressed." As Jabez D. Hammond wrote to Gerrit Smith in April: "I am sick, sick, sick of this vain political world. I had hoped that by mingling with one or [the] other of the two great parties that something good might be done for the cause of human liberty but I begin to despair." Preston King, once he sensed his error in expecting antislavery influences to mould a united Democratic party,

[70] Flagg to Charles S. Benton, Sept. 27, 1849, Benton Papers; Bailey to Sumner, Sept. 23, 1849, Sumner Papers; Bailey to Giddings, Sept. 29, 1849, Giddings-Julian Papers; *National Era*, Sept. 27, 1849; *Hartford Republican*, Oct. 11, 1849. See also Charles Sumner to Giddings, Oct. 19, 1849, Seth Gates to Giddings, Oct. 10, 1849, Giddings Papers; Salmon P. Chase to John F. Morse, Oct. 26, 1849, Sumner to Chase, Sept. 25, 1849, Chase Papers, LC; Chase to Sumner, Sept. 19, 1849, Chase, *Diary and Correspondence*, 186.

tried to head off reunification. But he tried too late. In June Barnburner chieftains Dix, Bryant, Butler, and John Van Buren cooled proposals for a national convention of the "friends of freedom." In September, hungry for spoils and anesthetized by the recent compromise
settlement at Washington, New York Democrats buried past quarrels
at a union convention in Syracuse. Delegates easily agreed upon Horatio Seymour, a moderate Hunker, as the party's candidate for governor
and with only twenty "nays" resolved to "congratulate the country
upon the recent settlement by Congress"—a pointed repudiation of the
Wilmot Proviso, since 1847 the touchstone of Barnburner orthodoxy.
Thereafter, though Democratic bickering continued, the Free Soil
party in New York was as dead as Blue Light Federalism.[71]

6

The Free Soilers' brief experiment in coalition politics had proved
neither a barren failure nor a resounding success. Architects of this
strategy could by 1852 point with satisfaction to the election of two
eloquent and trustworthy political abolitionists (not to mention fellow
travelers like Hamlin and Wade) to the United States Senate and several friends of free soil to Congress. With the slavery question now
front and center on the national stage—notwithstanding the alleged
"finality" of the compromise package—most Free Soilers deemed it
worth a great deal to have such a corps of antislavery advocates in
Washington. Equally valuable, at least in the eyes of proponents of
coalition, was the radicalizing influence of Free Soilers upon the major
parties with whom they cooperated. Rightly or wrongly, Free Soilers
viewed nearly every advance in the antislavery creed of their "old
line" allies as a product of third party pressure.

At the same time, coalition often hurt more than it helped. In seeking assimilation with one of the old parties, Free Soilers often succeeded only in driving off members partial to the other. Moreover, in
touting the antislavery credentials of one or another party with which

---

[71] Hammond to Smith, Apr. 29, 1850, Smith Papers; Muller, "Preston King," 495-
98; King to Azariah C. Flagg, June 27, 1850, and Flagg's endorsement to same,
Flagg Papers, Columbia University.

they sought an alliance, Free Soilers frequently discovered that they had undercut their own *raison d'être* and precipitated an exodus to the organization receiving their seal of approval. Conversely, conservative Democrats or Whigs sometimes balked at arranged marriages with Free Soilers, and by their stubborn resistance shattered hopes of an antislavery victory.

Furthermore, while coalition most often required no sacrifice of principle (beyond the bare fact of cooperation with a party with Southern ties), there were times when it did. In Massachusetts, for example, Free Soilers not only made sacrificial lambs of their own gubernatorial candidates in payment for Democratic favors, but, far less forgivable to purists like Palfrey and Adams, sometimes agreed to support Democrats on joint tickets without extracting from them a pledge to antislavery principles. In the end, many in the third party grew "disgusted with the bargain and sale" of coalition politics and returned to the view that, for the time being at least, independence was the only honorable course.[72]

Whatever the damage to Free Soil principles, coalition tactics left the party itself in tatters. In many states the organization simply ceased to exist. Only in Ohio and Massachusetts did it exhibit any real vitality by the close of 1851, and even there its power and influence had diminished. The gravest loss, of course, had come in New York, where the Barnburners' defection not only robbed Free Soil of its largest contingent but provided a ruinous example to Democratic Free Soilers in other states. "Had the Barnburners kept aloof from the Hunkers in 1849," Charles Sumner lamented, "the Democratic split would have been complete throughout the free States, and it would have affected sympathetically the Whig party."[73] To be sure, other forces—notably the Compromise of 1850—contributed to this erosion of third party strength. But much of their decline Free Soilers could blame on the backfiring of coalition. Those who had resisted its allure approached the 1852 campaign more certain than ever that principle and expediency alike demanded the preservation of a truly independent antislavery party.

[72] Quote from M. C. Williams to *National Era*, Feb. 20, 1851, in Smith, *Liberty and Free Soil Parties*, 242. Even Gamaliel Bailey had soured on coalition tactics by 1851. See, e.g., his response to Chase's decision to join the Democratic party, *National Era*, Sept. 11, 1851.
[73] Sumner to John Bigelow, Oct. 24, 1851, Pierce (ed.), *Letters of Sumner*, III, 255-56.

10

"The Darkest Day of Our Cause"

COMPOUNDING THE PROBLEMS of those who sought to build a strong, independent antislavery party was the deadening influence of the Compromise of 1850. The small band of Free Soilers in Congress at the time of the Compromise had fought strenuously against bills proposing to organize Utah and New Mexico without restriction on slavery and providing more stringent measures for the return of fugitive slaves. But their opposition, and that of antislavery Whigs and Democrats, had been unavailing, and not even the admission of California as a free state and the suppression of the slave trade in the District of Columbia struck Free Soilers as satisfactory compensation for the damage done to the cause of freedom. The so-called Compromise, they complained, was "like the handle of a jug, all on one side."[1]

Proslavery radicals called the Compromise a cup of hemlock, and some, like R. B. Rhett and William L. Yancey, openly espoused secession. But most Americans, North and South, rejoiced that the vexatious slavery issue had been put to rest and the Union saved. In Washington, men celebrated passage of the California and Utah bills with parades, speeches, bonfires, cannon salutes, and (scolded Joshua Giddings) "bacchanalian orgies" lasting through the night. Soon this scene was repeated (more sedately but no less enthusiastically) in city after city throughout the country—processions of speakers praising the authors of the Compromise and rebuking extremists whose recklessness had

[1] E. Plone to John P. Hale, Feb. 19, 1850, Hale Papers, NHHS. See also Salmon P. Chase to E. S. Hamlin, Feb. 2, 1850, Chase, *Diary and Correspondence,* 200-201.

raised the specter of civil war. Typical was the mass rally at Castle Garden in New York City on October 23, 1850, at which James W. Gerard chastized all abolitionists and upheld Daniel Webster's view that the law of nature more effectively curtailed slavery than any proviso that man might draft. Now, most Americans seemed to be saying, the distractions of slavery had been set aside and the nation might get on with the business of life.[2]

So successful was the Compromise of 1850 in dispelling the nation's apprehensions concerning slavery that seven years later William H. Seward could write that it had "brought on a demoralization over the whole country from which even New England has not yet adequately recovered. Nor has it quite passed away in New York." Even among Free Soilers the recent settlement produced a narcotic effect. In December 1850 the New Hampshire *Independent Democrat* complained that although much antislavery work remained, "the professed friends of freedom seem to be sleeping as though nothing needed to be done." Nine months later E. A. Stansbury, a prominent Vermont Free Soiler, grumbled: "The whole battle against slavery is yet before us. The past has witnessed only skirmishes. And yet the antislavery men are subsiding, like children, overcome with sleep, into a drowsy indifference to the portents of the future." Many Free Soilers (especially in New York) used the Compromise as an excuse to return to the old parties, while others concluded that it was wiser to lie low than to brave the winds of pro-Compromise sentiment.[3]

Yet dyed-in-the-wool political abolitionists vigorously resisted this trend. Objecting both to specific features of the Compromise (especially the Fugitive Slave Law and abandonment of the Wilmot Proviso) and to the idea that any moral issue could be resolved by compromise, antislavery politicians warned that this latest piece of legislative sleight-of-hand was doomed to failure. "Gentlemen flatter themselves that they have done a great deal for the peace of the country," John P. Hale lectured the United States Senate in September 1850.

> Everybody is pleased but a few "wild fanatics." . . . Sir, let
> not gentlemen deceive themselves. The pen of inspiration teaches

[2] Allan Nevins, *Ordeal of the Union*, 2 vols. (New York, 1947), I, 346-48, 354, 357; Giddings to Charles Sumner, Sept. 8, 1850, Sumner Papers.
[3] Seward to Cornelius Coles, Sept. 8, 1857, Seward Papers; *Independent Democrat*, Dec. 12, 1850; Stansbury to George W. Julian, Sept. 7, 1851, Giddings-Julian Papers; Loren P. Waldo to Gideon Welles, Feb. 15, 1851, Welles Papers, LC.

us that there was a time when a set of men cried "Peace! peace! but there was no peace." Let me tell you there is no peace to those who think they have successfully dug the grave in which the hopes, the rights, and the interests of freedom have been buried. No, sir, that peace will be short, and that rejoicing will most assuredly be turned into mourning.[4]

Events would prove Hale to be correct. Indeed, no sooner had President Millard Fillmore proclaimed the compromise measures "a final settlement of the dangerous and exciting subjects which they embraced" than the slavery issue flared up anew. Ironically, Southern friends of the Compromise were the first to reopen old wounds. The mercurial Senator Henry S. Foote of Mississippi (who had once threatened Hale with a lynching if ever he came to the South) did much of the damage with a superfluous resolution declaring the Compromise a "definitive settlement of the questions growing out of domestic slavery." In the end Congress reluctantly approved Foote's resolve, but not before it had provoked weeks of debate on the very subjects it sought to still. "What have we heard of all this session?" groused Massachusetts Senator Robert Rantoul. " 'Quiet agitation'; and quieting agitation is the noisiest business we have. . . ." And on the day the "finality resolution" cleared its last hurdle, Ohio's Lewis D. Campbell complained: " 'Agitation' is stopped (as we have just adjourned) *until to-morrow*, when no doubt some Southern man will take the floor and refresh our ears, with a harangue upon Southern interests and Northern aggression. I am heartily tired of hearing this eternal prating from these fellows."[5]

In other ways, too, Southern Congressmen persisted in stirring up debate on slavery. Henry Clay's request for a reexamination of ways to suppress the African slave trade touched off a brief discussion of the merits of slavery. So also did Senator James M. Mason's proposal to re-

---

[4] *Cong. Globe*, 31st Cong., 1st sess., 1860. See also James G. Birney, Diary, Feb. 10, 1850, Birney Papers, LC; C. F. Adams to George W. Julian, Sept. 14, 1850, Giddings-Julian Papers.

[5] *Cong. Globe*, 32nd Cong., 1st sess., 34-35 and *passim; Independent Democrat*, Mar. 18, 1852; Campbell to John Sherman, Apr. 5, 1852, John Sherman Papers, LC. Matters had come to such a pass, grumbled Representative Charles Chapman of Connecticut, that were a Congressman to die a resolution of condolence to his relatives probably could not pass without a rider reenacting the Fugitive Slave Law. Chapman to Gideon Welles, Apr. 13, 1852, Welles Papers, LC.

imburse Spanish owners of mutinous slaves aboard the *Amistad* who had been set free in 1841 by American courts, and David R. Atchison's petition to indemnify a Missouri master whose bondsman absconded while in the employ of the Army Quartermaster Corps. So often did Southerners introduce the slavery question into daily congressional affairs—final settlement or no final settlement—that political abolitionists were able to absolve themselves of responsibility for agitation. "The slavery question agitates itself," the *Boston Commonwealth* asserted in 1853, "and no power can silence this agitation, until slavery disappears, for it is the movement and struggle of an irreconcilable controversy between right and wrong."[6]

Northerners, of course, also did their bit to keep the slavery question simmering during these years of alleged quiescence—none more so than Harriet Beecher Stowe. Her immensely popular *Uncle Tom's Cabin*, which by the summer of 1853 had sold some 1,200,000 copies, not only spread a sugarcoated antislavery message more broadly than ever before, but, by provoking an angry Southern response, touched off a far-reaching series of literary and journalistic exchanges that kept slavery before the reading public for years to come. Mrs. Stowe herself joined in this debate by providing, in 1853, *A Key to Uncle Tom's Cabin*, a "chrestomathy of facts and figures" (many of them drawn from Theodore Weld's tract *Slavery as It Is*) designed to show that she had written merely "the truth." Soon there appeared melodramatic stage productions (Tom shows, they were called), etching lurid scenes of slavery's cruelty—"The Wild Flight and Escape of Eliza with her baby in her arms, across the river," "The genuine Auction Sale of Slaves upon the plantation," "Uncle Tom tied and beaten at the cruel whipping post"—into the minds of Northern audiences.[7] It was, however, the novel itself, especially its deft depiction of slavery as "a sys-

[6] *Cong. Globe*, 31st Cong., 2nd sess., 304-9, 385, 401-3; *National Era*, Jan. 23, Feb. 13, 1851; *Essex County Freeman*, Mar. 5, 1851; *Boston Weekly Commonwealth*, Dec. 10, 1853.
[7] Harriet Beecher Stowe, *Uncle Tom's Cabin or, Life Among the Lowly*, John Harvard Library edition, ed. by Kenneth S. Lynn (Cambridge, Mass., 1962), xvii, xxv-xxviii; Nevins, *Ordeal of the Union*, I, 102; J. C. Furnas, *Goodbye to Uncle Tom* (London, 1956), 259-84. The novel first appeared serially in the *National Era*, beginning June 5, 1851, and concluding April 1, 1852. Jewett & Co. of Boston published the text in book form in March 1852. The first dramatization of *Uncle Tom* was staged by C. W. Taylor at New York City's National Theater in August 1852.

tem so *necessarily* cruel and unjust" as to defeat even the attempts of an Augustine St. Clare to reform it, that hit Southerners hardest and quickened the North's awareness of slavery's continued corrosive presence.[8]

America's reaction to the visit of Louis Kossuth, exiled hero of Hungary's short-lived bid for independence, gave further proof that, if dormant, the slavery question was far from dead. For although most Northerners cheered and feted the "noble Magyar" from the moment he landed in New York early in December 1851, many Southerners felt jittery lest in honoring his struggle for self-determination abroad the nation pass implied censure on slavery at home.[9] Indeed, some antislavery spokesmen tried to do just that. When, for example, Senator Foote proposed appointment of a congressional committee to extend to Kossuth "assurances of the profound respect entertained for him by the people of the United States," John P. Hale at once sought to broaden this greeting to include an expression of sympathy for "victims of oppression everywhere." In the end, however, Congress settled for William Seward's compromise resolution, which simply extended a "cordial welcome" to the Hungarian patriot.[10]

Kossuth himself, though he tried to steer clear of the slavery question (thereby rousing the ire of the most radical abolitionists) could hardly avoid the subject of freedom. And "by turning the minds of all parties to the subject of universal liberty," Kossuth won the blessings of nearly all political abolitionists. ". . . Every speech he makes is the best kind of Abolition lecture," Ben Wade concluded. "This is felt keenly by our Southern brethren."[11] By the time he left the country in July 1852 much of Kossuth's allure had faded, Americans having grown weary of his insistent demand for their intervention in the affairs of Europe. Yet in the meantime the eloquent Magyar had by his very presence forced Americans to reexamine the ideals of their own revolution. And that kind of scrutiny, antislavery men contended, could not help but advance the cause of freedom.[12]

[8] Stowe, *Uncle Tom's Cabin*, i. Italics added.
[9] Benjamin Wade to Mrs. Wade, Dec. 10, 1851, Wade Papers.
[10] *Cong. Globe*, 32nd Cong., 1st sess., 21-24, 34-90.
[11] *National Era*, Jan. 1, 1852; George W. Julian to Joshua Giddings, Dec. 30, 1851, Giddings-Julian Papers; Wade to Milton Sutliff, Jan. 2, 1852, Sutliff Papers.
[12] *Indiana True Democrat*, Jan. 8, 1852; Van Deusen, *Seward*, 139-40.

2

The chief irritant to sectional harmony during these years was, of course, the stringent Fugitive Slave Law. Viewed by Southerners as an essential part of the Compromise of 1850, the new statute—which denied alleged fugitives the protection of habeas corpus, jury trial, and the right to give evidence—struck many Northerners as a dangerous perversion of fundamental civil liberties. While even moderates in slave states like Georgia and Mississippi threatened secession if the Fugitive Slave Law were not faithfully executed, most Yankees found the law objectionable and acquiesced in its operation reluctantly or not at all. Not only Emerson and Theodore Parker, but even the crusty Edward Everett declared that he would not obey the act. "I admit the right of the South to an efficient extradition law," Everett wrote to R. C. Winthrop, "but it is a right that *cannot be enforced*."[13] Throughout New England, upstate New York, and parts of the Old Northwest mass meetings railed against the "infernal" statute and warned slave catchers to look out for their skins. "The Fugitive Slave Bill has thrown into the cauldron of controversy new elements, and applied to it fiercer flames," noted Salmon P. Chase in the spring of 1851. Not even the Wilmot Proviso, said Charles Sumner, had offered such agitational advantages as the tyrannous extradition bill.[14]

What made the Fugitive Slave Act such an admirable agitational device was its many-sided vulnerability. To begin with, it served as a fresh reminder of slavery's basic immorality. Except for the awful spectacle of the auction block, no scene in slavery's chamber of horrors so aroused Northern moral sensibilities as did the image of the panting fugitive, struggling to escape his captors and their dogs. That it made possible the seizure and enslavement not only of recent runaways but of blacks who for years had lived useful and blameless lives in the North, simply compounded the law's—and hence slavery's—wickedness in the eyes of many patriotic Americans. The Reverend Charles Beecher vividly expressed a common sense of outrage when he thundered: "This law . . . is an unexampled climax of sin. It is the monster

[13] Quoted in Nevins, *Ordeal of the Union*, I, 380.
[14] Chase's speech at Toledo, May 30, 1851, quoted in *National Era*, June 19, 1851; Sumner to Theodore Parker, Apr. 19, 1851, Letterbook, Parker Papers.

iniquity of the present age, and it will stand forever on the page of history, as the vilest monument of infamy of the nineteenth century. Russia knows nothing like it. Hungary blesses God that *she* never suffered from anything worse than Haynau and nations afar off pause awhile from their worship of blocks of wood and stone, to ask what will those Christians do next." Under the Fugitive Slave Law, Theodore Parker snapped, Judas Iscariot would be judged a great patriot.[15]

Not only was the Fugitive Slave Act a moral disgrace, some argued, it was also unconstitutional. Particularly among antislavery Democrats this objection carried great weight. Even if one granted (as not everyone did) that the Constitution recognized property in persons and demanded the return of fugitive slaves to their masters, a good many held that the new extradition law overstepped constitutional bounds by making it a responsibility of the *federal* government to capture and carry back runaways. If the Fugitive Slave Law was not an invasion of states' rights, Gideon Welles grumbled, then neither were the Alien and Sedition Acts. "The South will themselves be convinced," he warned, "at no distant day, that the results of this amplification of the powers of the general government will be fatal to themselves, for if that government can override the state jurisdictions and seize persons in the free states to carry into slavery, that same government will under other auspices strech [*sic*] its power into slave states for the purposes of emancipation."[16] Even some antislavery Whigs and Free Soilers held that the 1850 law unconstitutionally aggrandized the powers of Congress at the expense of persons and states. Charles Sumner, for one, underscored his belief in its nullity by referring always to the Fugitive Slave *Bill*—never *Act*.[17]

Antislavery politicians also justified their opposition to the rendition law in terms of the North's commitment to free labor. Free state farmers and mechanics, Ohio's Lewis D. Campbell told Congress in 1850,

[15] Charles Beecher, *The Duty of Disobedience to Wicked Laws. A Sermon on the Fugitive Slave Law* (New York, 1851), quoted in Stanley W. Campbell, *The Slave Catchers: Enforcement of the Fugitive Slave Law, 1850-1860* (Chapel Hill, 1970), 50; Ralph A. Keller, "Northern Protestant Churches and the Fugitive Slave Law of 1850," Ph.D. dissertation, University of Wisconsin, 1969, p. 212.
[16] Welles to [?], Apr. 19, Oct. 16, 1851, Welles Papers, CHS. See also Salmon P. Chase to E. S. Hamlin, Dec. 21, 1850, Chase Papers, LC; John M. Niles to John A. Andrew, Apr. 5, 1851, quoted in *Boston Commonwealth and Emancipator*, Apr. 12, 1851; *Independent Democrat*, Mar. 18, 1852.
[17] Donald, *Sumner*, 188. See also Benjamin F. Wade to M. D. Bradley, Mar. 3, 1852, Sutliff Papers.

dependent upon their own labor for a livelihood, had no time to go chasing after every "somewhat darker" man they saw on the chance he might be a runaway slave. "If our Southern brethren, then, will have slaves," he declared, "and these slaves will run off to Ohio, they must capture them themselves."[18]

Indeed, what most affronted Northerners was the way the Fugitive Slave Law empowered federal marshals to organize local posses and to compel "all good citizens . . . to aid and assist" in the ugly business of slave catching. Many who had willingly turned their backs on slavery so long as it remained the South's peculiar institution, walled off below the Mason-Dixon line, now protested violently at being coerced into complicity with its defenders. By requiring citizen participation in the capture of runaways, a convention of New York Baptists protested, the law involved Northerners "in a business against which their moral sense and their best sympathies revolt with instinctive and unutterable aversion." Far from agreeing with the Free Soilers that freedom was national and slavery local, Southerners seemed bent on reversing that conception, on turning the North into "one vast hunting ground" where, declared the *American Baptist,* persons "of whatever complexion" were placed at the mercy of any Southerner who claimed them as his property. "If the Free States are not Free Soil for every slave that escapes to them," warned the *Boston Commonwealth,* "then they are virtually slave territory."[19]

As time passed, much of the initial uproar over the Fugitive Slave Law subsided. Union-minded Northerners preached the need to abide by all terms of the late Compromise, and except in New England the return of runaways met with little resistance. Yet although instances of obstruction were few, they were dramatic enough to keep antislavery—and proslavery—agitation simmering. The Hamlet case in New York, the rescue of the Crafts and Frederick Wilkins (alias Shadrach) and the rendition of young Thomas Sims from Boston, the Jerry rescue at Syracuse, the false arrest of Adam Gibson in Philadelphia, the bloody shoot-out at Christiana, Pennsylvania—these and similar episodes nagged at Northern consciences, defeating attempts to bury the slavery question once and for all.

[18] *Cong. Globe,* 31st Cong., 1st sess., Appendix, 178.
[19] Keller, "Northern Protestant Churches and the Fugitive Slave Law," 155, 161; *Boston Weekly Commonwealth,* July 10, 1852.

Antislavery Congressmen lagged somewhat behind their constituents in criticizing the Fugitive Slave Law,[20] but acts of resistance outside the Capitol inevitably touched off debate within, and by the spring of 1852 some were ready to propose repeal. William Seward in March and Charles Sumner in May presented petitions calling for revocation of the hated law. Each was easily tabled, though not without brief but heated discussion. Undaunted, Sumner in July moved for the immediate repeal of the Fugitive Slave Law. Again, the Senate gave short shrift to this attempt to "wash deeper and deeper the channel through which flow the angry waters of agitation." By a vote of 32 to 10 his colleagues denied Sumner permission to speak to his motion. A month later, under heavy pressure from his antislavery constituents, Sumner tried once more. This time he proposed an amendment to the civil appropriations bill providing that no funds be spent in executing the Fugitive Slave Act—"which said act is hereby repealed." Demanding the floor as his parliamentary right, Sumner then proceeded to bombard the Senate for nearly four hours on the iniquity of the Fugitive Slave Law.[21]

Within Congress, Sumner was preaching mainly to the unconvertible, and despite his eloquence he carried only three others with him on the vote for repeal: fellow Free Soilers Chase and Hale and the radical Whig Ben Wade. With the vastly larger audience beyond, however, Sumner's "Freedom National" address proved to be more successful. Thousands read it in newspapers like the *National Era* and the *New York Post* or bought the hot-selling pamphlet version.[22] If nothing else, Sumner's speech reminded the nation that even in the highest councils of government there were men who would not rest until slavery was deprived of all federal protection and driven back onto Southern soils, there to wither and die.

3

Yet while political abolitionists took heart in the persistent agitation of the slavery question, some professing to see signs of an upsurge in

[20] Joshua Giddings, who did speak up and who swore that "Agitation will never cease until the [Fugitive Slave] law ceases," complained early in 1851 that too many antislavery Congressmen had kept their "lips sealed in relation to the Fugitive Law during the entire session. . . ." Stewart, *Giddings*, 196-97.
[21] Donald, *Sumner*, 224-35.
[22] *Ibid*. 238-39.

---

reform sentiment, many bewailed the extent of public complaisance and chided Free Soilers themselves for "evident coldness and apathy" in the face of continued crisis. In Connecticut, complained the *Hartford Republican* in 1851, "those who vote our ticket, do so because they are men who cannot be induced to vote for any other," not because they had been won over—a brand of politics "too much like the boy's music that 'whistled itself.'" And taking stock on New Year's Day 1852, Charles Francis Adams fretted: "What we can do and whether we can accomplish anything really useful are questions I confess myself at present unable to solve. I think I could give an answer if our friends all over the country were of one mind. But it is plain to me the fact is otherwise." Antislavery Congressmen, he noted, "divide according to the political affinities of their constituents," some looking to the Whigs, others to the Democrats. "One thing seems now certain," Adams concluded, "—that there is little enthusiam in any quarter." "This is the darkest day of our cause," Sumner admitted in June 1852, adding with more hope than conviction: "but truth will prevail."[23]

There were many causes for Free Soil lethargy in these years. First of all, the backsliding of the Barnburners and the infatuation with coalition tactics had left the party reduced in numbers and wanting in organization. Second, the Compromise of 1850, while by no means stifling agitation, had cut some of the ground from under the Free Soilers. Even the *National Era* admitted that the issue of slavery in the territories had lost "much of its importance" due to the organization of the most valuable region, California, as a free state as well as the misguided popular impression that there was little danger of slavery in other parts of the West. In part for this reason, Salmon Chase expressed an unwillingness "to fight in a mere free soil party at the present time. I should be too uncertain whither it would drift."[24]

Still another source of discouragement to Free Soilers was a series of defeats suffered by antislavery Congressmen in their bids for reelection. Whereas the Thirty-first Congress (1849-51) had included twelve

---

[23] *Green Mountain Freeman*, Mar. 4, 1852, July 28, 1853; *Hartford Republican*, Apr. 17, 1851; Adams to Charles Sumner, Jan. 1, 1852, Sumner to Adams, June 21, 1852, Pierce (ed.), *Letters of Sumner*, III, 313. See also George W. Julian to Gerrit Smith, July 5, 1852, Smith Papers; John G. Palfrey to Sumner, July 5, 1852, Palfrey Papers.
[24] *National Era*, July 8, 1852; Chase to Charles Sumner, Feb. 26, 1851, Chase, *Diary and Correspondence*, 234.

Free Soil representatives, the Thirty-second counted only five—Allen, Tuck, Howe, Giddings, and Durkee—plus Wilmot and Preston King, who now styled themselves antislavery Democrats. The most telling losses had come in Massachusetts where, after a series of trials, John G. Palfrey lost to an orthodox Whig and in Indiana where the combined efforts of Whigs and Democrats defeated Giddings's protégé and future son-in-law, George W. Julian. Sumner's election to the Senate only partially compensated for Free Soil losses in the House.

So low had Free Soil fortunes sunk that some political abolitionists cherished hopes that one of the major parties might nominate a presidential candidate worthy of their support. Democratic Free Soilers for a time manifested a good bit of interest in Thomas Hart Benton, who had refused to sign Calhoun's "Southern Address" in 1849 and had voted for a free California and abolition of the District's slave trade in 1850. Whether he could be supported as a Democrat or only if he became the Free Soil nominee was left in the air.[25] More serious was the partiality of numerous Whig Free Soilers for General Winfield Scott, whose views concerning slavery were seductively vague. Especially among Massachusetts Free Soilers, Scott's candidacy possessed a substantial appeal. Charles Francis Adams, Stephen C. Phillips, and James W. Stone, among others, expressed a willingness to support Scott if the Whig national platform refrained from endorsing the Compromise.[26] Others simply urged that Free Soilers "hold themselves *absolutely uncommitted*, except to their principles" until the major parties tipped their hands.[27]

However, a great many Free Soilers, progressively disillusioned with coalitionist ventures and convinced of the venality of both Whigs and Democrats, had grown more and more insistent on the need for continued independence. In September 1851, "Friends of Freedom" from all but two Northern states gathered at Cleveland "to let the country know that we are not disbanded and do not intend to disband." Led by Joshua Giddings, George Julian, and former Liberty party stalwarts

[25] *Portland* (Me.) *Inquirer*, June 24, 1849; Salmon P. Chase to E. S. Hamlin, Dec. 21, 1850, Chase, *Diary and Correspondence*, 227. Friends of Sam Houston (the only Senator to vote for all parts of the Compromise of 1850) tried to induce Free Soilers to endorse their candidate, but got nowhere. See *Green Mountain Freeman*, Sept. 11, 1851; J. D. Baldwin to John M. Niles, Sept. 19, 1851, Welles Papers, LC.
[26] James W. Stone to Charles Sumner, June 6, 1852, Sumner Papers.
[27] Charles Sumner to Amasa Walker, Jan. 9, 1852, Amasa Walker Papers, MHS. See also Sumner to Francis W. Bird, Feb. 8, 1852, Francis W. Bird Papers, HLH.

like Samuel Lewis, Zebina Eastman, Francis J. LeMoyne, Sherman Booth, and Lewis Tappan, the delegates cheered a string of rousing speeches and embraced a strong set of antislavery resolutions that added to the 1848 Buffalo platform vigorous condemnation of the Fugitive Slave Law. Before adjourning the assembly also established a national committee to arrange for a nominating convention and prepare for the coming presidential campaign.[28]

By including in its deliberations idealists like Tappan and LeMoyne (neither of whom had supported Van Buren in 1848) as well as seasoned politicians like Giddings, Julian, and Charles Durkee, the Cleveland convention had refreshed a commitment to principle somewhat tarnished by recent experiments in coalition and the earlier association with Barnburner Democrats. And by denouncing the moral bankruptcy of both major parties, the convention had served notice that the bulk of Free Soilers intended to enter the 1852 campaign a united and independent force.[29]

As it happened, the actions of the major parties at their national conventions in June 1852 strengthened the hand of those who preached Free Soil autonomy. First the Democrats, who nominated New Hampshire dark horse Franklin Pierce, and then the Whigs, who chose Mexican War hero Winfield Scott over the incumbent Fillmore, pledged their adherence to the Compromise of 1850—the Fugitive Slave Act included—and warned against attempts to renew agitation over slavery. While Barnburner Democrats found Pierce perfectly acceptable and antislavery Whigs like Seward, Wade, and even Horace Mann held high hopes for Scott,[30] most Free Soilers were now surer than ever that whatever the possibility of state-level coalition, union with either major party in the impending presidential canvass was out of the ques-

---

[28] *National Era,* Oct. 2, 9, 1851.
[29] Stewart, *Giddings,* 205.
[30] Democrats like Preston King, Robert Rantoul, David Wilmot, and John Wentworth and Whigs like Seward, Mann, Greeley, and Wade nursed strong misgivings about their party's platform, but for a variety of reasons—personal ambition, party regularity and faith in party principles, confidence in the nominee or hopes of gaining influence over him—kept their peace. See, for example, Nevins, *Ordeal of the Union,* II, 21-23, 29; Preston King to Azariah C. Flagg, Aug. 16, 1852, Flagg Papers, Columbia University; Gideon Welles to C. F. Cleveland, June 14, 1852, Welles Papers, CHS; Charles Sumner to F. W. Bird, June 25, 1852, Sumner Papers; Horace Mann to Mrs. Mann, June 24, 1852, Mann to E. W. Clap, June 24, 1852, Mann Papers; Glyndon G. Van Deusen, *Horace Greeley: Nineteenth-Century Crusader* (Philadelphia, 1953), 169-71.

tion. "We have nothing left us but to make up the issue with both branches of the slave party . . . ," Charles Francis Adams decided in the aftermath of the Whig convention. "Whether few or many, an independent organization is our only resource." Even the wayward Chase concluded that separate nominations were now essential.[31]

Just who the third party presidential candidate should be had for some time been a matter of lively speculation. The names most frequently bandied about were nearly all former Democrats: John P. Hale, Salmon Chase, Henry Dodge, John M. Niles, John Charles Frémont, and Robert Rantoul—reflecting, it seems, both the bent of Free Soil platforms and a belief that votes might more easily be taken from Pierce than from Scott. Be that as it may, by the time Samuel Lewis, chairman of the national committee, issued a call for Free Democrats to assemble at Pittsburgh in August, most attention centered on Hale. His fame had grown after nearly five years in the Senate, and many old Liberty party hands wished to make amends for having dropped him in 1848. Now that the New York Barnburners had returned to the Democracy Hale seemed the most suitable candidate.[32]

A week before the Pittsburgh convention Hale confounded Free Soil leaders by flatly refusing to become a candidate. There had never been a more pressing need for effective antislavery action, he admitted, and he promised to support whatever ticket the Pittsburgh delegates might choose. But for private reasons (quite likely the hardships of campaigning and the impossibility of success) Hale asked that his name be withdrawn from consideration.[33]

Coming as it did on the very eve of the national convention, Hale's decision left Free Soil leaders in a real quandary. Learning of it while enroute to Pittsburgh, Charles Francis Adams grumbled: "I think I should not have started upon this mission had I been apprised of this early enough. Its effect will be to throw us into complete confusion."[34] Salmon Chase, next to Hale the most commonly mentioned candidate, had made too many enemies in his own state to be an attractive substitute, even if he could be prevailed upon to run. Other possible choices

[31] Adams to Charles Sumner, June 23, 1852, Sumner Papers; Chase to E. S. Hamlin, July 19, 1852, Chase Papers, LC.
[32] *Green Mountain Freeman*, Nov. 6, 1851; Joshua Leavitt to Charles Sumner, June 11, 1852; Sewell, *Hale*, 145.
[33] Sewell, *Hale*, 145-46.
[34] C. F. Adams, Diary, Aug. 6, 1852, Adams Papers.

either lacked sufficient prominence, or, like Joshua Giddings, seemed better fitted for congressional activities. The only alternative left, then, seemed to be to persuade Hale to change his mind. Accordingly, Austin Willey, a Free Soil editor from Maine, was deputized to telegraph the reluctant Senator, urging that he reconsider. At the same time Chase brought pressure to bear from Washington, quashing publication of Hale's letter of declination and beseeching his New Hampshire colleague to accept the Free Democratic nomination if it were tendered. Hale nonetheless remained mum, strengthened in his resolve by confidants like Amos Tuck, who contended that he was "of too much value to be used up, by being run at this time."[35]

Their entreaties unanswered, the Free Democratic delegates who crowded into Pittsburgh's Masonic Hall on August 11 had little choice but to press Hale's nomination anyway and trust to his sense of duty to answer their call. First, however, the convention had to nail together a statement of principles.[36] As reported by Joshua Giddings (on behalf of a committee that included among others Willey, Adams, and Gerrit Smith) the new platform was a somewhat more radical replica of the Free Soil manifesto of 1848. Indeed, its sixth article—which declared "that slavery is a sin against God and a crime against man, which no human enactment nor usage can make right; and that Christianity, humanity, and patriotism alike demand its abolition"—sounded a moralistic note at least as shrill as any to be found in earlier Liberty party platforms. Moreover, while again "leaving to the states the whole subject of slavery," the new platform dropped those passages that had previously expressed an explicit disavowal of congressional tampering with slavery in the South. And in urging diplomatic recognition of Haiti, a black republic born in insurrection, it took a stand as bold as it was unprecedented.

Doubtless the defection of "unreliable" elements (notably the Barnburners) as well as the presence of the Smith faction accounts for this shift in tone. Yet at the same time, the Pittsburgh platform smacked even more strongly of Democratic doctrines than had the Free Soil tenets of 1848. Not only did the party change its name to Free Demo

[35] Sewell, *Hale*, 146; George G. Fogg to Hale, Aug. 3, 1852, Hale Papers, BLD.
[36] Except where otherwise noted, the following account of the 1852 Free Democratic National Convention is based upon Schuyler C. Marshall, "The Free Democratic Convention of 1852," *Pennsylvania History*, XXII, No. 1 (Jan. 1955), 146-47; *National Era*, Aug. 19, 1852; McKee, *National Conventions and Platforms*, 80-84.

cratic, but it pointedly insisted on a strict construction of federal powers and added to its economic program a "demand that the funds of the
General Government be kept separate from banking institutions." This
heightened affinity for Democratic principles is not easy to explain. It
seems likely, however, that the greater success of Free Soilers in co-
alescing with Democrats than with Whigs, the influence of pro-Democratic theoreticians like Sumner and Chase, the Fugitive Slave Law's
vulnerability to states' rights doctrines, and a desire to undercut Franklin Pierce all helped to give the new creed its decidedly Jacksonian
flavor.

Despite such modifications, the Free Democrats held fast to the essence of the first Free Soil platform. As before, they called upon the
federal government to legislate against slavery wherever it possessed the
constitutional power to do so, held that Congress had "no more power
to make a slave than to make a king," and opposed the admission of any
more slave states to the Union. So also the Pittsburgh delegates reaffirmed their party's commitment to cheap postage, economical and
responsible government, river and harbor improvement, a tariff for
revenue only, and free homesteads. Even in what it did not say—especially the omission of any statement of concern for the rights of free
Negroes—the new platform resembled the old. New planks attacking
the Compromise of 1850 (in particular the unconstitutional and uncivilized Fugitive Slave Law), welcoming "emigrants and exiles from the
Old World," and recommending arbitration of international disputes
merely fleshed out and brought up to date an otherwise familiar set of
principles.

In committee, Gerrit Smith and F. J. LeMoyne had sought endorsement of equal political rights for blacks and women and recognition
of the principle that slavery, as a form of piracy, was everywhere illegal. Unsuccessful *in camera*, they carried their fight to the convention
proper, winning a partial victory in the form of a resolution (proposed
by Sherman Booth) that asserted the *moral* illegality of bondage but
stopped short of implying a right of physical resistance to slavery-sustaining statutes. Only a handful voted with Smith in favor of his
equal rights plank, the vast majority concurring in Joshua Giddings's
desire that the party not be "embarrassed by indefensible positions,"
that on such questions each man's conscience be his guide.[37] Then,

---

[37] Foner, "Politics and Prejudice," 252.

after one minor modification, the delegates, by a vote of 192 to 15, approved the proposed platform, politely tabled the rest of Smith's minority report, and turned to nominations. To no one's surprise, Hale was chosen on the first ballot; he received 192 of 208 votes cast. In a much closer battle Indiana's George Julian defeated the popular Samuel Lewis for second place on the Free Democratic ticket, thanks largely to the efforts of Henry Wilson and, apparently, the influence of Salmon Chase.[38]

All things considered, the Pittsburgh proceedings had been remarkably spirited and harmonious, and many came away with renewed confidence in the vigor and practicality of the political movement against slavery. "There was less hurrah than at Buffalo in '48," Austin Willey reported, "but in every element of real moral force, in dignity, sober earnestness, ability, and *principle*, Pittsburgh far exceeded Buffalo." Even Gerrit Smith praised Hale and Julian as "earnest and generous philanthropists" and at first decided to support them despite his misgivings concerning the party's creed. Others, however, had their doubts. Sumner hardly stirred, and Chase, while willing to back the Free Democratic candidates and platform, feared sinking his "individuality in this organization, which it seems to me, must be temporary."[39]

Northern blacks were also of two minds about the Free Democratic party. They were pleased that men "of sable hue" had been cordially welcomed at Pittsburgh and flattered that Frederick Douglass had been chosen a secretary of the convention and had taken his seat "amid loud applause." Douglass himself, his head perhaps a trifle turned by such attention, soon hoisted the Free Democratic ticket to his newspaper's masthead. Praising Hale as "a large-breasted philanthropist . . . a

---

[38] C. F. Adams, Diary, Aug. 12, 1852, Adams Papers; James W. Stone to Charles Sumner, Aug. 15, 1852, Sumner Papers; Riddleburger, *Julian*, 86.
[39] Austin Willey to John P. Hale, Aug. 19, 1852, Hale Papers, BLD; C. F. Adams, Diary, Aug. 13, 1852, Adams Papers; Adams to Sumner, Aug. 15, 1852, Pierce (ed.), *Letters of Sumner*, III, 316; *National Liberty Party* (broadside), 1852, NYHA; Harlow, *Smith*, 191; Donald, *Sumner*, 239-40; Chase to E. S. Hamlin, Aug. 13, 1852, Chase Papers, LC. Smith felt warmly enough toward Hale to entertain him in his Peterboro home in mid-September. However, when neither Hale nor Julian replied to Smith's printed letter asking their opinions concerning the political rights of women and blacks and the legality of slavery, he felt obliged to reconvene the Liberty party. That group—the Liberty Leaguers of 1848—met at Syracuse (Sept. 30) and nominated William Goodell and S. M. Bell of Virginia for President and Vice President. His principles thus preserved, Smith nonetheless continued to hope that Hale would poll a big vote. Hale to Mrs. Hale, Sept. 13, 1852, Hale Papers, NHHS; Smith to Henry Wilson, Oct. 15, 1852, Mann Papers.

dreaded foe of slavery" and Julian as "one of the truest and most disinterested friends of freedom whom we have ever met," Douglass called on all voting abolitionists to set aside paltering objections to the basically sound Pittsburgh platform and join him in support of the Free Democracy. "It can give us the wisdom of two heads instead of one," he lectured his Liberty party associates, "and the might of a multitude instead of a few." Black leaders in New England followed suit, organizing rallies in support of Hale and impressing on Negro voters the moral bankruptcy of Whigs and Democrats. At the same time, the omission of an equal rights plank rankled, and when Gerrit Smith mustered the tattered Liberty army once more, Douglass and a handful of other blacks changed front and joined him. Most Northern Negroes seem to have stuck by the Free Democracy, though perhaps with restrained enthusiasm—especially after it became apparent that the party's standard-bearers had no intention of publicly proclaiming their support of equal political rights for all citizens.[40]

Nobody, of course, least of all the candidates, expected the third party to carry so much as a single state in November. Yet the Free Democrats did not lack incentives. First, a vigorous campaign would stir up the faithful and sharpen the party's effectiveness in future wars. Second, even if defeated, Free Democrats believed they had a chance to influence public policy. As the *National Era* explained:

> The argument of 1848 is the argument for 1852. Triumph who may, the best safeguard for freedom, the surest restraint upon his Administration, will be the fact that three hundred thousand voters have spurned all party obligations, all party prejudices, all the seductions and intimidations of party, for the sake of giving a distinct testimony at the ballot-box in favor of Free Soil, Free Labor, and Free Men.[41]

Such testimony, moreover, might cleanse individual guilt as well as exert moral pressure on the nation's leaders. While former Liberty party abolitionists may have been most sensitive to this consideration,

---

[40] Foner, *Writings of Douglass*, II, 75-77, 206-9, 211-19; Quarles, *Black Abolitionists*, 186-87; Foner, "Politics and Prejudice," 251-53. It was characteristic of most Free Democrats that when one black delegate was refused service at a railway restaurant en route to Pittsburgh, all other delegates walked out. *Ibid.* 251-52.
[41] Salmon P. Chase to E. S. Hamlin, July 19, 1852, Chase, *Diary and Correspondence*, 243; *National Era*, July 8, 1852.

they were by no means its sole exponents. None put the matter more tellingly than did George Julian:

> It has been said truly that a man may commit murder by a vote [he wrote to his uncle in June 1852]. It was done repeatedly in the case of our infamous war with Mexico. In like manner we may involve ourselves in the guilt of slave holding by our votes. . . . Political action . . . is moral action, and moral action compounded; for our responsibility is multiplied by the objects which our action concerns. Political action, and party action especially, has made the slave power what it is, and I would fully as leave own and buy and sell slaves myself, as to help the old parties to build up and give life to the whole system.[42]

For many Free Democrats, however, the most immediate, tangible goal in 1852 was the defeat of Franklin Pierce and the Democratic party. Even before the Pittsburgh convention the *National Era* had pronounced old line Democracy the chief instrument of the Slave Power and recommended that Free Soilers pick a presidential candidate able to cut into the Democratic vote. Some complained of the *Era*'s indiscretion, but a good many third party leaders agreed with its analysis and championed Hale at least in part because he fit the bill so neatly. "It was the opinion from east and west," Austin Willey informed the Senator after the convention, "that you would take double the strength from Pierce which you will from Scott."[43] Antislavery Whigs (and a few Free Democrats) were more fearful that the popular Hale, despite his Democratic antecedents, would cost Scott Ohio and Indiana. Some (among them Thurlow Weed of New York) therefore beseeched him to decline the third party nomination. In the end, after nearly a month of deliberation, Hale reluctantly consented to run. But in the campaign that followed he as well as his supporters concentrated their efforts where damage to Pierce would be greatest. "I speak only in democratic towns," reported one Massachusetts Free Democrat, "—or rather, I *endeavour* to avoid all but Democratic towns."[44]

---

[42] Julian to David Hoover, June 17, 1852, Julian Papers. See also *Essex County Freeman*, Aug. 25, 1852.

[43] *National Era*, July 8, 1852; Joshua Giddings to Henry Wilson, Sept. 3, 1852, Tuck Papers; Henry Wilson to Charles Sumner, June 23, July 7, 22, 1852, Sumner Papers; Samuel Lewis to George W. Julian, Aug. 19, 1852, Giddings-Julian Papers; C. F. Adams to Hale, Aug. 15, 1852, Austin Willey to Hale, Aug. 19, 1852, Hale Papers, BLD.

[44] Horace Greeley, *Recollections of a Busy Life* (New York, 1868), 280; Thurlow

To the distress of Hale and his party, the campaign proved to be one of unparalleled dullness. Only the Free Democrats, it seemed, showed much enthusiasm. "In our recent travels in New York and New England," noted a *National Era* correspondent, "we should not have known, from any indications of popular feeling, that a Presidential election was pending." "Genl *Apathy* is the strongest candidate out here," one Whig wrote from Cincinnati. Both Whigs and Democrats shunned the slavery question and let Free Democratic challenges go unanswered.[45]

Judged by its results, the 1852 election appeared to be a disheartening setback for antislavery as a political force. Pierce, the greater of two evils in the eyes of most Free Democrats, overwhelmed General Scott, capturing all but four states. Hale polled only 156,667 ballots—roughly half Van Buren's total in 1848. In only four states did he receive as much as 10 per cent of the vote, and only one, Massachusetts, gave him more than 20 per cent. Nowhere, it seems, did the Free Democrats tip the scales in favor of either major candidate. State returns were equally bleak. Only in Ohio, where Joshua Giddings and Edward Wade carried the day, and in upstate New York, where a curious collection of antislavery Whigs, radical Liberty men, and some regular Democrats joined Free Democrats to elect a reluctant Gerrit Smith, were third party congressional candidates successful—a sharp drop from the twelve seats gained in 1848. Likewise, Free Democrats found themselves virtually without representation in state legislatures, wholly unable to exert pressure on either major party. In Massachusetts the once-formidable coalition fell victim to a Whig resurgence, killing chances that Horace Mann might be chosen as governor.[46]

Yet midst all the darkness Free Democrats perceived faint rays of light. Outside New York, where the Barnburners now solidly supported Franklin Pierce, the antislavery party showed substantial resiliency—its share of the presidential vote elsewhere slipping by only 2 per cent between 1848 and 1852. In Iowa and the slave states of Dela-

---

Weed to Hamilton Fish, Aug. 22, 23, Sept. 15, 1852, Hamilton Fish Papers, LC; Henry Wilson to Joshua R. Giddings, Aug. 21, 1852, Giddings Papers; George G. Fogg to John P. Hale, Aug. 3, 1852, Hale Papers, BLD; Hale to O. B. Matteson, Sept. 27, 1852, Seward Papers; W. B. Greene to Robert Carter, Oct. 1, 1852, Robert Carter Papers, HLH.
45 Sewell, *Hale*, 148-49; Blue, *Free Soilers*, 249-55.
46 *Ibid.* 255-68; Harlow, *Smith*, 312-14.

ware, Maryland, Virginia, Kentucky, and North Carolina Hale improved upon Van Buren's earlier showing, the last two states recording their first ballots ever for an antislavery candidate. And the loss of the Barnburners was less critical than it might first appear since, as George Julian recalled, "they were not Free Soil men, but Van Buren men, who hated General Cass." The vote for Hale provided a better index of political abolitionism, and, Julian added, "its quality went far to atone for its quantity." Better to compare Hale's tally with that of Birney in 1844—a 150 per cent increase.[47]

Free Democrats also drew satisfaction and hope from the collapse of the Whig party. Although many would have preferred to see the Democrats go under first (finding that organization more tightly knit and subservient to the South), most joined the *Independent Democrat* in rejoicing "that *one* of the two wings of the great slavery party of the country is dead, *dead*, DEAD." Besides, with Whiggery defunct, a fundamental restructuring of the American party system seemed inevitable. And in that process, antislavery spokesmen contended, the Free Democratic party would soon emerge as the dominant political force in the United States. Once again George Julian offered the most perceptive analysis, or at least the most cogent expression of Free Soil hopes. In a letter written upon the occasion of a testimonial banquet honoring Senator Hale in the spring of 1853 his recent running mate observed:

> One of these strongholds of slavery has perished, the other has thus been deprived of its antagonist, and must follow in its footsteps; for although intensely hostile, they have been the support of each other. Each has held the other in its orbit, whilst both have revolved round a common centre of antagonism, which was their spirit and their life. Henceforth we shall have the antagonism of slavery and freedom, and upon this issue the parties of the future are to be founded, and our great victory is to be won. Instead of being blinded by the assumed necessity of choosing between two evils, let us hail with delight the near approach of the 'good time coming,' when men shall march over their ruins to the ballot box with an eye single to the highest good of their country.

[47] Julian, *Political Recollections*, 129-32; Lewis Tappan to Editor of British & Foreign Anti-Slavery Society *Reporter*, Dec. 10, 1852, Abel and Klingberg (eds.), *Side-Light on Anglo-American Relations*, 308.

With the Democrats succeeding "to the position of general conservation and panic-making," and conscientious Whigs ready to form new alliances, the Free Democracy would sweep the country—"in eight years," said Joshua Leavitt, "if not in four: So I prophesy." It proved a remarkably accurate prediction.[48]

4

Buoyed by such hopes (however unrealistic the rest of the world might find them), Free Democrats exhorted one another to hold firm and prepare for the better days to come. In New England, John P. Hale, though recently defeated for reelection to the United States Senate, directed efforts to tighten and extend party organization. State elections in the fall of 1853 revealed how difficult the task would be. In Massachusetts Free Democrats could do no better than hold their own and, thanks to Whig gains, their coalition with regular Democrats lay in ruins. In Vermont, the party's fortunes became embroiled in a controversy over the Maine Liquor Law, with the result that its gubernatorial vote fell off slightly from earlier showings. Yet at least outside of Massachusetts (where feuding among Free Democrats over a proposed new constitution exacerbated prior differences concerning the wisdom of coalition), third party morale remained high throughout New England.[49]

Spirits were every bit as high and returns substantially greater in the Middle West. Encouraged by the shipwreck of national Whiggery and by evidence of internal feuding among Democrats, and convinced that inadequate preparation had needlessly curtailed Hale's vote in 1852, Free Democrats threw themselves into the task of party building with such gusto that in 1853 they made their best showing ever. In Indiana the third party drew some 1500 more votes than in the previous year, and George Julian repeatedly asserted that he had "never seen the Free Democrats . . . so much encouraged." Town elections in Michi-

---

[48] *Independent Democrat,* Nov. 4, 1852; Julian to F. W. Bird *et al.,* Apr. 29, 1853, Giddings-Julian Papers; Leavitt to R. H. Leavitt, Nov. 12, 1852, Joshua Leavitt Papers, LC.
[49] Hale to Anson Burlingame, Sept. 12, 1853, John P. Hale Papers, Phillips Exeter Academy; *Green Mountain Freeman,* Sept. 15, 1853; Blue, *Free Soilers,* 275-79.

gan witnessed a soaring third party vote. Prospects seemed even brighter in Ohio. There, after a vigorous and well-organized campaign, Free Democrats cast over 50,000 ballots for their gubernatorial candidate, Samuel Lewis, outpolling both Whigs and Democrats in Clinton County and throughout the Western Reserve. Lewis's total represented a nearly 60 per cent increase over the vote for Hale one year earlier. Even where there were no elections in this off year, as in Illinois and Iowa, Free Democrats tightened party lines and confidently prepared for the future.[50]

Just as heartening as the rise in Free Democratic strength was mounting evidence that antislavery Whigs throughout the Northwest (and to a lesser extent elsewhere) were growing receptive to combination with the third party. Much of the Free Democrats' success in Ohio stemmed from Whig crossovers; in parts of that state "People's" conventions chose mixed tickets of liberal Whigs and Free Democrats, and after the election even so conservative a Whig sheet as the *Cleveland Herald* admitted "that there are and ever have been reasons which should induce all considerate antislavery men to act together."[51]

Wisconsin Free Democrats carried cooperation with the Whigs still further and achieved even greater success than did their brethren in Ohio. This time the Whigs put out the first feelers, hinting at the efficacy of a joint nomination in the 1853 campaign. Governor L. J. Farwell, a radical antislavery Whig, popular with both parties, who was expected to head such a ticket, momentarily squelched such talk by adamantly refusing to seek reelection. After the Free Democrats had agreed to a slate of their own, however, Wisconsin Whigs (acting in accordance with Horace Greeley's advice in the *New-York Tribune*) came around. Two weeks before the election the two organizations formally united behind E. D. Holton, a veteran Liberty and Free Soil campaigner. A rump group of "Silver Gray" Whigs persisted in backing their own candidate, and that liability, together with the canvass' late start and the heavy Democratic beer vote cast by Germans who feared Free Democratic endorsement of prohibition, deprived the "People's" ticket of victory. Even so, Holton ran a respectable second to the Democrat

---

[50] *National Era*, Nov. 11, 1852; Smith, *Liberty and Free Soil Parties*, 261-77.
[51] *Ibid.* 269-76; *Independent Democrat*, July 14, 1853, quoting *Holmes County (Ohio) Whig, Painesville Telegraph, Lockport (N.Y.) Journal*.

Barstow, polling more than twice as many votes as any antislavery candidate in the state's history.[52]

The close of 1853 thus found political abolitionists still distinctly in the minority, yet very much alive. That their party and its cause had weathered repeated electoral setbacks and attempts to sweep the slavery question from public view, that it had survived with its fundamental principles still basically intact, became a source of pride and encouragement to embattled Free Democrats. Therefore, while shattered Whigs viewed the future with apprehension, most Free Democrats seem genuinely to have believed that there were good times coming. Congressional debate in February and March of 1853 over a bill to organize the Nebraska territory without slavery had once again revealed the snares of "finality." With the Whig party now defunct, Free Democrats might expect fresh recruits in this still smoldering war against slavery and the Slave Power. Although they had no way of knowing it, the Nebraska question would soon touch off an explosion so thunderous as to destroy even the illusion of sectional peace and to precipitate the formation of an antislavery alliance mightier than any that had gone before.

[52] Smith, *Liberty and Free Soil Parties*, 278-83. Holton received 21,886 votes to 30,405 for Barstow and 3304 for H. S. Baird, the die-hard Whig candidate. Wisconsin gave Van Buren 10,418 votes in 1848 and Hale 8814 in 1852.

II

"Party Ties Are Torn Wide Asunder"

EARLY IN JANUARY 1854 Senator Stephen A. Douglas of Illinois introduced a bill calling for the organization of the vast Nebraska territory, a bill that, in its final form, explicitly repealed the Missouri Compromise ban on slavery north of 36°30′. As Douglas himself had predicted, this proposal, which theoretically opened new pastures to slavery, raised a "hell of a storm" throughout the North. Before the tempest subsided it had splintered the Democratic party, smashed the last remnants of organized Whiggery, and crystallized antislavery elements from all parties into a formidable new political coalition. Some looked upon this new Republican party as the work of self-serving, outcast politicians, willing to risk chaos and disunion to further their own ambitions. To men like Sumner and Chase, Giddings and Hale, however, it seemed a logical, intensely gratifying culmination of years of agitation and principled resistance to slavery and Southern aristocrats. The "moral revolution" they had so long awaited now seemed near at hand.

Free Democrats, ever alert to aggression by the "slavocracy," had warned of the Nebraska earthquake months before it hit. In April 1853 the *National Era*, seeing in President Pierce's wholesale removal of judges in Minnesota, Oregon, Utah, and New Mexico an attempt to ensure proslavery decisions in the territories, urged antislavery Congressmen to seek explicit reaffirmation of the Missouri Compromise restriction in any bill for the organization of Nebraska. Editor Gamaliel

Bailey rang the alarm again in October, in response to the call of a meeting of Nebraska settlers for the prompt organization of the territory without restriction on slavery. Such "impertinent agitation," he averred, was but part of a larger "conspiracy of a base, blind sectionalism against the extension of Western empire." Freedom's defenders would need to be especially vigilant when Congress reconvened in December.[1] Other antislavery papers picked up the *Era*'s warning and stood ready to sound the tocsin when the Little Giant, bending before Southern pressure, repudiated the 1820 ban on slavery in the northern reaches of the Louisiana Purchase.[2]

In Congress, antislavery representatives began to organize well before the Kansas-Nebraska bill assumed its final shape. Sumner, Ben Wade, and William Seward were especially active, setting in motion petition and letter-writing campaigns to give voice to Northern outrage. Chase and Giddings, meanwhile, with stylistic assistance from Sumner and Gerrit Smith, drafted an "Appeal of the Independent Democrats in Congress to the People of the United States." In often violent language that address arraigned Douglas's measure "as a gross violation of a sacred pledge; as a criminal betrayal of precious rights; as part and parcel of an atrocious plot to exclude from a vast unoccupied region immigrants from the Old World and free laborers from our own States, and convert it into a dreary region of despotism, inhabited by masters and slaves."[3]

As one might expect, coming from the pens of such seasoned draftsmen, the "Appeal" proved a marvelously effective piece of antislavery propaganda. First printed in the *National Era* and *The New York Times* on January 24, the day after the introduction of the final Kansas-Nebraska bill, the "Appeal" was soon reprinted in newspapers across the North. With understandable pride, Chase called it "the *most valuable* of my works."[4] What made it so compelling was the deft way the "Appeal" moulded old arguments to fit the fluid circumstances of 1854. Without in any way seeming to lower tried and true antislavery prin-

[1] *National Era*, Apr. 14, Oct. 20, Nov. 17, 1853.
[2] *Essex County Freeman*, Nov. 23, 1853; Pierce (ed.), *Letters of Sumner*, III, 349; *Chicago Free West*, Dec. 8, 1853.
[3] Seward to Thurlow Weed, Jan. 8, 1854, Thurlow Weed Papers, University of Rochester; Wade to [Milton Sutliff?], Jan. 9, 1854, Sutliff Papers; Sumner to John Jay, Jan. 12, 1854, Jay Family Papers; *National Era*, Jan. 24, 1854; Robert W. Johannsen, *Stephen A. Douglas* (New York, 1973), 418-19.
[4] Chase to E. L. Pierce, Aug. 8, 1854, Chase, *Diary and Correspondence*, 263.

ciples, Chase and his fellow signators[5] developed a case against the Kansas-Nebraska "crime" calculated to attract the cooperation of groups hitherto outside the free-soil movement. Former Whigs, for instance, were assured that Henry Clay would have been the first to denounce Douglas's pretense that the Compromise of 1850 had implicitly nullified the prohibition of 1820. Churchmen were reminded that the Scriptures required "them to behold in every man a brother [an off-hand and thus camouflaged paraphrase of an old abolitionist motto] and to labor for the advancement and regeneration of the human race." American workingmen and European immigrants were warned that free labor would pay a heavy price for the passage of Douglas's bill. To all Northerners, the "Appeal" repeated stock Liberty party and Free Soil arguments concerning the Founding Fathers' intention to curtail slavery and the Slave Power's plot to extend it. If so sacred and solemn a compact as the Missouri Compromise were now to be tossed aside, merely to appease Southern bullies, fresh calamities would follow in thick succession. The Union itself might sicken and die.

As befit the crisis at hand, the "Appeal" concentrated on the danger of slavery encroachment. But in vilifying bondage as "legalized oppression and systematized injustice" and insisting that "the cause of human freedom is the cause of God," Chase and his colleagues reaffirmed their own dedication to still more radical goals.

Yet despite the skillful construction and wide circulation of the "Appeal," the Kansas-Nebraska bill at first aroused less popular protest than political abolitionists thought it deserved. "What a wicked business is the Nebraska-Kansas matter!" Theodore Parker fumed in February. "Men 'hate it but know it will pass'; the prominent men [of Boston] *do nothing*—not even call a convention!" Only the Free Soilers had been active, he complained. Three weeks later one of Chase's Philadelphia correspondents lamented: "Altho' a man cannot be found here who approves this gigantic attempt to make bitter as sweet and darkness as light, yet the public mind shows not the slightest sensibility, in these parts." As late as April 7 Neal Dow confessed to Hannibal Hamlin: "I am amazed at the supineness of our Maine people in relation to

---

[5] Besides Chase, Giddings, Sumner, Smith, Edward Wade of Ohio, and Alexander DeWitt of Massachusetts signed the document. Benjamin Wade, although not given a chance to sign, nonetheless also approved of the "Appeal" and endorsed its "every word" on the floor of the Senate. Trefousse, *Wade*, 85-86.

the Nebraska affair. . . ." His explanation for such passivity was that "the Measure is so Enormously wicked—that it is supposed to be impossible to pass it."[6]

Whether or not Dow's hunch was right, by the end of May when President Pierce signed the Kansas-Nebraska bill into law thunderous protest reverberated throughout the North. In city after city, merchants and mechanics, lawyers and draymen, clergymen and architects —many of them old foes of antislavery agitation, men new to political action—joined in petition campaigns and mass rallies to denounce Douglas's "treasonable scheme" and to swear war on doughfaces who voted for it. Conservative Whigs like Robert C. Winthrop, Hamilton Fish, and Thomas Ewing now stood shoulder to shoulder with Whiggish liberals and veteran Free Soilers in blistering the "Nebraska infamy." Even a good many Northern Democrats joined in the chorus of dissent. In Chicago Judge Mark Skinner, a self-styled Old Hunker and a friend of Douglas's, delivered the principal address at that city's first protest rally. And New Hampshire Democrat Henry F. French informed his brother Benjamin, Pierce's campaign biographer and crony: "The Nebraska peace measure is working as might be expected. Everybody almost is ready for a rebellion."[7]

Why all this uproar? Much of the clamor, it must be admitted, had little to do with slavery *per se*. As George Julian later recalled, many anti-Nebraska Whigs and Democrats "made the sacredness of the bargain of 1820 and the crime of its violation the sole basis of their hostility. Their hatred of slavery was geographical, spending its force north of the Missouri restriction. They talked far more eloquently about the duty of keeping covenants, and the wickedness of reviving sectional

[6] Parker to Charles Ellis, Feb. 12, 1854, Letterbook, Parker Papers; W. H. Furness to Chase, May 3, 1854, Chase Papers, LC; Dow to Hamlin, Apr. 7, 1854, Hannibal Hamlin Papers, University of Maine. See also William H. Seward to Thurlow Weed, June 12, 1854, Weed Papers; Theodore Parker, *The New Crime Against Humanity* (Boston, 1854), 34. The *Springfield* (Mass.) *Republican* confirmed Dow's analysis, explaining that when Douglas first proposed repeal of the Missouri Compromise "we looked upon it as an extravagant bid of that gentleman for Southern gratitude, to be made available in the Presidential campaign of 1856. We had no idea that it could become so formidable as to promise success." Once the paper came to perceive it as an *Administration* measure designed to unify the Democratic party its concern burst into flame. *Springfield Daily Republican*, Feb. 8, 1854.
[7] *New York Evening Post*, Jan. 31, 1854; Harriet B. Stowe to Charles Sumner, Feb. 23, 1854, Sumner Papers; Nevins, *Ordeal of the Union*, II, 125-32; Donald, *Sumner*, 256-57; H. F. French to B. B. French, May 30, 1854, Benjamin B. French Papers, LC.

agitation, than the evils of slavery, and the cold-blooded conspiracy to spread it over an empire of free soil." Others worried that the economic interests of free whites—a homestead law, for instance, and a northerly railroad line to the Pacific—would suffer from the creation of a Western slave belt.[8]

On the other hand there were many—especially Free Soilers but also radical Whigs and Democrats—who insisted that the Kansas-Nebraska Act was but the latest and most alarming in a long string of attempts to bend government to the service of slavery. Moreover, repeal of the Missouri Compromise seemed to betoken a heightened proslavery aggressiveness, a determination to overturn all existing legal barriers to bondage. Northerners had long noted that slavery was aggressive, observed the *New-York Tribune*, but previously many believed it "to be warring on the defensive side." Douglas's measure, the *Tribune* decided, had changed all that. No sooner had Congress approved the Kansas-Nebraska bill than antislavery journals began to warn of the next steps in the Slave Power's plot against freedom: introduction of slavery into all federal territories (including Minnesota and Oregon), creation through conquest of numerous slave states in the Caribbean and Central America, renewal of the African slave trade, and, most ominous of all, legalization of slavery in states now free.[9]

Whether because they sincerely feared slavery's encroachment upon free states or because they sought to dramatize the North's stake in the Kansas-Nebraska decision, antislavery leaders warned early and often of Southern plans to nationalize the peculiar institution. At a mass meeting of Free Soilers at Boston in February, Salmon Chase, John P. Hale, Henry Wilson, Anson Burlingame, and other speakers all stressed that the Kansas-Nebraska proposal "was a part of a continuous movement of slaveholders to advance slavery over the entire North." Pierce's former law partner, Asa Fowler, predicted that repeal of the

[8] Julian, *Political Recollections*, 136-37. After attending a Kansas meeting in New York City in June 1856 William Goodell disgustedly reported to Gerrit Smith: "The tone was for war, but not a word of sympathy with the Slave! Repeatedly the orators said 'It is no nigger *question!* We do not propose an *emancipation* crusade. We will defend the liberty of the *whites*'—and repeatedly the roof trembled with applause." Goodell to Smith, June 20, 1856, Smith Papers. See also Sarah J. Day, *The Man on a Hill Top* (Philadelphia, 1931), 126.

[9] *New-York Daily Tribune*, Jan. 11, 1854; *New York Evening Post*, Jan. 25, May 23, Aug. 11, 1854; *Green Mountain Freeman*, May 25, 1854; Julian, *Political Recollections*, 137-38; J. Z. Goodrich to [?], June 24, 1854, Slavery Manuscripts, Box I, NYHS; Gideon Welles to [?], May 1854, Welles Papers, CHS.

Missouri Compromise would soon be followed by attempts to reestab-
lish slavery in the mid-Atlantic states and New England. Already there
were signs that such fears were real, the *New York Post* warned in
March. A state assemblyman from New York City had recently proposed a law providing for the free transit of slaves through New York.
And law or no law, the *Post* claimed, "Gangs of men and women,
chained together, may yet be seen, marching up or down Broadway or
trembling on the Battery." Once admit that property in slaves was absolute, independent of positive legislation establishing bondage, and
masters might as freely bring their chattels into any state as into any
territory. It was the Kansas-Nebraska excitement, and not the later
Dred Scott decision, which first gave currency to the charge that slavery threatened to blot out freedom in every corner of the land. That
Northerners responded so spiritedly to such warnings shows how deep
and disturbing the idea of a Slave Power conspiracy had by then become.[10]

Whatever the wellsprings of popular protest against the Kansas-
Nebraska Act, its effect was unquestionably to radicalize Northern antislavery attitudes. Typical of many was the response of Maine's newly
elected Whig Senator, William Pitt Fessenden. "The thing is a terrible outrage," he wrote to his wife during the heat of the debate on
Douglas's bill, "and the more I look at it the more enraged I become.
It needs but little to make me an out & out abolitionist." Similarly,
James H. Duncan, a Whig Congressman from Massachusetts, recalled
a few years later: "I voted for the compromise measures of 1850 with
the exception of the Fugitive slave law, and had little sympathy with
abolitionists, but the repeal of the Missouri Compromise, that most
wanton and wicked act, so obviously designed to promote the extension of slavery, was too much to bear. I now advocate the freedom of
Kansas under all circumstances and at all hazards, and the prohibition
of slavery in all territory now free."[11] Indeed, the very election to the
Senate of Fessenden, who won support from both Whigs and Demo-

[10] *New-York Daily Tribune*, Feb. 17, 1854; *New York Evening Post*, Mar. 27, Aug.
11, 1854; *Galesburg* (Ill.) *Free Democrat*, Aug. 17, 1854; *Dover* (N.H.) *Enquirer*,
Sept. 3, 1854.
[11] Fessenden to Ellen Fessenden, Feb. 26, 1854, William Pitt Fessenden Papers,
Bowdoin College Library (microfilm in SHSW); Duncan to William Pitt Fessenden, Jan. 24, 1857, William Pitt Fessenden Papers, WRHS; *Wisconsin Free
Democrat*, May 31, 1854; Charles A. Jellison, *Fessenden of Maine: Civil War Senator* (Syracuse, 1962), 68-72.

crats for his strong antislavery and temperance views, and, even more,
of Connecticut's Francis Gillette—"one of the most radical of old-
fashioned abolitionists in the country," Sherman Booth had called him
—bore witness to the growing radicalism of Northern voters during
the early months of 1854.

Many now recognized what political abolitionists had preached for
years: that compromise with the slave interest was, if not immoral, impossible. "Wantonly and without excuse," railed the Whiggish *Poughkeepsie* (N.Y.) *Eagle*, "those who professed to desire quiet have commenced agitation, and shown that while they are willing to profit
by compromises to promote slavery, they will sustain none to preserve
freedom. They have rendered evil for good, rewarded our concessions
with insult and treachery, have rejected peace and chosen war; and
now on their guilty heads be the consequences." The only honorable
course remaining, the *Eagle* concluded, was for Northerners to wage
full-scale war against slavery at every point. "The repeal of the Nebraska bill, the abolition of slavery in the District of Columbia, and not
another slave state, or inch of slave territory, no more compromises and
no terms with traitors, must be their watch words and their rallying
cry." John Jay's prediction that Douglas would accomplish what no
abolitionist could do—"arouse the country to a sense of its danger and
a remembrance of its duty"—was amply borne out before the Nebraska
bill became law. Never before had the Free Soil platform possessed
such broad appeal.[12]

Free Democrats, of course, were delighted at the growing popularity of their doctrines. A few may even have exulted in the Kansas-
Nebraska Act's passage, believing that it would "sound the death knell
of all compromises, and make the agitation of the slavery question
endless."[13] Most, however, strove mightily to defeat Douglas's measure
and once it became law fought to repeal it. But nearly all were quick
to perceive the political opportunities it afforded and hastened to capitalize upon them. "Our position is now rather enviable," Joshua Gid-

[12] *Poughkeepsie Eagle*, Feb. 4, 18, May 27, 1854; Jay to Charles Sumner, Jan. 24,
1854, Sumner Papers. See also *New-York Daily Tribune*, Jan. 11, 1854; *Wisconsin
Free Democrat*, May 31, 1854; William H. Seward to Theodore Parker, June 23,
1854, Letterbook, Parker Papers.
[13] J. D. Baldwin to Gideon Welles, Feb. 23, 1854, Welles Papers, LC. Baldwin, an
abolitionist turned Free Soil editor, dissociated himself from "the more *red-hot*
abolitionists" who held such views. See also R. K. Darrah to Charles Sumner, July
1, 1854, Sumner Papers.

dings cheered as the Nebraska yeast began to work. "We lead the hosts of freedom."[14]

Most political abolitionists were more modest (and more realistic) than Giddings concerning their faction's place in the anti-Nebraska movement. All, however, shared his optimism about the future and were determined to make their influence tell. A few, notably Salmon Chase and Ichabod Codding, at first thought that this might best be done by preserving Free Democratic (or, as Chase preferred, Independent Democratic) autonomy, counting on liberal Whigs and Democrats to give it sufficient strength to turn back the Slave Power.[15] The vast majority of third party veterans, however, agreed that conditions demanded a fresh start—the formation of a mighty, wholly new alliance. "This war with slavery is too radical, too difficult, too long, too big for success without a power constructed especially for it," argued Austin Willey, among others. "Cromwell needed a better army and so do we." Political abolitionists all agreed, moreover, that whatever form the antislavery host now assumed its aims lay well beyond mere opposition to the Kansas-Nebraska Act. The ultimate goal was still the destruction of slavery everywhere, and the means were still those described in the Free Soil platforms of 1848 and 1852: divorce of government from slavery, no more slave states or slave territory, repeal of the Fugitive Slave Law.[16]

Free Democrats were by no means the only ones to glimpse political advantage amidst the chaos Douglas's bill produced. To many Northern Whigs the popular outcry against repeal of the Missouri restriction came as a godsend, bringing hopes of resurrection to a party all but dead. Pointing to the unanimous vote against the Nebraska bill by Northern Whig Congressmen and insisting that "the spreading of slavery over territory now free IS A LOCOFOCO MEASURE," some sought to rejuvenate the party of Webster and Clay and to make it the vehicle for an extended war against slavery. There was no reason, the *Poughkeepsie Eagle* contended in June 1854, why Whigs "should seek new

[14] Giddings to G. R. Giddings, Feb. 12, 1854, Giddings-Julian Papers.
[15] Chase to Codding, Apr. 15, 22, 1854, Ichabod Codding Papers, FHL.
[16] Willey to William Pitt Fessenden, July 12, 1854, Fessenden Papers, WRHS; Willey to Salmon P. Chase, Mar. 26, 1855, Chase Papers, LC; Henry Wilson to William H. Seward, May 28, 1854, Seward Papers; Gamaliel Bailey to James S. Pike, June 6, 1854, James Shepherd Pike Papers, Calais Free Library, Calais, Me.; C. P. Huntington to Charles Sumner, July 2, 1854, Sumner Papers; *Boston Weekly Commonwealth*, Sept. 16, 1854; *National Era*, Sept. 28, 1854.

party alliances or desert their own. No party could be found or formed which would represent a firmer and more unmistakable hostility to the aggressions of the slaveholding interest, than the Whig party of the Free States at this moment."[17] Such opinions were most common and longest held in states like New York, Massachusetts, and Pennsylvania, where Whiggery had survived the disaster of 1852 in reasonably good shape. But they also found expression in other parts of the North, particularly during the first half of 1854, reflecting, no doubt, the fear of moderate Whig leaders that hard-earned political power and prestige—not to mention basic Whig programs—might be lost unless Free Soilers and anti-Nebraska Democrats came over to their ground.[18]

In most parts of New England and the Middle West, however, free-soil Whigs, their state organizations already in shambles, early showed a willingness—even eagerness—to fuse with anti-Nebraska elements in other parties. In part, this readiness to set aside old loyalties and join in the creation of a completely new political party stemmed from an awareness that Free Soilers, antislavery Democrats, and even some radical Whigs would have nothing to do with the Whig organization on any terms.[19] More fundamentally, it derived from a realization that the old issues—banks, tariffs, roads, and canals—issues that had once bound Whiggery together, had lately slipped into the shade and that the now revitalized slavery question rendered old alliances outworn. "Well," wrote one Illinois Whig in April 1854, "Whig, Democrat & free soil are now all 'obsolete ideas,' and bygones are gone forever—and what shall we do next? What but unite on *principle* instead of *party*." That Southern Whig Congressmen had joined Administration Democrats "in violating the Missouri Compromise" seemed to some still further proof that national Whiggery was beyond saving.[20]

[17] *Dover Enquirer*, Feb. 21, 1854; *Poughkeepsie Eagle*, June 17, July 22, 1854.
[18] *Athens* (Ohio) *Messenger*, Apr. 14, 1854; *Boston Weekly Commonwealth*, Apr. 29, 1854; *National Era*, Nov. 9, 1854; Samuel E. Sewall to Charles Sumner, July 23, 1854, Sumner Papers; Washington Hunt to Thurlow Weed, Aug. 10, 1855, Weed Papers; Nevins, *Ordeal of the Union*, II, 316-18.
[19] Henry Wilson to Israel Washburn, May 28, 1854, Israel Washburn Papers, LC; Gamaliel Bailey to James S. Pike, May 30, 1854, Pike Papers; H. B. Stanton to Charles Sumner, May 31, 1855, Sumner Papers.
[20] J. B. Turner to Richard Yates, Apr. 8, 1854, Richard Yates Papers, Illinois State Historical Library, Springfield; *Poughkeepsie Eagle*, Oct. 20, 1855; *Dover Enquirer*, June 13, 1854, Nov. 1, 1855. See also Benjamin F. Wade to [Milton Sutliff], Apr. 21, 1854, Sutliff Papers. Some Whigs had written off their old party as lost long before the Kansas-Nebraska Act. One of the first to become fed up was Horace

Even a good many Democrats balked at the Kansas-Nebraska Act and soon joined Whigs and Free Soilers in establishing a new opposition party. Although the Administration had sought to make Douglas's measure "a test of Democratic orthodoxy," when it came to a decision in the House forty-four Northern Democrats voted for passage, forty-three against—a division that probably reflected rank-and-file sentiment as well. Longstanding loyalties and party discipline stringently applied kept many of the bill's Democratic critics—including old Barnburners like Azariah Flagg and Martin Van Buren—in line. Especially in the West, however, and among the younger Radicals of the East, mutiny was widespread. Disenchantment with Southern dictation and an increasing sense of powerlessness as the party moved into the hands of "Whiggish" Hunkers like Marcy and Buchanan combined with genuine antislavery convictions to persuade a substantial number of Democrats that patriotism and private advantage demanded a recasting of political alliances. Some, like Preston King, William Cullen Bryant, David Wilmot, and Oliver P. Morton, left the Democracy early, participating from the beginning in the organization of an anti-Nebraska, Republican party. Others—Hannibal Hamlin, Gideon Welles, Benjamin F. Butler, Francis P. Blair, and Lyman Trumbull, to name but a few—moved into opposition more hesitantly, after attempts to rededicate the party to "pure" Jeffersonian principles (including curtailment of slavery) had collapsed and after events in Kansas had dramatized the grave failings of Administration policy. By 1856 something like a quarter of the Republican party's strength came from former Democrats.[21]

These Democratic-Republicans brought with them, as Eric Foner has shown, a special, uncompromising attachment to antislavery principles.

Greeley. Surveying the wreckage of Whiggery after the 1852 election, the brilliant and cantankerous editor wrote: ". . . I have ceased to expect wisdom from the Whig party. It is like the duelist whose brains *couldn't* have been injured by the bullet through his head—'cause if he had had any brains, he wouldn't have been in any such predicament. . . . In the wide world there is just one obstacle to the carrying on of the government on Whig principles, and that is the Whig party." Greeley to Schuyler Colfax, Jan. 18, 1853, Greeley Papers.
[21] Gideon Welles to [Preston King], May [no day] 1854, April 23, 1855 (copies), King to Welles, Oct. 21, 1854, Welles Papers, CHS; Benjamin F. Butler to Ira Smith, July 4, 1854, Benjamin F. Butler Papers, New York State Library, Albany; Francis P. Blair, Sr., to Francis P. Blair, Jr., July 21, 1854, Blair Family Papers, LC; Francis P. Blair, Sr., to Martin Van Buren, Aug. 24, 1854, Benjamin F. Butler to Van Buren, Dec. 2, 1854, Van Buren Papers; *New York Evening Post*, Dec. 18, 1855, Jan. 31, Feb. 25, 1856; Foner, *Free Soil, Free Labor, Free Men*, 155-68.

Unlike the Whigs, they enlisted in the Republican party in the first place as a matter of choice, not necessity. Believing, as David Dudley Field put it, that the Democracy had become the mere "tool of a slave-holding oligarchy," they joined the opposition primarily to restrain Southern attempts to extend the peculiar institution. As a rule, those who felt most strongly that slavery was a social and moral evil, "entirely out of place in a Republic," bolted the Democratic party, while those who viewed it with indifference and feared the consequences of sectional turmoil remained in it. Moreover, once having cast their lot with the Republicans, Democratic come-outers continued to stress the slavery issue both because they were convinced of its transcending importance and because discussion of traditional economic questions might threaten party unity. Yet although they steadfastly resisted attempts to lower the new party's stand against slavery expansion, these former Democrats often added a racist note to Republican pronouncements, one which most Free Soilers and many ex-Whigs regretted.[22]

The first steps in forming a political union of all anti-Nebraska factions came even before Congress acted on Douglas's bill. On February 22, 1854, Michigan Free Democrats met at Jackson and nominated a state ticket headed by Kinsley S. Bingham, a "Free Soil Cass man" in 1848, and two former Whigs. Six days later, antislavery Whigs, Democrats, and Free Soilers in Ripon, Wisconsin, assembled in the town's Congregational church and pledged themselves, should the Kansas-Nebraska bill pass, to cast off old party affiliations and form a new "Republican" party dedicated to slavery restriction. In May, badgered by Preston King and the *National Era*'s Gamaliel Bailey (who complained that "Party names and prejudices are the cords that bind the Sampson of the North"), some thirty members of the House of Representatives likewise assumed the name "Republican" and agreed that a new political organization was essential if Southern aggressions were to be checked. By mid-summer statewide anti-Nebraska fusion conventions had been called in Michigan, Wisconsin, Ohio, Indiana, Iowa, and Vermont. In other free states anti-Nebraska forces cooperated closely —often nominating overlapping slates—without, as yet, formal union.[23]

22 *Ibid.* 168-85; Day, *Man on a Hill Top*, 130; James R. Doolittle to Horace A. Tenney, Feb. 6, 1858, Tenney Papers.
23 Francis Curtis, *The Republican Party: A History of its Fifty Years' Existence and a Record of its Measures and Leaders, 1854-1904*, 2 vols. (New York, 1904), I, 173-201; Andrew W. Crandall, *The Early History of the Republican Party, 1854-*

Not all of the new coalitions took the name Republican, and the degree of antislavery commitment varied substantially from state to state. Where radical elements were strong, as in Michigan, Wisconsin, and Vermont, the new party promptly christened itself Republican and ratified resolutions similar to the Free Soil–Free Democratic platforms of 1848 and 1852: denouncing slavery as "a great moral, social, and political evil," demanding its abolition in the District of Columbia and its exclusion from federal territories, urging repeal of the Fugitive Slave Law, and insisting that no other slave states be admitted to the Union. Where they were weak, or where organized Whiggery remained a force to be reckoned with, union at first took place under other names ("Whig," "Union," "People's") and on platforms often limited to a restoration of the Missouri Compromise. At times, in fact, it seemed that the second American party system had been replaced by no system at all. "Party ties are torn wide asunder," wrote William Herndon from Illinois a year after the Kansas-Nebraska eruption. Likewise, the *New York Post*, surveying Maine's political landscape in the fall of 1855, discerned "a perfect chaos of party movements." In addition to downeast Republicans, the *Post* identified three other active political groupings: anti-Nebraska Democrats allied with anti-Republican Whigs, pro-Nebraska Democrats who struggled to make the state's liquor law the chief issue, and nativist Know-Nothings. The citizens of Hartford, Connecticut, faced a bewildering array of twenty-three different parties in 1854.[24] Only slowly, awkwardly, with many a wrong step, did Northern politicians arrive at more stable party alignments.

2

Before Republicans could effectively challenge the "proslavery" Democracy, they had first to cope with the distractions of an astonishing young rival—the Native American or "Know-Nothing" party. Al-

1856 (Boston, 1930), 20-26; Gamaliel Bailey to James S. Pike, May 21, 1854, Pike Papers; *New-York Daily Tribune*, June 16, Oct. 16, 1854.
[24] *National Era*, July 20, 1854; *Wisconsin Free Democrat*, Sept. 5, 1855; Herndon to Charles Sumner, Feb. 15, 1855, Sumner Papers; *New York Evening Post*, Sept. 10, 1855; Ray A. Billington, *The Protestant Crusade, 1800-1860: A Study of the Origins of American Nativism* (New York, 1938), 390.

though its roots lay deep in the nation's past, this semi-secret nativist party had been organized in 1849 as the Order of the Star Spangled Banner. At first no more than a tiny political pressure group, what Horace Greeley dubbed the Know-Nothing party had become by 1854 a well-drilled organization of many thousands with political strength in the North and South. What made it a threat to the Republican party was that despite the Order's attempts to mute sectional controversy many Northern Know-Nothings combined hostility toward Catholics and foreigners with moderate antislavery attitudes. In a way, all three antagonisms were related: anti-foreign feeling was directed specifically against the Irish, most of whom were Catholic, and consistent foes of abolition. Each of these animosities, moreover, responded to apparent conspiracies against the American Way.[25]

When outrage over Kansas-Nebraska drove many Whigs and Democrats into rebellion, therefore, great numbers found a welcome refuge in the newly vital American party. Some of the displaced went over to the Know-Nothings because they too worried about the rising tide of Catholic immigration, which filled Eastern cities with hard-drinking brawlers and Democratic pawns, threatening job security, the established social order, and traditional American values. Thousands of others "flocked into the order," as Gideon Welles observed, "not that they approved of its principles, but for the purpose of relieving themselves from the obligations and abuses of the old organizations." Still others joined the Know-Nothing party– as did Henry Wilson of Massachusetts–determined to bend it to antislavery purposes. And, incidentally, to advance their own political fortunes at the expense of the Democratic party. When early in 1855 a solidly Know-Nothing Massachusetts legislature elected Wilson to the United States Senate, many concluded that Northern Know-Nothingism was at bottom an antislavery movement. In June, New Hampshire Know-Nothings lent support to this conclusion by joining with Free Democrats to return John P. Hale to the national Senate.[26]

[25] For general accounts of the Know-Nothing movement see *ibid*. 380-97; Nevins, *Ordeal of the Union*, II, 323-46, 397-404. Republican ideas concerning nativism are carefully examined in Foner, *Free Soil, Free Labor, Free Men*, chap. VII. Foner concludes, convincingly, I think, that most Republicans rejected political nativism as inherently at odds with their free labor ideology. For contradictory views, see Michael F. Holt, *Forging a Majority: The Formation of the Republican Party in Pittsburgh, 1848-1860* (New Haven, 1969); Formisano, *Mass Political Parties*, 233-65.
[26] Welles, "National & State Politics," manuscript draft in Welles Papers, CHS;

By no means did all anti-Nebraska men respond so warmly to political nativism. Even many who shared Know-Nothing antagonism toward aliens and Catholics and who stood four-square for temperance
vehemently protested the rise of nativism as a political force. The Order's secrecy, its ritualistic mumbo-jumbo, its conspiratorial insistence
that initiates vote for none but card-carrying nativists in all political
elections offended some who otherwise sympathized with the Know-
Nothing program. More important, the Order's subordination of antislavery to nativism struck many as a grave misallocation of priorities.
Whatever their views of Papists and immigrants, those who gave prece-
dence to the curtailment of slavery often concluded that Know-Nothingism obstructed that mission. Even in states like Massachusetts, some
lamented, Know-Nothings displayed a tepid brand of antislavery (inevitable, given the party's national ambitions and large complement of
conservative Whigs) that divided and weakened the free-soil movement. And in states like Illinois, as one political abolitionist observed
in 1855, "where the Anti-Slavery sentiment is not hale and strong, and
controlling, the whole tendency of 'Sam' [i.e. Know-Nothingism] is to
sponge it up or crush it out."[27]

Not only did the Know-Nothing party offer timid men a milk-and-
water alternative to the "true Antislavery Spirit" of Republicanism,
complained Salmon Chase, but in competing for anti-Nebraska voters
it led some Republican leaders "to urge an abatement or modification of
our Antislavery creed." Indeed, there were those who concluded that a
movement so subversive of the antislavery cause must have been
hatched by the Slave Power itself. George Julian, for one, politically
ostracized for his own attacks on the Know-Nothings, found it no acci-
dent that the rise of political nativism coincided with the crisis over
slavery in Kansas. "It was," he asserted, "a well-timed scheme to divide
the people of the free states upon trifles and side issues, while the South
remained a unit in defense of its great interest. It was the cunning

New York Evening Post, Nov. 9, 1855, June 5, 1856; Henry Wilson to Theodore
Parker, July 23, 1855, Letterbook, Parker Papers; Galesburg Free Democrat, Feb.
8, 1855; Hale to Thurlow Weed, Feb. 2, 1855, Weed Papers; Sewell, Hale, 157-62;
Michael F. Holt, "The Politics of Impatience: The Origins of Know Nothingism,"
Journal of American History, LX, No. 2 (Sept. 1973), 309-31.
[27] Foner, Free Soil, Free Labor, Free Men, 232, 260; Galesburg Free Democrat, Feb.
22, Mar. 15, Apr. 19, 1855; Chicago Daily Tribune, June 12, 1855; National Era,
Dec. 6, 1855; Harriet A. Weed (ed.), Autobiography of Thurlow Weed, 2 vols.
(Boston, 1883), II, 224-25.

attempt to balk and divert the indignation aroused by the repeal of the Missouri restriction, which else would spend its force upon the aggressions of slavery; for by thus kindling the Protestant jealousy of our people against the Pope, and enlisting them in a crusade against the foreigner, the South could all the more successfully push forward its schemes." Thus had one conspiracy begot another.[28]

A fair number of Republicans and proto-Republicans lashed out at the Know-Nothings for reasons of principle as well as practicality. Especially among old Liberty and Free Soil abolitionists and adherents of William H. Seward repugnance for nativist bigotry ran deep. Among political abolitionists none waged a longer or more costly war against nativism in every form than did Gamaliel Bailey. From the mid-1840s to his death in 1859, Bailey used the columns first of the Cincinnati *Philanthropist* and then of the *National Era* to protest ethnic and religious, as well as racial, discrimination. The Know-Nothing party he proclaimed a "detestable organization," the party "of caste and compromise," one that no thinking reformer could countenance, much less join. "You have no more right to disfranchise your brother man, seeking a home in this country," Bailey remonstrated in 1855, "than you have to disfranchise your colored neighbor: nor, have you a right to make membership in any religious sect, a disqualification for office. Know Nothingism, in its essential elements, is as repugnant to the doctrine of equal rights, as Slavery, and we should as soon think of reforming the one as the other." Not even the loss of "several thousand subscribers" to the *Era* stopped the editor's hard-hitting attacks on nativism.[29]

Nearly all other abolitionists of the Liberty–Free Soil school echoed Bailey's line. Papers like the *American Freeman* and politicians like James G. Birney and Henry B. Stanton had warned of the dangers and injustices of nativism as early as 1844.[30] The Free Democratic platform

[28] Chase to Sumner, July 16, 1858, *Diary and Correspondence*, 278; Julian, *Political Recollections*, 141-42. See also Julian to E. A. Stansbury, Sept. 14, 1855, Giddings-Julian Papers.

[29] *Cincinnati Weekly Herald and Philanthropist*, May 22, Oct. 21, 1844; *National Era*, Oct. 12, Nov. 23, Dec. 28, 1854, Apr. 19, May 3, Dec. 6, 1855; Bailey to John G. Palfrey, Oct. 19, 1856, Palfrey Papers; Bailey to James R. Doolittle, Oct. [no day] 1858, Doolittle Papers.

[30] Birney to Patrick Kelly *et al.*, June 10, 1844, quoted in *Cincinnati Weekly Herald and Philanthropist*, June 26, 1844; Stanton to Gerrit Smith, Nov. 23, 1844, Smith Papers; *American Freeman*, Sept. 8, 1847.

of 1852 boldly declared "that emigrants and exiles from the Old World
should find a cordial welcome to homes of comfort and fields of enterprise in the New; and every attempt to abridge their privilege of becoming citizens and owners of the soil among us ought to be resisted
with inflexible determination." And once the American party began its
startling ascent, it was "the *old* Liberty Guard," Bailey noted, together
with Free Soilers like Adams, Palfrey, Sumner, and (after a false start)
Giddings, who led the fight to purge Republicans of all nativist influence.[31] "The Republican party should be a standard-bearer of human
rights," insisted Charles Roeser, abolitionist editor of *Wisconsin's Democrat.* "We are against Black Slavery, because the slaves are deprived
of human rights. We are also against White Slavery, because such
Slavery will deprive the foreign-born of political rights."[32] Political
arithmetic—the preponderance of ethnic voters over Know-Nothings—
merely reinforced such liberal attitudes in states like Wisconsin.

Other anti-Nebraska elements also sharply criticized nativist principles and insisted that except for its deranging effect on old party
organizations no good could be expected from Know-Nothingism. Gideon Welles dismissed the American party as "a miserable piece of machinery" and argued that "A proscription of men on account of birth
is as odious certainly as that of color"—a position with which a good
many other free-soil Democrats agreed.[33] Owing to the influence of
William H. Seward a substantial number of liberal Whigs also lashed
out at "the Natives." The Whig party had traditionally been more suspicious of immigrants and Catholics than had the Democrats, and Conservative or "Silver Gray" Whigs, especially in New York, ran to the
Know-Nothing party with open arms after 1854. Seward, however, and
his "Woolly Head" followers, had for years defended the rights and
privileges of foreigners—even to the point of advocating public support
for parochial schools. Not only did the Sewardites object to nativism on
principle, believing that religious bigotry was wrong and that for
Americans to hate immigrants was "to hate such as their forefathers

[31] Bailey to Gerrit Smith, Jan. 2, June 6, 1855, Joshua Giddings to Smith, Jan. 21,
1856, Smith Papers; *National Era,* May 3, 1855.
[32] Quoted in *Wisconsin Free Democrat,* Apr. 16, 1856.
[33] Welles to Preston King, Nov. 25, 1854 (copy), Apr. 23, 1855 (copy), John Boyd
to Welles, Mar. 23, 1855, Welles Papers, LC; Welles to Edwin D. Morgan, July 22,
1856, Edwin D. Morgan Papers, New York State Library, Albany; *New York
Evening Post,* Aug. 16, 1854; Day, *Man on a Hill Top,* 132, 163-64.

were," but they protested the political advantage it gave to Democrats in states with sizable foreign-born populations. Seward and Greeley, for instance, both blamed nativism for Henry Clay's defeat in 1844.[34] Whig nativists, of course, looked elsewhere for culprits and fought Seward at every turn. By 1854 the Senator's backers recognized nativism as "our traditional, implacable enemy," ready to "cut Seward's throat the moment it can get hold of it."[35] Quite naturally, Whigs (and, later, Republicans) of Seward's persuasion greeted the meteoric rise of Know-Nothingism with a mixture of derision and alarm. So too did antislavery Whigs in other regions, especially in the West. Groping for political identity as the Whig party broke up around him, Abraham Lincoln explained to his friend Joshua Speed:

> I am not a Know-Nothing. That is certain. How could I be? How can any one who abhors the oppression of negroes, be in favor of degrading classes of white people? Our progress in degeneracy seems to me to be pretty rapid. As a nation, we began by declaring that *"all men are created equal."* We now practically read it "all men are created equal, *except negroes."* When the Know-Nothings get control, it will read "all men are created equal, except negroes, *and foreigners, and catholics."* When it comes to this I should prefer emigrating to some country where they make no pretense of loving liberty—to Russia, for instance, where despotism can be taken pure, and without the base alloy of hypocracy [*sic*].[36]

For a time, however, nativism, antislavery (and frequently temperance) moved very much in step. Especially in the industrializing

---

[34] Van Deusen, *Seward*, 44, 67-73, 101, 102; Van Deusen, *Greeley*, 73, 100-101; Lee Benson, *The Concept of Jacksonian Democracy: New York as a Test Case* (Princeton, 1961), 121, 213, 246; Lee H. Warner, "The Silver Grays: New York State Conservative Whigs, 1846-1856," Ph.D. dissertation, University of Wisconsin, 1970, p. 275.

[35] Horace Greeley to Schuyler Colfax, Sept. 7, 1854, Greeley Papers. See also Vivius W. Smith to Seward, Sept. 4, 1854, George E. Baker to Seward, Sept. 5, 1854, Seward Papers; Seward to Thurlow Weed, Mar. 13, 1856, Weed Papers; Jeter A. Isely, *Horace Greeley and the Republican Party, 1853-1861* (Princeton, 1947), 83; Van Deusen, *Seward*, 156-58; Foner, *Free Soil, Free Labor, Free Men*, 234-36.

[36] Aug. 24, 1855, Roy P. Basler (ed.), *The Collected Works of Abraham Lincoln*, 8 vols. (New Brunswick, N.J., 1953), II, 323. Lincoln's chief Illinois lieutenants, William Herndon and David Davis, shared his distaste for political nativism, although Herndon "cordially detested the Irish." See David Donald, *Lincoln's Herndon* (New York, 1948), 75; Willard L. King, *Lincoln's Manager, David Davis* (Cambridge, Mass., 1960), 109. See also Trefousse, *Wade*, 96-98.

Northeast, early cooperation between Know-Nothings and free soilers produced striking political triumphs. In Massachusetts, for example, nativists and free soilers joined beneath the Know-Nothing banner to make a clean sweep in 1854, electing eleven Congressmen, a governor, all state officers, all state senators, and all but two of 378 state representatives. The following year the nativist legislature not only sent Henry Wilson—a "hot shot from abolition cannon," Salmon Chase called him—to Washington, but voted to unseat Judge Edward G. Loring for his role in returning the fugitive Anthony Burns to slavery, enacted a tough new personal liberty law, and harshly condemned the Kansas-Nebraska Act.[37] In neighboring New Hampshire, the various anti-Nebraska factions—Whigs, Know-Nothings, and Independent Democrats—held separate conventions during the fall and winter of 1854-55, but except for governor and railroad commissioner nominated nearly identical tickets. Once again, the outcome warmed antislavery hearts: not only Hale but James Bell, an antislavery Whig, gained election to the United States Senate, and all three anti-Nebraska congressional candidates won easily.[38] Although the results were less spectacular, nativists, temperance advocates, and anti-Nebraska men also cooperated fruitfully in other parts of New England, particularly in Connecticut and Rhode Island.[39]

New York Know-Nothings formally set themselves apart from the anti-Nebraska forces, nominating the conservative Daniel Ullman for governor on a platform that sought to silence agitation over slavery. Yet even there, the firm of Seward, Weed, and Greeley found it prudent in 1854 to confer its gubernatorial nomination on Myron Clark, an antislavery prohibitionist turned Know-Nothing. This strategy paid

[37]Abbott, *Cobbler in Congress*, 59-76; Crandall, *Early History of the Republican Party*, 24; Chase to E. S. Hamlin, Feb. 9, 1855, Chase, *Diary and Correspondence*, 270. Although such distinguished names as Charles Francis Adams, S. C. Phillips, John G. Palfrey, Charles Allen, and Francis W. Bird refused to countenance involvement with nativism, the great bulk of Bay State Free Soilers (among them Wilson, Anson Burlingame, E. L. Keyes, and A. W. Alvord) willingly voted the Know-Nothing ticket in 1854. "Four fifths of the organization has left the standard of freedom to enlist itself against a shadow," Adams complained. Duberman, *Charles Francis Adams*, 198. The fledgling Republican party received fewer than 7000 votes, while more than 80,000 were cast for Know-Nothings.
[38]Sewell, *Hale*, 158-62.
[39]Robert D. Parmet, "The Know-Nothings in Connecticut," Ph.D. dissertation, Columbia University, 1966, chap. III; Charles Stickney, "Know-Nothingism in Rhode Island," *Publications of the Rhode Island Historical Society*, new series, I, No. 4 (Jan. 1894), 243-57.

off. Clark narrowly defeated Horatio Seymour, the "Soft" Democratic candidate, and early the next year Seward, with help from some anti-Nebraska Know-Nothings, won reelection to the United States Senate.[40] In Pennsylvania, despite friction and jealousy, antislavery Whigs and Know-Nothings cooperated sufficiently well in 1854 to claim twenty-one of twenty-five seats in the Thirty-fourth Congress for professed critics of the Kansas-Nebraska Act. Thereafter Know-Nothings and slavery restrictionists drew even closer together, giving to Pennsylvania Republicanism a stronger and more resilient strain of nativism than that in any other state.[41]

Throughout the West, where a vital Republican party quickly took wing, Know-Nothingism counted for less. Although foreign-born populations (mostly Germans and Scandinavians) were substantial—ranging from 9 per cent in Indiana to 33 per cent in Wisconsin—they were on the whole sober, frugal, industrious, and much esteemed by their native American neighbors. Far from appearing as a threat, they seemed to most Westerners a distinct blessing. "Our German settlers," observed one Illinois editor in 1855, "are valuable acquisitions to the state and are doing good service in opening up its waste places to the hand of cultivation. . . . It is seldom, indeed, that we hear of one being in the poor house or under the care of a pauper committee."[42] That so many Western immigrants (especially the Germans) also displayed strong antislavery propensities further weakened nativism's appeal in states like Illinois, Iowa, and Wisconsin.

Yet here and there, even in the Middle West, the Know-Nothings enjoyed a fleeting success, at times joining Republicans and other anti-Nebraska groups to overturn defenders of Administration policy. In Indiana the Know-Nothings seized control of the anti-Nebraska movement from the very beginning. Led by young Schuyler Colfax, an antislavery Whig, and Stephen S. Harding, an active Free Soiler, the

[40] Van Deusen, *Seward*, 158-61; Isely, *Greeley and the Republican Party*, 98-105.
[41] Warren F. Hewitt, "The Know Nothing Party in Pennsylvania," *Pennsylvania History*, II, No. 2 (Apr. 1935), 69-85; Holt, *Forging a Majority*, chaps. IV-VIII; Nevins, *Ordeal of the Union*, II, 342. The *New-York Daily Tribune* (Oct. 16, 1854) broke down Pennsylvania's anti-Nebraska contingent as follows: 1 Know-Nothing, 5 Democrats, and 15 Whigs. Presumably, all four pro-Nebraska Congressmen-elect were Buchanan Democrats.
[42] Billington, *Protestant Crusade*, 394-95; Foner, *Free Soil, Free Labor, Free Men*, 244-47. See also Eugene H. Roseboom, *The Civil War Era, 1850-1873* (Columbus, 1944), 287.

Know-Nothings easily controlled the state "People's party" convention in July 1854. The ticket nominated had in fact been fashioned two days earlier at a secret Know-Nothing conclave. Despite the protests of George Julian, who condemned "the accursed heresy of Nativism" and criticized the fusionists' retreat from the Buffalo platform of 1852, most Hoosier Free Soilers willingly cooperated with the Know-Nothings. Even one so dedicated as Rawson Vaile, long a supporter of Julian and editor of the state's leading Free Soil journal, defended Know-Nothings as worthy allies in the war against the Slave Power. In 1854, at all events, the People's party carried nine of eleven congressional districts and won control of Indiana's house of representatives. Not until after 1856 did antislavery begin to move independently of nativism in Indiana, and not until 1858, when the opposition at last took the name Republican and nominated two naturalized citizens for state office, did the break become complete.[43]

Antislavery and nativist forces also worked together in Ohio, although there the former was distinctly the dominant partner and the association more fleeting and unstable than in Indiana. In 1854 Ohio fusionists—Whigs, Know-Nothings, and Free Democrats—concentrating their fire almost exclusively on the Nebraska "fraud," carried seventy-eight of eighty-eight counties in the leading state contest and captured all twenty-one congressional seats. The following year, however, Salmon P. Chase's candidacy for governor forced a showdown of sorts between his Democratic-Free Soil backers and Whig–Know-Nothing fusionists, who preferred someone like Jacob Brinkerhoff—less conspicuously radical in his abolitionism and a member of the secret Order. Chase himself, hoping to improve his chances, adopted a somewhat conciliatory stance toward the Know-Nothings, criticizing the Order for its secrecy and indiscriminate proscription of Catholics and aliens yet admitting that some complaints "against papal influences or organized foreignism" were justified and expressing a willingness to cooperate with Know-Nothings so long as no sacrifice of principle were involved. But most of Chase's followers pulled no punches in their at-

---

[43] Riddleberger, *Julian*, 98-109, 111-16; Julian, *Political Recollections*, 144-46; Emma Lou Thornbrough, *Indiana in the Civil War Era* (Indianapolis, 1965), 81; Charles Zimmerman, "The Origin and Rise of the Republican Party in Indiana from 1854 to 1860," *Indiana Magazine of History*, XIII, No. 3 (Sept. 1917), 234-47; Carl F. Brand, "History of the Know Nothing Party in Indiana," *ibid*. XVIII, No. 1 (Mar. 1922), 47-81, No. 2 (June 1922), 177-206, No. 3 (Sept. 1922), 266-306.

tacks on nativism, pointing to the Know-Nothings' popularity in the South as proof that the Order could not be trusted where slavery was concerned.[44]

Although ostensibly a compromise, the actions of the state Republican convention in July 1855 in fact represented a victory for the Chase forces and a setback for political nativism. For while all other nominations went to Know-Nothings, that Order proved unable or unwilling to prevent Chase's nomination for governor. Moreover, the Republican platform gave no recognition whatsoever to nativist demands. During the campaign Chase continued to step gingerly. Fearful of alienating either nativists or foreign-born, he keyed his remarks to events in Kansas and the "Slave Power's" plot against freedom everywhere. Once this strategy paid off in his election, however, Chase threw his support unreservedly behind efforts to purge the Republican party of "dark-lantern" nativism. "Liberal" Know-Nothings were welcomed —even appointed to office—so long as their antislavery convictions remained strong. But foreign-born voters (especially influential Germans) were also openly wooed and rewarded with state offices. By 1856 nativism was dying as an independent political movement in Ohio. "Our Know-Nothings I think are upon the Reserve disposed to act generally with the Republicans," reported one of Ben Wade's free-soil correspondents. "They made all our nominations last Fall in this county, and they still make or control the nominations in this county, but it is under the *name* of Republicans; and to a great extent under its *spirit*." Barely 7 per cent of the state's voters supported Millard Fillmore on the American ticket in 1856. By 1857 even this die-hard remnant had given up the ghost.[45]

Matters were much the same in neighboring Michigan. There Know-Nothings, operating under a cloak of secrecy, also vied for control of the fledgling Republican or "Fusion" party. Nativist votes doubtless

[44] Roseboom, *Civil War Era*, 286-303; William E. Van Horne, "Lewis D. Campbel and the Know-Nothing Party in Ohio," *Ohio History*, LXXVI, No. 4 (Autumn 1967), 202-21; Hart, *Chase*, 152-55; Chase to Dr. Paul, Dec. 27, 1854, Chase Papers PHS; Chase to George W. Julian, Jan. 20, 1855, Joshua R. Giddings to Julian, May 30, 1855, Giddings-Julian Papers; Chase to [E. S. Hamlin], Jan. 22, Feb. 15, 1855 Chase to Lewis D. Campbell, May 25, 29, 1855 (copies), Chase Papers, LC; Columbus *Ohio Columbian*, Apr. 25, 1855.
[45] Roseboom, *Civil War Era*, 303-5, 315-16, 329; Salmon P. Chase to Kinsley S Bingham, Oct. 19, 1855, Chase Papers, PHS; Wade to Mrs. Wade, Mar. 7, 1856 Milton Sutliff to Wade, May 11, 1856, Wade Papers.

contributed to the triumph of anti-Democratic candidates in 1854, and the following year a spate of anti-Catholic and nativist bills in the state legislature testified to continued Know-Nothing influence. From the beginning, however, Republicans like Austin Blair condemned "the villainy of . . . a gigantic secret society based upon political and religious bigotry carried on by lying and fraud." By 1856, Michigan's Republican party lay firmly in the hands of men who insisted on the paramountcy of anti-Southern, antislavery principles. Fillmore polled a bare 1.3 per cent of the state's vote in 1856. Nativism was by no means dead, as the passage of stringent voter registration laws in 1859 and 1861 made plain. But slavery and "slavocrats" remained the chief objects of Republican abuse—not wild Irishmen or the Pope.[46]

As the slavery question waxed ever hotter (clashes between free state emigrants and proslavery "border ruffians" making "Bloody Kansas" a national byword), crusades against Popery and the Irish peril came to seem hopelessly, dangerously, beside the point. Already vulnerable because of its "un-American" secrecy and penchant for violence, the Know-Nothing party found it increasingly hard to cope with the forces of sectionalism. In the North, Know-Nothing successes proved as ephemeral as they had been spectacular. Not even the "North Americans'" repudiation of the national party's proslavery platform, nor the organization of a "Know-Something" party advocating temperance and antislavery as well as nativism, could prevent a mass exodus to Republican ranks once that party was fully formed. By 1856 the Republicans had established themselves nearly everywhere as the chief rivals of the Democrats—without having to embrace a particle of the nativists' platform.

The first clear sign that Republicans and not Know-Nothings would prosper came early in February 1856 with the election of Nathaniel P. Banks as Speaker of the United States House of Representatives. Although himself a former Know-Nothing of Democratic roots, the "Bobbin Boy of Massachusetts" had recently joined the Republican camp. With the American party holding the balance between Democrats and Republicans, House Republican leaders (with help from the party press) promoted Banks for the speakership in hopes of splintering the nativist party and drawing all antislavery representatives into

[46] Formisano, *Mass Political Parties*, 249-65, 272, 284-87. The Blair quote is on p. 261.

the Republican party. After weeks of dicker and dodge their labors were rewarded. On the one hundred and thirty-third ballot, after altering the rules to permit election by a simple plurality, a weary House chose Banks speaker by a margin of two votes over William Aiken of South Carolina.[47]

Gamaliel Bailey regretted that "extraneous influences" had been essential to Banks's victory, and he estimated that perhaps a third of Banks's support came from dyed-in-the-wool Know-Nothings. Yet even he admitted that by dividing Southern and Silver Gray Americans from members partial to Banks the speakership fight had materially strengthened the Republicans. Some thirty-five or forty nativists, Bailey claimed, now wished to slough off Know-Nothingism and henceforth to "act alone with the pure Republicans."[48] And, of course, in the speakership Republicans had claimed a prize of great practical and symbolic worth. Theodore Parker crowed that "Banks' election is the first victory of the Northern Idea since 1787," while Thurlow Weed excitedly told Banks: "The Republican Party is now inaugurated. We can now work 'with a will.'" To the aging "Father Giddings," who had managed Republican strategy in the House and who enjoyed the honor of swearing in the new Speaker, it seemed a victory worth waiting for. "I have attained the highest point of my ambition," he rejoiced. "*I am satisfied.*"[49]

As often before, Giddings was premature in his satisfaction. Banks soon proved to be a sore disappointment to Republican radicals—presiding over the House with commendable efficiency but maddening impartiality. More important, the conservatism of the Speaker's antislavery opinions—shared by many other Republicans—left still in the air the terms of Republican union. Where first organized, the party had been strongly influenced if not dominated by political abolitionists, and its platforms in states like Michigan and Vermont took high antislavery ground.[50] What would happen to its policies as more moderate

[47] Fred Harvey Harrington, "The First Northern Victory," *Journal of Southern History*, V, No. 2 (May 1939), 186-205.
[48] Gamaliel Bailey to Salmon P. Chase, Feb. 21, 1856, Chase Papers, LC. See also *Chicago Daily Tribune*, Feb. 6, 1856.
[49] Parker to Charles Sumner, Feb. 16, 1856, Letterbook, Parker Papers; Weed to Banks, Feb. 3, 1856, Nathaniel P. Banks Papers, Essex Institute, Salem, Mass.; George W. Julian, *The Life of Joshua R. Giddings* (Chicago, 1892), 326; Giddings to his daughter, Feb. 3, 1856, Giddings-Julian Papers.
[50] This was, of course, particularly true in states where moderate anti-Nebraska

refugees from Know-Nothingism and the older parties filled the Republican ranks remained to be seen. Giddings himself would soon discover that antislavery principles were threatened by false friends within as well as by enemies without the Republican gates.

3

On Christmas Day 1855 a small but distinguished company of antislavery politicians met at the Silver Spring, Maryland, home of Francis P. Blair, Sr. to lay plans for a national Republican organization. Present that day were Nathaniel Banks and Charles Sumner of Massachusetts, Preston King of New York, Governor Chase of Ohio, Gamaliel Bailey, editor of the *National Era*, and their host, Andrew Jackson's old friend *"Blar."* Between them they represented nearly every important antislavery faction and a variety of sectional interests, although the radicalism of Chase, Bailey, Sumner, and King overbalanced the more cautious views of Banks and Blair. All agreed that the movement already afoot for a national consultative convention of anti-Administration forces (instigated, apparently, by political friends of Chase) should be encouraged. Names of possible candidates were bandied about, but only Blair's favorite, the popular explorer-adventurer John Charles Frémont, was seriously considered. In the end, Blair and his influential guests decided to leave the question of nominees—indeed, the practicability of permanent fusion—to the talked-of anti-Nebraska conference, to be held sometime early in 1856.[51]

---

politicians initially held aloof from the Republican party, leaving antislavery radicals free to set whatever standards they wished. In Illinois the name Republican was first borne by avowed abolitionists, among them Owen Lovejoy, younger brother of the martyred Elijah, Ichabod Codding, and Zebina Eastman. Its earliest platforms called boldly for restriction of slavery to the states where it already existed, a ban on the admission of new slave states, and repeal of the Fugitive Slave Law. When, after the collapse of the state Whig party in 1855, the Republican party was reconstituted, this time under Abraham Lincoln's lead, the radicals found themselves outnumbered and the platform substantially toned down. See Magdol, *Lovejoy*, 106-20, 127-36, 141-48; George H. Mayer, *The Republican Party, 1854-1964* (New York, 1964), 38-40; John S. Wright, *Lincoln & the Politics of Slavery* (Reno, 1970), 92-96.

[51] William H. Seward to Thurlow Weed, Dec. 31, 1855, Weed Papers; Preston King to Gideon Welles, Jan. 3, 1856, Welles Papers, LC; John Niven, *Gideon Welles: Lincoln's Secretary of the Navy* (New York, 1973), 264-66; Crandall, *Early History of the Republican Party*, 50-53. Seward was apparently also invited to the

With support from such prominent antislavery politicians, the Republican chairmen of five Northern states arranged for an informal gathering at Pittsburgh on February 22. Its purpose was to perfect national party machinery and to provide for a nominating convention at some later date. Since all "Republicans of the Union" were invited to attend, a singularly large and varied assemblage answered the call to order. On hand were representatives of all the free states and at least five slave states, including spokesmen for virtually every shade of antislavery opinion—from radical political abolitionists like Owen Lovejoy and Joshua Giddings to such conservatives and moderates as Francis P. Blair and Oliver P. Morton. So too did antislavery Know-Nothings rub shoulders with German-American leaders like Cincinnati's eloquent Charles Reemelin.[52]

The tone of the Pittsburgh meeting, despite the presence of a vociferous radical contingent, was one of caution and moderation. An early sign that the delegates intended to tread lightly was the election of Blair, a Maryland slaveholder, as convention chairman. Free Soil stalwarts like Julian grumbled that Blair had "strangely misconceived the spirit and purpose of the convention," and indeed Blair's willingness to settle for the Missouri Compromise struck most delegates as hopelessly backward.[53] Yet the hope of gaining a foothold among slaveless Southerners and the fear of antagonizing antislavery Know-Nothings led even many radicals to urge restraint. Even Horace Greeley (an improbable advocate of caution, as he himself admitted) contended that at this stage the party's platform should be confined solely to "making every territory free." Only after that mission had been accomplished should other issues be taken up. Joshua Giddings sought to ridicule such pleas by telling an old story of two pious brothers, Joe and John, who had undertaken a settlement in the West. Joe (Greeley) prayed for assistance, giving to the Lord a detailed list of instructions. John, averse to such sacrilegious pettyfogging, prayed: "O Lord! We have

Silver Spring meeting, but declined because of his "rule" against participation "in plans or schemes for political action"!
[52] For general accounts of the Pittsburgh session, see George W. Julian, "The First Republican National Convention," *American Historical Review*, IV, No. 2 (Jan. 1899), 313-22; Julian, *Political Recollections*, 147-50; Isely, *Greeley and the Republican Party*, 152-54; Magdol, *Lovejoy*, 136-41.
[53] Julian, "First Republican National Convention," 317.

begun a good work; carry it on as You think best, and don't mind what Joe says."[54]

The convention, however, did mind what Joe said. Its platform, drafted chiefly by *New York Times* editor Henry J. Raymond, followed Greeley's prescription to the letter. Except for declaring war on the Pierce Administration and urging Kansas' prompt admission to the Union as a free state, the convention asked only that all "constitutional means" be used to prevent slavery in the territories. Not a word was said concerning the Fugitive Slave Law, slavery in the District of Columbia, or the admission of new slave states. Nor, despite strong support from Julian and others, did anything come of Reemelin's appeal for a plank against the mischief and bigotry of Know-Nothingism. "There is not a single warm and living position, taken by the Republican party," Frederick Douglass complained, "except freedom for Kansas." Antislavery radicals swallowed their disappointment at the Pittsburgh platform, however, and set their eyes on the vastly more important Republican national nominating convention called for June 17 at Philadelphia.[55]

Before that convention took place, events occurred in Washington and on the Kansas frontier that electrified the nation and strengthened the hand of antislavery radicals within the Republican party. In May, almost simultaneously, came news that proslavery raiders had "sacked" the free-state outpost at Lawrence, Kansas, and that Congressman Preston S. Brooks of South Carolina had bludgeoned Charles Sumner nearly to death as the Massachusetts abolitionist sat at his desk in the United States Senate. Many Southerners defended, or at least excused, both actions. Lawrence had been a sinkhole of abolition and treason, they said, and Sumner had courted "chastisement" by his savage, insulting attacks on the South and its leaders. But to free-soil Northerners the events of May stood as awful reminders of the violence inherent in slavery and the need for more active resistance to it.

Violence reigns in the streets of Washington [William Cullen Bryant apprised readers of the *New York Evening Post*] . . .

[54] *Ibid.* 316.
[55] *Proceedings of the First Three Republican National Conventions of 1856, 1860 and 1864, Including Proceedings of the Antecedent National Convention Held at Pittsburg, in February, 1856, as Reported by Horace Greeley* (Minneapolis, 1893), 10-11; Foner, *Writings of Douglass*, II, 392.

violence has now found its way into the Senate Chamber. Violence lies in wait on all the navigable rivers and all the railways
of Missouri, to obstruct those who pass from the free states into
Kansas. Violence overhangs the frontiers of that territory like
a storm-cloud charged with hail and lightning. Violence has carried election after election in that territory. . . . In short, violence is the order of the day; the North is to be pushed to the
wall by it, and this plot will succeed if the people of the free
states are as apathetic as the slaveholders are insolent.[56]

"Bloody Kansas" and "Bloody Sumner" would inevitably become issues in the 1856 presidential campaign, and among Republicans pressure
for a bold antislavery stand increased. As one of Ben Wade's correspondents asserted, "The south is *positive*—The 'ruffians' of Missouri
are *positive*—The Democratic Party is *positive*," and if the Republican
party were to succeed it too had to be positive. "Now," he concluded,
"is the beginning of the Second 'American Revolution.' "[57]

As one might expect, delegates to the Republican National Convention at Philadelphia displayed a somewhat more radical temper than
had the conferees at Pittsburgh. They also, if Murat Halstead is to be
believed, provided a moral as well as political counterpoint to the Democrats, who in raucous sessions a fortnight earlier had nominated James
Buchanan for President. "The crowd here is nearly as large, but not so
noisy as that which gathered at the travail of Democracy in Cincinnati," the young journalist reported. "There is but a slight quantity of
liquor consumed, very little profane swearing is heard, and everything
is managed with excessive and intense propriety."[58] Among those on
hand when National Chairman Edwin D. Morgan of New York gaveled the convention into session were such veteran political abolitionists
as David Wilmot, Thaddeus Stevens, Preston King, John P. Hale,
Amos Tuck, Joshua Giddings, Joseph M. Root, Henry Wilson, Charles
Francis Adams, John M. Niles, Kinsley S. Bingham, Owen Lovejoy,
and E. D. Holton, as well as such radicals-in-the-making as Daniel Clark
of New Hampshire, James M. Ashley of Ohio, and Zachariah Chandler
of Michigan. Moderate, even conservative, delegates also took part,

[56] Allan Nevins, *The Evening Post: A Century of Journalism* (New York, 1922),
253.
[57] Thomas F. Hicks to Benjamin Wade [June 19, 1856], Wade Papers.
[58] William B. Hesseltine and Rex G. Fisher (eds.), *Trimmers, Trucklers & Temporizers: Notes of Murat Halstead from the Political Conventions of 1856* (Madison, 1961), 87.

most of them old line Whigs like Indiana's Caleb B. Smith and the New York City merchant prince Moses Grinnell, or Border state representatives like Francis P. Blair.[59] But, as soon became apparent, antislavery activists commanded the salient position.

The convention was only minutes old when its temporary chairman, Judge Robert Emmet of New York, brought the delegates to their feet with a rousing speech that pointed with pride to the Free Soil platform of 1848 and appealed to the Declaration of Independence in support of his contention that slavery was a political (perhaps also a moral) evil that must be repressed and allowed to die. Permanent chairman Henry S. Lane of Indiana followed with an even more trenchant address. "The vital principle of the Republican party," he shouted, was the admission of a free Kansas and "no more slave States"—a principle grounded firmly in the natural rights of man. And if defiance of the Fugitive Slave Law were treason, Lane thundered, swinging his arms and smacking his fists for emphasis, the federal marshals might well get ready, "for he intended to declare it upon every stump during the campaign." Similar efforts by Lovejoy, Wilson, Hale, and others overwhelmed speeches like that of Caleb Smith, which emphasized the Republican party's nationalism and denied that it intended any interference with slavery in the states. Even moderates like Smith, moreover, insisted that freedom was national and slavery sectional and that Congress had a right to outlaw bondage in the territories.[60]

Few showed much surprise when the platform committee, headed fittingly enough by David Wilmot, reported a set of principles that, without alienating moderates, carried a distinctly radical edge. In somewhat veiled language, the platform reaffirmed the old Liberty and Free Soil contention that the federal government had a duty to abolish slavery wherever its jurisdiction reached. More bluntly, it demanded that Congress "prohibit in the territories those twin relics of barbarism —polygamy and slavery," and that Kansas be at once admitted to the Union as a free state. It denounced the Ostend Manifesto's call for the acquisition of Cuba as "the highwayman's plea, that 'might makes right.' " Finally, tacked like a tail to the antislavery kite, were demands for federal assistance in river and harbor improvement and in the con-

[59] *Proceedings of the First Three Republican National Conventions*, 35-42.
[60] *Ibid.* 15-20, 25-35, 72-74; Hesseltine and Fisher (eds.), *Trimmers, Trucklers & Temporizers*, 87-88.

struction of a railroad to the Pacific, "by the most central practicable route." The Republicans called on men of all parties to support these principles, rebuking all legislative attempts to impair the security of any group. This latter resolve—a gentle slap at Know-Nothingism—occasioned the only debate on the platform, and even then the brush was brief and inconsequential.[61] With mighty cheers the delegates approved the Wilmot committee's handiwork and turned to the task of nominations.

Well before Philadelphia the field of likely Republican standard-bearers had been narrowed to two: the dashing young "Pathfinder," John C. Frémont, and aging Supreme Court Justice John McLean of Ohio. Other possible candidates had by then either seen their hopes go flickering or, like William Seward, had let themselves be persuaded that the time was not yet ripe for success. (Greeley and Weed, Murat Halstead reported, wished "to keep Mr. William Seward nicely pickled away" until 1860.)[62] Salmon Chase coveted the nomination and possessed more than his share of admirers. Yet his Ohio friends had been "out-generalled" in the selection of delegates so that at Philadelphia nearly half the vote from his own state went to other candidates. It was not so much his antislavery radicalism that did Chase in, nor, as he complained, the fecklessness of his backers at the convention. Rather, it was his conspicuous inability to keep even his own troops in line that most undercut his claims to broad support. The chickens of 1849 had come home to roost.[63]

Of the two leading contenders for the Republican nomination, Frémont had a distinct edge. His reputation was that of soldier and Western explorer, and, except for a short stint as Senator from California, his political life had been wholly vicarious, drawn from that of his

[61] *Proceedings of the First Three Republican National Conventions*, 43-45. Originally, the platform had stated: "Believing that the spirit of our institutions, as well as the Constitution of our country, guarantees liberty of conscience and equality of rights among citizens, we oppose all proscriptive legislation affecting their security." Under pressure from Thaddeus Stevens, among others, the resolution was softened slightly by striking out "proscriptive" and substituting "impairing" for "affecting." A sharper, though less public rebuke to political nativism lay in the convention's refusal to treat collectively with the North American party, then meeting in convention at New York City. *Ibid.* 52-53, 55-58.
[62] Hesseltine and Fisher (eds.), *Trimmers, Trucklers & Temporizers*, 89. See also Van Deusen, *Seward*, 174-78.
[63] Chase to E. S. Hamlin, June 2, 1856, Chase Papers, LC; Chase to Charles Sumner, Jan. 18, 1858, Sumner Papers; Hart, *Chase*, 160-61.

illustrious father-in-law, Thomas Hart Benton. Indeed, the *Philadelphia Pennsylvanian* joked that if he were successful Republicans would head their ticket:

For President

col. j. frémont, son-in-law of

THOMAS HART BENTON.[64]

Yet in many ways, Frémont's very inexperience seemed an asset. Being closely identified with no party and having kept his peace on most issues, save for a firm but moderate commitment to free soil, Frémont offended few Republicans' sensibilities. Radicals were easily persuaded of his soundness on the slavery question, while more conservative types remarked on his Southern connections and trusted that his discretion would continue in the future. Realizing this, Frémont's promoters had encouraged him to refrain from public statements. Said one New Yorker, "the discontented of all parties can come to him so long as he is silent—as a *veiled prophet* he will have followers from the romance of his life and position but when he enters the arena of a public letter writer, the charm will be broken."[65] Some former Free Soilers protested the need for such devious promotion and, recollecting the Van Buren misadventure of 1848, cautioned against once again substituting "availability" for steadfastness. Frémont's candidacy, Gamaliel Bailey warned, was largely the work of "place hunters and politicians . . . demolished by a passion for immediate success." Yet most radicals among the Republicans found reassuring Frémont's vigorous defense of the free-state cause in Kansas, and, once Seward and Chase had withdrawn, gave him their backing.[66]

With few exceptions McLean's support came from old line Whigs who counted upon the Justice's popularity among Know-Nothings to

[64] Hesseltine and Fisher (eds.), *Trimmers, Trucklers & Temporizers*, 86.
[65] Isaac Sherman to Nathaniel P. Banks, Apr. 3, 1856, Nathaniel P. Banks Papers, LC.
[66] Bailey to Salmon P. Chase, Apr. 18, 1856, Chase Papers, PHS; Charles Francis Adams to Charles Sumner, Apr. 1, 1856, Ellis Gray Loring to Sumner, Apr. 9, 1856, Sumner Papers.

carry doubtful Middle states and who perhaps still hoped to preserve Whiggery's program if not its name. Abraham Lincoln had urged his nomination in order to hold in the Republican party tender-footed Whigs who would vote for Buchanan before they would support Chase, Seward, or even Frémont.[67] And Thad Stevens warned the convention that only McLean could prevent a Democratic victory in Pennsylvania.[68] The vast majority of delegates, however, found the seventyish Justice too old, cautious, and colorless, too reserved in his antislavery opinions, to head a vigorous young party. McLean's recent pronouncement that Congress had the power to exclude slavery from the territories, coming after years of evasion during which he had argued that slavery's local character made the Wilmot Proviso superfluous, struck even many moderates as too little, too late. "Good Heavens!" Lewis D. Campbell sarcastically exclaimed, "What a discovery! Verily this is the age of Progress! 'Vive la humbug!' "[69]

Sensing the hopelessness of his candidacy, McLean instructed his champions at Philadelphia to withdraw his name. Taken by surprise, the McLean men at first complied, then caucused and at last decided to ignore his wishes and put up a fight. They might better have saved themselves the trouble and their hero the embarrassment. An informal ballot showed 359 votes for Frémont, 190 for McLean, and four scattered among Banks, Sumner, and Seward. With "three times three perfect Davy Crockett war-whoops" the sweltering delegates then made Frémont's choice unanimous. After picking New Jersey's William L. Dayton for Vice President—a sop to the conservatives—the convention adjourned. Under the banner "Free Speech, Free Press, Free Men, Free Labor, Free Territory, and Frémont" the Republicans confidently faced the future.[70]

[67] Hesseltine and Fisher (eds.), *Trimmers, Trucklers & Temporizers*, 83, 85-86, 89-90; O. H. Browning to Lyman Trumbull, May 19, 1856, Lyman Trumbull Papers, LC; Lincoln to Lyman Trumbull, June 7, 1856, Basler (ed.), *Works of Lincoln*, II, 342-43.

[68] Fawn M. Brodie, *Thaddeus Stevens: Scourge of the South* (New York, 1959), 128-29.

[69] Campbell to Salmon P. Chase, June 7, 1856, Chase Papers, LC. See also Benjamin F. Wade to Milton Sutliff, May 8, 1856, Sutliff Papers; Sutliff to Wade, May 11, 1856, Wade Papers.

[70] *Proceedings of the First Three Republican National Conventions*, 60-66, 78. In the informal balloting Abraham Lincoln finished second to Dayton, 110 to 253. Others receiving substantial support were Nathaniel Banks (46 votes), David Wilmot (43), and Charles Sumner (35). *Ibid.* 64.

Except for "Old Fogy Whigs," most Republicans were more than happy with the results of the Philadelphia convention. Even conservatives, as it turned out, quickly acquiesced in the outcome; Frémont had been the second choice of many McLean men, and the nomination of Dayton, an old line Whig on good terms with nativists, salved many a wound.

Antislavery radicals were especially pleased, particularly with the platform. Those who met at Philadelphia, the *Indiana True Republican* later declared, had "organized the Republican party—a FREE SOIL PARTY in the fullest sense of the term, gave it a Free Soil baptism, and a Free Soil Platform, and sent it forth" to do battle with proslavery Democrats. Joshua Giddings extravagantly observed of the new party's credo: "I think it ahead of all other platforms ever adopted." Salmon Chase agreed. "Indeed," he confessed, "I cannot but suspect that the convention 'builded wiser than they knew.' I hardly believe that the majority understood what broad principles they were announcing. . . . It includes denationalization of slavery entire." Even George Julian, who complained of the "very mean scurvy pack of politicians" who controlled the Republican party in his state, said of the national platform, "I accept it, because I think I can stand upon it and preach from it the whole anti-slavery gospel." So long as they could give their own gloss to a platform that explicitly protested slavery expansion and contained the germ of denationalization, the radical Republicans were perfectly content. With victory apparently near, it mattered little to them that Republican dogma lacked the tactical precision and moral sharpness of earlier Liberty and Free Soil platforms.[71]

Predictably, Garrisonian moral suasionists and members of Gerrit Smith's recently formed Radical Abolition party took a more jaundiced view of the Republican party. Not only did such men protest its failure "to embrace the colored as well as the white man" and its timid

[71] *Indiana True Republican*, Sept. 2, 1858; Giddings to Julian, June 24, 1856; Chase to Julian, July 17, 1856, Giddings-Julian Papers; Julian to Salmon P. Chase, July 22, 1856, Chase Papers, LC. See also Hans Trefousse, *The Radical Republicans: Lincoln's Vanguard for Racial Justice* (New York, 1969), 100; Trefousse, *Wade*, 104; Stanton, *Random Recollections*, 185. *The National Era* (June 26, 1856) responded coolly to the nominations—especially of Frémont, who, it noted, had avoided the slavery question during his brief term in the Senate "except to record his vote once or twice against certain positions brought forward by Mr. Seward or Mr. Hale." Yet the paper praised the Philadelphia platform extravagantly, calling it "a bold proclamation of the sacredness of human rights" regardless of race, creed, or national origin.

demand for free soil instead of outright, universal emancipation, but they warned of the new party's tendency to compromise essential reforms. The decision of some prominent philanthropists to give funds to the Republican party instead of to hard-pressed antislavery societies merely aggravated such caveats.[72] A few even prayed for a Republican defeat in 1856. "If the Democrats succeed, it is hoped, and may reasonably be expected, that they will sufficiently outrage the rights and feelings of the north, to incite them (the north) to get up on their hind legs, and declare that they are men," argued Lysander Spooner. "But if the free soilers succeed, I fear they will be so well satisfied with themselves, that they will aim at nothing further, and will continue to go on all fours, like good honest asses, as they always have done."[73]

Yet most ultra abolitionists mixed praise with their censure, admitting with Garrison that "as between the three rival parties, the sympathy of every genuine friend of freedom must be with the Republican party, in spite of its lamentable shortcomings."[74] Priding themselves on having infused in Republicanism "whatever of bone and sinew it may possess," most Garrisonians saw in the new party evidence that the war against slavery had entered its final phase. Although Republicans warred less with slavery than with the "Slave Power," abolitionists rejoiced to see at last a party free of Southern trammels. Besides, the *National Anti-Slavery Standard* maintained, abolitionists and slaveholders both knew "that when men begin to hate slavery on their own account, they will not stop till they have learned to hate it for that of the slaves. As Fisher Ames once said, 'There's no such thing as blowing a barrel of gunpowder half way down!' "[75] Not least, Garrisonians ac-

---

[72] Lewis Tappan to Frederick Douglass, Nov. 27, 1856, Tappan to William Slade, Dec. 30, 1856, Letterbook, Tappan Papers; Theodore Parker, *Some Thoughts on the New Assaults Upon Freedom in America*. . . . (Boston, 1854), 37; Gerrit Smith to Lewis Tappan, July 6, 1855, William Goodell to Smith, June 18, 1856, Smith Papers; *Liberator*, Mar. 7, July 11, 1856, Aug. 14, 1857; *National Anti-Slavery Standard*, Aug. 2, 16, 1856; Irving H. Bartlett, *Wendell Phillips: Brahmin Radical* (Boston, 1961), 206.

[73] Spooner to George Bradburn, May 25, 1856, Lysander Spooner Papers, NYHS. See also *National Anti-Slavery Standard*, Aug. 9, 23, 1856; Theodore Parker to William H. Fish, Nov. 17, 1856, Letterbook, Parker Papers. Such arguments were often designed more to head off abolitionist votes for Frémont, so as to keep moral suasion pure, than to abet the Democrats.

[74] *Liberator*, Sept. 5, 1856.

[75] *National Anti-Slavery Standard*, Nov. 16, July 26, 1856. See also [Twenty-second] *Annual Report, Presented to the American Anti-Slavery Society, by the Executive Committee . . . 1855,* (New York, 1855), 69-76; [Twenty-third] *An-*

corded respect to the Republican party because it gave promise of accomplishing its admittedly limited objectives. For the Radical Abolition party—as for the earlier Liberty party—Garrison showed only contempt. "I see that Lewis Tappan, [Frederick] Douglass, McCune Smith, [William] Goodell and Gerrit Smith have called a convention for the purpose of nominating candidates for the Presidency and Vice Presidency of the United States!!" he scoffed in March 1856. "Can anything more ludicrous than this be found inside or outside of the Utica Insane Asylum? It is really sad to see so good a man as Gerrit Smith befooled in this manner."[76] In fact, however, Smith looked upon his tiny party as purely an agitational device that would, by swelling antislavery feeling, give a boost to Frémont. Smith, although himself the Abolition candidate for President, gave $500 to the Republican campaign in 1856.[77]

Pleased that the Republican platform was sound so far as it went, and thrilled at the prospect of rescuing the national government from the Slave Power's grip, a good many radical abolitionists threw their support to Frémont. Even among Garrisonians there were some who broke ranks and actively campaigned for the Republican ticket. One such was Samuel J. May. One of Garrison's oldest and closest friends, a founder of the New England and American Anti-Slavery societies, and an early member of the New England Non-Resistance Society, May startled his associates with a Fourth of July address at Syracuse urging other abolitionists to join him in working for a Republican victory. "If you will have free soil, a free press, free speech, and be yourselves free men," he cried, "—then go to the polls and vote for Frémont." During the canvass May stumped extensively throughout upstate New York on behalf of the Republican candidates, defending his actions ably in the antislavery press.[78] Lydia Maria Child, another early friend of Garrison and for several years editor of the *National Anti-Slavery Standard*, shared May's hopes for Frémont and, although barred by her sex from voting, put her lively pen to work on his be-

nual Report, Presented to the American Anti-Slavery Society, by the Executive Committee . . . 1856 (New York, 1856), 10-14.
[76] Garrison to Samuel J. May, Mar. 21, 1856, Garrison Papers.
[77] Smith to William Goodell, Aug. 15, 1856, quoted in *National Era*, Sept. 4, 1856; Gerald Sorin, *Abolitionism: A New Perspective* (New York, 1972), 143.
[78] *National Anti-Slavery Standard*, Aug. 2, 9, Sept. 6, 13, 1856; *American Anti-Slavery Society Annual Report, 1856*, 69; May to Theodore Parker, Sept. 20, 1856, Garrison Papers.

half. (One of her contributions, a verse critical of Pierce, drew condemnation from Democrats. "I couldn't help it," she explained to her husband David. "His name wouldn't rhyme to anything but curse. . . .") So fervently did Lydia Child pray for Frémont's election that when in October a five-year-old neighbor girl heard from her father that western Pennsylvania had gone Republican she called out, "*Miss* Child! Pennsylvany's all right," and ran away.[79]

Garrison himself opposed such "backsliding." But it was a sign of new times that he made no move to ostracize May or Mrs. Child as he once had the followers of James G. Birney. Indeed, by 1856 the *Liberator*'s editor had come to occupy a middle position within abolitionist circles, mediating between Republican fellow travelers on the one hand and, on the other, doctrinaires like Stephen and Abby Kelley Foster, who insisted that Republicans were to the antislavery crusade "what respectable, moderate drinkers are and have been to the Temperance cause"—more dangerous than unvarnished sinners. Although it was hardly perceptible at the time, Garrison had begun a drift toward political reinvolvement which by the Civil War would make him an effective ally of Abraham Lincoln and the Republican party.[80]

Black as well as white abolitionists found much to criticize in the Republican party, yet they too expressed hopes for its improvability and in the end gave it strong support. Even Frederick Douglass, who subscribed to the Radical Abolition party's doctrine that Congress had a right and duty to abolish slavery everywhere in the United States, had by August switched his backing from Gerrit Smith to Frémont and Dayton. "Their election," he told readers of *Frederick Douglass' Paper*, "will prevent the establishment of Slavery in Kansas, overthrow Slave Rule in the Republic, protect Liberty of Speech and of the Press, give ascendancy to Northern civilization over the bludgeon and bloodhound civilization of the South, and [put] the mark of national condemnation on Slavery, scourge doughfaces from place and from power, and inaugurate a higher and purer standard of Politics and Government." That the Democrats labeled their opponents "Black Republicans" and charged them with plotting disunion and "running off

[79] L. M. Child to Mrs. S. B. Shaw, [no day], Oct. 27, 1856, in *Letters of Lydia Maria Child* (Boston, 1883), 78-80, 85-86; L. M. Child to David Lee Child, Oct. 27, 1856, Antislavery Collection, Cornell University.
[80] *Liberator*, June 6, Sept. 5, 1856; *American Anti-Slavery Society Annual Report, 1856*, 64, 70-71.

niggers," of course only strengthened Negro attachment to Republicanism. Nearly all black voters, therefore, followed the lead of Douglass, Henry Highland Garnet, and others and clambered aboard the Frémont bandwagon.[81]

4

Unlike the Free Democrats four years earlier, the Republicans entered the 1856 campaign bursting with optimism. With good reason they counted all New England, New York, Ohio, Michigan, Wisconsin, and Iowa as safe for Frémont. If but two of the swing states—Pennsylvania, New Jersey, Indiana, or Illinois—could be added to that list the long-awaited victory of freedom over slavery would be an accomplished fact. Much of the Republican effort, therefore, centered in these Border free states; party luminaries like Seward, King, Wilson, Burlingame, and Hale joined Wilmot, Stevens, and others in stumping Pennsylvania and New Jersey while such practiced campaigners as Giddings, Banks, and Wade reinforced party regulars in Indiana and Illinois.

Republicans faced opposition everywhere, not only from Democrats but also from the nativist American party. Although antislavery "North Americans" had bolted the American convention which in February had nominated Millard Fillmore for President, most of them joining the Republican party instead, enough conservative Whigs preferred the American party's "Union-saving" program to make it a force worthy of concern. The Republicans' chief rivals, however, were the Democrats—superbly organized, well financed, ably led, and blessed with a candidate whose recent stint as Minister to England had kept him out of the Kansas-Nebraska controversy and whose seat of power was the key state of Pennsylvania. By contrast, the Republicans—for all their dedication and high spirits—lacked funds and organizational efficiency, while their standard-bearer (as perhaps befit an explorer) possessed no base of strength of his own. Even Frémont's father-in-law, the redoubtable Benton, backed Buchanan.[82]

While both Democrats and Whig-Americans strove to tar Republi-

[81] Foner, *Writings of Douglass*, II, 401; Quarles, *Black Abolitionists*, 187-89.
[82] Nevins, *Ordeal of the Union*, II, 487-505.

cans with the brush of abolitionism, to charge Frémont (falsely) with Catholicism, and to raise the specter of disunion should he be elected, the Republican party concentrated its campaign efforts almost exclusively on the Kansas question and the weakness of popular sovereignty. If one makes allowances for his open enmity, more than a little truth can be found in Robert C. Winthrop's complaint that Republican propaganda monotonously repeated the same old recipe:

> One-third part Missouri Compromise repeal, without one grain of allowance for the indisputable fact that it was proposed and supported by Northern men and could not have been carried without their aid; one-third Kansas outrages by Border Ruffians, without one scruple of doubt as to the wisdom of Northern measures which, reasonable or unreasonable, have furnished so much of the pretext and provocation; one-third disjointed and misapplied figures, and a great swelling of words and vanity, to prove that the South is, upon the whole, the very poorest, meanest, least productive, and most miserable part of creation, and therefore ought to be continually teased and taunted and reproached and reviled, by everybody who feels himself better off.[83]

Here and there other issues—free homesteads, the tariff, construction of the Pacific railroad—entered into the debate, and the unstated question of nativism undoubtedly swayed many voters. But insofar as they were able, Republican campaigners made antislavery—Bloody Kansas and Bloody Sumner—the focus of attention.[84]

Given its fledgling state, the Republican party put on a stunning performance in 1856. For although Buchanan won the presidency by collecting 174 electoral votes to Frémont's 114 and Fillmore's eight, the margin of victory proved exceedingly slim. Frémont swept all but five free states—Pennsylvania, New Jersey, Indiana, Illinois, and California. North of the National Road he had been nearly invincible. Most encouraging of all to Republicans, even in the free states Frémont had lost the Democratic party's strength showed signs of erosion. The capture of Pennsylvania and the switch of a few thousand votes in Indiana or Illinois would assure a Republican victory another time. Senator

[83] Quoted in Ruhl J. Bartlett, *John C. Frémont and the Republican Party* (Columbus, 1930), 31n. See also *New-York Daily Tribune*, Oct. 24, Nov. 3, 1856; *Harrisburg* (Pa.) *Weekly Telegraph*, Aug. 14, 1856.
[84] Bartlett, *Frémont and the Republican Party*, 25-36; Nevins, *Ordeal of the Union*, II, 501-2; Isely, *Greeley and the Republican Party*, 177-95.

William Pitt Fessenden of Maine struck a common note when he observed soon after the election: "We are beaten, but we have frightened the rascals awfully. They cannot help seeing what their doom must inevitably be, unless they abandon their unrighteous ways. I am grieved that we could do no more, but surprised that we accomplished so much in so short a time."[85] Having scant faith that the rascals would ever mend their errant ways, the Republicans—though "tired and sore and a little inclined to rest and quiet"—began at once to prepare for a reversal of fortunes in 1860.[86]

[85] Quoted in Jellison, *Fessenden*, 97.
[86] Isely, *Greeley and the Republican Party*, 194-95.

12

Freedom National

AFTER 1856 THE REPUBLICAN PARTY broadened its creed to include other issues besides antislavery. Frémont's defeat and the Panic of 1857 convinced most Republicans that exclusive reliance on the slavery question (not to say Kansas) jeopardized their party's future. By 1859, therefore, economic issues began to appear in Republican state platforms and in 1860 the party's national convention added to antislavery planks demands for a protective tariff and free homesteads, as well as river and harbor improvement and a Pacific railroad. Like their antislavery predecessors, Republicans had concluded that the "one idea" was too narrow a platform for a party aspiring to power.

Yet there can be no question that hostility toward slavery lay at the very core of Republican ideology, that nearly everywhere it overshadowed and subsumed all other issues.[1] Nor can there be much doubt that by 1860 the vast majority of Republicans viewed bondage as a curse and sought not merely to arrest its spread but to place it on the road to ultimate extinction. Small wonder that seasoned political abolitionists looked upon the Republican party as a logical extension of the Liberty and Free Soil organizations.

[1] There were, of course, exceptions. In eastern Pennsylvania, for instance, the tariff question bulked particularly large after 1857, and despite the national party's formal rebuffs to xenophobia local groups sometimes relied on nativist appeals to enlist voters in the Republican cause. See *Harrisburg Weekly Telegraph*, July 15, 1858; James E. Harvey to John Sherman, Oct. 14, 1859, Sherman Papers; James M. Brown to Salmon P. Chase, Feb. 6, 1860, John A. C. Gray to Chase, Mar. 19, 1860, Chase Papers, LC; Holt, *Forging a Majority*, 207-9, 215-19, 286-88.

Where slavery was concerned, the Republicans' lowest common denominator was the principle of the Northwest Ordinance and the Wilmot Proviso. The Founding Fathers having intended that freedom be made national and slavery sectional, Republicans contended, it became "both the right and the imperative duty of Congress" to prevent the South from engrafting its peculiar institution upon the Western territories.[2]

In seeking to impress upon voters the crucial importance of the territorial issue, Republicans relied chiefly upon a free labor ideology long familiar to veterans of the Liberty and Free Soil parties.[3] If not an "irrepressible conflict," then at least a fundamental antagonism existed between the free labor society of the North and the slave labor society of the South, Republican spokesmen repeatedly insisted. And the stakes of that contest, they took pains to point out, were at least as high for whites as for blacks. As the *New York Post* put it in 1857:

> We are opposed to the extension of slavery because it degrades labor; it demoralizes the character; it corrupts the young; it diminishes the productive power of the soil and the productive power of its population; it depreciates the value of all kinds of property; it is an obstacle to compact settlements, and, as a consequence, to every general system of public instruction, literary or religious; it develops bad passions without providing any means of disciplining or controlling them, and generates a lawless state of society; and finally, under our Constitution, it con-

[2] See, e.g., Edward Wade's speech in the U.S. House of Representatives, Aug. 2, 1856, *Cong. Globe*, 34th Cong., 1st sess., Appendix, 1076-81; *New-York Daily Tribune*, Apr. 2, 1857; *New York Evening Post*, July 10, 1860; James W. Grimes's inaugural address as Governor of Iowa, Dec. 9, 1854, quoted in William Salter, *The Life of James W. Grimes, Governor of Iowa, 1854-1858: A Senator of the United States, 1859-1869* (New York, 1876), 61; *Proceedings of the First Three Republican National Conventions*, 43, 132. A very few Republican politicians went further, embracing the notion that the Constitution was an antislavery instrument which justified direct assaults on slavery *everywhere* in the United States. See the speech of Congressman Amos P. Granger of New York, Apr. 4, 1856, *Cong. Globe*, 34th Cong., 1st sess., Appendix, 295-97.
[3] Foner, *Free Soil, Free Labor, Free Men*, esp. chaps. I-II, IX. The free labor ideology possessed special force, Foner suggests, because it appealed both to proponents of modernization (by placing a premium on internalized *self*-discipline) and to "those whose objective was to preserve the pre-modern status of the independent artisan" (by securing a Western safety-valve against economic exploitation and by idealizing a society of upwardly-mobile, self-employed individuals). Foner, "The Causes of the American Civil War: Recent Interpretations and New Directions," *Civil War History*, XX, No. 3 (Sept. 1974), 206-9.

fers upon slave proprietors a political representation based upon
property, which is denied to other citizens.[4]

The Constitution forbade frontal assaults on slavery in the states, but
Northerners might win a partial victory, at least, by saving the territories for development by resourceful, enterprising, and virtuous free
laborers from Europe and America. Such a victory would not only
prevent slavery's rape of virgin lands in the West, but, by emboldening
antislavery elements within the South, would undermine the institution where already rooted. "The great Anti Slavery sentiment of Virginia[,] Kentucky & Missouri," wrote one of Charles Sumner's correspondents, "will only take heart when they shall find that it can be &
will be sustained by action in Congress and the free states."[5]

When Republicans spoke of the territories, of course, they usually
had Kansas in mind. Yet Kansas, though vitally important in itself,
seemed even more significant as a precedent for the future. Time and
again, in private correspondence and public pronouncements, Republicans expressed the conviction (apparently shared by such proslavery
leaders as Missouri's Senator David R. Atchison) that in the fate of
Kansas lay the fate of all other territories—and ultimately of the nation.
"If it is free, the world, in germ, is free," William Herndon reflected,
"and if slave—ah! there is the question." Likewise, the *Lansing State
Republican* declared: "Make Kansas a free State, and a bulwark is established beyond which it is almost impossible for slavery to pass. Make
Kansas a Slave State, and a highway is opened for the rush of tens of
thousands of petty despots with their helpless victims into the wide
spread Territories beyond. . . . This generation gives Slavery its
death-blow, or infuses into the system a vigor which may prolong
its existence for centuries."[6]

To the Republicans, therefore, the issue of slavery in the territories
was of more than symbolic importance. As they saw it, congressional
prohibition of slavery expansion was essential not only because such

[4] *New York Evening Post*, Apr. 14, 1857.
[5] Charles W. Elliott to Sumner, July 14, 1854, Sumner Papers. See also Cassius M.
Clay to Gerrit Smith, Nov. 20, 1857, Smith Papers.
[6] Herndon to Charles Sumner, Jan. 8, 1857, Sumner Papers; *Lansing State Republican*, Apr. 8, 1856. See also *Dover Enquirer*, Nov. 8, 1855; *New-York Daily Tribune*,
Oct. 24, 1856; Edward E. Hale to Charles Sumner, Nov. 12, 1855, Sumner Papers;
Theodore Parker to Charles Sumner, Jan. 14, 1856, Letterbook, Parker Papers; *Chicago Daily Tribune*, Sept. 7, 1857.

action would declare the moral unacceptability of slavery everywhere, but because it seemed the only safe way to protect the interests of free settlers and to curb an arrogant and aggressive slavocracy.

Most Northern Democrats, as well as Republicans, hoped to keep slavery out of the territories. But their formula for doing so, Republicans found woefully weak. Even before the Dred Scott decision and attempts to force the proslavery Lecompton constitution upon the settlers of Kansas, Republicans had denounced as humbug the Democratic doctrine that the people of a territory should be left "perfectly free," as the Kansas-Nebraska Act phrased it, "to form and regulate their domestic institutions in their own way, subject only to the Constitution of the United States." And after the near-success of the Lecompton "fraud," and the Dred Scott dictum that settlers might legislate for but not against slavery, Republican contempt for "popular sovereignty" intensified—notwithstanding what Abraham Lincoln dubbed Stephen A. Douglas's interminable "explanations explanatory of explanations explained." Most Republicans agreed with Lincoln that the Democratic doctrine was "as thin as the homeopathic soup that was made by boiling the shadow of a pigeon that had starved to death," and rejected it out of hand.[7]

Republican aversion to popular sovereignty (or, as it was sometimes called, "squatter sovereignty") rested partly on moral, partly on political considerations. Radicals especially, but also many moderate Republicans, protested that popular sovereignty treated slavery as a morally neutral question, one which, in Senator Douglas's parlance, might be "voted up or voted down" as territorial settlers saw fit. So long as Republicans considered slavery morally wrong, Lincoln proclaimed—"an unqualified evil to the negro, to the white man, to the soil, and to the State"—they could in good conscience have nothing to do with a theory which acknowledged that slavery had "equal rights with liberty."[8]

To the argument that "the sacred right of self government" counseled congressional nonintervention in the internal affairs of the terri-

[7] Gideon Welles to [James T. Pratt], Mar. [no day] 1854 (copy), Welles Papers, LC; Francis P. Blair, Jr., to Nathaniel P. Banks, Jan. 28, 1856, Nathaniel P. Banks Papers, Illinois State Historical Library; Lincoln's debate with Douglas at Quincy, Ill., Oct. 13, 1858, Lincoln's speech at Columbus, Ohio, Sept. 16, 1859, Basler (ed.), *Works of Lincoln*, III, 279, 405.
[8] Lincoln's speech at Edwardsville, Ill., Sept. 11, 1858, Lincoln to John D. Defrees, Dec. 18, 1860, *ibid.* III, 92, IV, 155; Salmon P. Chase to William H. Seward, Mar. 10, 1858, Seward Papers.

tories Republicans had a ready answer. It was all well and good, they said, to keep hands off when only mundane issues were at stake. "Here, or at Washington," Lincoln asserted, "I would not trouble myself with the oyster laws of Virginia, or the cranberry laws of Indiana." But territories were not states and slavery expansion, far from being an insignificant question, was "the great Behemoth of danger." Whether the territories would become the preserve of freemen—dotted with prosperous farms and bustling cities, amply nurtured by churches and schools—or whether they would fall under slavery's deadening hand, seemed to Republicans a matter of legitimate *national* concern, not something that might safely be left to prairie pioneers. To say, as Douglas's brand of popular sovereignty seemed to, "that if any *one* man, choose to enslave *another*, no *third* man shall be allowed to object," struck Republicans like Abraham Lincoln as a gross perversion of democratic principles.[9]

Like the Free Soilers before them, most Republicans also rejected the contention of Northern Democrats that popular sovereignty would in practice provide as effective a barrier to slavery expansion as congressional prohibition would. Its great flaw as an antislavery instrument, they maintained (dismissing as specious Douglas's "Freeport doctrine" that without the support of local police regulations slavery could not exist an hour anywhere), was that it permitted bondage a toehold. And once entrenched, Republicans maintained, the institution would be devilishly hard to dislodge. Not only would slaveholders exert a disproportionate influence during the territorial stage—thanks to their wealth, leisure, and political connections—but when the time came to form a state constitution, men would find the practical difficulties of liquidating an already established form of property to be virtually insurmountable. Had not the slave states themselves repeatedly complained that this was so? Once again, therefore, voters were urged to heed the poet's injunction that to bend the twig was to shape the tree.[10]

Republicans also sharply challenged the notion that congressional

[9] Lincoln's speech at Peoria, Ill., Oct. 16, 1854, Lincoln's "House Divided" speech at Springfield, Ill., June 16, 1858, Basler (ed.), *Works of Lincoln*, II, 265, 270, 462; Salter, *Grimes*, 47-48.
[10] *New York Evening Post*, Feb. 9, Aug. 11, 1854; *Galesburg Free Democrat*, Feb. 9, 1854; Edward Dodd to Thurlow Weed, Apr. 4, 1856, Weed Papers; *Independent Democrat*, Sept. 17, 1857; *Chicago Daily Tribune*, July 3, 1857.

proscription was unnecessary—that popular sovereignty would do the job—because soil and climate had already ruled against slavery in the territories. They rightly perceived that the theory of geographical determinism was a double-edged sword: if one admitted that nature barred slavery in certain latitudes, one had also to admit that it invited it in others. And even if soil and season could be counted on to rescue Oregon from slavery, what would prevent the South—once the popular sovereignty formula gained recognition—from carrying its peculiar institution through annexation into Mexico, Central America, or the West Indies? As for Kansas, Republicans often pointed out that it lay along the same parallel as Missouri, Kentucky, Maryland, and Virginia. If slavery survived in those states, why might it not in Kansas as well? Only the Northwest Ordinance had kept "the monster out" of Indiana and Illinois, and then only after a desperate struggle. Indeed, argued the *Chicago Tribune*, slavery was as suited to the temperate as to the torrid zone. "Repeal all the organic and statutory inhibitory laws, in the Free States," it warned, "and Slavery will travel back to New England, New York and Pennsylvania. The codfish and cotton aristocracy would speedily purchase slaves for house and body servants even though the artizans and farmers should reject the employment of servile labor."[11]

To many Republicans, the enactment of a severe slave code for New Mexico in 1859 offered convincing proof that slavery knew no natural limits. It mattered little that as late as 1861, after eight years of Democratic rule, only two dozen slaves could be found in all of New Mexico—most of them female domestics in the service of federal officials. What counted most was that once again the "soothing, let-alone, do-nothing policy" of popular sovereignty had been revealed a sham and bondage had been legalized even in a region "known to be arid, sterile, and mountainous."[12] With the aid and comfort of pro-Southern Administrations in Washington, New Mexico's tiny slave interest had forced upon the territory's "ignorant, superstitious, and degraded"

---

[11] *Chicago Daily Tribune*, Mar. 19, 1856. See also *New-York Daily Tribune*, Feb. 24, 27, 1854, Jan. 23, 1855, Oct. 6, 1856; *Athens* (Ohio) *Messenger*, June 23, 1854; *Boston Commonwealth*, Mar. 18, 1854; *New York Evening Post*, Aug. 1, 1855; Salter, *Grimes*, 45-47. At least some proslavery propagandists shared the Republicans' scorn for the natural limits theory. See William S. Jenkins, *Pro-Slavery Thought in the Old South* (Chapel Hill, 1935), 103; Barney, *Road to Secession*, 12.
[12] *New-York Daily Tribune*, Mar. 28, 1859, Feb. 25, 1859; *National Era*, Mar. 31, 1859; Duberman, *Adams*, 235.

masses a code that not only upheld property in slaves but imposed a penalty of up to ten years in jail and a $5000 fine for anyone convicted of aiding runaways. Once bondsmen became cheaper and more readily available (perhaps, Republicans fretted, as a result of a reopening of the African slave trade), slavery might be expected to expand. New Mexico's mines, some noted, were ideally suited to slave labor. "A gang of slaves once shut into a deep mine could be flogged and worked in the greatest security," the *Chicago Tribune* luridly speculated. And from a political standpoint, it of course made little difference how many slaves there were. As Horace Greeley remarked, Delaware claimed a minuscule slave population—barely 1.5 per cent of the whole —yet it was as much a slave state as Mississippi, and regularly sent loyal defenders of the slave oligarchy to represent it in Congress.[13]

Not quite all Republicans shared these views (which, in any event, may have been inflated for political effect). The failure of Kansas to confirm such dire predictions, together with Stephen A. Douglas's bold denunciation of the Lecompton chicanery, had by the late 1850s inclined some Republicans toward a more favorable opinion of popular sovereignty. William H. Seward, for one, subscribed "to some extent" to the "isothermal theory" (which he believed would keep even so southerly a territory as New Mexico free of slavery), and in 1858 he announced his willingness to cooperate with Douglas Democrats in support of genuine popular sovereignty.[14] So too did Massachusetts Congressman Eli Thayer, whose work on behalf of the New England Emigrant Aid Company convinced him that free state settlers, properly organized and financed, needed no help from Congress to extinguish slavery from their midst.[15] Particularly among conservative Republicans a growing fear of disunion bred a willingness to support popular sovereignty—at least until such time as their party gained the power to implement non-extension. Such opinions, however, found favor with very few Republicans. In 1858 Indiana's was the only state Republican organization not to reaffirm the Philadelphia platform of 1856, and in 1860 the party once again upheld its adherence to the principle of non-extension. When the secession crisis came, Lincoln and his party stood

[13] *Chicago Daily Tribune*, Feb. 8, 1861; *Illinois State Journal*, Mar. 23, 1859; *Harrisburg Semi-Weekly Telegraph*, Mar. 23, 1859; *New-York Daily Tribune*, Feb. 25, 1861; John Jay to Charles Sumner, Feb. 4, 1861, Sumner Papers.
[14] Van Deusen, *Seward*, 189, 191.
[15] *Dictionary of American Biography*, XVIII, 403.

ready to risk disunion rather than surrender their demand for the positive exclusion of slavery from all federal territories.[16]

2

A number of influential Republicans, among them Abraham Lincoln, voiced fears that the "care not" attitude implicit in popular sovereignty would encourage attempts to make slavery the law of the land—in states as well as territories, in the North as well as the South. Even before the Dred Scott decision, some Republicans warned that to regard human bondage as simply another form of property was to open the door to its infinite expansion. Only by insisting that it was indeed a peculiar institution, rightfully existing only where established by positive law, might slavery be held at bay. Fears aroused by the Kansas-Nebraska Act have already been noted. The decision of Pennsylvania Judge John K. Kane in the Passmore Williamson case of 1855—that slaveholders might legally retain possession of their chattels when traveling with them through Northern states—occasioned further warnings of "a plan to force slavery upon the free states as well as upon the territories." There was no valid distinction, argued the *New York Post*, "between the power of a state *in transitu* or *in domicilii*." Once recognize rights in slave property beyond the limits of a slave state, Ohio Congressman Benjamin Stanton contended in 1856, and masters might soon insist upon their right to take and, if need arose, sell their chattels anywhere. "If this principle is to be established," he cautioned, "the free States must provide themselves with stocks and whipping-posts, and slave-pens, and slave-markets, and all the paraphernalia of a slave plantation. The struggle, therefore, that is now pending is in reality a struggle for the extension of slavery over the whole Confederacy, and the establishment of it in all the States."[17]

---

[16] *Indiana True Republican*, May 5, 12, June 2, 1859; Eli Thayer to John Sherman, Aug. 27, 1860, J. D. Baldwin to Sherman, Aug. 4, 1860, Sherman Papers; Kenneth M. Stampp, *And the War Came: The North and the Secession Crisis, 1860-1861* (Baton Rouge, 1950).

[17] *New York Evening Post*, July 28, 31, 1855; *Cong. Globe*, 34th Cong., 1st sess., Appendix, 410 (Apr. 23, 1856). Slavery was a local institution, dependent upon positive law, Republicans explained, because slaves, as men, could not be made "brute beasts or chattels" except by force, which would be legalized only by positive law. Common and civil law deemed even wild animals not absolute but

The Supreme Court's decision in Dred Scott *v*. Sandford, handed down on March 6, 1857, boldly underscored such warnings. Chief Justice Roger B. Taney's opinion that since property in a slave was no different from other property neither Congress nor a territorial assembly could debar slavery from any territory struck Republicans as profoundly ominous—as much for its seeming tendency as for its immediate effect. Although Horace Greeley belittled the decision as a piece of *obiter dicta* "entitled to just so much moral weight as would be the judgment of a majority of those congregated in any Washington barroom," he and many other Republican leaders were quick to note its implications for free states as well as territories. "The inference is plain," the *New-York Tribune* commented on short reflection. "If slaves are recognized as property by the Constitution, of course no local or State law can either prevent property being carried through an individual State or Territory, or forbid its being held as such wherever its owner may choose to hold it." Now, Greeley ominously asserted, "Mr. Toombs can call the roll of his chattels on the slope of Bunker Hill; auctions of black men may be held in front of Faneuil Hall, and the slave-ship, protected by the guns of United States frigates, may land its dusky cargo at Plymouth Rock."[18]

Coming from so partial a court (all but the two dissenting Justices, McLean and Curtis, were Democrats and six of the nine were decidedly pro-Southern) and so soon after repeal of the Missouri restriction, it is hardly surprising that many Republicans professed to find in the Dred Scott decision evidence of a slowly unfolding conspiracy to promote slavery and the Democratic party at the expense of free labor and states' rights.[19]

---

defeasible property, which dissolved the moment they regained their natural and normal state. Moreover, the *New York Evening Post* (July 10, 1860) declared, experience had proven slavery detrimental to "the commercial and moral condition of society, so that society will not tolerate it except under the strictest legal provisions." See also *New-York Daily Tribune*, Apr. 2, 1857.

[18] *Ibid*. Mar. 7, 11, 1857. See also *New York Evening Post*, Mar. 9, 1857; *Chicago Daily Tribune*, Mar. 11, 16, 1857; *Poughkeepsie Eagle*, Mar. 14, 1857; *Independent Democrat*, Mar. 19, 1857; *Lansing State Republican*, Mar. 24, 31, 1857; *Galesburg Free Democrat*, Mar. 26, 1857; *Galena Weekly Northwestern Gazette*, Oct. 12, 1858. Greeley's reference was to Senator Robert Toombs of Georgia, reputed to have boasted that one day he would muster his slaves on Bunker Hill. Toombs denied having made any such statement. See Pleasant A. Stovall, *Robert Toombs: Statesman, Speaker, Soldier, Sage* (New York, 1892), 119.

[19] Preston King to Gideon Welles, Mar. 9, 1857, King Papers; *Chicago Daily Tribune*, Mar. 11, 1857; *New York Evening Post*, Mar. 7, 1857.

Seventy years ago [the *Harrisburg Telegraph* editorialized in 1859] the Democrats drew a line around the States, and said to the Slave Trader, "thus far you may go, but no farther." This was the Jeffersonian Proviso. Thirty years ago they rubbed out part of the line, and said to him, "You may go into the lands South, but not into the lands North." This was the Missouri Compromise. Five years ago they rubbed out the rest of the line, and said to him, "We leave it to the Settlers to decide whether you shall come in or not." This was the Nebraska Bill. Now they turn humbly to him, hat in hand, and say, "Go where you please; the land is all yours, the National flag shall protect you, and the National Troops shoot down whoever resists you." This is the Dred Scott decision.[20]

That the Olympian Supreme Court had now seemingly joined Southern oligarchs and doughfaces like Pierce and Buchanan in a "conspiracy against Freedom" disturbed even many Northern Democrats. The dying Thomas Hart Benton somehow summoned the energy to produce a 190-page treatise which upheld Congress' supreme authority over the territories and lambasted the Court for meddling in purely political questions. Similarly, one New York Democrat confessed: "I feel quite mortified for the course of this *Tawny* Lion of Gen. Jackson—it is a great drawback on his fame." And while Stephen A. Douglas strained to square the Dred Scott decision with his version of popular sovereignty (arguing that the right to bring slaves into a territory remained "a barren and worthless right" unless buttressed by "appropriate police regulations and local legislation"), some of his followers discerned a sellout to the South. The Dred Scott opinion, declared Democratic journals in Wisconsin and Illinois, revealed "a conspiracy between a portion of the Supreme Court Judges, Buchanan and the South . . . to retard the progress of freedom, and confirm the claims of the slave power to universal supremacy."[21]

Republicans, of course, hammered hardest at the conspiracy thesis. By 1858 it had become a staple of Republican propaganda, and Abraham Lincoln exploited it fully in his canvass that year against Douglas. "Stephen and Franklin and Roger and James," Lincoln charged in his

---

[20] *Harrisburg Semi-Weekly Telegraph*, Mar. 30, 1857.
[21] William N. Chambers, *Old Bullion Benton: Senator from the New West* (Boston, 1956), 433-35; Johannsen, *Douglas*, 568-72; Sycamore (Ill.) *DeKalb Co. Republican Sentinel*, Apr. 2, 1857, quoting with its endorsement the *Beloit* (Wis.) *Journal*.

House Divided speech of June 1858, had plotted to sustain slavery in the territories. And, he warned, unless the "care not" doctrine were purged from the public mind, the next step in their conspiracy might be another Supreme Court decision declaring that no *state* might exclude slavery from its limits.[22]

Such accusations were unquestionably overdrawn, perhaps often deliberately so. Republicans were hard put to reconcile Douglas's fight against the Lecompton fraud with alleged complicity in a proslavery plot, and in later speeches Lincoln softened his remarks somewhat, admitting that evidence of a plot was wholly circumstantial and that Douglas himself might have served more as dupe than as conspirator. Yet circumstantial (trout-in-the-milk) evidence can be powerfully persuasive, and Lincoln and his followers pointed to real, not imaginary, events when they leveled their charges of a plot against freedom. Whatever the nature of their collaboration (to use a less loaded and probably more accurate word than "plot" or "conspiracy"), there can be no denying that Pierce, Buchanan, Taney, and Douglas had lately moved in step to expand rather than curtail slavery's domain. In first discarding the Missouri Compromise line, and then by judicial mandate (with presidential endorsement) denying any legislative right to ban slavery from the territories, Democratic policy-makers had revealed a *tendency* toward encouraging the spread of slavery. And that tendency, as Lincoln not unreasonably observed, gained strength both from the moral indifference inherent in popular sovereignty and from Taney's ruling that where the Constitution was concerned Negroes "had no rights which the white man was bound to respect." Lincoln's prophecy that the people of Illinois might one day awake to discover that the Supreme Court had made their's a slave state never came to pass, of course. That it did not, however, is perhaps better explained by the rush of events and the resistance of the Republican party than by judicial wisdom or restraint.[23]

In fact, when Lincoln warned that the Slave Power's next step might be to obtain a court ruling protecting slave property in *all states* he may have had in mind a case already before New York courts, one

---

[22] Basler (ed.), *Works of Lincoln*, II, 461-69. See also Lyman Trumbull's speech at Chicago, Aug. 7, 1858, reported in the *National Era*, Sept. 2, 1858.
[23] For a brilliant exposition of this point of view, see Jaffa, *Crisis of the House Divided*, chaps. XI-XII.

which many feared would, on appeal, give Taney and his associates a pretext to do just that. In November 1852, a Virginia couple, Jonathan and Juliet Lemmon, brought with them to New York City, aboard the steamer *Richmond City*, eight slaves—ranging in age from two to twenty. The Lemmons planned to remain in New York only a few days while awaiting passage to Texas, their ultimate destination. Soon after they landed, however, one Louis Napoleon, a Negro, discovered their slaves and promptly petitioned Superior Court Justice Elijah Paine for a writ of habeas corpus on their behalf. Paine complied, and, after hearing arguments on both sides, he set the slaves free. New York state laws, he declared, extinguished all right to slave property, "except in the single instance of fugitives from labor, under the Constitution of the United States."[24]

Although private citizens reimbursed the Lemmons for the loss of their chattels, the State of Virginia, believing that Paine's decision undermined the value of slave property everywhere, carried an appeal to the New York Supreme Court. In December 1857 that court upheld Judge Paine's order, only one of five Justices dissenting. Once again, an appeal was made—this time to the New York Court of Appeals—and once again, in March 1860, the prior ruling was reaffirmed. Liberty being man's natural condition, slavery was rooted in physical force and could be sustained only by positive law. And a majority of the Justices proclaimed that since New York statutes expressly declared that no person held as a slave might be brought on any pretense within the state, the Lemmons's title to their human "property" had expired the moment the *Richmond City* docked at Manhattan. New York had clearly and firmly reasserted its determination to keep the least part of slavery from its soil.[25]

What worried many Republicans, however, was that the Taney Court might take a quite different view. The arguments of Charles O'Conor, counsel for the appellant, which included a plea that all good citizens vindicate slavery's "essential justice and morality in all courts and places before men and nations," seemed to presage an appeal to the nation's highest court.[26] Such a review, Republicans feared, might es-

[24] New York Court of Appeals, *Report of the Lemmon Slave Case* (New York, 1861), 3-12.
[25] *Ibid.* 13-146; Chester L. Barrows, *William M. Evarts: Lawyer, Diplomat, Statesman* (Chapel Hill, 1941), 83-87.
[26] *Lemmon Slave Case*, 28-46, 107-21, esp. 120.

tablish not only the slaveholders' right to carry their chattels through
"free" states, but also the right to hold such property in any of the
United States.[27] Whether these fears were fully justified must remain
a mystery, for the Civil War and the Thirteenth Amendment soon cut
short all thought of a final court appeal. Yet it would be wrong to describe them as wholly fanciful.

3

Nearly all Republicans would have agreed with Salmon P. Chase's admirably succinct statement of the Republican creed: "No slavery
outside the slave states."[28] The slogan neatly expressed the party's
determination both to block slavery's advance into any territory or
free state and to abstain from any *direct* assault on the institution where
already established. Like the Democrats' popular sovereignty formula,
however, it concealed—and hence accommodated—widely variant points
of view. Some, like Chase, read into this slogan (as into the national
platform of 1856) a demand for the complete separation of government
and slavery and for a war of attrition against bondage by all constitutional means. Others took a more conservative, negative view of the
party's mission—stressing the danger of Slave Power aggression and
softpedaling or ignoring altogether the plight of the slave. Timothy
Howe of Wisconsin, himself a proponent of this latter position, at-
tested to the variety of Republican attitudes toward slavery when he
lectured a more radical associate: "Yes! nobody knows better than I do
that there are thousands of Republicans in the State, whose flaming
zeal against Slavery would consume every article in the way of its extinction. But do you not know also that there are thousands in the state
who condemn slavery as a bad policy not as a wrong principle, who
will vote against it but will not fight ag[ains]t it—and that there are
other thousands still who hate slavery as they hate all despotism, but

[27] *Boston Weekly Commonwealth*, Jan. 29, 1853; *Chicago Daily Tribune*, Mar. 16,
1857; *New-York Daily Tribune*, Oct. 6, 1857, Jan. 28, 1860; *Galesburg Free Democrat*, Nov. 11, 1857; *Chicago Press & Tribune*, Jan. 28, Apr. 11, 1860; *Independent
Democrat*, Feb. 16, 1860. The slaves involved in the Lemmon case settled in
Canada. See John Jay to William H. Seward, Mar. 16, 1857, Seward Papers.
[28] Quoted (favorably) in the *Lansing State Republican*, May 13, 1856.

who would no more consent to strike slavery in So[uth] Carolina than Despotism in Russia?"[29]

At one time or another virtually all leading Republicans warned of the machinations of an aggressive slavocracy and played upon the self-interest of whites. What distinguished antislavery conservatives was the priority, the emphasis, they gave to such arguments, and their unwillingness, based upon fears of disunion and a solicitude for property rights in general, to give needless offense to the South. Republicans to a man agreed that Southern rapacity must be checked, slavery's special privileges destroyed. "Are we," asked conservative Congressman Henry Bennett of New York, "to have a government of the people, a real representative Republican Government? or are the owners of slave property, small in number but with the power now in their hands, and strongly intrenched in every department, to rule us with arbitrary and undisputed sway?"[30] But when moderate and radical Republicans agreed with John Wesley that slavery was "the sum of all villainies," and called non-extension but a first step toward universal emancipation, party conservatives refused to go along.

To conservative Republicans like Orville H. Browning of Illinois, Tom Corwin of Ohio, and Hamilton Fish of New York—most of them old line Whigs who neither forgot nor forgave the abolitionists' role in the 1844 defeat of Henry Clay—slavery's evils were chiefly economic and political, bearing even more destructively on whites than on blacks. "We do not base our opposition to the extension and nationalization of Slavery upon our pity for the condition of the slaves . . . ," explained one Republican paper in Illinois. "We base our opposition to the spread of Slavery upon the effects of that institution upon the slaveholders and all other citizens of Slave States and the influence it thus exerts upon our national character and destiny."[31] The mission of the Republican party, conservatives maintained, was purely defensive—the protection of "Free White American Labor" from slavery's grasping, disruptive, demoralizing tendencies. Typical was the appeal of the *Pennsylvania Weekly Telegraph* during the campaign of 1860:

> We say to the government, give us protection to our labor that we may advance the national prosperity by developing the un-

[29] Howe to Horace Rublee, Apr. 3, 1859, Timothy O. Howe Papers, SHSW.
[30] *Cong. Globe,* 34th Cong., 1st sess., Appendix, 698 (June 30, 1856).
[31] *Galena Weekly Northwestern Gazette,* Sept. 2, 1856.

bounded resources of our country. We say to the South, keep your domestic institutions, if you choose; we desire not to infringe on your rights or to disturb you in your domestic relations, but we demand equal courtesy at your hands. —You must not carry your blighting institution of Slavery into the public Territories to compete with, degrade and impoverish our White Labor. . . . Keep your negroes at home, gentlemen, and if you choose to go into the Territories, do as we do. . . . We not only offer you equal terms in this respect, but we invite you to the free West, and would give you homes when you reach it.[32]

So timid were the antislavery beliefs of conservative Republicans that after 1858, when in a fair election Kansas settlers decisively rejected the proslavery Lecompton constitution, some pronounced slavery a dead issue and urged their party "to quit the everlasting cry about negroes, Bleeding Kansas, etc." Mossbacks like Corwin, distressed at the lingering effects of the Panic of 1857, carped that people had let the country "go to the dogs, economically" while they fought over the Negro. Especially in the Middle states, the late 1850s found business-oriented Republicans arguing the conservatism of their party on the slavery question and seeking to focus attention on other issues, particularly the tariff.[33]

Conservatives were by no means the only Republicans to boast of their party's responsibility and restraint or to pose as the champions of free white labor. Political expediency, if nothing else, forced all factions to reckon with popular prejudices—in particular, to deny Democratic charges that Republicans were prepared to sacrifice the stability of the Union and the rights and interests of white men in a reckless crusade for Negro freedom. Nationwide veneration of the Constitution and deep attachment to the federal Union—refreshed annually by Fourth of July oratory and daily by the infinite interaction of an increasingly mobile and business-minded people—demanded reassurances from all Republicans of their basically conservative intent, of their de-

---

[32] June 20, 1860. See also *Galena Weekly Northwestern Gazette*, Jan. 10, 1860; J. B. Turner to Richard Yates, [1856], Yates Papers.
[33] S. J. Watson to George W. Julian, July 23, 1860 (quoting a speech of Davie Kilgore in Muncie, Ind.), Giddings-Julian Papers; Daryl Pendergraft, "Thomas Corwin and the Conservative Republican Reaction, 1858-1861," *Ohio State Archae ological and Historical Quarterly*, LVII, No. 1 (Jan. 1948), 1-23. For an extended account of the ideology of conservative Republicans, see Foner, *Free Soil, Free Labor, Free Men*, 186-205.

termination to abide by the compromises of the Constitution.[34] So too, deep and widespread racial prejudice made it politically imperative that, when vindicating the basic civil rights of blacks, Republicans not overlook the rights of whites. "This may be a narrow and illiberal prejudice," the *New York Post* remarked; "it may work a foul injustice to the colored class; nevertheless the prejudice exists, and while it exists it is idle to attempt to organize a national party based exclusively or principally upon sympathy with African blood."[35]

Once again, therefore, Republican editors (like Liberty and Free Soil publicists earlier) cranked out reams of copy, and party orators shouted hundreds of speeches, underscoring the white man's stake in slavery restriction. Once again Republican opinion-makers drew invidious comparisons between prosperous Vermont and benighted, decaying Virginia; once again slavery's degrading effect upon free labor was spelled out in full. "Regardless of the moral bearings of this [Kansas] question," Horace Greeley editorialized, "—of opening a market for the sale of tens of millions of human beings with immortal souls—for their sale at the auction block like hogs or sheep, and their doom to toil, like beasts of the field, without reward—look at the economical aspect. The food, raiment, and shelter of a Southern slave costs less than $30 a year. Northern freemen, can you ever compete with labor paid at this rate?"[36]

Though pitched at self-interested whites, these remarks nonetheless reveal a sensitivity to slavery's moral dimension and an implicit determination to harry the institution from the land. Indeed, most other Republicans—notwithstanding their solicitude for Northern rights and their disclaimers of aggressive designs against the South—shared Greeley's deep repugnance for slavery. And, like him, most desired to do all that was constitutionally possible not only to close it off but to help it to an early grave. Abraham Lincoln doubtless went too far

[34] For representative statements in this vein, see *New-York Daily Tribune*, Dec. 20, 1856, Aug. 21, 1858, Feb. 11, 1860; Salter, *Grimes*, 49-50; *Chicago Daily Tribune*, Sept. 29, 1857; *Illinois State Journal*, July 28, 1858; Richard Henry Dana, Jr., to John G. Palfrey, Dec. 4, 1859, Palfrey Papers; Samuel H. Hammond, *Speech of the Hon. S. H. Hammond, of the 27th Senate District [of New York], on the Governor's Message* (Albany, 1860), 13; *Dover Enquirer*, Feb. 21, 1861.
[35] *New York Evening Post*, Apr. 14, 1857.
[36] *New-York Daily Tribune*, Nov. 3, 1856. See also *ibid.* Dec. 20, 1856, Dec. 17, 1860; *National Era*, Sept. 13, 1855; *Chicago Daily Tribune*, Feb. 21, June 2, 1857; W. B. Thrak [?] to Benjamin F. Wade, Aug. 5, 1856, Wade Papers.

when he accused Douglas Democrats of utter indifference to the injustice of human bondage. But he displayed a shrewd understanding of his own party when he boasted: "Now, I confess myself as belonging to that class in the country who contemplate slavery as a moral, social and political evil, having due regard for its actual existence amongst us and the difficulties of getting rid of it in any satisfactory way, and to all the constitutional obligations which have been thrown about it; but, nevertheless, desire a policy that looks to the prevention of it as a wrong, and looks hopefully to the time when as a wrong it may come to an end."[37]

As one might expect, the old Liberty and Free Soil guard thundered loudest against the immorality of slavery and insisted most strongly that universal emancipation was the Republican party's goal. In Congress such veteran political abolitionists as Charles Sumner, Henry Wilson, John P. Hale, Joshua Giddings, Owen Lovejoy, Charles Durkee, and John Fox Potter stung Southern representatives to fury with violent attacks on the evil of slavery and prayers for its early demise. "Barbarous in origin," snapped Sumner, in the most bitter of all such speeches; "barbarous in its law; barbarous in all its pretensions; barbarous in the instruments it employs; barbarous in consequences; barbarous in spirit; barbarous wherever it shows itself, Slavery must breed Barbarians."[38] Only slightly less blistering and morally charged were the speeches of former Whig radicals like Benjamin F. Wade, Thaddeus Stevens, Zachariah Chandler, and, at times, William H. Seward. So commonplace had political abolitionism become, that in 1855 Giddings closed a letter describing his latest speech with an offhand admission that "the time has gone bye when a good speech on slavery is to attract attention. There are so many of them now made by others that no man can distinguish himself in that way."[39]

Outside Washington radical Republicans felt even freer to excoriate slavery's wickedness and demand a program for its reduction. "Should we here [in Congress] use words that some of our friends use at home," Henry Wilson explained to an impatient Theodore Parker, "we should play into the hands of our enemies. . . ." Back home such trammels, while not wholly absent, counted for less, and Republican antislavery

[37] Lincoln's reply to Douglas at Galesburg, Ill., Oct. 7, 1858, Basler (ed.), *Works of Lincoln*, III, 225-26.
[38] Quoted in Donald, *Sumner*, 354.
[39] Giddings to Molly Giddings, Jan. 12, 1855, Giddings-Julian Papers.

pronouncements at times bore a strikingly—critics said fanatically—radical aspect. "American Slavery," asserted New Hampshire's leading Republican newspaper, "is an atrocious outrage upon the natural and inalienable rights of man. It can no more be justified upon ethical or christian principles, than can widow-burning or cannibalism." The Galesburg, Illinois *Free Democrat* blasted the institution as "one of the worst evils that ever afflicted humanity, . . . a great injury to man and a sin against God." While disavowing unconstitutional tactics, square-jawed Owen Lovejoy told a party convention at Joliet in June 1858: "For myself, I hate slavery with a deathless and earnest hatred, and would see it exterminated, as some time by some means it must be."[40]

Even the *New York Post,* normally more solicitous of white interests, at times assailed the inhumanity of bondage itself. Responding to articles in the Democratic *Boston Courier* which alleged that Southern slaves were treated with greater kindness and familiarity than were free Negroes in the North, the *Post* conceded the beneficence of many masters. But, it went on, "the impunity with which cruelties may be practiced on the slave, and the absence of any wholesome check on the excesses of passion, place the whites under frequent temptations to treat their negroes as no other human being should ever treat another." Besides, "convenience and interest" frequently led to such enormities as the "selling [of] children from the arms of their parents, and breaking up [of] marriages with as little ceremony as they would sell an ox from his mate." These, plus the "frightful immoralities" endemic to plantation life, were the bitter fruit of slavery.[41]

Radical Republicans were equally forthright concerning the emancipationist aims of their party. Non-extension, they made plain, was but the first step in a comprehensive, perfectly constitutional battle plan for "the destruction of slavery the world over." A very few, indeed, contemplated even more extreme action—abolition in the states by action of the federal government.[42] Many more were ready if need

[40] Wilson to Parker, Feb. 28, 1858, Letterbook, Parker Papers; *Independent Democrat,* Jan. 19, 1860; *Galesburg Free Democrat,* Sept. 29, 1854; Magdol, *Lovejoy,* 203.
[41] *New York Evening Post,* July 28, 1859.
[42] C. S. Seldon, editor of the *Galesburg Free Democrat* and a man of open abolitionist sympathies, editorialized on June 7, 1855: "Individually we are willing to go as far in opposition to American Slavery as any man—even to the abolition of it in all the States by action of the Federal Government, but at the same time we are willing to reach that point step by step." Two months later (Aug. 9, 1855), however, he sounded a more cautious, characteristically Republican note: "Slavery is a

be to risk disunion in order to speed the annihilation of slavery. Ben
Wade, for one, exclaimed as early as 1854: "I go for the death of Slavery, whether the Union survive it or not. With me the Rubicon is
past. . . ." Most, of course, hoped desperately to avoid a splintering of
the Union, and nearly all insisted that the campaign against slavery be
waged within constitutional bounds. But Republican radicals made no
secret of their determination to destroy "the infernal institution in the
shortest time."[43]

More moderate Republicans—men like William Pitt Fessenden, Samuel Bowles, Edwin D. Morgan, John Sherman, Caleb Smith, and Abraham Lincoln—exhibited greater patience, greater reverence for the
Union and the Republican party as ends in themselves, and less cru-
sading zeal than did their radical colleagues. Yet on the whole they
shared the radicals' hatred of slavery as well as the Slave Power and
viewed the destruction of both as the prime task of their party. Ohio's
Congressman (soon to be Senator) John Sherman stated the moderate
position on slavery as concisely as anyone in a letter to Lydia Maria
Child in February 1860. In response to the abolitionist's entreaty that
he and others of his party more boldly exert the moral power of antislavery, Sherman answered that "A chronic disease, which has been the
growth of centuries, cannot be cured in a day or a generation." But, he
maintained, the Republican non-extension policy would produce "the
gradual and peaceful, but eventually certain eradication of this great
social and political evil. . . ." Once slavery was shut in upon itself,
time would work the cure. "It will do so," he insisted, "slowly but
surely; not by violence and bloodshed, but by the operation of natural
causes, the promptings of self interest, and the enlightened dictates of a
true Christian philanthropy." Mrs. Child must have been less than ec-
static at this response. Yet it reveals just the same a sincere, if infinitely
patient, commitment to *emancipation* which was strong enough to hold
moderate Republicans to their more radical brethren—and, to an extent,
to the Lydia Childs as well.[44]

State institution, and Congress has, perhaps, no power to interfere with it there—
at least, not one voter in one hundred in the North will concede to it such power."
[43] Both quotations are from Wade to [Milton Sutliff], Apr. 21, 1854, Sutliff Papers.
See also George W. Julian to Thomas Wentworth Higginson, Oct. 24, 1857
(copy), Giddings-Julian Papers. For the radical Republicans' attitude toward the
Union, see Foner, *Free Soil, Free Labor, Free Men*, 139-41.
[44] *Ibid.* 205-25; Child to Sherman, Dec. 13, 1859, Sherman to Child, Feb. 8, 1860
(copy), Sherman Papers.

4

As Congressman Sherman indicated, the confinement of slavery within
present bounds was the constitutional remedy most often prescribed by
Republican politicians. Even those who envisioned more aggressive
measures later, recognized that non-extension was a logical and effective way to begin the work of abolition—that, as one California Republican put it, "it is time enough to carry the war into *Africa,* when we
have checked the march of Hannibal in *Rome.*" Many Northerners
conceded Congress' power to abolish slavery in the territories, Salmon
Chase reminded Theodore Parker, but precious few believed that such
power extended to the states. That being so, a practical reformer would
take hold where prospects of success were greatest. "Let us," recommended Horace Greeley, with reference to the repeal of the Missouri
restriction, "make our platform so broad and liberal that all who stand
for Public Faith may come to the aid of those whose animating purpose
is the extension of Freedom; and let us by proving our capacity to win
one victory, open the way for winning many more."[45]
In explaining non-extension's potential for abolition in states as well
as territories, Republicans reiterated long-familiar arguments. Slavery's
wastefulness, its exhaustion of the soil, its potentiality for insurrections
as concentration of blacks increased, all indicated that only by expand-
ing into fresh lands could the institution survive. Its staunchest defenders admitted as much. The upper South, especially, depended upon
slavery expansion to sustain the trade in surplus slaves which alone
made bondage profitable to Delaware, Maryland, and Virginia.[46] Moreover, Republicans contended, by forbidding slavery in the territories
Congress would stigmatize the institution everywhere, thus adding to
the moral burdens of an already beleaguered South. "There is no doubt
that every inch of ground preserved from slavery is an everlastingly
eloquent and inflammatory argument against slavery," the *New York
Post* observed during the 1860 campaign; "there is no doubt that the

[45] Cornelius Cole to William H. Seward, May 3, 1856, Seward Papers; Chase to
Parker, July 17, 1856, Letterbook, Parker Papers; Greeley to William M. Chace
et al., May 9, 1856 (copy), Greeley Papers.
[46] *Independent Democrat,* July 24, 1856, May 12, 1859; *Lansing State Republican,*
Mar. 3, 1857; *New-York Daily Tribune,* May 16, 1857, Apr. 8, 1859; *New York
Evening Post,* Nov. 15, 1858; *National Era,* Jan. 27, 1859.

election of Lincoln to the Presidency will put all states of the Union upon the inquiry whether slave labor is, on the whole, as profitable in any sense of the word or anywhere as free labor, and the conviction that it is not may be so general and so deep that abolition doctrines may become as rife and as irresistible before many years in the slave states, as they now are in Massachusetts or Michigan."[47]

In one way only did Republicans significantly modify earlier arguments in favor of slavery restriction. Whereas Liberty men and Free Soilers had usually glossed over the likelihood that non-extension would work its abolition magic only very slowly, Republicans at times made a positive virtue of that fact. It was in the interest of all concerned—blacks as well as whites—that the overthrow of so long and deeply entrenched an institution as slavery proceed gradually. Not only did Southern whites deserve time to prepare for so radical an alteration of their social and economic system, it was said, but the slaves themselves would benefit from prior instruction in the responsibilities of freedom. Non-extension, by stimulating *voluntary* abolition within the South, would provide the time and necessary inducements for an orderly transition from slavery to freedom.[48]

For some Republicans, slavery restriction seemed all that was wise or necessary. However, for many more (moderates, to some extent, as well as radicals) it represented but one aspect of a more general plan to cripple and destroy slavery by attacking it wherever Congress possessed the constitutional power to do so. As Salmon Chase explained to a receptive Joshua Giddings:

> My idea is this: Let those who are prepared to do so take the ground of no Slavery outside of Slave States & no favor of the National Government to Slavery anywhere; boldly avowing that we expect as the consequence of such action that slavery will be abolished every where . . . by the State Governments. Let us get rid of that cold indifference to Slavery as a system which some of our prominent men seem so anxious to display. Let us condemn it as it deserves to be condemned every where, & insist that every obligation of duty, patriotism & honor binds us against

[47] Sept. 26, 1860. See also *Indiana True Republican*, Dec. 2, 1858.
[48] See, e.g., *Chicago Daily Tribune*, Aug. 3, Sept. 29, 1857; *Weekly Chicago Press & Tribune*, Nov. 3, 1859; *National Era*, Sept. 18, 1856. Abraham Lincoln approvingly observed in 1858: "I do not suppose that in the most peaceful way ultimate extinction would occur in less than a hundred years at least. . . ." Basler (ed.), *Works of Lincoln*, III, 181.

any allowance of it where we are politically responsible for it; which is every where outside of those states; & to protest against it & by moral means seek its overthrow wherever we are morally responsible for it, & that is every where that our influence can reach.[49]

Although not always in perfect agreement among themselves, advocates of the "denationalization" of slavery spelled out in some detail what such a policy might mean. In addition to the exclusion of slavery from all territories—present and future—radical spokesmen called for abolition in the District of Columbia and on the high seas, an end to the interstate slave trade, a ban on new slave states, and repeal or drastic modification of the Fugitive Slave Law. All such federal props as the use of the Army and Navy to capture runaway slaves would be promptly dismantled. Republican postmasters would protect the free flow of mail to the South—including, presumably, antislavery literature. Deprived of special favor, turned in upon itself, subjected to constant moral agitation from without, slavery would wither and die.[50]

But would Southerners acquiesce in such a catastrophic design? Would those who now lustily praised slavery as a positive good, as the cornerstone of a superior civilization, meekly submit to coercion from without—constitutional or otherwise—and voluntarily, if grudgingly, become the agents of emancipation? However improbable it may seem in hindsight, most Republicans apparently gave affirmative answers to these questions—when, indeed, they bothered to ask them at all—down to the very moment when secession began. Two weeks after Lincoln's election as President, less than a month before South Carolina dissolved its ties to the Union, the *Lansing State Republican* forecast that the patriotic masses of the South would soon recognize "that the principles of the Republican party are politically right, and soundly National."[51]

[49] Chase to Giddings, Jan. 7, 1857, Giddings Papers. See also Chase to John Sherman, May 6, 1858, Sherman Papers; Giddings's speech to U.S. House of Representatives, Jan. 12, 1859, *Cong. Globe*, 35th Cong., 2nd sess., 343-46.
[50] *Galesburg Free Democrat*, Jan. 3, 1854, June 7, 1855; Columbus *Ohio Columbian*, Feb. 21, 1855; speech of Henry Wilson in New York City, May 8, 1855, quoted in *New York Evening Post*, May 9, 1855; Salmon P. Chase to Theodore Parker, Mar. 25, 1858, Letterbook, Parker Papers; *New-York Daily Tribune*, Dec. 4, 1858; *Sycamore True Republican*, Mar. 8, 1858; *National Era*, Jan. 27, 1859; *Lansing State Republican*, Sept. 11, 1855, Nov. 7, 1860.
[51] *Ibid.* Nov. 21, 1860.

Republican hopes for the South rested chiefly on the region's slaveless white majority. Cognizant of the fact that almost three-quarters of
all free Southerners owned no slaves at all, and that half of all slave
owners held fewer than five, Republicans blithely assumed that there
was a reservoir of antislavery feeling in the South just waiting to be
tapped. A grave miscalculation, to be sure, but one which was perfectly understandable—almost inevitable—given Republican ideology.
For not only did the Republicans' own enchantment with free labor
doctrines blind them to contrary views in a society fearful of the consequences of emancipation, but having for years preached of a Slave
Power *conspiracy* against freedom it was all too easy for them to believe that once the plot had been unmasked and the planter oligarchs
exposed as the selfish tyrants they were, slaveless yeomen would join in
the battle against class oppression.

At all events, Republicans in the 1850s expected the actual work of
emancipation to proceed peacefully, through the operation of state Republican parties in the South. The first step would be to break the
planter aristocrats' hold over the Southern masses. Then, once channels
of discussion were open, the fight against slavery itself might begin.
Progress might be slow, but it would be irresistible. Like its Northern
branch, Theodore Parker predicted in 1859, the Republican party of
the South would "go through changes like a Caterpillar and come out
winged and handsome as a Butterfly at the end."[52]

The Liberty and Free Soil parties had also looked to a day when the
"natural" antislavery sentiment of Southern yeomen would assert itself, but except for encouragement to and through Cassius M. Clay's
Lexington *True American* and John C. Vaughan's *Louisville Examiner*
(which ably promoted emancipation in Kentucky in the late 1840s)
they advanced no plan to mobilize it.[53] Republicans, on the other hand,
developed a number of schemes designed to win free labor recruits in
the South. Of these easily the most quixotic was the attempt of Eli
Thayer and John C. Underwood to establish a Republican beachhead
in western Virginia. By colonizing the Old Dominion with enterprising

[52] Parker to Francis Jackson, Sept. 13, 1859, Letterbook, Parker Papers. See also
Galesburg Free Democrat, July 26, 1856; *National Era*, Aug. 7, 1856; *New York
Evening Post*, Nov. 7, 1856; Salmon P. Chase to [Theodore Parker], July 17,
1856 (copy), Chase Papers, PHS.
[53] David L. Smiley, *Lion of White Hall: The Life of Cassius M. Clay* (Madison,
1962), 80-106, 115; *Louisville Examiner*, June 19, 1847–Mar. 3, 1849.

Northern immigrants they hoped to demonstrate convincingly the superiority of free labor to slave labor—"filling our valleys with arts and
manufactures and doubling the value of our lands," trilled Underwood,
". . . making our hillsides smile with plenteous beauty and our deserts
blossom like the rose, converting our grog shops into school houses and
temples for the worship of Almighty God."[54]

To realize this grandiose dream, Thayer and Underwood, in May
1857, organized the American Emigrant Aid and Homestead Company.[55] Thayer, a conservative Republican Congressman from Massachusetts whose New England Emigrant Aid Company had sponsored
antislavery imperialism in Kansas, was elected president; Underwood, a
transplanted New Yorker (once a Liberty party candidate for Congress) who had for a decade made Virginia his home, became secretary. With the backing of several prominent New York businessmen—
all apparently more intent on profits than on antislavery—and with
encouragement from much of the Republican press, Thayer, Underwood & Co. began the work of colonization. Their plan called for the
purchase of cheap Virginia lands, a quarter of which would be given
away, in town lots or small farms, to industrious workers and husband-
men from Northern states or from Europe. Once this first wave of pioneers had, with the company's assistance, established factories and
farms, schools and churches, another quarter of the lands would be
sold at cost. In time, it was hoped, the remaining half of the company's
holdings could be sold at a handsome profit to men and women attracted by the obvious prosperity of these progressive new communities. Thus might Thayer, Underwood and associates do well by doing
good.

At first all went surprisingly well. In the spring of 1857 the company
purchased a large tract in western Virginia, along the Ohio River.
Thayer christened it Ceredo, after Ceres, the goddess of grain. During
the summer a town was born, as eager settlers threw up homes, stores,
a school, a church, a newspaper, and various small industries. By the

[54] Underwood to Samuel M. Janney, Aug. 9, 1857, quoted in Patricia Hickin,
"John C. Underwood and the Antislavery Movement in Virginia, 1847-1860,"
Virginia Magazine of History and Biography, LXXIII, No. 2 (Apr. 1965), 162.
[55] The following account of Northern colonization in Virginia rests chiefly on
Hickin, "John C. Underwood," and George W. Smith "Ante-Bellum Attempts
of Northern Business Interests to 'Redeem' the Upper South," *Journal of Southern
History*, XI, No. 2 (May 1945), 177-213.

end of 1858 Underwood boasted (perhaps hyperbolically) that the company had established free labor colonies in ten or twelve Virginia counties, with a population "nearer five thousand than five hundred." Land values in Ceredo had doubled, he claimed, and in addition to the *Wheeling Intelligencer* three other "good sound Republican weeklies" had begun publication in western Virginia—all preaching the disadvantages of slavery and asserting the rights of non-slaveholders. If properly supported, Underwood confidently proclaimed, such efforts would swiftly "revolutionize public sentiment in all border states."[56]

Yet whatever its initial promise, the Thayer-Underwood project soon came on hard times. The effects of the Panic of 1857, rifts within the company, and rising local resentment against what the *Richmond Enquirer* called "the Abolition Plot Against Virginia"—especially after John Brown's raid on Harpers Ferry in 1859—all helped to blight the venture. In 1860 Republican settlements in Virginia could muster fewer than 2000 votes for Lincoln, and during the Civil War Confederate sympathizers ransacked Ceredo. War's end found only 175 colonists still hanging on. To be sure, seeds had been planted which, in a small way, contributed to independence in 1863 for the new, Republican state of West Virginia. As a peaceful solution to the slavery question, however, and as a business enterprise, the free labor experiment never really had a chance.

Another Republican approach to the problem of winning support from slaveless Southern whites was to persuade them that emancipation would end the competition of black (slave) labor without danger of black equality. Especially in the upper South, Republicans stressed the economic benefits of abolition and sought ways to allay fears of its racial consequences. The influential Blair family was especially insistent on this point. In letters, pamphlets, and speeches, Francis P. Blair and his sons Frank, a Congressman from Missouri, and Montgomery, a distinguished Maryland attorney and counsel for Dred Scott, contended that the Republican party should promise not only free homesteads in the West, but also the colonization of free blacks in Central America. For, the elder Blair argued, "unless northern men make it plain by the whole tenor of their course on the subject of slavery that they aim at the deliverance of their own blood, not the african, from the mischief slavery entails on the country, they will find that every

[56] Underwood to William H. Seward, Nov. 12, 1858, Seward Papers.

non slaveholder is but an enlisted soldier to fight the battles of slave-holders & nullifyers. . . ." If, on the other hand, Northern Congress-men coupled gradual emancipation with the prompt removal of free Negroes from the country, "the whole yeomanry of the South" would join in putting down the "oligarchy of masters" which had so long op-pressed them.[57]

Not all Republicans, by any means, shared the Blairs' passion for col-onization.[58] But most shared their desire to win the support of Southern yeomen, and even some radicals conceded the expediency, if not the propriety, of appeals to poor white interests. For, as one abolitionist editor noted, "though it is better to put away evil upon righteous than upon selfish principles, yet it is better to put it away through any mo-tives than to persist in its practice."[59]

Most famously, of course, Republicans sought to build a following in the South by exploiting the appeal of Hinton Rowan Helper's *The Im-pending Crisis*. Himself a negrophobic store clerk and small farmer from backcountry North Carolina, Helper dedicated his book (published in June 1857) to "THE NON-SLAVEHOLDING WHITES OF THE SOUTH." His purpose, he announced, was neither to vilify masters nor to glorify blacks, but simply to demonstrate slavery's deadening effect upon South-ern economic life. "Yankee wives" had given "the fictions of slavery; men should give the facts." Armed with history books and census re-ports, Helper proceeded for some 420 pages to air "the facts" in a way that powerfully affirmed the superiority of free labor to slave labor sys-tems. By virtually every conceivable index, he argued—imports and ex-ports; land and crop values; manufacturing output; per capita wealth; investment in railroads and canals; patents on inventions; school attend-ance; number of post offices, libraries, newspapers, and churches; literary achievement—the North far outstripped the South. Only by abolishing the peculiar institution, which made slaves of poor whites as well as of blacks, could the South be saved "from falling into the vortex of utter ruin." To stimulate emancipation, Helper proposed (among other steps in a detailed eleven-point program) a stiff tax on all slaves, the returns to be used to subsidize the removal of freedmen to Africa, Cen-

[57] Francis P. Blair, Sr., to F. P. Blair, Jr., Jan. 20, Feb. 5, Mar. 19, 1857, Blair Family Papers; William E. Smith, *The Francis Preston Blair Family in Politics*, 2 vols. (New York, 1933), I, 371-73, 443-52.
[58] See below, p. 332.
[59] *Galesburg Free Democrat*, Aug. 26, 1857.

318 BALLOTS FOR FREEDOM

tral America, or some "Comfortable Settlement" in the United States.[60]

Southern frenzy against Helper's "incendiary" tract (anyone caught circulating the book in North Carolina faced a public whipping and a year in jail for the first offense, and hanging if caught a second time), was matched by Republican delight at having found such impressive corroboration of their faith. Horace Greeley was the first to recognize the propaganda value of Helper's book. Lengthy and glowing reviews in the *New-York Tribune*, and puffs in other Northern journals as various as *Hunt's Merchant Magazine and Commercial Review* and the *National Anti-Slavery Standard* soon netted a sale of 13,000 copies. Before long, with the aid of endorsements from sixty-eight of the ninety-two Republican members of the House of Representatives and the financial assistance of such party notables as Greeley, Thurlow Weed, and Governor Edwin D. Morgan of New York, Helper had produced an abridgment (*The Compendium of the Impending Crisis of the South*), perhaps 100,000 copies of which Republicans distributed as campaign documents in 1859 and 1860. In the event, Helper's writings were used most extensively among Democrats in the southernmost tier of *free* states. Censorship, suppression, illiteracy, and the poor whites' stake in slavery as an instrument of white supremacy and racial control all stifled Helper's appeal in the South. Yet to Republicans the very fact that so few in his intended audience could or wished to read his polemic gave it a kind of ironic validation.[61]

Of all the slave states, Republicans looked upon Missouri as the most likely to succumb to antislavery pressures from within and without. One sign of the institution's frailty in that state was a relative drop in the number of slaves. While Missouri's white population more than trebled between 1840 and 1860, its slave population failed to double. What most encouraged Republicans, however, was the emergence in the mid-1850s of a full-blown antislavery movement—one which stressed the interests of white laborers and preached the need for black emigration, but which pressed for a program of gradual emancipation

[60] Hinton Rowan Helper, *The Impending Crisis of the South: How to Meet It* (New York, 1857). The second edition of this work, published in 1860, and the abridged version, printed as a Republican campaign document, revealed a somewhat less radical tone than the original. The basic argument, however, remained the same. For a recent critique of that argument, see Fogel and Engerman, *Time on the Cross,* esp. 163-69.
[61] Hugh C. Bailey, *Hinton Rowan Helper: Abolitionist-Racist* (Montgomery, Ala., 1965), 41-60.

at home as well as a ban on slavery in the territories. Led by Frank Blair, Jr., and B. Gratz Brown, editor of the St. Louis *Missouri Democrat*, Missouri emancipationists displayed a growing radicalism which Northern Republicans found particularly heartening.[62]

Brown's speech to the Missouri legislature in February 1857 anticipated many of Hinton Helper's arguments. Like Helper, Brown set aside humanitarian appeals to end slavery as "impotent." Besides, he explained, his concern was "not so much the mere emancipation of the black race, as it is . . . THE EMANCIPATION OF THE WHITE RACE. I seek to emancipate the white man from the yoke of competition with the negro." The gradual destruction of slavery, Brown maintained, coupled with the removal of all freedmen from the state, would encourage white immigration, foster trade and commerce, benefit railroad and mining interests, and enhance the value of Missouri lands. Already, he warned, the writing was on the wall. The 1856 state census revealed that in only twelve of Missouri's 107 counties was slavery holding its own. Elsewhere the institution was clearly on the wane: 25 counties reported an actual decrease in slave population since 1851 and the rest showed whites far outstripping blacks. It would be pointless as well as shortsighted to resist so inexorable a drift.[63]

Equally cheering to Northern Republicans were the occasional successes of Missouri emancipationists. Proslavery forces still commanded too much strength to make feasible the creation of a Frémont ticket in 1856, but Frank Blair won election to Congress that year as a Free Soil Democrat. Already, in fact, Blair and Brown were quietly working toward the formation of a Republican party in Missouri. In 1857 James S. Rollins, running on a free labor platform, came within 300 votes of winning the governorship, and both that year and the next St. Louis elected antislavery mayors. These were small beginnings, but Republicans in other states attended them with interest and concern. For if slavery could peacefully be swept from one state, the example would encourage similar movements elsewhere. "The redemption of Missouri

[62] Perry McCandless, *A History of Missouri, 1820 to 1860* (Columbia, Mo., 1972), 277-88; Smith, *Blair Family*, I, 373-75, 400-403, 415-17, 429, 439-43; Allan Nevins, *The Emergence of Lincoln*, 2 vols. (New York, 1950), I, 164, II, 149-51; *National Era*, Apr. 5, 1855; *Galesburg Free Democrat*, Feb. 21, 1856; *Chicago Daily Tribune*, Feb. 17, 1857.
[63] *Speech of the Hon. B. Gratz Brown, of St. Louis on the Subject of Gradual Emancipation in Missouri* (St. Louis, 1857), 5, 7-13, 25.

is the great turning point of the battle for Free Labor," William Seward remarked in 1858. "The rescue of Kansas was only carrying an out-post. The State of Missouri is the castle of St. Juan d'Ulloa. When this shall fall, we have an easy conquest."[64] Whether, or when, Republicans could have carried Missouri had the Civil War not intervened is, of course, a moot point. It is worth noting, however, that in 1860 Abraham Lincoln polled over 17,000 votes in Missouri—more than half the vote for Breckenridge and nearly a third of that for Douglas and Bell.

[64] Seward to James W. Webb, Oct. 1, 1858, Seward Papers. See also *Galesburg Free Democrat*, Mar. 5, 1847; *Sycamore True Republican*, Mar. 8, 1859.

13

"Black Republicans"

As THE PLANS OF HELPER, the Blairs, and Gratz Brown made clear, there was unquestionably a racist side to prewar Republicanism. Moreover, such bigotry was by no means confined to Border state Republicans. Particularly in the lower Middle West (south of the National Road) and among former Democrats, Republicans might easily be found who viewed all blacks with callous indifference or outright hostility. Abraham Lincoln's renowned repertoire of jokes and anecdotes included many which demeaned blacks, including a coarse "story of the old Virginian strapping his razor on a certain member of a young negro's body. . . ." The epithet "nigger" fell as easily from the lips of Lincoln's law partner, Billy Herndon, as from any planter, and Ben Wade, in summing up his first impressions of Washington, groused: "On the whole it is a mean God forsaken Nigger riden [sic] place. The Niggers are certainly the most intelligent part of the population but the Nigger smell I cannot bear, yet it is in on and about every thing you see."[1]

[1] Benjamin Quarles, *Lincoln and the Negro* (New York, 1962), 39-40; Herndon to Lyman Trumbull, May 20, June 16, July 12, 1856, Trumbull Papers; Wade to Mrs. Wade, Dec. 29, 1851, Wade Papers. Lincoln himself occasionally used the word "nigger," usually when paraphrasing remarks of Douglas or some other Democrat. Never, however, did Lincoln, Herndon, or, so far as I know, any Republican publicly indulge in such virulent racism as Douglas displayed during the 1858 debates, especially his sneers at "Lincoln's ally, . . . FRED. DOUGLASS, THE NEGRO." See Basler (ed.), *Works of Lincoln*, III, 20, 55-56, 171-72, 317; Don E. Fehrenbacher, "Only His Stepchildren: Lincoln and the Negro," *Civil War History*, XX, No. 4 (Dec. 1974), 293-310; George M. Fredrickson, "A Man but Not a Brother: Abraham Lincoln and Racial Equality," *Journal of Southern History*, XLI, No. 1 (Feb. 1975), 39-58.

Some sought to keep not only slaves but all blacks out of Western territories. Even radical Republicans often denied that their party favored full social and political equality for blacks. At best, the *Chicago Press & Tribune* pointed out, the Republican party's program for Negroes was negative and indirect: to curtail and slowly to suffocate slavery. Only with regard to *white* rights was its stand affirmative and constructive: free territories, free homesteads, internal improvements and tariff reform. Time and again Republicans proclaimed that theirs was "preeminently the white man's party."[2]

The Republicans' negrophobia showed most clearly when it came to social intercourse between the races. Seldom did they protest Jim Crow laws and customs which isolated and oppressed Northern Negroes. At times, in fact, they helped to buttress the walls of segregation. In 1857, for instance, Ohio Republicans passed a law excluding blacks from the state militia—a restriction in accord with long-standing practice, but one which opened their party to charges of hypocrisy. "Black Republicans regard the nigger as good enough to make political capital with," twitted the Democrats, "but consider his skin too black, nose too flat and heel too long to be permitted to unite with them in a corn stalk muster."[3]

Republicans also denounced the incessant Democratic slur that they intended an amalgamation of the races. Only the counterfeit logic which turned a horse-chestnut into a chestnut horse, Abraham Lincoln protested, could conclude "that, because I do not want a black woman for a *slave* I must necessarily want her for a *wife*."[4] Not only did they deny the charge, but Republicans turned it back upon their opponents. Slavery was the real fountainhead of miscegenation, they often insisted; the Democracy was the party of amalgamation. "In its ranks are half a million *fathers* of mulatto children," claimed the *Chicago Tribune*. "Nearly every Southern leader in that party, is a blood relation of negroes, either as parent, brother, uncle, or nephew. And the same may be said of the rank and file. . . . The Republicans, at most, only propose to improve the *political* condition of the blacks, but the Democracy insist on improving the breed. We submit to casuists which

[2] *Chicago Press & Tribune*, Feb. 25, 1860; *Illinois State Journal*, July 15, 1857.
[3] *Ohio Patriot*, quoted in *Athens Messenger*, June 26, 1857.
[4] Speech at Springfield, Ill., June 26, 1857, Basler (ed.), *Works of Lincoln*, II, 405.

party is most in favor of Negro Equality." Similarly, the *Illinois State Journal* seized upon one Democrat's taunt, "I would rather sleep with a nigger than a Republican," as proof that Douglasites endorsed racial mixing![5]

Even political equality was more than most Republicans were willing to accord Northern blacks. Lincoln had good company when he forthrightly opposed admitting blacks to the ranks of voters, jurors, or officeholders. Horace Greeley, himself an advocate of Negro enfranchisement, asserted that "the great body" of Western Republicans objected to equal suffrage, as did more than half of those in the East. Such sketchy evidence as there is would seem to bear Greeley out. In Republican-controlled Iowa, voters turned down a Negro suffrage amendment by a 6 to 1 margin in 1857. In New York, a Republican-sponsored attempt to repeal the state's discriminatory voting law met a similar fate in 1860. Although aware of the united opposition of "drunken Irishmen, and ignorant Dutchmen, controlled by sham Democrats," Frederick Douglass refused to absolve Republicans of blame for the defeat. "Had the Republican party been as true to the sacred cause of liberty and equality, as the Democratic party always proves itself to slavery and oppression," he declared, "the invidious and odious discrimination against our equal citizenship would have been blotted out. . . ." Instead, the hullaballoo for Lincoln and Hamlin had drowned out the black man's plea, and though the Republican ticket carried New York, equal suffrage suffered a decisive setback. "The black baby of Negro Suffrage was thought too ugly to exhibit on so grand an occasion," Douglass remarked bitterly.[6]

A fair number of Republicans—again chiefly from the Border states and Middle West—doubted the wisdom or feasibility of racial integration on any terms and supported attempts to colonize Negroes abroad. Republican interest in so drastic a solution to racial problems reflected a widespread revival of colonization sentiment in the 1850s. "Romantic racialists" like Harriet Beecher Stowe and Henry Ward Beecher, pessimistic abolitionists like James G. Birney, frustrated Northern Ne-

---

[5] *Chicago Daily Tribune*, Sept. 1, 1857; *Illinois State Journal*, Oct. 20, 1858.
[6] Lincoln's debate with Douglas at Charleston, Ill., Sept. 18, 1858, Basler (ed.), *Works of Lincoln*, III, 145; *New-York Daily Tribune*, Sept. 26, 1857, Jan. 1, 1859; Berwanger, *Frontier Against Slavery*, 41-42; Foner, *Writings of Douglass*, II, 525, 530-32.

groes like Martin R. Delany, and crusty conservatives like William Henry Ruffin all joined Republican colonizationists in promoting black expatriation.[7]

Among Republicans, colonization's chief theoretician was Frank Blair, Jr. Heeding the advice of his distinguished father, who told him he might become famous by taking the colonization lead, young Frank not only devoted his maiden address in Congress to that theme, but circulated literature, buttonholed politicians, and crisscrossed the North preaching the virtues of a peaceful separation of the races. "Whether as a slave or a free man," Blair argued, "the presence of multitudes of the black race is found to be fatal to the interests of our race; their antagonism is as strong as that of oil and water, and so long as no convenient outlet, through which the manumitted slave can reach a congenial climate and country willing to receive him, is afforded, the institution of slavery stands on compulsion." The solution, then, to the twin problems of slavery and race lay in the voluntary emigration of free Negroes, under federal auspices, to some tropical land. Blair preferred Central America (Honduras struck him as ideal) to Africa because it was closer—hence more conducive to the development of trade—and less barbarous, and because free black settlements there might serve as a barrier to Slave Power expansion.[8]

Blair's proposal outraged proslavery Democrats but found substantial favor within his own party. In the Senate, James R. Doolittle of Wisconsin introduced a resolution similar to Blair's and pressed upon fellow Republicans the need to nail a colonization plank into the party's platform. Not only was colonization politically advantageous, he maintained, but it was "right, humane, & the only true solution of the negro question."[9] Preston King was already on record in support of black expatriation, and Lyman Trumbull, Henry Wilson, and Benjamin

[7] Fredrickson, Black Image in the White Mind, 115-17, 147-48; William G. McLoughlin, The Meaning of Henry Ward Beecher: An Essay on the Shifting Values of Mid-Victorian America, 1840-1870 (New York, 1970), 198-99.
[8] Francis P. Blair, Sr., to F. P. Blair, Jr., Feb. 5, 17, June 19, 1857, Blair Family Papers; Cong. Globe, 35th Cong., 1st sess., 293-98 (Jan. 14, 1858); Frank P. Blair, Jr., The Destiny of the Races of this Continent (Washington, D.C., 1859); Frank P. Blair, Jr., Colonization and Commerce (n.p., 1859).
[9] Cong. Globe, 35th Cong., 1st sess., 3034 (June 14, 1859); Doolittle to Edwin D. Morgan, Jan. 29, 1860, Weed Papers. See also Doolittle to Thurlow Weed, Aug. 23, Sept. 6, 1859, Jan. 23, 1860, Weed Papers; Doolittle to John Fox Potter, July 25, 1859, Nov. 7, 1860, John Fox Potter Papers, SHSW; Doolittle to Mrs. Doolittle, Dec. 2, 1860, Charles C. Sholes to Doolittle, May 21, 1860, Doolittle Papers.

Wade soon lent their powerful voices to the cause. So too did Governors Dennison of Ohio, Bissell of Illinois, Kirkwood of Iowa, and Randall of Wisconsin, as well as such prominent Republican newspapers as the *Albany Evening Journal, The New York Times,* the *New York Evening Post,* the *National Era,* and the *Chicago Tribune.* Abraham Lincoln, likening American Negroes to the children of Israel who "went out of Egyptian bondage in a body," advocated transferring "the African to his native clime." Even so radical a political abolitionist as Gerrit Smith praised Blair as a "philanthropic, largehearted statesman," and approved his colonization scheme—provided that it remained entirely voluntary and in no way robbed blacks of self-respect.[10]

There was, as the support of idealists like Smith and even many Negroes revealed, a humanitarian side to the colonization movement of the 1850s. Except for Edward Bates, the Missouri conservative who believed that compulsion might be used as a last resort, nearly all Republican colonizationists insisted that blacks ought not be driven out against their will. Moreover, not only was colonization often justified as an antislavery measure (encouraging manumissions, blasting Southern dreams of a Caribbean slave empire), but Blair and others insisted that their aim was not further to oppress blacks but "to exalt the destiny of all the races of this continent." Only in a congenial tropical clime, free from the enmity and despotism of whites, might American Negroes find prosperity and true happiness.[11]

Yet for all that, colonization rested on the belief that blacks were not only different from but inferior to whites, and the language of many of its proponents was anything but benign. Blair himself spoke of the "sable race, bred in the pestilence of Africa," as "a blot on the fair prospect of our country." James Shepherd Pike, Washington correspondent of the *New-York Tribune,* bluntly proclaimed that "the ignorant

---

[10] Francis P. Blair, Sr., to F. P. Blair, Jr., Mar. 19, 1857, Blair Family Papers; Blair, Jr., *Destiny of the Races,* 29-38; *Cong. Globe,* 35th Cong., 1st sess., Appendix, 172-73 (Wilson), 36th Cong., 1st sess., 154-55 (Wade); William Dennison, Jr., to Benjamin F. Wade, Nov. 30, 1859, Feb. 6, Mar. 12, 1860, Wade Papers; Smith, *Blair Family in Politics,* I, 445-46; *Albany Evening Journal,* Aug. 29, 1859; *New York Times,* July 9, 1859; *New York Evening Post,* Jan. 19, 1858, Jan. 30, Sept. 26, 1860; *National Era,* Feb. 24, 1859; *Chicago Daily Tribune,* Dec. 4, 1860; Basler (ed.), *Works of Lincoln,* II, 409; Gerrit Smith to F. P. Blair, Jr., Apr. 7, 1858, Blair Family Papers.
[11] Marvin R. Cain, *Lincoln's Attorney General: Edward Bates of Missouri* (Columbia, Mo., 1963), 99-100; Blair, Jr., *Destiny of the Races,* 4. See also *New-York Daily Tribune,* Feb. 1, 1859.

and servile race will not and cannot be emancipated and raised to the enjoyment of equal civil rights with the dominant and intelligent race; they will be driven out." Senator Trumbull championed colonization in a speech studded with racist slurs.[12] And one of Ben Wade's correspondents cynically confided:

> . . . I like this new touch of colonizing the niggers. I believe practically it is a d—n humbug. But it will take with the people. Our creed runs into what the French call a *Cul de sac*, which I take to be a road with the end chopped off. If we are to have no more slave states what the devil are we to do with the surplus niggers?
> Your plan will help us out on this point. But practically I have not much faith in it. You could not raise twenty five cents from a Yankee to transplant a *nigger* to South America.[13]

There can be little question that the effect, if not the intent, of the Republican colonizationists' program was to strengthen the already prevalent notion that the United States was white man's country, that progress, prosperity—perhaps the Union itself—depended upon "sloughing off" American blacks.

Yet too much can be made of this racist element in the Republican party. For one thing, a belief in white superiority was nearly universal throughout the western world, and Republicans saw as clearly as anyone that political success depended upon some measure of accommodation to the reality of racism.[14] To set aside moral questions and concentrate on slavery's destructive effect upon *whites* was "a narrow method," the *Chicago Tribune* admitted in an editorial headlined "THE WHITE MAN'S PARTY." But, it went on, "so inveterate are the prejudices of color; so deep rooted, even in the Slave States, is the conviction that the African is a being of an inferior order; . . . so low, under the depressing influence of 'the institution,' has the national morality de-

---

12 Blair, Jr., *Destiny of the Races*, 21; Robert F. Durden, *James Shepherd Pike: Republicanism and the American Negro, 1850-1882* (Durham, N.C., 1957), 32; Trumbull's speech at Chicago, Aug. 7, 1858, quoted in *National Era*, Sept. 2, 1858.
13 D. R. Tilden to Wade, Mar. 27, 1860, Wade Papers.
14 Aileen Kraditor notes that even Garrisonian abolitionists complemented their moral messages with appeals to white self-interest. E.g., she cites an essay by Ellis Gray Loring in the *Liberator* which attempted to show slavery's bearing on "the esteem in which labor was held, the prosperity of the Northern economy, the morals of the young, and the peace of the community." *Means and Ends in American Abolitionism*, 263-64n.

scended, that this method, narrow and incomplete as it is, holds out the only promise of success. We are not Jesuits to justify the use of bad means to accomplish a good end; but we can maintain that any combatant has the right to employ such weapons in his armory as he chooses."[15]

Invariably, moreover, Republican racist pronouncements palled beside the brutish negrophobia of Northern Democrats. Recurrent sneers of "nigger," a fondness for dialect quotes of illiterate blacks, contemptuous talk of the Negro's smell, his wide nose, thick lips, and woolly head—such were the stock-in-trade of a great many Democratic editors and politicians. They called Republicans the "nigger party," rank amalgamationists peddling a "Congo creed."[16] A few Northern Democrats went so far as to defend slavery itself. The day would come, predicted the *Dover* (N.H.) *Gazette,* when even "Black Republicans" would agree that slave labor was essential to the South, "that cotton, sugar, rice and tobacco fields, tilled by negroes under the guidance and control of superior intelligence, are better . . . than marshes and jungles inhabited by the alligator and the runaway nigger."[17] D. J. Van Deren, editor of the *Mattoon Gazette,* even advocated the reestablishment of slavery in Illinois.[18] That Republicans at times fought fire with fire—especially during election years—need come as no surprise.

What is surprising, perhaps—given the bigotry of the age—is that nearly all Republicans defended the Negro's manhood and insisted that he be accorded those inalienable rights set forth in the Declaration of Independence. Most would have agreed with Abraham Lincoln that there was a physical difference between whites and blacks which would "forever forbid the two races living together on terms of social and political equality." Yet most would also have agreed with him that "not withstanding all this, there is no reason in the world why the negro is not entitled to all the natural rights enumerated in the Dec-

[15] *Chicago Daily Tribune,* May 30, 1857.
[16] See, e.g., *Quincy* (Ill.) *Herald,* Sept. 22, 1856, and selections from Democratic newspapers in *Athens Messenger,* Oct. 9, 1857. There were, to be sure, exceptions. E.g., Edward L. Mayo, Democratic editor of the *DeKalb County Republican Sentinel,* scandalized Illinois Douglasites and many Republicans by contending that free Negroes "should enjoy all the privileges of the whites where they reside." See Sycamore *DeKalb County Republican Sentinel,* July 26, Aug. 9, Oct. 11, 1858; Sycamore *True Republican,* Aug. 3, 1858.
[17] Quoted in *Dover Enquirer,* June 30, 1859.
[18] *Chicago Daily Tribune,* Aug. 6, 1857; *Illinois State Journal,* Sept. 2, 1857.

laration of Independence, the right to life, liberty and the pursuit of happiness." He could agree with Senator Douglas, said Lincoln at Ottawa, that the Negro "is not my equal in many respects—certainly not in color, perhaps not in moral or intellectual endowment." But, he continued, "in the right to eat the bread, without leave of anybody else, which his own hand earns, *he is my equal and the equal of Judge Douglas, and the equal of every living man.* [Great applause.]"[19] To say, as Douglas did, that the Declaration was intended to include only white men and not "the whole human family," was to dehumanize the Negro and thereby not only "deny, or dwarf to insignificance, the wrong of his bondage," but "crush all sympathy for him, and cultivate and excite hatred and disgust against him. . . ."[20]

Republicans reacted with particular vehemence to Chief Justice Taney's Dred Scott pronouncement that Negroes, far from being citizens, had historically possessed "no rights which the white man was bound to respect." The New York City Nineteenth Ward Republican Association condemned this finding as "a most atrocious, inhuman and malignant stab at the happiness of a much wronged and still crushed and bleeding race." Maine Republican legislators asked for, and received, a court ruling upholding the right of Negroes to citizenship and suffrage in that state. In Wisconsin a Republican mass meeting held on June 17, 1857, called upon Congress to safeguard the rights of *all* Americans, "without regard to Birth, Creed or Color." If Taney's dictum were allowed to stand, the *Lansing State Republican* asked, what would prevent unprincipled whites from reducing every Negro to slavery? The Court's sorry legalization of the "prejudice of color," proclaimed the *Chicago Tribune*, contradicted the tenets of American republicanism, found no support in the Constitution, and stood "condemned by the increasing light of civilization, and the advance of christianity in the universal mind." More frivolous arguments also cropped up. One black woman, it was said, capitalized on the Dred Scott ruling by paying freight rather than passenger rates when traveling by rail.[21]

[19] Basler (ed.), *Works of Lincoln*, III, 16.
[20] *Ibid.* II, 409. See also *Chicago Daily Tribune*, June 26, 1855; William Seward to Lucian Barbour *et al.*, July 2, 1855, Seward Papers; *Illinois State Journal*, July 15, 1857; Salter, *Grimes*, 101; Joshua Giddings to Augustus Ganter, Nov. 2, 1857, quoted in Adrian *Michigan Expositor*, Jan. 2, 1858; *Chicago Weekly Press & Tribune*, July 29, 1858; *Wisconsin Weekly Free Democrat*, Sept. 15, 1858.
[21] *Lansing State Republican*, Mar. 24, Apr. 24, 1857; *Chicago Daily Tribune*, Apr. 10, Aug. 22, 1857; *Milwaukee Daily Sentinel*, May 24, June 19, 1857. See also *New*

In short, most Republicans denied that black inferiority gave title to oppression. Instead of adding to the burdens of an already downtrodden race, many maintained, sensible whites should help blacks to make the most of such abilities as they possessed. Supposing it was true that Negroes were an ignorant and degraded people, Joshua Giddings lectured one bigoted constituent: "have they less claim upon our sympathy? Are we at liberty to rob the poor? to oppress the weak? to despise the humble?" He, for one, thought not. And although the Republican platform stopped short of such radicalism, Giddings announced it his purpose "not merely to protect them, but to inform, educate, refine and raise them to a moral elevation, far higher and broader" than America's negrophobic society would yet entertain. If blacks were an inferior race, argued Senator Francis Gillette of Connecticut, "why not have the justice and magnanimity to remove their civil disabilities, and let them rise, and no longer exhibit toward them the dastardliness of an overgrown bully, who pounces upon the weak and defenseless?" "All I ask for the negro," said the more moderate Lincoln, "is that if you do not like him, let him alone. If God gave him but little, that little let him enjoy."[22]

A few radical Republicans even questioned the prevailing belief in the *innate* inferiority of blacks to whites. Certainly nothing could be more unfair, one New Hampshire Republican pointed out, than "to virtually exclude colored people from schools, and crush them under a mountain weight of prejudice against color, and then disparage them for lack of intelligence. . . ."[23] Despite staggering handicaps, Gamaliel Bailey declared, Northern Negroes had made great strides forward—often surpassing the accomplishments of Southern poor whites. And where free of the millstone of prejudice, some observed, American blacks demonstrated remarkable ability. "On the whole," concluded the

---

York Evening Post, Mar. 10, 1857; *Madison* (Wis.) *Daily State Journal*, Mar. 17, 1857.

[22] Giddings to Augustus Ganter, Nov. 2, 1857, quoted in *Michigan Expositor*, Jan. 2, 1858; *Cong. Globe*, 33rd Cong., 2nd sess., Appendix, 230-31 (Feb. 23, 1855); Basler (ed.), *Works of Lincoln*, II, 520. See also *Chicago Daily Tribune*, June 26, 1855; John Sherman's speech at Cincinnati, quoted in *Indiana True Republican*, Nov. 1, 1860.

[23] "Narrow Axe" in *Dover Enquirer*, Feb. 28, 1856. See also *New-York Daily Tribune*, Mar. 8, 1859; Sewell, *Hale*, 209-10. William Seward held that "philosophy meekly expresses her distrust of the asserted natural superiority of the white race. . . ." *Cong. Globe*, 31st Cong., 1st sess., Appendix, 268 (Mar. 11, 1850).

New-York Tribune, which devoted a series of articles to the subject, "the condition of the exiled negroes in Canada does not give much color to the theory of the inferiority of the negro race. . . . It may well be doubted whether a similar number of white refugees of any country, with no more advantages to begin with than they, would have succeeded any better." One Ohio Republican even contended that originally the still-predominant colored races had comprised "*all of mankind*," and that whites had developed as an aberrant strain, first in the Caucasian mountains. Therefore, he maintained, "if there are any rights arising from color origin or superior numbers, they are on the opposite side & in favor of making slaves of white men."[24]

Whether skeptical or (much more likely) fully persuaded of white racial supremacy, most Republicans exhibited a far greater willingness than Democrats to combat the poisons of prejudice and guarantee blacks at least the most basic civil liberties. At a minimum, nearly all agreed, Negroes were entitled to buy, sell, and hold all forms of property; to testify, enter suits, or serve as jurymen in any court; and to come and go as they wished, without harassment or restraint. "We do not say the black man is, or shall be, the equal of the white man; or that he shall vote or hold office, however just such [a] position may be," explained Joshua Giddings; "but we assert that he who murders a black man shall be hanged; that he who robs the black man of his liberty or his property shall be punished like other criminals. We deny that crime depends upon the complexion of him against whom it is committed."[25]

In accordance with such views, Republicans battled on many fronts —sometimes at high political cost—to secure legal equality for blacks. A prime target of many Republicans were the statutes, proposed or already enacted, barring the entry of free Negroes into a number of Western states. In Ohio Republicans thrice thwarted Democratic attempts to pass a Negro exclusion law, and in Indiana and Illinois Republicans proved virtually the only critics of such "unchristian and diabolical" legislation. Even in Kansas, where settlers from the Border slave states augmented the influence of Midwestern racists, Yankee Republicans headed off demands for Negro exclusion. Although Democrats warned that Kansas would become "a sort of Botany Bay [for]

---

[24] *National Era*, June 9, 1859; *New-York Daily Tribune*, Nov. 27, 1857; Charles Whittlesey to Benjamin F. Wade, Mar. 14, 1860, Wade Papers.
[25] *Cong. Globe*, 35th Cong., 2nd sess., 346 (Jan. 12, 1859).

all the lazy, worthless, vagabond Free negroes of the other States," the Wyandotte Constitution under which Kansas entered the Union in 1861, while it provided for segregated schools and lily-white suffrage, placed no restrictions on black immigration.[26]

When Oregon applied for admission to the Union with a constitution which not only prohibited Negroes from taking up residence but also denied them the right to hold real estate, enter contracts, or "maintain any suit," the mass of Republicans were appalled. The party press denounced such discrimination as "absurd, unnecessary and tyrannical," "a disgrace to any Christian or civilized country," a brutal vestige of barbarism.[27] In Congress, only ex-Democrats Preston King and Lyman Trumbull, among Republicans, had a good word to say for the Negro article—and even King confessed that if he were a resident of Oregon he would have voted against it. "In point of needless and gratuitous barbarity," said Representative Clark B. Cochrane of New York, it was without parallel in American history. A "refined and consumate barbarity," Abbott of Maine called it; an "infamous atrocity," shouted Ohio's Bingham. Senator Seward entered a "decided protest" against such rank discrimination, and William Pitt Fessenden solemnly announced that he could never vote to admit a state which would exclude his dark-skinned "fellow-citizens" of Maine. Massachusetts Senator Henry Wilson pronounced the anti-Negro clauses "unconstitutional, inhuman, and unchristian," and boasted that he lived in a commonwealth that recognized "the absolute and perfect equality of all men of all races." Such declarations struck no sympathetic chord from the other side of the aisle. Rather, they set off a flurry of what had become the standard Democratic riposte: charges that Black Republicans were bent upon an indiscriminate mixing of the races.[28]

In the end, six of seventeen Republican Senators (Hale, Wilson, Fessenden, Hamlin, Trumbull, and Durkee) and seventy-three of eighty-

---

[26] Foner, *Free Soil, Free Labor, Free Men*, 286; Berwanger, *Frontier Against Slavery*, 97-118; *Galena Weekly Northwestern Gazette*, June 30, 1854; *Chicago Daily Tribune*, Jan. 23, 1854, July 28, 1857. In 1855 free state voters ratified a Negro-exclusion clause in the extralegal Topeka constitution by a 3 to 1 margin. It was never implemented.

[27] *Chicago Tri-Weekly Tribune*, May 7, 1858; *Poughkeepsie Eagle*, Feb. 19, 1859; *Galesburg Semi-Weekly Democrat*, Feb. 16, 1859. See also *New York Evening Post*, Feb. 14, 1859; *New-York Daily Tribune*, Feb. 14, 1859. Cf. *New York Times*, Feb. 14, 1859; *Springfield* (Mass.) *Republican*, Feb. 16, 1859.

[28] *Cong. Globe*, 35th Cong., 1st sess., 1964-66, 2206-7, 2nd sess., 947, 950, 974-86, Appendix, 193.

eight Republican Representatives voted against the admission of Oregon, even as a free state. Trumbull based his opposition on "proslavery" domination of Oregon politics, and some argued that it was unfair to admit Democratic Oregon and not Republican Kansas. But for most, the "cruel and inhumane" Black Code proved the stumbling block.[29]

Republicans demonstrated a greater willingness to encourage colonization as the ultimate solution of the racial problem in the United States. Yet never did the Blair-Doolittle program win recognition in official Republican platforms, and if critics of colonization chorused more softly than its friends, it was because they saw no need to do more. Most Republicans recognized that voluntary migration would not work—because of staggering costs and black opposition—and not even conservatives had the stomach for forcible repatriation.[30] Some feared that the removal of free Negroes would "fortify slavery." Others argued the need for their labor. Far from their being a curse, Greeley's *Tribune* asserted, "there is no reason to believe that, if afforded fair play, the protection of the laws, and opportunities for industry and education, free negroes might not make useful citizens." Once the popular mind grasped the proper moral "relation of the superior to the inferior, the fortunate to the unfortunate, or the strong to the weak," reasoned another Republican editor, the Negro would no longer seem a problem and might be welcomed as an integral and useful element in American society.[31]

Because education was deemed essential to the self-improvement of *all* Americans, some Republicans gave at least passing attention to schooling for blacks. Republicans Sumner and Wilson had already led a successful campaign against segregated schools in Massachusetts on the grounds that separate facilities were inherently unequal.[32] In Kan-

[29] *National Era*, Feb. 17, 1859; *New-York Daily Tribune*, Feb. 14, 1859; Lyman Trumbull to Editor, *Chicago Times*, May 21, 1858 (copy), Trumbull Papers; Trumbull to Salmon P. Chase, Feb. 7, 1859, Chase Papers, PHS.
[30] E.g., the conservative *Illinois State Journal* (Jan. 26, 1859) criticized the Missouri legislature for considering a bill to expel all free Negroes from the state and to pay expenses by confiscating their property. "Of course all this is in accordance with the decision that negroes have no rights which white men are bound to respect. It is all right, undoubtedly, in the minds of the National Democracy, to sell free men and confiscate their property."
[31] *Cong. Globe*, 31st Cong., 1st sess., 268 (Mar. 11, 1850); *New-York Daily Tribune*, May 29, 1857; *Wisconsin Weekly Free Democrat*, June 16, 1858. See also *Galesburg Free Democrat*, Feb. 1, 1855; Joshua Giddings to Augustus Ganter, Nov. 2, 1857, quoted in *Michigan Expositor*, Jan. 2, 1858.
[32] *Supra*, pp. 183-84.

sas Republicans as well as Democrats approved the establishment of Jim Crow schools, although radicals like George W. Brown castigated the "miserable hypocrites" who preached but feared to practice the elevation of blacks.[33] In neighboring Iowa, on the other hand, Republicans succeeded in opening the public schools to children of all races. When Ben M. Samuels, the Virginia-born Democratic candidate for governor, sought to nullify this decision, alleging that white children's morals would be corrupted by association with Negroes who were vulgar, vicious, "and full of nigger songs," the *Chicago Tribune* gibed: "The issue is thus made up: One hundred infant darkies, armed to the teeth with 'nigger songs,' against the hosts of Iowa Democracy, led on by a Virginia snob [Samuels]. We bet on the little niggers."[34]

Elsewhere, Republicans strove to eliminate glaring inequities in educational funding. Horace Greeley crusaded in the pages of his *New-York Tribune* for an end to the discrimination which in two decades permitted school expenditures per white student forty times greater than those per black. And in Congress Senator John P. Hale moved to amend a District of Columbia school bill so that the taxes of Negroes might be used to support schools for their own children. He proposed no establishment of mixed schools, Hale declared, merely "simple justice." The capital's blacks were "an oppressed and degraded people," he said, and it ill-befitted "the magnanimity of their superiors to collect their money and to use it to educate their own [white] children."[35]

Natural and civil rights were one thing to Republicans, political rights quite another. Even one so radical as Joshua Giddings held that "The right of suffrage is not a natural right," and refrained from forcing "any doubtful issue" into the Republican platform. Yet notwithstanding the political risks involved, Republicans proved vastly more liberal than Democrats wherever the question of Negro suffrage was debated. New York Negroes had a perfect right to complain of Republican apathy toward the equal suffrage referendum in 1860. The fact remains, however, that Seward, Weed, Greeley, and most other Republican leaders in the state had long advocated an impartial franchise. When the issue was raised in the 1857 New York legislature, Republican members voted unanimously in favor of suffrage exten-

[33] Berwanger, *Frontier Against Slavery*, 117.
[34] *Chicago Daily Tribune*, Sept. 14, 1857.
[35] *New-York Daily Tribune*, Mar. 8, 1859; *Cong. Globe*, 35th Cong., 1st sess., Appendix, 371 (May 15, 1858).

sion, Democrats solidly against. A second roll call in 1860 showed much the same pattern, and in the popular referendum of that year over half the Republican voters approved equal suffrage, while a good many more abstained. New York Democrats, who had labored to make it a party issue, branding their opponents as the party of "Amalgamation" and "Nigger Equality," overwhelmingly rejected the proposed amendment.[36]

Wisconsin Republicans shinnied even further out along the black suffrage limb.[37] In response to petitions circulated by Milwaukee Negroes late in 1855, leading Republicans resurrected the question of black voting rights, and by 1857 they had made it a party issue. Elisha W. Keyes, the Republican kingpin in Madison, put his name to one of the instigating petitions; Republican presses—especially the *Wisconsin Free Democrat*, the *Racine Advocate*, and the *Milwaukee Sentinel*—pushed the reform forward; and Republican representatives shepherded a bill for equal suffrage through the legislature and into a statewide referendum. In a report more radical than any Free Soil pronouncement, Joseph T. Mills, on behalf of the Assembly Judiciary Committee, recommended universal suffrage as a fundamental right belonging to all men—and women. He castigated "the barbarous and unmanly dogma that human rights are qualities of color, to be analyzed and determined by the prism of prejudice or hereditary hatred." Unless ignorance or lack of education could be reduced to some practical and temporary test, the Mills report concluded, "no race can be proscribed in the Republic without establishing a precedent which may be applied with fatal effect to all proscribed and despised minorities."

Not all Wisconsin Republicans, to be sure, shared such opinions. The *Whitewater Register* complained of attempts to "abolitionize the Republican party," and Timothy Howe testified to intraparty disagreements when he wrote: "We have left them in profound doubt whether if they enlisted in the fight they were to be led by Jno. Fremont or Gerrit Smith." Nor were Republicans altogether alone in supporting

[36] *Chicago Press & Tribune*, Oct. 12, 1860, quoting *Ashtabula Sentinel; New-York Daily Tribune*, Sept. 7, 26, 1857, Aug. 7, Sept. 17, 1860; Litwack, *North of Slavery*, 88; Foner, *Free Soil, Free Labor, Free Men*, 285-86; Phyllis F. Field, "Republicans and Black Suffrage in New York State: The Grass Roots Response," *Civil War History*, XXI, No. 2 (June 1975), 136-47.
[37] The following discussion rests upon Fishel, "Wisconsin and Negro Suffrage," 185-89; Robert N. Kroncke, "Race and Politics in Wisconsin, 1854-1865," M.A. thesis, University of Wisconsin, 1969, pp. 22-37.

Negro suffrage. No less a Democrat than James B. Cross, that party's candidate for governor, turned out to have signed an equal suffrage petition. As the 1857 campaign developed, however, Republicans increasingly accepted black enfranchisement as their own measure, just as Democrats backed away. At its state convention in June the Republican party pronounced itself "utterly opposed to the proscription of any man on account of birthplace, religion, or color." Conversely, Democrats adopted a platform which denounced "the odious doctrine of negro equality" in general and the suffrage amendment in particular. While some Republican papers avoided the question and others expressed a willingness to abide by the people's decision, a sizable number came out strongly for manhood suffrage. The Manitowoc *Wisconsin's Democrat*, a German Republican journal, the *Berlin Courant*, the *Racine Advocate*, the *Monroe Sentinel*, and the *River Falls Journal* were especially insistent on the need for reform. And the *Milwaukee Sentinel*, which posted "For Extension of Suffrage" at its masthead, urged its readers on election eve to "REMEMBER that this is a contest where a great and living principle is involved—the inalienable right of every human being to life, liberty, and the pursuit of happiness."

The returns disheartened Wisconsin blacks and their Republican allies. Voters rejected Negro suffrage, 40,915 to 23,074, even though Republicans elected their candidate for governor, Alexander Randall, by a narrow margin—clear evidence, claimed the Democratic *Wisconsin Patriot*, that "even the Republicans themselves are hostile to this, their great hobby." In this there was some truth. Still, 35 per cent of those who voted on the question—and well over 60 per cent of the Republicans—endorsed Negro suffrage. By the standards of antebellum America, it was a remarkable showing.

In a way, of course, Wisconsin and New York were the exceptions which proved the racist rule. Nearly everywhere else the issue cropped up during the 1850s—in Ohio, Minnesota, Iowa, Kansas—Republican support for black suffrage proved negligible. Moreover, even many of the most forceful Republican advocates of equal voting rights often patronized Negroes and turned hostile at the first sign of black militance. Horace Greeley, for instance, scolded a Convention of Colored Persons in New York City for protesting legislative foot-dragging on the state suffrage amendment in 1857:

The fact that one negro quietly and resolutely cultivating his own land—no matter though there be but few acres of it—[wrote the editor] training up his children as well as the atmosphere of prejudice and brutality which surrounds him will permit, and worshipping the God of the oppressed in patient favor and humble faith—is doing more to hasten and secure the full emancipation of his race than a hundred who are shouting and blowing at Conventions, is so manifest that only supereminent knavery or transcendent stupidity can affect not to see it.[38]

Such condescension grates hard on modern ears. Yet even some blacks at the time, and Booker T. Washington forty years later, preached much the same message. That the antebellum Republicans were not freedom riders, that they were often indifferent and sometimes hostile to black Americans, need come as no surprise. The remarkable fact is that the Republicans, like the Free Soilers before them, showed a willingness to recognize the Negro's humanity and to protect his most basic freedoms which went well beyond the narrow racism of most other contemporary Americans, North and South.

2

One measure of the relative liberality of Republicans on the issue of slavery and race lies in the developing response of blacks and radical white abolitionists to the Republican party. In the years between Frémont's defeat and Lincoln's victory, American Negroes and their closest white allies found much to criticize in the new Northern party. Yet at the same time many showed a growing appreciation of its accomplishments and principles and a conviction that whatever their shortcomings, the Republicans were infinitely preferable to the "proslavery," negrophobic Democrats.

Some black spokesmen, to be sure, continued to stress Republican failings and to deny any significant difference between the major parties. "Despotism is the avowed object of one, whilst self-interest is the all controlling power and ruling motive of the other," complained one contributor to the *Anglo-African Magazine*. "The philanthropic doctrine of equal rights is totally ignored." Similarly, H. Ford Douglass, a black leader from Illinois, insisted that no party deserved "the sym-

[38] *New-York Daily Tribune*, Sept. 26, 1857.

pathy of anti-slavery men, unless that party is willing to extend to the black man all the rights of a citizen." As matters stood in Illinois, he protested, "if we sent our children to school, Abraham Lincoln would kick them out, in the name of Republicanism and anti-slavery!" A few even contended (like certain white abolitionists) that Republicans represented a greater threat to Negro advancement than did their opponents, if only for the false hopes they raised. "Under the guise of humanity, they do and say many things," complained the black editor Thomas Hamilton, "—as, for example, they oppose the re-opening of the slave-trade. . . . They oppose the progress of slavery in the territories, and would cry humanity to the world; but . . . their opposition to slavery means opposition to the black man—nothing else. Where it is clearly in their power to do anything for the oppressed colored man, why then they are too nice, too conservative, to do it. . . ."[39]

Embittered by the broad streak of white supremacy they discerned in both major parties, and weary of injunctions to wait patiently, tending their gardens, until the dominant race should find them worthy of equal rights, some Negroes turned their backs on America. "I must admit, that I have no hopes in this country—no confidence in the American people," confessed Martin R. Delany. Such men rejected political involvement and urged instead the creation of an independent black republic abroad.[40]

Most Northern blacks, however, rejected emigration as "unwise, unfortunate, and premature." Determined to win a respectable place in American society, they pinned their hopes, for better or worse, on the Republican party. Blacks had little choice but to cast their lot with the Republicans, if only because the Democrats were such rabid racists. As Frederick Douglass remarked in 1860: "If the Negro should discriminate between the various organized forces of this country against him, he would point to the Democratic party as pre-eminent in unscru-

[39] Charles M. Wilson, "What Is Our True Condition?" (Jan. 1860), quoted in Litvack, North of Slavery, 274; Douglass's speech at Framingham, Mass., July 4, 1860, Anglo-African, Mar. 17, 1860, both quoted in James M. McPherson, The Negro's Civil War (New York, 1965), 4-7.
[40] Leon F. Litwack, "The Emancipation of the Negro Abolitionist," in Martin Duberman (ed.), The Antislavery Vanguard: New Essays on the Abolitionists (Princeton, 1965), 150-54; Litwack, North of Slavery, 257-62; Quarles, Black Abolitionists, 215-18; Victor Ullman, Martin R. Delany: The Beginnings of Black Nationalism (Boston, 1971), chaps. IX-XII; Howard H. Bell, "A Survey of the Negro Convention Movement, 1830-1861," Ph.D. dissertation, Northwestern University, 1953, pp. 206-16, 225-53.

pulous malignity and heartless cruelty. Attracting to itself all that is low, vulgar, coarse, brutal and mobocratic in the nation, it has poured down upon the Negro all these elements of wrath and poison. The vital element of the party has been hatred of Negroes and love of spoils."[41]

The Republican party, on the other hand, offered hope, if not complete satisfaction. Its success, one Chicago Negro maintained, "cannot help but benefit first the country, next the Free Colored Man and next the Slave." Negro conventions in Ohio, New York, and New England endorsed the Republican cause.[42] During the 1860 presidential campaign, black Republican "Wide Awakes" paraded and raised "Lincoln Liberty Trees" in Boston, Brooklyn, and Pittsburgh. Samuel Smothers, a black Indiana educator, noting that "The best anti-slavery men in the nation are rallying under the Republican banner," concluded that Negroes ought to look to that party "for the ultimate abolition of slavery throughout the entire nation, and the elevation of our race to social and political equality." Frederick Douglass, though he announced his intention to vote for Gerrit Smith's minuscule Radical Abolitionist party, admitted that "the Republican party carries with it the anti-slavery sentiment of the North" and prayed for Lincoln's victory.[43] In the end, Democratic attempts to smear Lincoln as a "nigger worshipper" and his running mate Hamlin as a mulatto brought even some of the Republicans' sharpest critics around. H. Ford Douglass, for one, changed his tune in the closing days of the campaign. "I love everything the South hates," he told a rally in Boston, "and since they have evidenced their dislike of Mr. Lincoln, I am bound to love you Republicans with all your faults." Thus, ironically, did eligible Northern blacks vote "almost solidly" for a presidential candidate who disapproved their right to do so.[44]

Initial black reaction to the Republican triumph in 1860 ranged from misguided rapture to guarded optimism. One Baltimore Negro, painfully ignorant of the President-elect's racial views, boldly boarded a white streetcar, insisting that because of Lincoln's victory he was as free to ride as any man. Similarly, a Kentucky correspondent complained to Lincoln that blacks in Logan County had "commenced the

[41] Foner, *Writings of Douglass*, II, 493.
[42] W. R. Bonner to Lyman Trumbull, Jan. 17, 1860, Trumbull Papers; Bell, "Negro Convention Movement," 192-93, 205; Litwack, *North of Slavery*, 274-75.
[43] McPherson, *Negro's Civil War*, 10; Foner, *Writings of Douglass*, II, 514-15.
[44] Quarles, *Lincoln and the Negro*, 56-57; Quarles, *Black Abolitionists*, 190.

work of poisoning and Incendiaryism," in the belief that his election had given them freedom. At the other extreme, Frederick Douglass worried that the Republicans' success might blight more thoroughgoing abolitionism. Yet even he found reason to rejoice at the election's outcome. Not only would it quench recent attempts to revive the foreign slave trade and make "more unpopular and odious" the recapture of fugitive slaves, Douglass decided, but it had "demonstrated the possibility of electing, if not an Abolitionist, at least an *antislavery reputation* to the Presidency of the United States." The future looked perilous, but with peril came hope.[45]

As a rule, radical white abolitionists remained even more critical than blacks of the Republican party's failings. The Republicans' narrow, non-extension platform, their "excessive prudence," their shameful scrambling to dissociate themselves from genuine abolitionists, their tendency to undercut more radical activity, and their neglect of Negro rights all reinforced the conviction of avowed abolitionists that Republicanism was an exceedingly unreliable antislavery force.[46] Some, in fact, still maintained that the Republican party was a "false friend," and as such "more difficult to deal with, and more dangerous than a frank and open enemy."[47] The eccentric Stephen S. Foster had been hawking this line since the end of 1855, and after 1856 he stepped up the attack. Together with his wife, Abby Kelley Foster, and Parker Pillsbury, Foster repeatedly sought to bind the Massachusetts and American Anti-Slavery societies to resolutions denouncing the Republican party as abolition's greatest enemy.[48]

Always, however, the Foster-Pillsbury resolutions failed to win more than splinter support. For the vast majority of ultra abolitionists, in-

[45] Quarles, *Lincoln and the Negro*, 57; Foner, *Writings of Douglass*, II, 526-30.
[46] Theodore Parker to John P. Hale, Dec. 19, 1856, Parker to Charles Sumner, Feb. 27, 1857, Letterbook, Parker Papers; Charles Batcheller to William Lloyd Garrison, June 30, 1857, Joseph A. Howland to Samuel May, Jr., Aug. 12, 1857, Garrison to N. R. Johnston, Oct. 15, 1860 (copy), Garrison Papers; Lydia M. Child to Lyman Trumbull, Dec. 25, 1859, Trumbull Papers; Child to Charles Sumner, June 17, 1860, Sumner Papers; *Annual Reports of the American Anti-Slavery Society, by the Executive Committee, for the Years Ending May 1, 1857, and May 1, 1858* (New York, 1859), 33; *Liberator*, Sept. 28, 1860; *National Anti-Slavery Standard*, Mar. 31, 1860.
[47] "H.W.G." in *ibid*. Sept. 18, 1858.
[48] *Liberator*, Dec. 21, 1855, Feb. 1, 8, May 16, June 6, 1856, June 26, 1857, Feb. 4, June 4, 1859; *National Anti-Slavery Standard*, Mar. 31, 1860. See also Larry Wertheim, "Garrisonian Abolitionists and the Republican Party, 1854-1861," seminar paper, University of Wisconsin, 1972, pp. 16-22, 32-36.

cluding William Lloyd Garrison, continued to view the Republican party not as a dangerous adversary but as an imperfect accomplice in the destruction of slavery. Garrison still rebuked Republicans for their fealty to a "proslavery" Constitution and their milk-and-water platform. But when the Foster-Pillsbury clique stamped even Charles Sumner a "villain" and argued that the antislavery cause had more to fear from Republicans than from Democrats, the editor demurred. "There is a good deal of pro-slavery in the [Republican] party, perhaps," Garrison told the Massachusetts Anti-Slavery Society Convention in 1859, "but [also] a great deal of warm and genuine anti-slavery —sympathy, generosity, kindness, pity for the slave. . . ." While insufficient in itself, the curtailment of slavery's growth was a useful work, and abolitionists ought to wish Republicans well, "for we also desire to save the great West from the encroachments of the Slave Power. . . ." His hope, said Garrison, lay "in the great Republican party"—not where it then stood, but where it tended. He thought it especially unfair that the Fosters and Pillsbury, after obtaining contributions from prominent Massachusetts Republicans on the ground that antislavery lectures helped to weaken "satanic Democracy" and strengthen Republicanism, nonetheless damned the Republican party as the slave's worst enemy.[49]

Most Republicans felt distinctly uncomfortable at any hint of close relations with the Garrisonians—"This little coterie of common scolds," the *New-York Tribune* called them—and incidents like Garrison's public burning of the United States Constitution ("a covenant with death, and an agreement with hell") did nothing to change their minds.[50] The Disunion Convention at Worcester, Massachusetts, in January 1857 failed woefully in its mission to unite abolitionists and radical Republicans in support of disunion, even though some politicians went along because they were "sick of the Southern gas on the subject."[51]

---

[49] Joseph A. Howland to Garrison, Aug. 10, 1857, Garrison Papers; *Liberator*, Feb. 4 1859; Garrison to Abby Kelley Foster, Sept. 8, 1859, Stephen S. Foster Papers. See also Theodore Parker to T. J. Moore, Aug. 2, 1858, Letterbook, Parker Papers; Wendell Phillips to Abby Kelley Foster, June 30 [1859?], Foster Papers. As before, Garrison heaped ridicule on Gerrit Smith's Radical Abolitionist party, whose punyness ("a mere baker's dozen"), not principles, made it farcical in his eyes. See *Liberator* Sept. 7, 1860; Garrison to Samuel J. May, Sept. 26, 1860, Garrison Papers.
[50] *New-York Daily Tribune*, Feb. 20, 1860. See also Harrisburg *Pennsylvania Telegraph*, Nov. 21, 1855.
[51] Henry Wilson to Theodore Parker, Mar. 14, 1857, Letterbook, Parker Papers

Yet behind the scenes, Republicans like Charles Sumner, Henry Wilson, John Andrew, Joshua Giddings, Salmon P. Chase, William Seward, and John P. Hale, plied abolitionist papers with documents and speeches and engaged in cordial correspondence with Garrison, Theodore Parker, David and Lydia Maria Child, and others of that stripe. William Herndon called on Garrison during a visit to Boston in 1858, expecting to find "a shrivelled-cold-selfish-haughty man, one who was weak and fanatically blind to the charities and equities of life. . . ." Instead he found him "warm, generous, approachable, and communicative"—a campfire of friendliness in an otherwise frosty Boston.[52] A few of the more radical Republican editors and politicians publicly confessed to the charge of abolitionism, although never in the Garrisonian, disunionist sense. Even some who considered abolitionists impatient and impractical extremists granted them "the virtues of devotion, self-sacrifice and heroism." The *Chicago Tribune* jeered at Stephen A. Douglas: "We tell you that by the side of many of these men you sneer at as 'Abolitionists,' who, whatever may be their errors, are still examples of that sublime fanaticism which dares and does for truth and right, you are simply contemptible. . . ."[53]

As election day approached in 1860, the abolitionists displayed a growing good will toward the Republicans. The *Liberator* and the *National Anti-Slavery Standard*, while discouraging votes for that "half-a-loaf" party, nonetheless made it clear that their "sympathies and best wishes" lay with the Republicans. Oliver Johnson, editor of the *Standard*, struck a common note when he remarked in October: "Deficient as the Republican party is, I regard its success as the beginning of a new and better era. Let Stephen Foster and his sympathizers say what they will, to me it seems utterly preposterous to deny that Lincoln's election will indicate growth in the right direction." A fair number of Garrisonians—among them Sidney Howard Gay, Theodore Til-

---

Thomas, *The Liberator*, 391-93; Tilden G. Edelstein, *Strange Enthusiasm: A Life of Thomas Wentworth Higginson* (New Haven, 1968), 194-201.
[52] Child, *Letters*, xiii; *Liberator*, May 14, 1858; Giddings to Garrison, Mar. 3, Apr. 27, 1858; Herndon to Garrison, Apr. 16, May 29, 1858, Garrison Papers; Seward to Parker, Mar. 26, June 28, 1858, Seward Papers; Herndon to Parker, Apr. 7, May 29, 1858, Letterbook, Parker Papers.
[53] *Galesburg Free Democrat*, Sept. 29, 1854, Jan. 25, Apr. 26, 1855; *Green Mountain Freeman*, June 29, 1854; *National Era*, Oct. 12, 1854; *Indiana True Republican*, Dec. 30, 1858; *Poughkeepsie Eagle*, July 7, 1860; *Chicago Daily Tribune*, July 17, 1857.

ton, David Lee Child, and Moncure D. Conway—capitulated entirely, giving political as well as moral support to the Republicans.[54]

Most, following Garrison's lead, held themselves above the fray. But once the returns were in, even outspoken critics joined in the hosannas over Lincoln's victory. Wendell Phillips, who five months earlier had pilloried Abraham Lincoln as "The Slave-Hound of Illinois," now rejoiced that "for the first time in our history the *slave* has chosen a President of the United States." Even more enthusiastically Samuel May, Jr., exclaimed: "Is not the result *wonderful?* Not that L. & his administration will be likely to do anything antislavery, but in view of the fact that *the North* has stood fast, and, in face of all the Southern threats & bombast & defiance, chosen the candidate which the South had denounced." "It is not the harvest," wrote Edmund Quincy, "but it is the green blade that must go before it." Coming from such radical sources, even such qualified jubilation as this bespoke the antislavery character of the Republican party.[55]

[54] *Liberator*, Sept. 28, 1860; *National Anti-Slavery Standard*, Sept. 29, 1860; Oliver Johnson to J. Miller McKim, Oct. 11, 1860, Antislavery Collection, Cornell University; James M. McPherson, *The Struggle for Equality: Abolitionists and the Negro in the Civil War and Reconstruction* (Princeton, 1964), 14. See also Elizur Wright, Jr., to [Beriah Green], Oct. 8, Nov. 3, 1860 (typed copy), Wright Papers, BPL; William Lloyd Garrison to J. M. McKim, Oct. 21, 1860, Garrison Papers.
[55] McPherson, *Struggle for Equality*, 26-28.

14

Politics and Principles

THOSE WHO SOUGHT to keep the Republican party squarely on an anti-slavery course, were, by and large, successful. Although less radical than the men of earlier antislavery parties (or Gerrit Smith's tiny band of Radical Abolitionist diehards), the Republicans managed to preserve basically intact the root principle of all such organizations, one broached in the American Anti-Slavery Society's "Declaration of Sentiments" as long ago as 1833—"to abolish slavery in those portions of our territory which the Constitution has placed under . . . [Congress'] exclusive jurisdiction." Yet the party's sterner antislavery advocates had to weather a series of attempts during the prewar years to dilute the Philadelphia platform of 1856. The most conspicuously radical of the Republican pronouncements of this period—including Lincoln's House Divided, Seward's Irrepressible Conflict, and Sumner's Barbarism of Slavery speeches—were more or less explicitly aimed at overcoming such retrogressive efforts. By the time of the secession crisis, antislavery radicals and moderates had won the battle for control of the Republican party. Led now by Abraham Lincoln, a man of firm if temperate antislavery principles, Republicans stood ready to risk disunion rather than surrender another inch to slavery. And the war came.

The pressures on Republicans to modify their original antislavery doctrines and to welcome into their alliance a hodgepodge of anti-Lecompton Democrats, conservative Whigs, and Know-Nothings derived from many sources. Frémont's defeat in 1856 was in itself evidence that something had to be done to broaden the Republican party's appeal, especially in swing states like Pennsylvania, New Jersey, Indiana, and Illinois. The success of the Pennsylvania People's party (a coalition of Republicans and Know-Nothings) suggested one way to proceed. By moderating its antislavery pronouncements and stressing local issues and the tariff question, the People's party swept to impressive victories in 1858 and 1859.[1] Why, some Republicans asked, might not the same policy profitably be applied nationally? The Panic of 1857, by deflecting attention from "the possible fate of the slaves or their masters" to the actual distress at home, encouraged this tendency toward fusion and a playing down of the slavery issue.[2] A weariness of agitation in conservative quarters and the settlement of the Kansas imbroglio by the English Act referendum in August 1858 also contributed to a willingness to set antislavery concerns aside, at least temporarily. "Times are so dull that we seem just creeping along on the cold surface of the world," observed the normally cheerful Billy Herndon in January 1859. "There is nothing to animate—elate—fire us up to the blazing point." At no time since 1853, he complained, had the antislavery fires burned so low as during the year just past.[3]

The first large-scale effort to broaden the Republican confederation at the expense of its antislavery creed got underway late in 1857. It began following overtures from Stephen A. Douglas, hitherto an arch villain to all Republicans, and was directed toward some sort of alliance between disaffected, anti-Administration Democrats and the Republican party. Already smarting under a long train of slights from President Buchanan, angered at the mockery Kansas' Lecompton constitution made of popular sovereignty (permitting a sham referendum on slavery only), and increasingly aware of the force of anti-Southern feeling in Illinois, Douglas broke openly with the Administration in December 1857. "If this constitution is to be forced down our throats, in violation of the fundamental principle of free government, under a mode of submission that is a mockery and insult," he threatened, "I will resist it to the last."[4]

[1] Holt, *Forging a Majority*, chap. VI.
[2] *Chicago Daily Tribune*, Oct. 29, 1857.
[3] *New York Times*, Nov. 24, Dec. 1, 1858; Herndon to Lyman Trumbull, Jan. 21 1859, Trumbull Papers.
[4] Quoted in Johannsen, *Douglas*, 591.

Even before this declaration of war on Buchanan and the pro-Southern wing of his party, Douglas had begun a discreet but earnest search for support from the Republicans. In November Charles H. Ray, senior editor of the *Chicago Tribune*, reported that the Little Giant was "playing the part of injured innocence" and exclaiming: "By G–d sir, I made Mr. James Buchanan, and by G–d sir, I will unmake him." Douglas even sent an emissary to the *Tribune*'s office to ask that it not pitch into him while he fought the Republicans' fight. This diplomacy was extended after Douglas's return to Washington in December. In a series of private talks with such Republican leaders as Horace Greeley, Henry Wilson, Nathaniel P. Banks, Schuyler Colfax, Anson Burlingame, and Benjamin Wade, Douglas declared his determination to follow his principles wherever they might lead, and he pleaded for Republican cooperation in defeating the "Lecompton swindle."[5]

Although fully aware of his self-serving motives (Wade called him a "pirate," driven "by stress of weather into our port"), and unwilling to trust him very far, all Republicans welcomed Douglas's attacks on the Administration. Even Herndon at first admitted that "Douglas is more of a man than I took him to be: he has got some nerve at least." Greeley urged that a group of young Republican Congressmen call on Douglas from time to time to sustain him in his newly found independence. Neither side committed itself beyond the Lecompton struggle, although Douglas hinted at the formation of "a great Constitutional Union" party to resist Jefferson Davis and other Southern disunionists, and rumors flew of secret deals concerning the election of 1860. Yet though commitments were few, hopes were many. Some confidently predicted that Douglas and his Northern followers would soon join the Republican party. "He is as sure to be with us in the future as Chase, Seward or Sumner," Henry Wilson certified. "I say nothing about motives . . . but he is to be with us and he is today of more weight than *any ten men* in the country."[6] To smooth Douglas's transit to Republicanism, or, failing that, to splinter the Democratic

5 Ray to Lyman Trumbull, Nov. 24, 1857, Trumbull Papers; Douglas to Colfax, [Dec. 1857], Memorandum of Interview, Burlingame and Colfax with Douglas, at his residence, Dec. 14, 1857, 8:30 to 11:30 p.m., Schuyler Colfax Papers, Indiana State Library; Wade to Mrs. Wade, Dec. 20, 25, 1857, Wade Papers.
6 Herndon to Lyman Trumbull, Dec. 16, 1857, Trumbull Papers; Greeley to Schuyler Colfax, [December, 1857?], Memorandum of Interview, Burlingame and Colfax with Douglas . . . Dec. 14, 1857, Colfax Papers; Wilson to Theodore Parker, Feb. 28, 1858, Letterbook, Parker Papers.

346 BALLOTS FOR FREEDOM

party, some prominent Republicans went so far as to support his bid for reelection to the Senate against Abraham Lincoln.

Those most conspicuous in this Republicans-for-Douglas movement represented two quite different groups. First, there were antislavery conservatives, many of them content with popular sovereignty, who welcomed any chance to vitiate Republican radicalism. Republicanism, it seemed to men like Senator James Dixon of Connecticut, had thus far been "bigotted [sic] & narrow, . . . only another name for Abolitionism." Douglas offered an opportunity to engraft upon the Republican party sounder, more responsible elements. If it meant lowering the party's platform to allow the Douglasites to scramble aboard, some were more than willing to pay the price.[7]

A second set of Republicans, smaller but more influential, supported Douglas's candidacy purely as a matter of expediency. Horace Greeley was easily the most prominent of this group, but the *Atlantic Monthly*, *Boston Traveller*, *Springfield Republican*, and *Albany Evening Journal*, as well as politicians like Henry Wilson and Anson Burlingame, also extolled the benefits of reelecting Douglas.[8] For the Little Giant himself, few had much respect. Greeley privately considered him "a low and dangerous demagogue," and later told Herndon that Douglas was "like the man's hog who (he said) 'didn't weigh so much as he expected, and he always knew he wouldn't.' "[9] All, moreover, were firm in their antislavery sympathies. Yet believing that Douglas's bold stand against Lecompton deserved reward (if only to encourage others to defy the South) and seeing a chance to rebuke the "Slave Power" and further divide the Democracy, they did what they could to return the Senator to Washington. "We *know* that Mr. Lincoln will prove an excellent senator if elected," the *New-York Tribune* noted in May 1858; "we *believe* Mr. Douglas cannot henceforth be otherwise. . . . There

[7] Dixon to Gideon Welles, Mar. 2, 6, 8, 17, Apr. 2, 1858, Welles Papers, LC; *New York Times*, May 10, 1858; *Indiana True Republican*, July 15, Aug. 26, 1858; Johannsen, *Douglas*, 634-35.
[8] Don E. Fehrenbacher, *Prelude to Greatness: Lincoln in the 1850's* (Stanford, 1962), 61; E. L. Pierce to Salmon P. Chase, Nov. 5, 1858, Chase Papers, LC; *New-York Daily Tribune*, Mar. 3, 1858; Greeley to Schuyler Colfax, May 6, 17, 1858, Greeley Papers; William H. Herndon to Lyman Trumbull, Apr. 24, 1858, Trumbull Papers. Herndon incorrectly listed the *National Era* as one of those Republican newspapers "disposed to side with Douglas." For the *Era's* denial, see its issue of Apr. 29, 1858.
[9] Greeley to F. Newhall, Jan. 8, 1859, quoted in Isely, *Greeley and the Republican Party*, 238; Greeley to William H. Herndon, Dec. 4, 1859, Greeley Papers.

would be rejoicings in every slave-mart over the tidings that he has been superseded, though his successor were [Owen] Lovejoy or [Ichabod] Codding." If nothing else, Greeley later explained, Republican support of Douglas would destroy his political bases in the South by deepening "the impression that he is a disguised Abolitionist, and virtual ally of the Black Republicans."[10]

Greeley and Co. soon learned, however, that the rest of their party had different ideas. Outside the East, Republican enthusiasm for Douglas proved negligible, and even there the movement never really took hold. While delighted at Douglas's defiance of the "Buchaneers," most Republicans remained dissatisfied with popular sovereignty and mistrustful of its leading proponent. "Douglas is just what he always was," Ben Wade warned Salmon P. Chase, "a mere Demagogue not to be trusted. He is at heart now with the worst of the Buchanan Tribe, and has not one sentiment in common with us. *Be not deceived.*" The endorsement Illinois Douglas men gave in April to the Democratic national platform of 1856 reinforced such feeling, and except in Indiana Republican state conventions rebuked fusion by reaffirming the Philadelphia platform.[11]

Understandably, Illinois Republicans were even more suspicious of Douglas and were also resentful of the attempt of Easterners to sell them out. Most found it hard to forget the Senator's earlier abuse of their party and its doctrines or to trust his sudden conversion. In April William Herndon pleaded with Greeley: "Bate your eulogisms on Douglas a little—because every puff is at the expense of Republicans in Illinois. . . . Were we—the Republicans—this day to run Douglas for any office in Illinois it would crush us and our principles so fine that God alone could find the powdered fragments. . . . We in Illinois like Douglas' treason, but do not think the traitor absolutely or even relatively Divine." After Lincoln's nomination in June, Herndon spoke even more bluntly. Douglas, he said, was "the greatest liar in the world." Democratic Republicans like Lyman Trumbull and Norman

---

[10] *New-York Daily Tribune,* May 17, 1858; Greeley to Schuyler Colfax, Feb. 28, 1860, Colfax Papers.
[11] William Dennison to Joshua Giddings, Feb. 23, 1858, Salmon P. Chase to Giddings, May 5, 1858, Giddings Papers; Wade to Chase, May 29, 1858, Chase Papers, PHS; George E. Baker to William H. Seward, July 11, 1858, Seward Papers; Carl Schurz to Gerrit Smith, Sept. 14, 1858, Smith Papers; Chase to Charles Sumner, Sept. 10, 1859, Sumner Papers; *Indiana True Republican,* July 15, Aug. 26, 1858.

Judd took the same hard line. Only among old line Whigs, fearful of radical tendencies they perceived in the Republican party, were there any appreciable defections to Douglas.[12]

Faced with such obstinacy, even Greeley beat a partial retreat. Not, however, before he had profoundly alienated Illinois Republicans who pinned on him much of the responsibility for Lincoln's defeat. "I say d—n Greely [sic] and Co.," cursed a downstate politico. "They have done more harm to us in Illinois than all others beside not excepting the d—n Irish."[13] Bitterness bred paranoia, and some, including Herndon, muttered that Lincoln had fallen victim to a conspiracy. Greeley and Seward, it was widely rumored, had agreed to help Douglas in his senatorial campaign in exchange for the Little Giant's continued opposition to Lecompton and, perhaps, a boost for Seward's presidential hopes in 1860. In fact such charges appear to have been groundless, and Seward's posture in 1858 had been one of neutrality, not active aid to Douglas. Yet even neutrality seemed a kind of treason to Illinois Republicans. In a matter of months Seward's aloofness had cost him a fund of good will it had taken him years to amass. "If the vote of Illinois can nominate another than Seward," wrote one peevish Republican with an eye on 1860, "I hope it will be so cast." Ironically, the just vanquished Abraham Lincoln would be the man to take up Seward's slack.[14]

2

Disappointed in their attempts to forge an alliance with Douglas Democrats, Republican fusionists pressed ahead on another front. More than any other group, it had been the conservative Whigs and Know-Nothings who had done in the Republican ticket in 1856. Had their

[12] Herndon to Greeley, Apr. 8, July 20, 1858, Greeley Papers; Norman B. Judd to Lyman Trumbull, Mar. 7, 1858, Trumbull Papers; Trumbull to Salmon P. Chase, June 17, 1858, Chase Papers, PHS; Fehrenbacher, *Prelude to Greatness*, 61-63, 118. See also William H. Bissell to Trumbull, Jan. 9, 1858, Trumbull Papers; Herndon to Charles Sumner, Apr. 10, 1858, Sumner Papers; Herndon to William H. Seward, June 27, 1858, Seward Papers; Joseph A. Ware to William Pitt Fessenden, May 21, 1858, Fessenden Papers, WRHS; *Chicago Daily Tribune*, Apr. 21, May 1, 11, June 18, 1858.
[13] Quoted in Fehrenbacher, *Prelude to Greatness*, 117.
[14] *Ibid.* 117-18; Herndon to Theodore Parker, Nov. 8, 28, 1858, Letterbook, Parker Papers; Van Deusen, *Seward*, 191-92; King, *Davis*, 126.

votes gone to Frémont instead of Fillmore, the outcome might well have been different. What was needed, some thought, was a formula by which Northern conservatives—and perhaps Whiggish (or "Opposition") elements in the upper South—might be drawn into Republican ranks without driving off the party's radical antislavery wing.

A few ultraconservatives suggested simply that agitation of the slavery question be stopped. If experience proved anything, *The New York Times* maintained, it was that abolitionist agitation retarded, not advanced, the cause of emancipation. "Ten years of absolute silence would do more than fifty of turmoil and hostility, towards a peaceful removal of the evil." In short, the Republican party might advance both its own fortunes and the antislavery cause if it concentrated on conventional matters of political economy. For its pains, however, the *Times* got only lectures from more radical Republican sheets on the virtue and necessity of continued agitation.[15] No more successful in winning Republican minds was the proposal of Nathan Sargent. An old Whig journalist and onetime sergeant-at-arms of the House of Representatives, Sargent appealed in 1858 and 1859 to conservative leaders on both sides of the Mason-Dixon line to form a national party, headed by "a statesman of the old school, of elevated and conservative views,"—that is, an advocate of higher tariffs and checks on immigration. If an official platform were deemed necessary, he contended, it need say no more than "Opposition to the opening of the Slave-trade; & eternal hostility to the rotten democracy." Democratic-Republican sources predictably and quite properly saw in all of this an attempt to adulterate party principle by binding "the live body of Republicanism to the dead carcass of silver gray Whiggery," and even former Whigs bluntly told Sargent that his was a blueprint for disaster. "It would gain nothing in the South, and lose every thing in the North," predicted Abraham Lincoln.[16]

Somewhat less reactionary, much more widely debated, but in the end equally unavailing were the efforts of Greeley's *New-York Tribune* to harmonize the divergent strands of Republicanism. Often enormously quixotic, a sucker for many a fad, the white-coated, cherubic

[15] *New York Times*, Nov. 24, Dec. 1, 1858; *National Era*, Feb. 3, 1859.
[16] *Indiana True Republican*, July 8, 1858; *New York Post*, quoted in *ibid.*; Cassius M. Clay to William H. Seward, July 10, 1858, Seward Papers; Lincoln to Sargent, June 23, 1859, Basler (ed.), *Works of Lincoln*, III, 387-88.

Greeley considered himself the most hardheaded thinker in the Republican organization. And nothing could be more impractical, he insisted, than to overestimate the depth and extent of antislavery attitudes in the United States. "I assume I differ from you mainly in this respect," he wrote to Salmon Chase in September 1858, "—I do not believe that the People of the Free States are heartily Anti-Slavery. Ashamed of their subserviency to the Slave Power they may well be; convinced that Slavery is an incubus and a weakness, they are quite likely to be; but hostile to Slavery as wrong and crime, they are not, nor (I fear) likely soon to be." That being so, Greeley argued, Republicans would be best advised to soft-pedal antislavery for a while and concentrate instead on a program of fiscal retrenchment. Abolition of the Army, he suggested, would make a more rousing war cry than the abolition of slavery.[17]

In December 1858 Greeley revealed that he was willing to go still further to build an effective, if watered-down, antislavery coalition. Having failed in an earlier attempt to bring Republicans and Know-Nothings together in New York (the gubernatorial nomination had been his hoped-for reward), Greeley now proposed through the *Tribune*'s columns that those two organizations make common cause in 1860. The Republicans, he counseled, might choose the presidential candidate, letting Whig–Know-Nothings pick a running mate. All would then support this joint ticket, "each party and each State making its own platform" and taking its own name. Or, Greeley advised, Republicans might let the Whig–Know-Nothings have the presidential nomination in exchange for second place on the ticket and a public agreement "that the Administration thus formed shall do all in its power to confine Slavery within the limits of the existing Slave States."[18]

This proposal, as Greeley admitted later, received nothing but censure from the parties concerned. But convinced that without fusion and compromise Republicanism would fail, the *Tribune*'s scrappy editor persisted. Toward the end of April 1859 Greeley repeated his call for a

[17] Greeley to Chase, Sept. 28, 1858, Chase Papers, PHS. See also Greeley, *Recollections of a Busy Life*, 389-90.
[18] Isely, *Greeley and the Republican Party*, 248-52; *New-York Daily Tribune*, Dec. 9, 1858.

fusion of all groups opposed to the Administration and to slavery expansion, one which would welcome enlightened slaveholders as well as antislavery Northerners of every hue. "We believe that Maryland, Delaware, and Missouri, with possibly Kentucky, Tennessee and North Carolina, may be carried in 1860 for a National ticket which shall be frankly but inoffensively hostile to the Extension of Slavery," he declared. While preferring "an original Republican" like Chase or Seward for President, Greeley realized that that might be out of the question. The *Tribune* stood ready, therefore, "heartily and zealously" to support someone like John Bell of Tennessee, Edward Bates of Missouri, or John M. Botts of Virginia, provided assurances were given that if the candidate were elected, he would use the powers of the presidency to confine slavery to its present bounds. "Victory is clearly within reach of the Opposition," Greeley assured his many readers, "—a victory over which both Republicans and Conservatives will have ample reason to rejoice. Let it not be fooled away by a childish strife about names."[19] In his own eyes, Greeley now held the position of the rich gentleman who paid from his own pocket for a village church and then told his townsmen:

> I've built you a meeting-house,
> And bought you a bell;
> Now go to meeting
> Or go to h——![20]

To Greeley's vexation, most of his parishioners preferred hell. Only here and there did other Republicans respond favorably to the *Tribune*'s battle plan.[21] The overwhelming majority, on all parts of the antislavery spectrum, vehemently rejected it. Greeley's "shuffling policy," nearly all agreed, would mean death to their party and its principles. The *Indiana True Republican* spoke for many when it warned that "there is infinitely more hazard of weakening our forces by insulting the predominant Anti-Slavery sentiment of the party, by a

[19] *Ibid.* Jan. 24, Apr. 26, 1859.
[20] Greeley to James S. Pike, Feb. 26, 1860, quoted in Isely, *Greeley and the Republican Party*, 266.
[21] See, e.g., *Poughkeepsie Eagle*, Apr. 30, 1859; Keene *New Hampshire Sentinel*, May 6, 1859; Concord *New Hampshire Statesman*, May 14, 1859. All these newspapers had once been Whig.

paltering, half hearted course, than there is probability of gain from the odds and ends of pro-slavery conservatism."[22] Not only antislavery radicals but German-Americans of all sorts made it clear that they would bolt the party before they would make any concessions to Know-Nothings.[23] In any event, some argued, concessions were unnecessary. Most conservatives would choose the Republican camp anyway, and no matter how flaccid its platform or benign its candidates, *no* antislavery party could ever hope to win a single slave state. Border state moderates concurred. "I could not carry a single Southern State as your candidate," wrote Kentucky's John J. Crittenden, one of Greeley's favorites, "—and how many could you carry North with me for your candidate? The party would sink me in a Slave State, and I should sink the party in the Free States."[24] Even if by some miracle a patchwork opposition party did turn out the rascally Democrats, most Republicans agreed, it would collapse of its own weight unless united by strong, sustaining principles.[25]

Greeley conceived of his policy as a means of hastening the triumph of antislavery doctrines. But to many Republicans it seemed that his sights were set on victory at any cost, that he proposed cutting the heart out of Republicanism for the sake of political success. And hungry though they were for the loaves and fishes of office, few in the party would go that far. "A triumph of any party which will not inaugurate and carry forward the reforms demanded by the country, will be equivalent to defeat," the *Chicago Press & Tribune* maintained.[26]

Already upset by Greeley's recent willingness to accept popular sovereignty as a legitimate and effective antislavery instrument, radical

22 *Indiana True Republican*, May 26, 1859. See also *Wisconsin Weekly Free Democrat*, Dec. 22, 1859; F. D. Parish to John Sherman, Dec. 23, 1858, Sherman Papers; Gamaliel Bailey to Gerrit Smith, Apr. 9, 1859, Smith Papers; *Harrisburg Weekly Telegraph*, June 1, 1859; Abraham Lincoln to Mark W. Delahay, May 14, 1859, Basler (ed.), *Works of Lincoln*, III, 379.
23 Carl Schurz to John F. Potter, Dec. 24, 1858, Potter Papers; *New York Evening Post*, Aug. 20, 1859; Gustav Koerner to Lyman Trumbull, Dec. 23, 1859, Trumbull Papers.
24 *Weekly Chicago Press & Tribune*, Apr. 28, May 5, 1859, *Independent Democrat*, May 26, 1859; G. D. Prentice to Orville H. Browning, Jan. 9, 1860, Orville H. Browning Papers, Illinois State Historical Library.
25 S. York to Lyman Trumbull, Dec. 6, 1858, Trumbull Papers; *Indiana True Republican*, Dec. 23, 1858; *Lansing State Republican*, June 7, 1859.
26 *Weekly Chicago Press & Tribune*, Apr. 14, 1859. See also Charles Francis Adams to Charles Sumner, Mar. 2, 1859, Sumner Papers; Preston King to Gideon Welles, July 20, 1859, Welles Papers, LC.

and moderate Republicans exploded at his pitch for a platform and ticket "inoffensively hostile" to slavery's spread. Even some conservatives insisted that congressional exclusion of slavery from the territories remained the Republican touchstone, and they disdained "to accommodate the weak stomachs" that could not bear "the doctrine that slavery is local and freedom the natural right of man."[27] The party's radical voices took the occasion to remind other members that Republicanism had an even deeper commitment—not only to slavery restriction but to slavery repression and slavery extinction. The salvation of the nation, editorialized the *St. Paul Minnesotian*, depended "upon the vigorous carrying out of the not to be disguised determination of the Republican party, that the States of this Union shall be all free; that not a chain shall clank nor a whip crack over human beings guilty of no crime, anywhere under the broad folds of the American flag."[28] Only a platform clearly *offensive* to slaveholders would satisfy the party's rank and file, New Hampshire's ranking Republican journal claimed.[29]

To the *Tribune*'s suggestion that some Southern Opposition leader be placed atop the Republican ticket in 1860, the reaction was predictably cold. Some conservatives and even a few moderates like Lincoln were willing, for a time, to entertain the possibility, provided a Bates or a Bell would agree to run on the original Republican platform. And even the radical editor of the *Chicago Tribune*, Joseph Medill, toyed briefly with a Chase-Bell combination. But most Republicans agreed with the *Sycamore True Republican* that "we want no half-way men —no compromise candidates." And after publication of Bates's letter, to a committee of New York Whigs, which dismissed slavery as "a pestilent question" that might better be set aside in favor of economic development, Greeley himself was taken aback. "I'm afraid Bates has killed himself," he confessed at the time.[30]

[27] Edward Kent to William P. Fessenden, Jan. 12, 1859, Fessenden Papers, WRHS.
[28] *St. Paul Minnesotian*, quoted (approvingly) in *Sycamore True Republican*, Mar. 3, 1859. See also *National Era*, Dec. 16, 30, 1858, Jan. 27, 1859; *Galesburg Semi-Weekly Democrat*, May 14, 1859; *Indiana True Republican*, May 19, 1859; Joshua R. Giddings's speech of Jan. 12, 1859 to the U.S. House of Representatives, *Cong. Globe*, 35th Cong., 2nd sess., 343-46; Benjamin F. Wade to Milton Sutliff, Jan. 20, 1859, Sutliff Papers.
[29] *Independent Democrat*, May 12, 1859.
[30] Lincoln to Mark W. Delahay, May 14, 1859, Lincoln to Theodore Canisius, May 17, 1859, Basler (ed.), *Works of Lincoln*, III, 379, 380; Medill to Salmon P. Chase, Apr. 26, 1859, Chase Papers, PHS; *Sycamore True Republican*, May 3, 1859, Greeley to Schuyler Colfax, Apr. 25, 1859, Greeley Papers. See also *Lansing State*

354   BALLOTS FOR FREEDOM

By mid-1859, then, the "trimmers and dodgers" were in retreat. Bates's letter had alienated many, despite heroic attempts by Greeley and Colfax to provide it with an antislavery exegesis. The demand of the Opposition party of Kentucky for a federal slave code for the territories further chilled enthusiasm for a union of all anti-Administration groupings. Republican state conventions in Maine, New Hampshire, Vermont, New York, Ohio, Michigan, Wisconsin, Iowa, and Minnesota all cold-shouldered the fusionists. Even the conservative Tom Corwin, taking heat from his Ohio constituents, felt obliged to reiterate his aversion to popular sovereignty and to uphold the right and duty of Congress to prohibit slavery in the territories. Although the *New-York Tribune* continued to plug gamely for the candidacy of Bates (that "fossil of the Silurian era," one critic called him), it candidly admitted that the party's response to fusion had been decidedly "adverse."[31]

3

For a short time it appeared that Republican dismay at John Brown's reckless raid into Virginia might turn the tide in a more conservative direction. News of the Harpers Ferry calamity hit Republican radicals hard. "I very much fear that old Brown has furnished the unhorsed democracy with ammunition to renew the fight," fretted Joseph Medill, "and that our party will suffer in the eyes of the *conservative* class." Republican back-pedaling to regain the support of frightened conservatives, some feared, might jeopardize the party's antislavery integrity. Most distressed were the supporters of William Seward, who was still considered a radical (thanks mainly to his Irrepressible Conflict speech of the year before) and wrongfully accused of complicity in Brown's bloody assault. His once-promising chances of nomination for the presidency in 1860 suddenly looked much more bleak.[32]

Republican, May 17, 1859; *Indiana True Republican*, June 2, 16, July 21, 1859; *Independent Democrat*, June 2, 9, 1859; Thurlow Weed to Zachariah Chandler Aug. 26, 1859, Zachariah Chandler Papers, LC; Austin Willey to William P. Fessenden, Nov. 4, 1859, Fessenden Papers, WRHS.
[31] *Indiana True Republican*, July 21, Sept. 15, 1859; *Independent Democrat*, Sept 22, 1859; Josiah Morrow (ed.), *Life and Speeches of Thomas Corwin: Orator Lawyer, and Statesman* (Cincinnati, 1896), 369-80; Van Deusen, *Greeley*, 241-43 *New-York Daily Tribune*, Oct. 12, 1859.
[32] Medill to Salmon P. Chase, Oct. 30, 1859, Chase Papers, PHS; James A. Briggs t(

To Northern conservatives and adherents of the *New-York Tribune* policy, however, the clouds of October contained a silver lining. "Don't be downhearted about the Old Brown business," Greeley urged one confidant the day before Brown's trial began. "Its present effect is bad, and throws a heavy load on us in this State." But the ultimate effect would be good: "It will drive the Slave Power to new outrages. It settles the Charleston coffee of Douglas. It will probably help us to nominate a moderate man for Pres[iden]t on our side. It presses on the 'irresistible conflict,' and I think the end of Slavery in Virginia and the Union is ten years nearer than it seemed a few weeks ago." More conservative Republicans would have been put off by Greeley's reference to an irrepressible conflict between North and South, freedom and slavery. But they did agree that events at Harpers Ferry made fusion with the Southern Opposition party more advantageous than ever before. Speeches like that of Maryland's Henry Winter Davis, who blamed Brown's raid on the reckless course of Southern fire-eaters, encouraged Republican conservatives in false hopes that such a union —which "would disarm the clamor now raised"—was still possible. Arguing that hoped-for Southern allies would never accept "an ultra or rigidly representative man, who ding-dongs on slavery only," they again joined Greeley in singing the praise of conservative candidates like Edward Bates.[33]

As it turned out, however, the John Brown affair did little to soften Republican antislavery attitudes. Far from facilitating a union of all anti-Democratic forces, Harpers Ferry frightened the Southern Opposition so thoroughly that henceforth all talk of intersectional coalition was just so much hot air. Moreover, the Republican response to the Brown episode proved surprisingly aggressive. The attempted insurrection itself, of course, drew nothing but condemnation from Republicans of all types, in and out of Congress. Party prints damned it as an act of treason born of madness, an "utterly repugnant," hopelessly counter-productive act of violence.[34] John P. Hale assured the United

---

Chase, Oct. 19, 1859, Lewis Clephane to Chase, Oct. 31, 1859, W. S. Mills to Chase, Nov. 25, 1859, Chase Papers, LC; Lewis Dyer to Lyman Trumbull, Jan. 3, 1860, Trumbull Papers; John W. Jones to John Sherman, Oct. 25, 1859, Sherman Papers.
[33] Greeley to Schuyler Colfax, Oct. 24, 1859, Greeley to William Herndon, Dec. 4, 1859, Greeley Papers; James E. Harvey to John Sherman, Oct. 31, 1859, Sherman Papers.
[34] See, e.g., *Albany Evening Journal*, Oct. 19, 1859; *New York Times*, Oct. 20,

States Senate that those with whom he was allied "have never made, and never will make, an appeal to slaves. . . . Their appeal, so far as I know, is to the enlightened conscience and the patriotism, not of the slaves, but of their masters." During the state elections that autumn, some Republicans prescribed double doses of Tom Corwin as the best antidote to Democratic charges that Republicanism meant "negro stealing" and insurrection.[35]

Yet even while the 1859 campaign raged (and still more afterward), many Republicans freely praised Brown's motives and most blamed the peculiar institution and proslavery Democrats for the blood spilled at Harpers Ferry. At worst, several party publicists argued, Brown remained less a felon or a traitor than were Southern filibusters and "border ruffians"—and he, at least, had worked to free, not to enslave or oppress. Many spoke favorably of Brown's courage, resolution, and magnanimity. Privately, even conservatives granted the misguided warrior good intentions. He had no doubt that Brown was guilty and would be convicted, Timothy Howe confided to another Wisconsin Republican as the Harpers Ferry trial began. But, he went on, "in 'Heaven's Chancery' it may appear that Brown struck not wisely but bravely, not selfishly but benevolently, not for his own good but the good of his fellows."[36] Once Brown had gone bravely and serenely to the gallows, Republicans freely expressed respect for the man if not for his deed. Typical, at least of radical opinion, was the response of the Concord, New Hampshire, *Independent Democrat:* " 'Old Brown' has gone from earth, and while the enterprise in which he engaged, may be condemned, yet the popular heart recognizes in him a hero—a misguided, perchance, hallucinated, but an honest, fearless, Christian man, who dared do what he thought was right."[37]

1859; *Weekly Chicago Press & Tribune*, Oct. 20, 27, 1859; *Poughkeepsie Eagle* Oct. 22, 1859; *Galesburg Semi-Weekly Democrat*, Oct. 22, 1859; *Illinois State Journal*, Oct. 26, Nov. 2, 1859; *Dover Enquirer*, Oct. 27, 1859; *New York Evening Post* Oct. 18, 31, 1859.
[35] *Cong. Globe*, 36th Cong., 1st sess., 15; John W. Jones to John Sherman, Oct. 25 1859, Sherman Papers.
[36] *Weekly Chicago Press & Tribune*, Oct. 20, 1859; *Dover Enquirer*, Dec. 8, 1859 *New York Evening Post*, Oct. 31, 1859; *Poughkeepsie Eagle,* Dec. 3, 1859; Howe to Horace Rublee, Oct. 26, 1859, Horace Rublee Papers, SHSW.
[37] Dec. 8, 1859. See also *New-York Daily Tribune*, Dec. 3, 1859; George Hoadly to Salmon P. Chase, Dec. 3, 1859, Chase Papers, LC; William Herndon to Theodore Parker, Dec. 15, 1859, Letterbook, Parker Papers; *Indiana True Republican*, Dec

More insistently, Republicans contended that the real villain was not poor old John Brown but "the great Monstrosity" at which he had struck—human bondage. The violence in Virginia was of a piece with the bloodshed in Kansas, filibustering in Central America, lynch laws to suppress free speech, and the code duello—all products of the violence inherent in slavery itself.[38] Southerners ought to take a hard look, many Republicans maintained, at an institution at once so monstrous and fragile that a bare handful of fanatics could strike terror throughout an entire region.[39] Goodly numbers of Northerners had already done just that, reported the *Aledo* (Ill.) *Record*, gaining thereby a heightened appreciation "of the inherent wrongfulness of slavery *in itself*, without reference to parallels of latitude." If Brown had been right in forcibly resisting "border-ruffianism" in Kansas, had he been altogether sinful in Virginia?[40] Most Republicans answered this question affirmatively, yet in a way which focused attention on the still-greater sin of slavery.

Republican trimming on the slavery question was most conspicuous within the halls of Congress. During the first few weeks of the Thirty-sixth Congress (which convened on December 5, 1859, only three days after John Brown's body had been cut from the gallows) Republicans in both houses scrambled so hard to dissociate themselves from Harpers Ferry and Helper's *Impending Crisis* that sometimes their constituents complained. William Herndon, for one, accused his party's representatives of "grinding off the flesh from their knee caps, attempting . . . to convince the Southern men that we are *cowards*." It was enough to make one ashamed to be a Republican. To Theodore Parker he pungently remarked: "I am like the little girl who accidentally shot off wind in company. She said 'I wish I was in hell a little while.' I feel like I wanted to scorch off the disgrace of our kneeling whining cowardice."[41]

22, 1859; Henry G. Pearson, *The Life of John A. Andrew, Governor of Massachusetts, 1861-1865*, 2 vols. (Boston, 1904), I, 101-4.
[38] *New York Evening Post*, Oct. 18, 1859; *Albany Evening Journal*, Oct. 19, 1859; *Poughkeepsie Eagle*, Nov. 12, 1859.
[39] *Ibid.* Oct. 22, 1859; *Galena Weekly Northwestern Gazette*, Oct. 25, 1859; S. L. Emery to John Sherman, Dec. 7, 1859, Sherman Papers.
[40] Quoted in *Indiana True Republican*, Dec. 22, 1859.
[41] Herndon to Parker, Dec. 15, 1859, Letterbook, Parker Papers. See also Martin Kellogg to John Sherman, Jan. 3, 1860, Sherman Papers.

Much to the disgruntlement of Northern radicals, Republicans in the House muted their antislavery remarks while, for two months and forty-four ballots, a battle raged over the speakership (won, ultimately, by William Pennington, a conservative Republican from New Jersey).[42] And in the Senate William Seward sought to rub from his cloak some of the stains of extremism—and thereby improve his presidential "availability"—with a much-publicized speech stressing the basic nationalism and conservatism of Republican doctrines. Denouncing John Brown's abortive insurrection as "an act of sedition and treason" and denying that Republicans contemplated unconstitutional aggression against slavery in the states, the New York leader assured the South that his party already felt "the necessity of being practical in its care of the national health and life." Gone was any hint of the higher law or the irrepressible conflict.[43]

That by such silence or conciliation Republican lawmakers were merely riding out the storm, not preparing to surrender principle, became clear in March 1860. Near the end of that month Congressman Harrison Blake of Ohio, without fanfare, introduced the following resolution:

> Whereas the chattelizing of humanity and the holding of persons as property is contrary to natural justice and the fundamental principles of our political system, and is notoriously a reproach to our country throughout the civilized world, and a serious hindrance to the progress of republican liberty among the nations of the earth: Therefore,
> Resolved, that the committee on the Judiciary be, and the same are hereby, instructed to inquire into the expediency of reporting a bill giving freedom to every human being and interdicting slavery wherever Congress has the constitutional power to legislate on the subject.

Just what prompted Blake, a virtual unknown then serving his first term in Congress, is uncertain. Quite likely he intended his resolution as a corrective to antislavery views he thought too conservative, unrepresentative of Republican opinion. If so, he largely fulfilled his pur-

[42] Nevins, *Emergence of Lincoln*, II, 116-23; George S. Boutwell to Charles Sumner, Jan. 21, 1860, Francis W. Bird to Sumner, Jan. 20, 23, 1860, Sumner Papers.
[43] *Cong. Globe*, 36th Cong., 1st sess., 910-14 (Feb. 29, 1860).

pose. For although the House voted down the resolution without debate, 60 to 109, Republicans gave it strong backing. All but one of the affirmative votes and only fourteen of the negative came from Republicans. Casting ballots for the resolution were prominent moderates like John Sherman and Schuyler Colfax as well as such radicals as Charles Francis Adams, Galusha Grow, and Owen Lovejoy. Most of those who abstained and even some who voted "nay" approved the substance of Blake's declaration and would have endorsed it had they not been paired (as were Thad Stevens, James Ashley, and several others) or thought it too loosely drawn. David Kilgore of Indiana, for example, opposed the resolution merely because in seeking freedom for "every human being" it appeared to include common criminals as well as slaves. In response to Southern queries, in fact, Kilgore not only declared his belief in Congress' power to interdict slavery in the territories and the District of Columbia, but admitted that the exercise of such power might well topple the peculiar institution in the states as well. Blake's proposal created little stir either then or later. Yet a perceptive observer might have found in its reception evidence of widespread Republican determination to use every constitutional weapon to uproot slavery from the land.[44]

Better than any other Republican politician, Abraham Lincoln caught the prevailing temper of his party. In dozens of speeches during the fall and winter of 1859-60—throughout the Middle West, New York, and New England—Lincoln hammered away at two themes: that slavery was first and foremost a moral question, and that the Republican party must firmly resist all attempts to compromise away its principles. Especially did he fight against the substitution of an amoral, "insidious" popular sovereignty for what he insisted had been the true policy of the Founding Fathers: federal prohibition of slavery expansion.[45] Lincoln's tone was invariably evenhanded and good-tempered, but his message was at all times uncompromising:

> Republicans believe that slavery is wrong [Lincoln told Ohio audiences in 1859]; and they insist, and will continue to insist

---

[44] *Ibid.* 1359-62. Luther C. Carter, a Know-Nothing from New York, was the only non-Republican to support Blake's resolution—and he was listed by the *Congressional Globe* as an American-Republican.
[45] Basler (ed.), *Works of Lincoln*, III, 400-489, 495-504, 522-54; IV, 1-30.

upon a national policy which recognizes it, and deals with it, *as a wrong*. There *can* be no letting down about this.[46]

Even Lincoln's renowned address at Cooper Institute, New York City, on February 27, 1860, was conciliatory only to a point. To the Southern people and their Northern allies he offered assurances that his party intended no invasion of vested rights, and he denounced as "malicious slander" the charge of Republican complicity in John Brown's raid. To fellow Republicans he counseled forebearance and understanding whenever possible. Yet in sharp distinction to Seward's speech of two days later, Lincoln repeatedly reminded his audience of slavery's moral dimension.

> All they ask [he observed in closing], we could readily grant, if we thought slavery right; all we ask, they could as readily grant, if they thought it wrong. Their thinking it right, and our thinking it wrong, is the precise fact upon which depends the whole controversy. Thinking it right, as they do, they are not to blame for desiring its full recognition, as being right; but, thinking it wrong, as we do, can we yield to them? . . . Wrong as we think slavery is, we can yet afford to let it alone where it is, because that much is due to the necessity arising from its actual presence in the nation; but can we, while our votes will prevent it, allow it to spread into the National Territories, and to overrun us here in these Free States? If our sense of duty forbids this, then let us stand by our duty, fearlessly and effectively.[47]

Instead of trying to paper over sectional differences, as Seward had done, Lincoln faced them head on, urging Republicans to stand firmly by their original creed. In this, and in his insistence on recognizing the black man's humanity and on treating slavery as a moral wrong, Lincoln won favor with party radicals. At the same time, his manifest humility, reasonableness, and sense of fair play appealed to more conservative Republicans. As one perceptive New Yorker wrote to Lincoln soon after the Cooper Institute address: "It has produced a greater effect here than any other single speech. It is the real platform in the eastern states and must carry the conservative element in New York, New Jersey, and Pennsylvania."[48] Already the Illinoisian's name was beginning to crop up in presidential speculations.

[46] *Ibid*. III, 433.
[47] *Ibid*. III, 522-50.
[48] Quoted in Nevins, *Emergence of Lincoln*, II, 188.

4

Admitting the importance of behind-the-scenes bargaining by Lincoln's managers, it seems nonetheless true that the Republican presidential nomination went in 1860 to the man from Illinois largely because of his firm yet moderate antislavery beliefs. The front-running William H. Seward led for two ballots but failed on the third not only because of his widespread (if suspect) reputation as a radical, but because some Republicans mistrusted his recent waffling on the slavery question. The New Yorker's support in 1858 for an Administration bill to en-large the Army—ostensibly to police the Mormons in Utah, but really, claimed others, to suppress free state forces in Kansas—had set many Republicans to wondering. So too Seward's encouragement of Douglas, his vote to admit Oregon despite its Jim Crow constitution, and his recent Senate speech in which he had conciliatorily referred to the South as the "capital states" and to the North as the "labor states" all gave pause to Republican radicals. As one of William Pitt Fessenden's correspondents put it in 1858, it often appeared that Seward was "seek-ing an opportunity to distinguish himself as a compromiser. But he ought to consider that the day for compromises has long since gone by. . . ."[49]

Other Republican hopefuls were equally flawed. Salmon P. Chase suffered not only for his ultra political abolitionism but also from his inability to unite the entire Ohio delegation behind him. Edward Bates, for all of Horace Greeley's help, never really had a chance. Outside the border South, Republicans had long since rejected his brand of conservatism. In the end it was Abraham Lincoln who emerged as the most "available" candidate, as much for the steadfastness as for the moderation of his antislavery views.

If anything, radical Republicans were more pleased with "Honest Abe's" nomination than conservatives were. "As to Lincoln," declared old Joshua Giddings, "I would trust him on the subject of slavery as

[49] Virgil H. Hewes to Fessenden, Feb. 9, 1858, Fessenden Papers, WRHS. See also William H. Herndon to Charles Sumner, Feb. 11, 1857, Sumner Papers; Thurlow Weed to Seward, Mar. 11, 1858, May 6, 1860, Seward Papers; Joshua R. Giddings to Salmon P. Chase, Feb. 14, 1859, Miscellaneous Manuscripts, NYHS; C. Robin-son to Chase, Feb. 3, 1860, Chase Papers, LC; Allan Tomlin to Richard Yates, May 22, 1860, Yates Papers.

362   BALLOTS FOR FREEDOM

soon as I would Chase or Seward. I have been well acquainted with
him and think I understand his whole character. I know him to be
honest and faithful." In its post-convention editorial the Centreville
Indiana True Republican praised Lincoln as one who had sternly resisted pressures to run up the white flag of popular sovereignty. Better
still, it noted, "He not only believes in the rights of Germans and Irishmen but includes even negroes, in his interpretation of the self-evident
truths of the Declaration of Independence." Even Gerrit Smith found
Lincoln an admirable choice, confiding to Giddings: "I feel confident
that he is in his heart an abolitionist." He added, prophetically, "Lincoln will be President—and his victory will be regarded by the South
as an Abolition victory—not less so than if you yourself were elected
President."[50]

In the main, Republican radicals also applauded their party's 1860
platform. To be sure, new planks calling for a protective tariff, free
homesteads (an old Liberty League and Free Soil demand), and full
observance of immigrant rights made it a somewhat broader document
than that of 1856. Yet slavery remained the party's central concern,
and the resolutions dealing with it took much the same ground as before. While, it is true, the phrase "whenever necessary" now qualified
the previous insistence upon congressional exclusion of slavery from
all territories, the new platform made no secret of the Republicans'
determination to use federal power to keep the institution in check.
Not only did the resolutions committee beat down Horace Greeley's
suggestion that the party declare merely that slavery could exist only
where previously established by law, but it explicitly denied the power
of any legislative body to legalize slavery in a territory and denounced
popular sovereignty as "deception and fraud."[51]

Much has been made of the fact that only Joshua Giddings's dramatic threat to bolt the convention forced the delegates to restore to
the 1860 platform a full restatement of the egalitarian doctrines of the
Declaration of Independence. Yet symbolic though it was, the im-

[50] Giddings to George W. Julian, May 25, 1860, Giddings-Julian Papers; *Indiana True Republican*, May 24, 31, 1860; Smith to Giddings, June 2, 1860, Giddings Papers. Cf. Joseph Lyman to Charles Sumner, June 19, 1860, Sumner Papers.
[51] *Proceedings of the First Three Republican National Conventions*, 131-33; William B. Hesseltine (ed.), *Three Against Lincoln: Murat Halstead Reports the Caucuses of 1860* (Baton Rouge, 1960), 147.

portance of this incident ought not to be exaggerated. For while the original set of resolutions did not detail Jefferson's catalogue of natural rights, it did at least copy that part of the earlier Philadelphia platform which declared "That the maintenance of the principles promulgated in the Declaration of Independence and embodied in the Federal Constitution is essential to the preservation of our Republican institutions. . . ."[52] Some conservatives may have found Jefferson's language inflammatory, and they may have hoped to sweep it out of sight. Most, however, appear to have had no strong objections to explicit reaffirmation of the rights of "life, liberty and the pursuit of happiness." In the end, restoration was ordered by a margin of two to one. Democrats gibed that the Republican platform was "like the pedlers [*sic*] suspenders 'short enough for any boy and long enough for any man'. . . ."[53] But moderate and radical Republicans were proud of their work and confident that the principles of 1856 were still very much intact.[54]

In the months that followed, Lincoln's champions waged a spirited if cautious campaign designed to attract conservatives and to reassure the South without alienating Republican radicals and moderates. In addition to a full defense of their free-soil tenets, party orators played heavily upon exposés of corruption in Buchanan's Administration (juxtaposing homey vignettes of "Honest Abe"); touted the advantages of homesteads, tariffs, and a Pacific railroad; and wooed foreign-born voters with biting attacks on nativism. It proved a successful formula. In a four-cornered contest against Northern and Southern Democrats and the conservative Constitutional Union party, Lincoln and the Republicans swept every free state save New Jersey, which they split with Douglas. The 180 electoral votes thus gained were more than enough to secure the prize antislavery pioneers had so long awaited. "Thank God! Lincoln is chosen!" exulted Joshua Leavitt, one of the founders of the first antislavery party. "What a growth since 1840." John Greenleaf Whittier also cheered "the triumph of our principles—so long delayed."

---

[52] *Proceedings of the First Three Republican National Conventions*, 133-37, 140-43; Hesseltine (ed.), *Three Against Lincoln*, 152-56.
[53] J. J. Kitcham's report of J. C. Allen's speech, July 7, 1860, Yates Papers.
[54] *Indiana True Republican*, May 31, 1860; Foner, *Free Soil, Free Labor, Free Men*, 132-33.

More soberly, he added in his letter to Salmon Chase: "Well God has laid the great responsibility upon us! We must take it up & bear it."[55]

5

Bear it they did. Southern firebrands, seeing clearly the threat (it mattered not how distant) the Republican program posed to their domestic institutions, began on the morrow of Lincoln's election to take their states out of the Union. Throughout the ensuing crisis, urged on by their constituents, Republicans in Congress stood firm against Southern threats and the backsliding of a few "weak-kneed" Northern brethren, refusing to recede a "hair's breadth" from their party's national platform.[56] In their determination to resist all debilitating compromises on the slavery question, Republican lawmakers found themselves steadied from above as well as below. Although he refrained from public statements during the interregnum between his election and his inauguration, Abraham Lincoln left little doubt of his utter hostility to any trimming on the territorial question. Characteristic was his advice ("Private & confidential") to Illinois Congressman Elihu B. Washburne. "Prevent, as far as possible, any of our friends from demoralizing themselves, and our cause, by entertaining propositions for compromise of any sort, on 'slavery extension,'" he wrote in mid-December. "There is no possible compromise upon it, but which puts us under again, and leaves all our work to do over again. Whether it be a Mo. line, or Eli Thayer's Pop. Sov. it is all the same. Let either be done, & immediately filibustering and extending slavery recommences. On that point hold firm, as with a chain of steel."[57]

Neither Lincoln nor most other members of his party had believed that it would take a civil war to break the sectional logjam. And when reconciliation proved impossible and the war came, they were slow to see the propriety—and the necessity—of using the powers the war gave

[55] Nevins, *Emergence of Lincoln*, II, 261-317; Leavitt to Salmon P. Chase, Nov. 7, 1860, Whittier to Chase, Nov. 9, 1860, Chase Papers, LC. See also S. L. Harding to George W. Julian, Nov. 18, 1860, Giddings-Julian Papers.
[56] Stampp, *And the War Came*, 136-58.
[57] Lincoln to Washburne, Dec. 13, 1860, Basler (ed.), *Works of Lincoln*, IV, 151.

them to abolish slavery once and for all.[58] When, however, Congress and (somewhat more tardily) the President did grasp the military as well as moral advantages of abolition, they moved quickly to dismantle the peculiar institution by any means at hand. And always in the van were veteran political abolitionists like Charles Sumner, Henry Wilson, Benjamin Wade, and John P. Hale in the Senate, and Owen Lovejoy, Thaddeus Stevens, and George W. Julian in the House—men who measured the sweetness of victory by the length of the road they had come.

For the black freedmen, defeats, betrayals, and disillusionment—as well as hope and opportunity—lay ahead. But for a time, at least, those blacks and whites, moral suasionists and political abolitionists, who had seen slavery to its grave could stand proud.

[58] Some were more prescient than others. Joshua Giddings confided to Gerrit Smith (Dec. 24, 1860): "I am inclined to think your prediction in regard to blood-shed will prove true—; but I am more than ever confident that 'the day of emanci-pation must come; but (as Mr. [John Quincy] Adams said) whether it comes in blood or in peace I know not, but whether in blood or in peace *Let it come.*'" Smith Papers.

Manuscripts Cited

Charles Francis Adams Papers, Massachusetts Historical Society

Antislavery Collection, Cornell University

Nathaniel P. Banks Papers, Essex Institute

Nathaniel P. Banks Papers, Library of Congress

Nathaniel P. Banks Papers, Illinois State Historical Society

Charles S. Benton Papers, State Historical Society of Wisconsin

Francis W. Bird Papers, Houghton Library, Harvard University

James G. Birney Papers, Library of Congress

James G. Birney Papers, Clements Library, University of Michigan

Blair Family Papers, Library of Congress

Orville H. Browning Papers, Illinois State Historical Library

Benjamin F. Butler Papers, New York State Library

Robert Carter Papers, Houghton Library, Harvard University

Moses A. Cartland Papers, Hougton Library, Harvard University

Zachariah Chandler Papers, Library of Congress

Salmon P. Chase Papers, Library of Congress

Salmon P. Chase Papers, Pennsylvania Historical Society

David L. and Lydia M. Child Papers, Boston Public Library

Ichabod Codding Papers, Friends Historical Library, Swarthmore College

Schuyler Colfax Papers, Indiana State Library

Richard Henry Dana Papers, Massachusetts Historical Society

Moses M. Davis Papers, State Historical Society of Wisconsin

John A. Dix Papers, Columbia University

James R. Doolittle Papers, State Historical Society of Wisconsin

William Pitt Fessenden Papers, Bowdoin College

William Pitt Fessenden Papers, Western Reserve Historical Society

Hamilton Fish Papers, Library of Congress

Azariah C. Flagg Papers, Columbia University

Azariah C. Flagg Papers, New York Public Library

Theodore Foster Papers, Michigan Historical Collections, Ann Arbor

Stephen S. Foster Papers, American Antiquarian Society

Benjamin French Papers, Library of Congress

Frey Family Papers, New-York Historical Society

William Lloyd Garrison Papers, Boston Public Library

Joshua R. Giddings Papers, Ohio Historical Society

Giddings-Julian Papers, Library of Congress

Horace Greeley Papers, New York Public Library

John P. Hale Papers, Dartmouth College

John P. Hale Papers, New Hampshire Historical Society

John P. Hale Papers, Phillips Exeter Academy

Hannibal Hamlin Papers, University of Maine

George Frisbie Hoar Papers, Massachusetts Historical Society

Timothy O. Howe Papers, State Historical Society of Wisconsin

Jay Family Papers, Columbia University

John Jay Collection, Columbia University

Charles Francis Jenkins Collection, Friends Historical Library, Swarthmore College

George W. Julian Papers, Indiana State Library

Preston King Papers, St. Lawrence University

Joshua Leavitt Papers, Library of Congress

Ellis Gray Loring Papers, Houghton Library, Harvard University

John McLean Papers, Library of Congress

Horace Mann Papers, Massachusetts Historical Society

Miscellaneous Manuscripts, New-York Historical Society

Edwin D. Morgan Papers, New York State Library

Marcus Morton Papers, Massachusetts Historical Society

John M. Niles Papers, Connecticut Historical Society

John G. Palfrey Papers, Houghton Library, Harvard University

Theodore Parker Papers, Massachusetts Historical Society

Amos A. Phelps Papers, Boston Public Library

Calvin W. Philleo Papers, Connecticut Historical Society

James S. Pike Papers, Calais Free Library, Calais, Maine

William Plumer Papers, New Hampshire State Library

John Fox Potter Papers, State Historical Society of Wisconsin

Albert G. Riddle Papers, Western Reserve Historical Society

Horace Rublee Papers, State Historical Society of Wisconsin

William H. Seward Papers, University of Rochester

John Sherman Papers, Library of Congress

Slavery Manuscripts, New-York Historical Society

Gerrit Smith Papers, Syracuse University

Lysander Spooner Papers, New-York Historical Society

Thaddeus Stevens Papers, Library of Congress

Alvan Stewart Papers, New-York Historical Society

Alvan Stewart Papers, New York State Historical Association, Cooperstown

Charles Sumner Papers, Houghton Library, Harvard University

Milton Sutliff Papers, Western Reserve Historical Society

Lewis Tappan Papers, Library of Congress

Horace A. Tenney Papers, State Historical Society of Wisconsin

Nathan M. Thomas Papers, Michigan Historical Collections, Ann Arbor

Samuel J. Tilden Papers, New York Public Library

Charles T. Torrey Papers, Congregational Christian Historical Society, Boston, Massachusetts

Seymour B. Treadwell Papers, Michigan Historical Collections, Ann Arbor

Lyman Trumbull Papers, Library of Congress

Amos Tuck Papers, New Hampshire Historical Society

Martin Van Buren Papers, Library of Congress

Benjamin F. Wade Papers, Library of Congress

Amasa Walker Papers, Massachusetts Historical Society

Israel Washburn Papers, Library of Congress

Thurlow Weed Papers, University of Rochester

Gideon Welles Papers, Connecticut
Historical Society
Gideon Welles Papers, Library of
Congress
Gideon Welles Papers, New York Pub-
lic Library
Weston Family Papers, Boston Public
Library
John G. Whittier Papers, Friends His-
torical Library, Swarthmore College

Samuel Willard Papers, Illinois State
Historical Library
Elizur Wright Papers, Case-Western
Reserve University
Elizur Wright, Jr. Papers, Boston Pub-
lic Library
Elizur Wright, Jr. Papers, Library of
Congress
Richard Yates Papers, Illinois State His-
torical Library

Index

374